Hello!

You hold in your hands the latest edition of the Ball Blue Book® Guide to Preserving. The 37th edition is filled to the brim with more than 75 new recipes, with handy tips and tricks for better fresh preserving. Every new edition of this guide is a chance to reflect contemporary tastes—but we are making sure never to lose sight of the values that make fresh preserving so special—after all, the Ball Blue Book® Guide has been around since 1909.

With that said, welcome back all of our preserving veterans! And thank you. Thank you for your passion—for canning before it was cool and for keeping the tradition alive.

But if you're new to this whole thing: don't worry. Sure, you've got a thing or two to learn, but we promise it'll be fun (really!). Fresh preserving is equal parts art and science: there are rules to follow, but there's always more than enough room to express yourself.

We're certainly canning experts—the first official Fresh Preserving Test Kitchen was started in 1976—but we love all kinds of fresh preserving; from dehydrating to freezing, you'll find recipes for all inside. We've also added a brand new section devoted to dishes made with fresh preserved food, so you can put whatever you've made to work right away.

Our team of food experts developed and tested these recipes themselves and worked hard to put as much detail into them as possible. You should never feel lost or alone when making something new and awesome. The folks who love home canning are here to help.

So grab a few jars and let yourself Shine Through.

Judy Harrold

Judy Harrold

Jarden Home Brands
Ball Blue Book® Editor, Contributor and
Ball® Fresh Preserving Kitchen expert since 1981.

Contents

14

96

70

120

Savor and share

garden-fresh flavor
any time of the year

You Choose™
Looking to create something a little different? Look for this symbol for proven and tasty recipe variations.

Our Tip™
The Ball® Fresh Preserving Kitchen experts share tips and techniques to simplify preparation. Look for this symbol in recipes.

What You Need to Know

Nearly all food requires some type of preservation treatment to maintain its quality and safety, so that it may be enjoyed long after harvesting or purchasing. Home canning, also referred to as processing, preserving, and jarring, allows you to store many perishable foods on your pantry shelf for up to one year. Understanding how home canning prevents the natural occurrence of food deterioration caused by microorganisms is the basis to achieving a successful outcome, so that you can proudly share the foods you preserve with your friends and family.

Simple techniques used for everyday meal preparation are some of the same techniques used to minimize deterioration of food quality when home canning. For example, washing an apple is helpful in removing some surface spoilage microorganisms. Peeling the apple reduces even greater numbers of the spoilage microorganisms. However, once the protective peel is removed from the apple, the flesh begins to darken due to enzyme activity. If left untreated, the apple becomes brown and undesirable. This is Mother Nature's way of ensuring that you don't eat food that could potentially be harmful to your health. Another technique frequently used in meal preparation, which is also used to prepare food for home canning, is blanching. Blanching food helps control enzymes long enough for you to complete recipe preparation and fill the jars before processing.

You may then wonder—what does home canning contribute to extending the seasonal quality of food?

The normal cycle of food decay is interrupted when food is home canned according to the tested recipes, processing methods, and specific processing times in this book. Heating food in a sealed jar to a specific temperature for a precise length of time destroys the normal levels of heat-resistant microorganisms present in food and forces air from the jar. The vacuum seal that forms prevents new microorganisms from entering the jar and contaminating its contents. Storing processed, sealed jars at the correct room temperature, 50° to 70°F, is the last essential step to ensure flavorful, nutritious, safe foods are at hand when you're ready to serve them.

Now that you know the basic principles behind home canning, it's also helpful for you to understand how acidity and temperature affects molds, yeasts, bacteria, and enzymes—*the spoilers.*

Molds and Yeasts

Molds are fungi that grow as silken threads in food. A portion of the mold cannot be seen, while part may appear as fuzz on top of food. Certain molds can produce mycotoxins that are harmful to eat. Yeasts are also fungi that cause food to ferment, thus making it unfit to consume. Fortunately, the acid in food protects against the growth of bacteria; however, molds and yeasts are ever-present and continue to grow if left untreated. Molds and yeasts are easily destroyed at temperatures between 140° and 190°F. Processing high-acid foods according to a tested recipe in a boiling-water canner heats foods to 212°F, which is adequate to destroy the molds and yeasts without destroying the quality of food (see figure 1).

Bacteria

Bacteria are not easily destroyed by heat. In fact, certain bacteria actually thrive at the temperatures that destroy molds and yeasts. Salmonella is destroyed when held at 140°F. Staphylococcus aureus, or "staph," is destroyed if food is kept above 140°F. However, staph bacteria produce a toxin that must be destroyed by heating food in a sealed jar to 240°F, for the time specified by a tested home canning recipe (see figure 1).

The bacterium Clostridium botulinum is also readily destroyed by boiling; however, its toxin-producing spores cannot be destroyed at 212°F. Furthermore, this botulism-causing bacterium thrives on low-acid foods in the absence of air within a moist environment—exactly the conditions inside a sealed jar of canned vegetables, meats, or other types of low-acid foods. Due to bacterial spores and the toxin they produce, low-acid foods must be processed at 240°F (see figure 1). This high temperature can only be reached using a pressure canner, since the steam it creates can achieve temperatures hotter than boiling water.

Enzymes

Enzymes are present in all living things. They promote the normal organic changes necessary to the life cycle of food. Their action can cause food to change color, flavor, and texture, making it unappetizing. Enzymes are easily inactivated by heat beginning at 140°F. Like molds and yeasts, enzymes are easily inactivated using the boiling-water process.

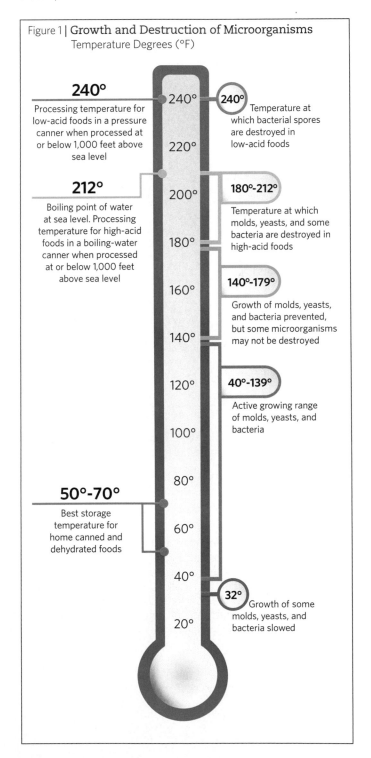

Figure 1 | **Growth and Destruction of Microorganisms**
Temperature Degrees (°F)

240° Processing temperature for low-acid foods in a pressure canner when processed at or below 1,000 feet above sea level

212° Boiling point of water at sea level. Processing temperature for high-acid foods in a boiling-water canner when processed at or below 1,000 feet above sea level

50°-70° Best storage temperature for home canned and dehydrated foods

240° Temperature at which bacterial spores are destroyed in low-acid foods

180°-212° Temperature at which molds, yeasts, and some bacteria are destroyed in high-acid foods

140°-179° Growth of molds, yeasts, and bacteria prevented, but some microorganisms may not be destroyed

40°-139° Active growing range of molds, yeasts, and bacteria

32° Growth of some molds, yeasts, and bacteria slowed

Understand the pH Value of Foods

For the purpose of home canning, all food is divided into two classifications, high-acid and low-acid, determined by the amount of natural acid present in food or the acidification of food to a specific pH level. The importance of pH, or acidity, is that it determines which home canning method must be used to safely preserve foods, enabling them to be stored at room temperature. Figure 2 lists common foods and their relative acidity.

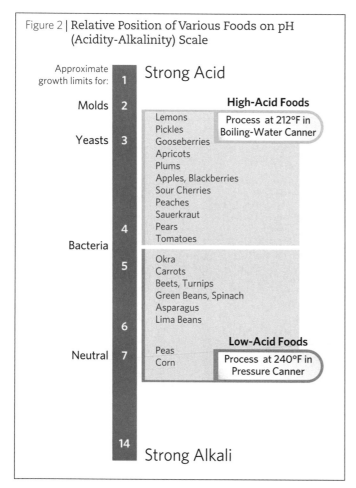

Figure 2 | Relative Position of Various Foods on pH (Acidity-Alkalinity) Scale

Approximate growth limits for:

Strong Acid

1

Molds — 2

High-Acid Foods

Lemons
Pickles
Gooseberries

Process at 212°F in Boiling-Water Canner

Yeasts — 3

Apricots
Plums
Apples, Blackberries
Sour Cherries
Peaches
Sauerkraut
Pears
Tomatoes

Bacteria — 4

Okra
Carrots
Beets, Turnips
Green Beans, Spinach
Asparagus
Lima Beans

5

6

Low-Acid Foods

Neutral — 7

Peas
Corn

Process at 240°F in Pressure Canner

14

Strong Alkali

High-Acid Food and Acidified Food

Foods having naturally high levels of acid, or those with a sufficient amount of acid added to increase the pH level to 4.6 or lower, may be processed using a boiling-water canner. Generally, fruits and soft spreads are classified as high-acid foods. Figs, rhubarb, and tomatoes require the addition of an acidulant (acid). Fermented foods, such as sauerkraut and brined pickles, or foods pickled using 5% acidity vinegar, are also classified as high-acid foods. An acidulant (acid) in the form of citric acid, bottled lemon juice, citrus fruit, or 5% acidity vinegar, when called for in a recipe, helps ensure the correct pH level is maintained. Recipes prepared using a combination of high-acid and low-acid foods must still register a pH of 4.6 or lower in order for them to be safely processed using a boiling-water canner.

Low-Acid Food

Foods having very little natural acid, those with a pH higher than 4.6, must be processed using a pressure canner. Foods in this category include vegetables, meats, poultry, and seafoods. Soups, stews, meat sauces, and other recipes that combine high-acid and low-acid foods, but register a pH higher than 4.6, must also be processed using a pressure canner.

Select the Correct Canning Method

The heat processing method required for any specific food type is determined by the pH—acidity or alkalinity—of the specific food or recipe to be canned. Only two proven methods are used to preserve the recipes in this book—boiling-water processing and pressure processing. Heat processing methods and processing times given for each recipe must be followed exactly as stated. Processing methods and times are not interchangeable; interchanging them may result in food loss or illness.

Boiling-Water Method

Foods naturally high in acid and acidified foods having a pH of 4.6 or lower may be processed using the boiling-water method (see figure 2). Fruits, soft spreads, tomatoes, pickled foods, and other acidified foods can be safely processed in a boiling-water canner when the tested recipes and tested processing times in this book are followed. Boiling-water processing times in this book are based on processing at or below 1,000 feet above sea level. Processing times must be increased if you are located at a higher elevation; refer to the Altitude Chart (see figure 5).

Are you wondering how boiling-water processing works?

1. Filled home canning jars fitted with two-piece vacuum caps are submerged in simmering water that covers the jars by 1 inch.

2. With the lid on the canner, the water is brought to a rolling boil, where it is held for the entire processing time. Heat transfers through the food by convection, conduction, or both, depending on the type of food.

3. The correct combination of temperature (212°F) and tested processing time from this book destroys molds, yeasts, and certain bacteria, and also inactivates enzymes that cause deterioration and spoilage of food.

Here is what to look for when selecting a boiling-water canner:

Boiling-water canners are commonly available in stainless steel, enamel on steel (graniteware), and aluminum. The standard size (approximately 21-quart liquid capacity) holds up to seven home canning quart jars. Boiling-water canners come equipped with a lid and rack.

Figure 3 | Boiling-Water Canner Features

Lid

Base

Rack

Lid—Used to help keep the water boiling during the entire processing period.

Base—Deep enough to hold the size of jar being processed with 1 inch of water covering the two-piece cap, and an additional 2 inches of air space to prevent boil-over. A canner that has a flat bottom may be used on gas or electric burners, while a canner that has a ridged bottom may operate more efficiently when used on gas burners.

Rack—Holds jars off the bottom of the canner and keeps jars upright during processing.

7

Figure 4 | Pressure Canner Features

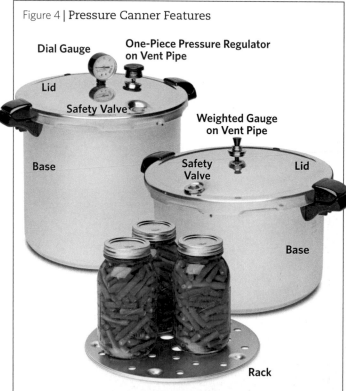

Dial Gauge

One-Piece Pressure Regulator on Vent Pipe

Lid

Safety Valve

Weighted Gauge on Vent Pipe

Base

Safety Valve

Lid

Base

Rack

Lid—Locks or clamps securely onto the base and may be fitted with a gasket, vent pipe, and safety valve.

Gauge—Measures the pressure in the canner. The gauge may be either a three-piece or one-piece weighted gauge or a dial gauge.

Base—Holds jars for processing without obstructing the lid.

Rack—Elevates the jars off the bottom of the canner to allow the steam to circulate around the jars.

Pressure Method

The pressure method is necessary to safely can vegetables, meats, poultry, seafoods, and recipes containing a combination of low-acid and high-acid foods, like meat sauce and beef stew. Foods such as these having a pH higher than 4.6 must be processed at a temperature of 240°F and held there for the time specified by a tested recipe. This high temperature is necessary to destroy all bacteria, their spores, and the toxins they produce, and is achieved only when using a pressure canner.

A pressure canner creates a controlled steam environment that is hotter than the boiling point of water. At 10 pounds pressure, a weighted gauge canner reaches 240°F at 1,000 feet above sea level or lower. Processing times in this book are based on using a weighted gauge pressure canner and processing at an elevation of 1,000 feet above sea level or lower. Pressure must be increased if you are located at a higher elevation or using a dial gauge pressure canner; refer to the Altitude chart (see figure 5).

Are you wondering how pressure processing works?

1. Filled home canning jars fitted with two-piece vacuum caps are placed in the pressure canner, which contains about 2 quarts (about 2 inches) of simmering water.

2. The canner lid is adjusted to the locked position. Heat is increased to medium-high and steam is allowed to escape through the vent pipe for 10 minutes.

3. The weighted gauge is then placed onto the vent pipe. When the gauge indicates the canner is pressurized to 10 pounds (psi), steam circulating inside the canner has reached 240°F, where it is held for the entire processing period. Heat transfers through the food by conduction.

4. The correct combination of temperature and tested processing time destroys molds, yeasts, and bacteria and their toxin-producing spores. It also inactivates enzymes that cause deterioration and spoilage of food.

For information about using your specific pressure canner model, refer to the owner's manual.

Here is what to look for when selecting a pressure canner:

Pressure canners are typically made of heavy-gauge aluminum. The standard size (about 22-quart liquid capacity) typically holds five to seven home canning quart jars. Pressure canners come equipped with a locking lid, lid gasket (for some models), dial or weighted pressure gauge, pressure regulator (for some models), and rack.

Dial Gauge—must be tested for accuracy once each year. If the gauge is inaccurate by 1 pound (psi) or more at 5, 10, or 15 pounds pressure, it must be replaced with a new, accurate gauge. Dial gauge pressure canners are fitted with a one-piece pressure regulator to help maintain temperature. Visually monitor the dial gauge throughout the entire processing period to ensure accurate temperature is maintained. Refer to the owner's manual for dial gauge testing information.

Weighted Gauge—available in adjustable 5, 10, and 15 pounds (psi) and non-adjustable 15 pounds (psi) styles. A weighted gauge does not require testing for accuracy. Slow movement of the weighted gauge during the entire processing period indicates accurate temperature is maintained. When using a non-adjustable gauge, process at 15 pounds (psi) for the same length of time as indicated for 10 pounds (psi). Do not shorten processing time.

Know Your Altitude for Canning

Barometric pressure is reduced at high altitudes, affecting the temperature at which water boils. This means boiling-water and pressure processing methods must be adjusted to ensure the safety of home canned food. Additional processing time must be added when using the boiling water method. Increased temperature is required when using the pressure method. The Altitude Chart gives adjustments for both methods at various elevations (see figure 5).

Processing times and temperatures for recipes in this book are based on canning at an elevation of 1,000 feet above sea level or lower. If you are processing at a higher elevation or using a dial gauge canner, refer to the Altitude Chart for adjustments (see figure 5).

Contact your Natural Resources Conservation Service, Cooperative Extension Service, or Public Library Service for the altitude in your area.

Gather Your Canning Equipment

Improvements in canning equipment, small appliances, and kitchen utensils help to make home canning a simple, safe, and efficient method of preserving food at home. Most equipment used for home canning is readily available in a well-equipped kitchen. A little pre-planning to check that all equipment and ingredients are on hand in advance of the intended canning day will allow you time to acquire any items you may need.

Figure 5 | Altitude Chart

Boiling-Water Method

The processing times given in this book for high-acid foods are based on canning at or below 1,000 feet above sea level using the boiling water method. When processing at altitudes higher than 1,000 feet above sea level, adjust the processing time according to this boiling-water canner chart.

Boiling-Water Canner Altitude Adjustments	
Altitude In Feet	Increase Processing Time
1,001 to 3,000	5 Minutes
3,001 to 6,000	10 Minutes
6,001 to 8,000	15 Minutes
8,001 to 10,000	20 Minutes

Pressure Method

The pressure method is used for low-acid foods. The pounds pressure given for low-acid foods in this book are based on using a weighted gauge canner and processing at or below 1,000 feet above sea level. When using a dial gauge canner or processing at altitudes higher than 1,000 feet above sea level, adjust pounds pressure according to this pressure canner chart.

Pressure Canner Altitude Adjustments		
Altitude in Feet	Weighted Gauge	Dial Gauge
0 to 1,000	10	11
1,001 to 2,000	15	11
2,001 to 4,000	15	12
4,001 to 6,000	15	13
6,001 to 8,000	15	14
8,001 to 10,000	15	15

Glass Home Canning Jars

Home canning jars, sometimes referred to as Mason jars, are the only glass jars recommended for home canning. They come in a variety of sizes with decorative embossing to meet everyday needs and for gift-giving occasions. Ball® brand jars are manufactured to the correct specifications and sizes for the tested recipes in this book, as well as for recipes offered by the USDA.

Ball® jars have two distinguishable shapes: standard and tapered. Standard home canning jars are easily recognized by their square-round side wall that curves slightly to form a shoulder as it connects to the neck of the jar where threads begin to form. Standard jars come in regular and wide mouth openings. They are typically available in 8-ounce, 16-ounce, 32-ounce, and 64-ounce sizes.

Tapered home canning jars are designed with a straight side wall and have a smaller circumference at the bottom than at the opening. The straight side wall connects to the neck of the jar where threads begin to form. It is this tapered shape that makes these jars uniquely suited for the dual functions of home canning and home freezing. Tapered jars are designed with regular and wide mouth openings. You can find them in 4-ounce, 8-ounce, 12-ounce, 16-ounce, and 24-ounce sizes.

The glass used to manufacture Ball jars can withstand both the high temperature of pressure canning and the sub-zero temperature of freezing—but only tapered jars are suitable for freezer storage.

Metal Lids and Bands

Home canning two-piece vacuum caps come in regular or wide mouth sizes. The set consists of a flat metal lid and a threaded band. The lid has a lacquer finish to help prevent the natural corrosive reaction that occurs when high-acid foods come in contact with metal. It also has a flanged edge sized to the width of the jar rim and lined with sealing compound. Lids are needed to help form a vacuum seal and to ensure microorganisms do not enter the jar and contaminate the food after heat processing. Lids may be used only one time for home canning.

Metal bands, in regular or wide mouth sizes, complete the cap set. Bands are threaded to adjust evenly onto home canning jars. Adjust bands to fingertip tightness so they fit comfortably onto jars without being forced. The sole purpose of the band is to hold the lid in place during processing. After jars are processed and a vacuum seal is formed, bands are no longer needed. They may be removed before storing jars. If maintained in good condition, bands can be reused multiple times.

Canning Utensils

Specially-designed utensils help make home canning easier and safer. Most pieces may be purchased where home canning supplies are sold. You will find these canning utensils to be very helpful.

Jar Funnel

Jar Lifter

Bubble Remover & Headspace Tool

What You Need to Do

Based on your family's needs and your gift-giving list, decide the types of food and recipes to be canned. Determine the number of jars and closures you'll need, along with the jar sizes and styles best suited for your selected recipes. Examine canning equipment to ensure canners and utensils are in good working condition. Plan to complete only those recipes which may be easily prepared and processed within the time you have available. For the most nutritious and flavorful results, can your produce immediately after harvesting or purchasing. If it becomes necessary to hold produce for more than a couple of hours, store produce properly to minimize the effects of deterioration from enzymes and microorganisms. Refer to the Home Canning Planning Guide (see page 183).

Start With A "Good" Recipe

What is meant by "use only a recipe tested for home canning?"

A recipe needs more than good flavor to be considered safe for home canning. Not all recipes undergo the necessary evaluation to determine accurate processing temperature and processing time that will yield a shelf-stable home canned food. Factors like jar size, accurate measurements, the use of only those ingredients listed in the recipe, among other factors, are all part of the equation when tested processing methods and tested processing times are established.

That's why it's important to choose recipes from a reliable resource with the knowledge of food chemistry and process testing to ensure safe, nutritious results that will store on your pantry shelf safely for up to one year.

Preparing the recipes in this book does not require special culinary skills. Begin by reading the recipe you selected all the way through in order to gain a clear understanding of the instructions before you start. Set aside enough time to prepare and process the recipe without interruption. Next, assemble all equipment and ingredients. Use a standard food scale, measuring cups, and measuring spoons as appropriate to prepare your recipe. Techniques used to prepare and cook ingredients are important, so do not deviate from the recipe instructions.

Each recipe will instruct on what temperature the food should be when packed into the jars. You will find recipes that call for some ingredients to be raw when packed into the jars and covered with hot brine, syrup, fruit juice, or water—this is the "Raw Pack" method.

Other recipes require all ingredients to be fully cooked and hot before being packed into the jars—this is the "Hot Pack" method. Maintaining accurate fill temperature is essential for the safety of home canned food. Changes made in the preparation of the recipe may adversely affect heat penetration and could possibly yield an underprocessed food product that is not shelf-stable.

Get Ready to Can

Before each canning session, examine all the equipment you plan to use to ensure it's in good working condition, including canners, jars, lids, and bands. Guidelines given in this book for the use of home canning jars, lids, and bands must be followed for safe handling, cleaning, and processing.

Canners

Boiling-Water Canner—Examine the canner lid and base for dents, holes, or warping that would interfere with heat distribution. The wire rack may become corroded after repeated use, but is easily cleaned using a soft abrasive cleaner or fine steel wool pad. Replace all parts that show signs of wear or defect. Replacement racks can usually be purchased separately.

Pressure Canner—Some canners are fitted with replaceable gaskets and safety valves that must be examined carefully for cracking or warping. Clean the vent pipe with string or a small brush to remove residue that might block the passage of steam. Test the locking mechanism on the lid and check the lid and canner base for warping. If the canner has a dial gauge, it must be tested annually for accuracy prior to use. Replace all parts that show signs of wear or defect.

Jars

Visually examine jars for defects or damage that prevent their use. Discard unusable jars. Wash new and previously used jars in hot, soapy water. Do not use brushes with wire components, steel wool or abrasive materials or cleansers, as they may damage the glass. Jars must be heated for 10 minutes before being filled to help prevent breakage due to thermal shock. Submerge jars in enough water to cover by one inch. Bring water to a simmer, 180°F, maintaining this temperature until the jars are ready for use. Remove jars one at a time as they are needed for filling. A dishwasher may also be used to clean and pre-heat jars. Wash and dry jars using a complete regular cycle just prior to the time you need them. Hold jars in the closed dishwasher to keep them hot, removing one at a time as needed. These two methods are the only methods recommended for pre-heating jars for canning.

Lids and Bands

Choose the appropriate size of lid and band for the jar you select. New lids with sealing compound must be used each time you home can. Bands may be reused if they are in working condition. Wash lids and bands in hot, soapy water. Do not use abrasive materials or cleansers that might scratch or damage the coatings applied to the lids and bands. Rinse them under hot water. Dry lids and bands and set aside until they are needed.

Follow the "How-To" of Processing

As with recipe preparation, jar size selection, and accurate processing temperature, it is equally important to the overall success of canning that jars are filled properly and lids and bands are applied correctly. Fill one jar at a time, rather than working assembly line-style. Remove one jar from preheating, fill jar to the correct headspace, adjust the lid and band, then immediately place the sealed jar onto the rack. Repeat until all jars are filled or the recipe is gone. Following these basic steps will help make the process efficient and easy to complete.

1. Filling Jar—There are two methods for packing food into jars: Raw Pack and Hot Pack. Each recipe in this book designates the correct method to use. For some recipes, either option is acceptable.

Raw Pack—Foods that would be delicate after they are cooked, such as peaches, are usually easier to handle if they are raw packed. Uncooked whole or cut food is placed into the jar. It is packed firmly without crushing. Hot brine, syrup, fruit juice, or water is added just to cover or as stated in the recipe.

Hot Pack—This method is preferred when the food to be canned is relatively firm and handles well. Whole or cut food is first cooked in brine, syrup, fruit juice, or water. It may be removed from the cooking liquid and placed into the jar without crushing. Hot brine, syrup, fruit juice, or water is added just to cover or as stated in the recipe. The hot pack method is preferred for nearly all vegetables, meats, poultry, seafoods, and many fruits. Fruit canned without sweetener is always hot packed.

2. Measuring Headspace—Headspace is the unfilled space in the jar between the food or liquid and the rim of the jar. Each recipe will specify the correct headspace to use. As a general rule, leave 1-inch headspace for low-acid foods, vegetables, and meats; 1/2-inch headspace for high-acid foods like fruits, tomatoes, pickles, and relishes; 1/4-inch headspace for fruit juices, jams, jellies, and other soft spreads (see figure 6).

3. Removing Air Bubbles—Air bubbles must be removed after filling the jar. Even though air bubbles may not be visible, they can be trapped between pieces of food or in thick liquid. Place a nonmetallic spatula inside the jar between the food and the side of the jar. Gently press the spatula against the food to release trapped air. Repeat several times around the inside of the jar. Do not use a metal knife or other metal utensils since metal can scratch the glass, making the jar susceptible to breakage.

4. Cleaning Jar Rim—Particles of food or syrup remaining on the jar rim can prevent a vacuum seal. Wipe the jar rim with a clean, damp cloth.

5. Adjusting Lid and Band—Center a lid on the jar so that only the sealing compound is in contact with the jar rim. Place a band over the lid and adjust it until fingertip-tight.

Filling Jar

Measuring Headspace

Figure 6 | **Measuring Headspace**
(Diagram is not to scale)

Rim of Jar

1/4"
1/2"
1"

Proper Fill Levels of Food in Jar
Measure headspace from the rim of the jar to the top of the food.

6. **Processing**—Processing methods and processing times apply only to individual recipes in this book as stated. Processing methods and/or processing times are not interchangeable.

Boiling-Water Processing

- Place filled jar on the rack that is elevated above simmering (180°F) water in boiling-water canner. Repeat until all jars are filled. Lower the rack into simmering water.

- Jars should be covered by 1 inch of simmering water. Add boiling water, if needed. Place lid on canner. Adjust heat to medium-high and bring water to a rolling boil.

- Set timer for the length of time stated in the recipe. Maintain a rolling boil throughout the entire processing period. After processing is completed, turn off heat and remove canner lid. Let canner cool 5 minutes before removing jars.

Pressure Processing

- With rack inside the canner, add approximately 2 quarts of water (about 2 inches), or follow manufacturer's instructions. Bring water to a simmer (180°F).

- Place filled jar on the rack in canner. Repeat until all jars are filled. Lock canner lid securely in place. Adjust heat to medium-high. After steam flows evenly from the vent pipe, continue to exhaust steam for 10 minutes.

- Place gauge on vent pipe. The canner should pressurize in about 5 minutes. After the gauge indicates recommended pounds of pressure (psi) is reached, adjust heat to maintain the correct pressure for the entire processing period. Set timer for the length of time stated in the recipe. Monitor the process to ensure the pressure does not fluctuate.

- Turn off heat after processing period is completed. Let the canner cool naturally. After the canner has depressurized and returned to zero pressure, remove the gauge. Unlock lid and lift it off the canner base so that the steam escapes away from you. Let canner cool 10 minutes before removing jars.

7. **Cooling**—Remove jars from canner using a jar lifter. Set jars upright on a dry towel or cutting board to cool for 12 hours, leaving 1 to 2 inches of space between jars so they cool at an even rate. Do not invert, move, or store jars while they are still warm, as this may cause seal failure and loss of food. Bands may loosen during the processing period. If this occurs, do not retighten bands, as doing so may interfere with the seal that is already forming.

8. **Testing Seals**—After the jars have cooled at least 12 hours, test the lids to determine if the jars are vacuum sealed. Press the center of the lid to determine if it is concave. Remove the band. Gently try to remove the lid with your fingertips. If the lid is concave and cannot be removed with your fingertips, the jar is vacuum sealed.

9. **Storage**—Carefully wash jars and lids using a clean, damp cloth to remove residue that may have siphoned from the jar during processing. Wash, rinse, and dry bands. Sealed jars may be safely stored without bands or, if you prefer, bands can be carefully applied onto the jars before storing. Label jars with the recipe name and processing date. Store jars in a cool (50° to 70°F), dry, dark place for up to one year.

Note: The processing methods and processing times given in this book are tested using only home canning products marketed by Jarden Home Brands.

Removing Air Bubbles

Cleaning Jar Rim

Adjusting Lid and Band

Testing Seal

Fruits & Juices

Fruits are one of the most iconic canned items. And it makes sense—after all, what other food has so many varieties, uses, or flavor combinations? Nothing else brightens a winter day like the taste of summer fruit perfectly preserved. Begin with canned fruits to create healthful desserts and sophisticated sauces and condiments, or you can simply eat them straight from the jar! Being able to choose the ingredients yourself gives you the ability to manage your family's healthy choices, too.

Getting Started

Here you'll find recipes that use fruits in a variety of ways with creative flavor combinations designed to inspire you at mealtime. Most fruits are naturally acidic, which makes them some of the easiest foods to preserve. Canning a few jars of your favorite fruits prepared whole, sliced, sauced, and juiced gives you even more versatility for serving, cooking, baking, and gifting.

Reap the sweet rewards of eating well

Whether it's to meet special dietary requirements or simply in order to make healthy eating choices, preserving fresh fruits gives you more control over the quality of foods you eat. We'll show you how to reduce sugar without losing flavor, among other healthy choices.

Build your success on food science

Because fruits are highly acidic, they're safe to process using the boiling water method. The boiling water method will heat fruits to a temperature hot enough to destroy the spoilers—molds, yeasts, and enzymes. Simply follow the instructions for measuring and preparing ingredients, selection of jar size, and processing time.

Understand how altitude affects canning

The processing times given for fruits, sauces, and juices in this section apply when canning at 0 to 1,000 feet above sea level. Barometric pressure affects the boiling point of water, so if you are canning at a higher elevation, refer to the Boiling-Water Canner Altitude Adjustments (see page 9).

Good Things to Know

Fruits

Harvest or purchase only the best quality fruit when it is at its peak for flavor, texture, and color. Discard mushy, overripe, and diseased fruit. Prepare only the amount of fruit needed for the recipe(s) you are able to complete at one time. Store remaining fruit where it will keep the freshest for a day or two. Refrigerate tender fruit, like berries and apricots. Apples, pears, and other firm fruits can be stored at room temperature.

Sweeteners

Fruits may be canned in sugar syrup, fruit juice, or water. Unless the recipe gives exact ingredients for the syrup, you have flexibility to vary the level of sweetness for personal preference or to meet dietary requirements. However, sugar does aid in retaining a bright color, firm texture, and full flavor of the fruit after processing. An important rule to follow when omitting all sugar from canned fruit is to use only the hot pack method—meaning the fruit must be heated in water or fruit juice until hot throughout before filling jars.

Non-sugar sweeteners may be used when canning fruit. Each has unique properties and usage recommendations. Select the type best suited for the specific recipe to be prepared. Non-sugar sweeteners that are sensitive to heat or prolonged storage should be added just before serving canned foods. Read the manufacturer's recommendations for more information.

Antioxidants

Light-colored fruit such as apples, peaches, pears, and apricots darken after peeling or cutting due to oxidation—exposure to air. This harmless discoloration can be prevented by pre-treating the fruit with an antioxidant combined with water. The solution acts as a barrier to prevent air from turning the fruit brown. Common antioxidants include: citrus juice, citric acid, ascorbic acid (vitamin C), and a blend of ascorbic and citric acids. Ball® Fruit-Fresh® Produce Protector is a blend of ascorbic and citric acids that prevents fresh cut fruits from darkening.

To prepare the pre-treatment solution using Fruit-Fresh, combine 3 rounded tablespoons of Fruit-Fresh and two quarts of water in a large bowl. Place prepared fruit in the mixture until needed. Drain fruit before filling jars for RAW PACK and before cooking in syrup, fruit juice, or water for HOT PACK.

Spices and Flavorings

Spices and herbs add flavor and interest to a number of fruit recipes in this book. Ground spices are used unless otherwise specified. Use whole, crushed, or slivered spices and herbs only when listed in the recipe. Substituting ground spices or herbs in place of their whole form may adversely affect the flavor and appearance of the recipe. Occasionally, whole spices and herbs are tied in a spice bag or several layers of cheesecloth so they can be easily removed before filling jars.

Wines, liqueurs, and extracts also impart their unique characteristics to the overall flavor of a recipe. It is not necessary to use the most expensive brands; however, their natural attributes of flavor and color should be considered in order to complement the fruit.

Syrups for Canning

Whole, halved, and sliced fruit is canned in a liquid which helps preserve its flavor, color, and texture, as well as transferring heat throughout the product during processing. The liquid may be a sweet syrup, fruit juice, or water. Fresh fruit juice, bottled fruit juice, and fruit juice made from frozen concentrate, either sweetened or unsweetened, may be used as the liquid for canning fruit. If fruit juice or water is used instead of sugar syrup, the HOT PACK method and processing time must be followed.

Select any sweetness level you prefer unless the recipe gives specific instructions for the amount of sweetener to add. The Syrups for Canning chart provides guidelines for preparing a variety of syrups sweetened with sugar, honey, and corn syrup. To make syrup for canning fruit, combine sugar (or other sweetener) and water in a saucepan. Bring the mixture to a boil, stirring until sugar dissolves. Reduce heat to a simmer (180°F); keep syrup hot until it is needed, but do not let it evaporate. Each quart jar of fruit requires about 1 to 1½ cups of syrup.

Figure 7 | **Syrups for Canning**

Syrup Type	% of Sugar	Sugar	Sweetener	Water	Yield
Extra-Light	20%	1½ Cups		5¾ Cups	6 Cups
Light	30%	2¼ Cups		5¼ Cups	6½ Cups
Medium	40%	3¼ Cups		5 Cups	7 Cups
Heavy	50%	4¼ Cups		4¼ Cups	7 Cups
Corn Syrup		1½ Cups	1 Cup Corn Syrup	3 Cups	6 Cups
Honey		1 Cup	1 Cup Honey	4 Cups	5 Cups

Note: Each syrup recipe yields enough syrup to can 3 to 4 quart jars of fruit.

Fruits

Apples

Yield: about 6 pint or 3 quart jars

7½ to 9 pounds apples
    (about 23 to 27 medium)

Ball Fruit-Fresh Produce
    Protector

1 batch Syrup for Canning,
    see page 16

PREP Wash apples under cold running water; drain. Core and peel apples. Cut apples into ¼-inch slices, quarters, or halves. Treat apples with Fruit-Fresh to prevent darkening (see page 16).

COOK Prepare Syrup for Canning in a large saucepan. Bring mixture to a boil. Drain apples. Add apples to hot syrup; gently boil 5 minutes.

FILL Pack hot apples into a hot jar, leaving ½-inch headspace. Ladle hot syrup over apples, leaving ½-inch headspace. Remove air bubbles. Clean jar rim. Center lid on jar and adjust band to fingertip-tight. Place jar on the rack elevated over simmering water (180°F) in boiling-water canner. Repeat until all jars are filled.

PROCESS Lower the rack into simmering water. Water must cover jars by 1 inch. Adjust heat to medium-high, cover canner and bring water to a rolling boil. Process pint or quart jars 20 minutes. Turn off heat and remove cover. Let jars cool 5 minutes. Remove jars from canner; do not retighten bands if loose. Cool 12 hours. Test seals. Label and store jars.

Tempt your taste buds with a variety of canned apples stored on your pantry shelf. Preserve Northern Spy for its juicy sweetness and tart bite, Gala variety for its sweetness and touch of spicy overtones, or the straightforward Fuji for its sweet flavor notes.

Apples for Baking

Yield: about 8 pint or 4 quart jars

10 to 12 pounds Granny
    Smith apples (about
    30 to 36 medium)

Ball Fruit-Fresh Produce
    Protector

1 cup sugar

2 cups water

1 tablespoon lemon juice,
    fresh or bottled

PREP Wash apples under cold running water; drain. Core and peel apples. Cut apples lengthwise into ¼- to ½-inch slices. Treat apples with Fruit-Fresh to prevent darkening (see page 16).

COOK Combine sugar, water, and lemon juice in a large saucepan. Bring mixture to a boil, stirring until sugar dissolves. Drain apple slices. Add apple slices to hot syrup; gently boil 5 minutes.

FILL Pack hot apple slices into a hot jar, leaving ½-inch headspace. Ladle hot syrup over apple slices, leaving ½-inch headspace. Remove air bubbles. Clean jar rim. Center lid on jar and adjust band to fingertip-tight. Place jar on the rack elevated over simmering water (180°F) in boiling-water canner. Repeat until all jars are filled.

PROCESS Lower the rack into simmering water. Water must cover jars by I inch. Adjust heat to medium-high, cover canner and bring water to a rolling boil. Process pint or quart jars 20 minutes. Turn off heat and remove cover. Let jars cool 5 minutes. Remove jars from canner; do not retighten bands if loose. Cool 12 hours. Test seals. Label and store jars.

This recipe is prepared using light syrup. Refer to Syrups for Canning (see page 16) for other options.

Use any variety of apples good for baking to help maintain shape and texture such as Granny Smith, Fuji, Winesap, and Rome Beauty.

Apple Rings

Yield: about 6 pint or 3 quart jars

10 pounds apples (about
    30 to 40 medium)

Ball Fruit-Fresh Produce
    Protector

4 cups sugar

4 cups water

Red food coloring (optional)

PREP Wash apples under cold running water; drain. Core apples but do not peel. Slice apples crosswise into ¼-inch rings. Treat apple rings with Fruit-Fresh to prevent darkening (see page 16).

COOK Combine sugar and water in a large saucepan. Add a few drops of red food coloring, if desired. Bring mixture to a boil, stirring until sugar dissolves. Boil 5 minutes. Remove saucepan from heat. Drain apple rings. Add apple rings to hot syrup and let stand 10 minutes. Bring apple rings and syrup to a boil. Reduce heat to a simmer (180°F); simmer 30 minutes. Remove apple rings from syrup; keep hot. Return syrup to a boil.

FILL Layer hot apple rings loosely into a hot jar, leaving ½-inch headspace. Ladle hot syrup over apple rings, leaving ½-inch headspace. Remove air bubbles. Clean jar rim. Center lid on jar and adjust band to fingertip-tight. Place jar on the rack elevated over simmering water (180°F) in boiling-water canner. Repeat until all jars are filled.

PROCESS Lower rack into simmering water. Water must cover jars by 1 inch. Adjust heat to medium-high, cover canner and bring water to a rolling boil. Process pint jars 15 minutes or quart jars 20 minutes. Turn off heat and remove cover. Let jars cool 5 minutes. Remove jars from canner; do not retighten bands if loose. Cool 12 hours. Test seals. Label and store jars.

Spiced apple rings can be made by adding stick cinnamon, whole cloves, or other whole spices tied in a spice bag. Add spice bag to the syrup during recipe preparation. Remove spice bag before canning apple rings.

Use any variety of apples good for cooking to help maintain shape and texture, such as Granny Smith, Braeburn, and Cortland.

Apple Wedges in Cinnamon Red Hot Syrup

Yield: about 6 pint jars

8 to 10 pounds apples (about
    24 to 30 medium)

Ball Fruit-Fresh Produce
    Protector

1½ cups sugar

½ cup cinnamon red hot
    candies

2 sticks cinnamon

2 teaspoons whole cloves

1 teaspoon ginger

2 cups water

1½ cups vinegar, 5% acidity

⅔ cup light corn syrup

2 tablespoons red food
    coloring (optional)

PREP Wash apples under cold running water; drain. Core and peel apples. Cut apples lengthwise into eighths. Treat apples with Fruit-Fresh to prevent darkening (see page 16).

COOK Combine all ingredients, except apples, in a large saucepan. Bring mixture to a boil, stirring until sugar dissolves.

Boil 5 minutes. Drain apple wedges. Add apple wedges to hot syrup. Cover pan and simmer (180°F) 5 minutes.

FILL Pack hot apple wedges into a hot jar, leaving ½-inch headspace. Ladle hot syrup over apple wedges, leaving ½-inch headspace. Remove air bubbles. Clean jar rim. Center lid on jar and adjust band to fingertip-tight. Place jar on the rack elevated over simmering water (180°F) in boiling-water canner. Repeat until all jars are filled.

PROCESS Lower the rack into simmering water. Water must cover jars by 1 inch. Adjust heat to medium-high, cover canner and bring water to a rolling boil. Process pint jars 15 minutes. Turn off heat and remove cover. Let jars cool 5 minutes. Remove jars from canner; do not retighten bands if loose. Cool 12 hours. Test seals. Label and store jars.

Applesauce

Yield: about 6 pint or 3 quart jars

7½ to 10½ pounds apples (about 22 to 32 medium)

Ball Fruit-Fresh Produce Protector

1 to 1½ cups water

1¾ cups to 2½ cups sugar (optional)

PREP Wash apples under cold running water; drain. Remove stem and blossom ends from apples. Peel apples, if desired. Cut apples into quarters. Treat apples with Fruit-Fresh to prevent darkening (see page 16).

COOK Drain apple quarters. Combine apples and water in a large saucepan. Cook over medium heat until soft, stirring to prevent sticking. Remove from heat. Purée mixture using an electric food strainer or food mill to remove peels and seeds. Return apple pulp to saucepan. Add sugar, if desired, stirring until sugar dissolves. Bring applesauce to a boil (212°F), stirring to prevent sticking. Maintain temperature at a boil (212°F) while filling jars.

FILL Ladle hot applesauce into a hot jar, leaving ½-inch headspace. Remove air bubbles. Clean jar rim. Center lid on jar and adjust band to fingertip-tight. Place jar on the rack elevated over simmering water (180°F) in boiling-water canner. Repeat until all jars are filled.

PROCESS Lower the rack into simmering water. Water must cover jars by 1 inch. Adjust heat to medium-high, cover canner and bring water to a rolling boil. Process pint or quart jars 20 minutes. Turn off heat and remove cover. Let jars cool 5 minutes. Remove jars from canner; do not retighten bands if loose. Cool 12 hours. Test seals. Label and store jars.

 Applesauce can be made without the addition of sugar. Use a juicy, sweet apple like Honeycrisp, Golden Delicious, Gala, or Fuji when omitting sugar from the recipe. Try spicing up a batch or two by adding your favorite ground spices during the last 5 minutes of cooking.

 Red-skinned apples impart a rosy color to applesauce if they are not peeled before cooking. Prefer a creamy yellow color? Peel the apples before cooking.

Chunky Applesauce: Coarsely crush half of the cooked apples and purée the other half; combine mixtures. Process as for Applesauce.

Apricots

Yield: 6 pint or 3 quart jars

6 to 7½ pounds apricots (about 48 to 60 medium)

Ball Fruit-Fresh Produce Protector

1 batch Syrup for Canning, see page 16

PREP Wash apricots under cold running water; drain. Apricots may be canned with or without the peel. To peel apricots, blanch in boiling water 30 to 60 seconds. Immediately transfer to cold water. Cut off peel. Cut apricots in half and remove pits and fibrous flesh. Treat apricots with Fruit-Fresh to prevent darkening (see page 16).

COOK

RAW PACK—Prepare Syrup for Canning in a medium saucepan. Bring mixture to a boil. Reduce heat to a simmer (180°F). Drain apricots.

HOT PACK—Prepare Syrup for Canning in a large saucepan. Bring mixture to a boil. Reduce heat to a simmer (180°F). Drain apricots. Cook apricots in syrup, one layer at a time, until hot throughout.

FILL

RAW PACK—Pack apricots, cavity side down and layers overlapping, into a hot jar, leaving ½-inch headspace. Ladle hot syrup over apricots, leaving ½-inch headspace.

HOT PACK—Pack hot apricots, cavity side down and layers overlapping, into a hot jar, leaving ½-inch headspace. Ladle hot cooking syrup over apricots, leaving ½-inch headspace.

Remove air bubbles. Clean jar rim. Center lid on jar and adjust band to fingertip-tight. Place jar on the rack elevated over simmering water (180°F) in boiling-water canner. Repeat until all jars are filled.

PROCESS Lower the rack into simmering water. Water must cover jars by 1 inch. Adjust heat to medium-high, cover canner and bring water to a rolling boil. Process pint jars 20 minutes or quart jars 25 minutes. Turn off heat and remove cover. Let jars cool 5 minutes. Remove jars from canner; do not retighten bands if loose. Cool 12 hours. Test seals. Label and store jars.

Apricots in Pineapple Juice No sugar added

Yield: about 6 pint or 3 quart jars

6 to 7½ pounds apricots (about 48 to 60 medium)

Ball Fruit-Fresh Produce Protector

5 cups unsweetened pineapple juice, fresh or bottled

PREP Wash apricots under cold running water; drain. To peel apricots, blanch in boiling water for 30 to 60 seconds. Immediately transfer to cold water. Cut off peel. Treat apricots with Fruit-Fresh to prevent darkening (see page 16).

COOK Drain apricots. Heat apricots in a small amount of water, one layer at a time, until hot throughout. Heat pineapple juice just to a boil.

FILL Pack hot apricots into a hot jar, leaving ½-inch headspace. Ladle hot pineapple juice over apricots, leaving ½-inch headspace. Remove air bubbles. Clean jar rim. Center lid on jar and adjust band to fingertip-tight. Place filled jar on the rack elevated over simmering water (180°F) in boiling-water canner. Repeat until all jars are filled.

PROCESS Lower the rack into simmering water. Water must cover jars by 1 inch. Adjust heat to medium-high, cover canner

and bring water to a rolling boil. Process pint jars 20 minutes or quart jars 25 minutes. Turn off heat and remove cover. Let jars cool 5 minutes. Remove jars from canner; do not retighten bands if loose. Cool 12 hours. Test seals. Label and store jars.

Berries

Blackberries, Black Raspberries, Blueberries, Currants, Elderberries, Huckleberries, Red Raspberries, etc.

Yield: about 6 pint or 3 quart jars

4½ to 9 pounds berries

1 batch Syrup for Canning, see page 16, for RAW PACK
-OR- Sugar for HOT PACK

PREP Wash berries under cold running water; drain. Discard crushed, bruised, or diseased berries. Measure berries.

COOK

RAW PACK—Prepare Syrup for Canning in a medium saucepan. Bring mixture to a boil. Reduce heat to a simmer (180°F).

HOT PACK—Combine berries and ¼ cup to ½ cup sugar for each quart of berries. Let stand 2 hours in a cool place. Cook berries over medium-low heat until sugar dissolves and berries are hot throughout.

FILL

RAW PACK—Fill a hot jar with berries using a non-metallic utensil to gently pack berries without crushing, leaving ½-inch headspace. Ladle hot syrup over berries, leaving ½-inch headspace.

HOT PACK—Ladle hot berries and juice into a hot jar, leaving ½-inch headspace. If there is not enough syrup for all jars, add simmering water (180°F), leaving ½-inch headspace.

Remove air bubbles. Clean jar rim. Center lid on jar and adjust band to fingertip-tight. Place jar on the rack elevated over simmering water (180°F) in boiling-water canner. Repeat until all jars are filled.

PROCESS Lower the rack into simmering water. Water must cover jars by 1 inch. Adjust heat to medium-high, cover canner and bring water to a rolling boil. Process pint or quart jars 15 minutes. Turn off heat and remove cover. Let jars cool 5 minutes. Remove jars from canner; do not retighten bands if they are loose. Cool 12 hours. Test seals. Label and store jars.

Note: Use RAW PACK for red raspberries and other berries that do not hold their shape well when heated. Use HOT PACK for blueberries and other berries that do hold their shape when heated. Add 1 to 2 tablespoons fresh or bottled lemon juice in each quart jar of elderberries to improve flavor, if desired.

Create an assortment of flavorful tastes by combining two or three varieties of berries in the same batch. Combine your choice of berries, using an equal amount of each, in a large bowl; toss gently to blend. Process berries using the RAW PACK or HOT PACK method. Oh, don't forget to process a mixed batch following the recipe Berries for Baking!

Fresh herbs enliven the flavor of almost any berry. Toss a sprig or two of mint, rosemary, or thyme into the syrup as it cooks. Remove herbs before canning.

Berries for Baking: Omit sugar from recipe and cook in a small amount of water until berries are hot throughout; process as for HOT PACK berries.

Brandied Cherries

Yield: about 6 pint jars

6 pounds dark sweet cherries	½ cup lemon juice, fresh or bottled
1 cup sugar	1¼ cups brandy
1 cup water	

PREP Wash cherries under cold running water; drain. Stem and pit cherries.

COOK Combine sugar, water, and lemon juice in a large saucepan. Bring mixture to a boil, stirring until sugar dissolves. Reduce heat to a simmer (180°F). Add cherries and simmer until they are hot throughout. Remove saucepan from heat. Stir in brandy.

FILL Pack hot cherries into a hot jar, leaving ½-inch headspace. Ladle hot syrup over cherries, leaving ½-inch headspace. Remove air bubbles. Clean jar rim. Center lid on jar and adjust band to fingertip-tight. Place jar on the rack elevated over simmering water (180°F) in boiling-water canner. Repeat until all jars are filled.

PROCESS Lower the rack into simmering water. Water must cover jars by 1 inch. Adjust heat to medium-high, cover canner and bring water to a rolling boil. Process pint jars 10 minutes. Turn off heat and remove cover. Let jars cool 5 minutes. Remove jars from canner; do not retighten bands if loose. Cool 12 hours. Test seals. Label and store jars.

Note: Brandied Cherries will be evenly flavored in about 4 weeks.

Brandied Peaches

Yield: about 3 pint jars

4 to 5 pounds small peaches (about 16 to 20 small)	6 cups sugar, divided
	1 teaspoon salt
	1 quart water
Ball Fruit-Fresh Produce Protector	¾ cup peach brandy

PREP Wash peaches; drain. To peel peaches, blanch in boiling water for 30 to 60 seconds. Immediately transfer to cold water. Cut off peel. Treat peaches with Fruit-Fresh to prevent darkening (see page 16).

COOK Combine 3 cups sugar, salt, and water in a large saucepan. Bring mixture to a boil, stirring until sugar dissolves. Drain peaches. Gently boil peaches in syrup, one layer at a time, for 5 minutes or until hot throughout. Transfer cooked peaches to a large bowl. Boil syrup 5 minutes; pour hot syrup over peaches. Cover peaches and refrigerate 12 to 18 hours. Drain peaches, reserving syrup. Combine syrup and 3 cups sugar in a large saucepan. Bring mixture to a boil, stirring until sugar dissolves. Pour hot syrup over peaches. Cover peaches and refrigerate 12 to 18 hours. Gently boil peaches in syrup until hot throughout.

FILL Pack hot peaches into a hot jar, leaving ½-inch headspace. Add 4 tablespoons peach brandy. Ladle hot syrup over peaches, leaving ½-inch headspace. Remove air bubbles. Clean jar rim. Center lid on jar and adjust band to fingertip-tight. Place jar on the rack elevated over simmering water (180°F) in boiling-water canner. Repeat until all jars are filled.

PROCESS Lower the rack into simmering water. Water must cover jars by 1 inch. Adjust heat to medium-high, cover canner and bring water to a rolling boil. Process pint jars 10 minutes. Turn off heat and remove cover. Let jars cool 5 minutes. Remove jars from canner; do not retighten bands if loose. Cool 12 hours. Test seals. Label and store jars.

Note: Brandied Peaches will be evenly flavored in about 4 weeks.

Brandied Pears

Yield: about 4 quart jars

10 pounds pears (about 30 to 35 medium)	6 cups sugar
	4 cups water
Ball Fruit-Fresh Produce Protector	3 cups brandy

PREP Wash pears under cold running water; drain. Cut pears in half lengthwise, core, and peel. Treat pears with Fruit-Fresh to prevent darkening (see page 16).

COOK Combine sugar and water in a large saucepan. Bring mixture to a boil, stirring until sugar dissolves. Drain pears. Cook pears in syrup, one layer at a time, until just tender, about 5 minutes. Transfer pears to a large bowl; keep hot. Continue cooking syrup to thicken, about 15 minutes. Remove syrup from heat. Stir in brandy.

FILL Pack hot pears into a hot jar, cavity side down and layers overlapping, leaving 1/2-inch headspace. Ladle hot syrup over pears, leaving 1/2-inch headspace. Remove air bubbles. Clean jar rim. Center lid on jar and adjust band to fingertip-tight. Place jar on the rack elevated over simmering water (180°F) in boiling-water canner. Repeat until all jars are filled.

PROCESS Lower the rack into simmering water. Water must cover jars by 1 inch. Adjust heat to medium-high, cover canner and bring water to a rolling boil. Process quart jars 15 minutes. Turn off heat and remove cover. Let jars cool 5 minutes. Remove jars from canner; do not retighten bands if loose. Cool 12 hours. Test seals. Label and store jars.

Note: Brandied Pears will be evenly flavored in about 4 weeks.

 Our Tip Use any type of brandy to flavor pears. Use white brandy for a clear syrup.

Cherries

Yield: 6 pint or 3 quart jars

6 to 7 1/2 pounds sweet cherries

1 batch Syrup for Canning, see page 16 for RAW PACK -OR- Sugar for HOT PACK

PREP Wash cherries under cold running water; drain. Stem cherries. Cherries may be canned with or without pits. If pits are left in, prick each cherry with a thin metal skewer to help prevent the skins from bursting open. When canning without the pits, measure cherries after the pits are removed.

COOK

RAW PACK—Prepare Syrup for Canning in a medium saucepan. Bring mixture to a boil. Reduce heat to a simmer (180°F).

HOT PACK—Measure cherries. For each quart of cherries, measure 1/2 to 3/4 cup sugar. Combine cherries and sugar in a large saucepan. Cook cherries over medium-low heat until hot throughout, stirring until sugar dissolves. If cherries are not pitted, add just enough water to prevent sticking.

FILL

RAW PACK—Fill a hot jar with cherries using a non-metallic utensil to gently pack cherries without crushing, leaving 1/2-inch headspace. Ladle hot syrup over cherries, leaving 1/2-inch headspace.

HOT PACK—Ladle hot cherries and juice into a hot jar, leaving 1/2-inch headspace. If there is not enough syrup for all cherries, add simmering water (180°F), leaving 1/2-inch headspace.

Remove air bubbles. Clean jar rim. Center lid on jar and adjust band to fingertip-tight. Place jar on the rack elevated over simmering water (180°F) in boiling-water canner. Repeat until all jars are filled.

PROCESS Lower the rack into simmering water. Water must cover jars by 1 inch. Adjust heat to medium-high, cover canner and bring water to a rolling boil. Process RAW PACK pint or quart jars 25 minutes. Process HOT PACK pint jars 15 minutes or quart jars 20 minutes. Turn off heat and remove cover. Let jars cool 5 minutes. Remove jars from canner; do not retighten bands if loose. Cool 12 hours. Test seals. Label and store jars.

Note: Use medium or heavy syrup when canning sour cherries; refer to Syrup for Canning (see page 16).

 Our Tip When removing cherry pits using a hand-held cherry pitter, slip a heavy-duty plastic sandwich bag over your hand to contain splattering juice. A metal cake tester is the perfect little tool to use for pricking cherries so they don't burst open when canned.

Cherries for Baking: Use only cherries with pits removed. Heat the cherries in water or extra-light syrup until hot throughout. Extra-light syrup will help the cherries retain their natural fruit color. Process this recipe as for HOT PACK cherries.

Cinnamon Pears in Apple Juice No sugar added

Yield: about 6 pint and 3 quart jars

6 to 9 pounds pears (about 18 to 27 medium)	3 to 6 sticks cinnamon
	5 cups unsweetened apple juice
Ball Fruit-Fresh Produce Protector	

PREP Wash pears under cold running water; drain. Cut pears in half lengthwise, core, and peel. Treat with Fruit-Fresh to prevent darkening (see page 16).

COOK Drain pears. Cook pears in a small amount of water, one layer at a time, until hot throughout. Heat the apple juice just to a boil.

FILL Pack hot pears, cavity side down and layers overlapping, leaving 1/2-inch headspace. Put one cinnamon stick into jar. Ladle hot juice over pears, leaving 1/2-inch headspace. Remove air bubbles. Clean jar rim. Center lid on jar and adjust band to fingertip-tight. Place jar on the rack elevated over simmering water (180°F) in boiling-water canner. Repeat until all jars are filled.

PROCESS Lower the rack into simmering water. Water must cover jars by 1 inch. Adjust heat to medium-high, cover canner and bring water to a rolling boil. Process pint jars 20 minutes or quart jars 25 minutes. Turn off heat and remove cover. Let jars cool 5 minutes. Remove jars from canner; do not retighten bands if loose. Cool 12 hours. Test seals. Label and store jars.

Crabapples

Yield: about 6 pint or 3 quart jars

4 pounds crabapples (about 24 to 36 small)	1 batch Syrup for Canning, see page 16

PREP Wash crabapples under cold running water; drain. Prick whole crabapples in several places using a thin metal skewer to help prevent peel from bursting open, although peel may crack when cooked.

COOK Prepare Syrup for Canning in a large saucepan. Bring mixture to a boil. Reduce heat to a simmer (180°F); simmer 5 minutes. Cook crabapples in syrup, one layer at a time, until hot throughout.

FILL Pack hot crabapples into a hot jar, leaving ½-inch headspace. Ladle hot syrup over crabapples, leaving ½-inch headspace. Remove air bubbles. Clean jar rim. Center lid on jar and adjust band to fingertip-tight. Place jar on the rack elevated over simmering water (180°F) in boiling-water canner. Repeat until all jars are filled.

PROCESS Lower the rack into simmering water. Water must cover jars by 1 inch. Adjust heat to medium-high, cover canner and bring water to a rolling boil. Process pint or quart jars 20 minutes. Turn off heat and remove cover. Let jars cool 5 minutes. Remove jars from canner; do not retighten bands if loose. Cool 12 hours. Test seals. Label and store jars.

 For spiced crabapples, tie 1 stick cinnamon, 1 tablespoon allspice, and 1 tablespoon whole cloves in a spice bag and add it when cooking syrup. Remove spice bag before filling jars.

Cranberry Sauce – Jellied

Yield: about 4 half-pint or 2 pint jars

4¼ cups cranberries (about 1½ pounds)

1¾ cups water
2 cups sugar

PREP Wash cranberries under cold running water; drain. Discard crushed, bruised, or diseased cranberries.

COOK Combine cranberries and water in a large saucepan. Boil over medium-high heat until skins burst open. Purée mixture using an electric food strainer or food mill to remove peels and seeds. Return mixture to large saucepan. Add sugar to cranberry mixture and cook over medium-high heat, stirring until sugar dissolves. Boil mixture almost to the gelling point (see page 43).

FILL Ladle hot cranberry sauce into a hot jar, leaving ½-inch headspace. Remove air bubbles. Clean jar rim. Center lid on jar and adjust band to fingertip-tight. Place jar on the rack elevated over simmering water (180°F) in boiling-water canner. Repeat until all jars are filled.

PROCESS Lower the rack into simmering water. Water must cover jars by 1 inch. Adjust heat to medium-high, cover canner and bring water to a rolling boil. Process half-pint or pint jars 15 minutes. Turn off heat and remove cover. Let jars cool 5 minutes. Remove jars from canner; do not retighten bands if loose. Cool 12 hours. Test seals. Label and store jars.

 To serve jellied cranberry sauce as a mold or sliced, process in Ball Half-Pint (8-ounce) Regular Jars or Ball Pint (16-ounce) Wide Mouth Jars for easy removal.

Cranberry Sauce – Whole Berry

Yield: about 6 pint jars

2 quarts cranberries (about 2½ pounds)

4 cups sugar
4 cups water

PREP Wash cranberries under cold running water; drain. Discard crushed, bruised, or diseased cranberries.

COOK Combine sugar and water in a large saucepan. Bring mixture to a boil over medium-high heat, stirring until sugar dissolves. Boil 5 minutes. Add cranberries. Continue boiling, without stirring, until skins burst open.

FILL Ladle hot cranberry sauce into a hot jar, leaving ½-inch headspace. Remove air bubbles. Clean jar rim. Center lid on jar and adjust band to fingertip-tight. Place jar on the rack elevated over simmering water (180°F) in boiling-water canner. Repeat until all jars are filled.

PROCESS Lower the rack into simmering water. Water must cover jars by 1 inch. Adjust heat to medium-high, cover canner and bring water to a rolling boil. Process pint jars 15 minutes. Turn off heat and remove cover. Let jars cool 5 minutes. Remove jars from canner; do not retighten bands if loose. Cool 12 hours. Test seals. Label and store jars.

Figs

Yield: about 6 pint or 3 quart jars

7½ pounds figs (about 45 to 50 small)

1 batch Syrup for Canning, see page 16

Bottled lemon juice or Ball® Citric Acid

PREP Wash figs under cold running water; drain. Whole, unpeeled figs are canned with stem intact. Blanch whole figs 2 minutes in boiling water; drain.

COOK Prepare Syrup for Canning in a large saucepan. Bring mixture to a boil over medium-high heat. Add figs to syrup and gently boil 5 minutes.

FILL Add 1 tablespoon bottled lemon juice or ¼ teaspoon citric acid to a hot pint jar; 2 tablespoons bottled lemon juice or ½ teaspoon citric acid to a hot quart jar. Pack hot figs into jar, leaving ½-inch headspace. Ladle hot syrup over figs, leaving ½-inch headspace. Remove air bubbles. Clean jar rim. Center lid on jar and adjust band to fingertip-tight. Place jar on the rack elevated over simmering water (180°F) in boiling-water canner. Repeat until all jars are filled.

PROCESS Lower the rack into simmering water. Water must cover jars by 1 inch. Adjust heat to medium-high, cover canner and bring water to a rolling boil. Process pint jars 45 minutes or quart jars 50 minutes. Turn off heat and remove cover. Let jars cool 5 minutes. Remove jars from canner; do not retighten bands if loose. Cool 12 hours. Test seals. Label and store jars.

Fruit Sauce

Apricots, Peaches, Pears, Nectarines, Berries, etc.

For Sauce: Follow recipe for Applesauce (see page 18). Pack in half-pint or pint jars. Process half-pint or pint jars 20 minutes.

 Fruit Sauce can be made with or without sugar, making this recipe perfect to prepare in individual servings for babies, for young children, and for diet-conscious individuals. Process individual servings in Ball 4-ounce Jelly Jars for 20 minutes.

Gooseberries

Yield: about 6 pint or 3 quart jars

4½ to 9 pounds gooseberries

1 batch Syrup for Canning, see page 16

PREP Wash gooseberries under cold running water; drain. Use scissors to snip off stem and blossom ends.

COOK Prepare Syrup for Canning in a large saucepan. Bring mixture to a boil over medium-high heat. Reduce heat to a simmer (180°F).

FILL Ladle ½ cup hot syrup into a hot jar. Fill jar with gooseberries, using a non-metallic utensil to gently pack gooseberries without crushing, leaving ½-inch headspace. Ladle additional hot syrup over gooseberries, if needed, leaving ½-inch headspace. Remove air bubbles. Clean jar rim. Center lid on jar and adjust band to fingertip-tight. Place jar on the rack elevated over simmering water (180°F) in boiling-water canner. Repeat until all jars are filled.

PROCESS Lower the rack into simmering water. Water must cover jars by 1 inch. Adjust heat to medium-high, cover canner and bring water to a rolling boil. Process pint jars 15 minutes or quart jars 20 minutes. Turn off heat and remove cover. Let jars cool 5 minutes. Remove jars from canner; do not retighten bands if loose. Cool 12 hours. Test seals. Label and store jars.

Grapefruit

Yield: about 6 pint or 3 quart jars

6 to 7½ pounds grapefruit (about 7 to 9 medium)

1 batch Syrup for Canning, see page 16

PREP Wash grapefruit under cold running water; drain. Peel grapefruit, cutting deep enough to remove white pith and membrane. Cut membrane along each side of one section and remove grapefruit pulp in one piece. Repeat until all sections are removed. Discard seeds.

COOK Prepare Syrup for Canning in a medium saucepan. Bring mixture to a boil over medium-high heat. Reduce heat to a simmer (180°F).

FILL Pack grapefruit into a hot jar, leaving ½-inch headspace. Ladle hot syrup over grapefruit, leaving ½-inch headspace. Remove air bubbles. Clean jar rim. Center lid on jar and adjust band to fingertip-tight. Place jar on the rack elevated over simmering water (180°F) in boiling-water canner. Repeat until all jars are filled.

PROCESS Lower the rack into simmering water. Water must cover jars by 1 inch. Adjust heat to medium-high, cover canner and bring water to a rolling boil. Process pint or quart jars 10 minutes. Turn off heat and remove cover. Let jars cool 5 minutes. Remove jars from canner; do not retighten bands if loose. Cool 12 hours. Test seals. Label and store jars.

 Grapefruit comes in many varieties, with varying levels of sweetness. Select the sugar syrup that best complements the sweetness of the grapefruit.

 Try grapefruit canned in brown sugar syrup for breakfast. Spoon grapefruit and syrup into individual oven-safe ramekins; add a dab of butter and a dash of cinnamon. Heat the ramekins under a broiler until the grapefruit is hot and bubbly.

Grapes – Ripe

Yield: about 6 pint or 3 quart jars

6 pounds grapes

1 batch Syrup for Canning, see page 16

PREP Wash grapes under cold running water; drain. Stem grapes.

COOK Prepare Syrup for Canning in a medium saucepan. Bring mixture to a boil over medium-high heat. Reduce heat to a simmer (180°F).

FILL Ladle ½ cup hot syrup into a hot jar. Fill jar with grapes using a non-metallic utensil to gently pack grapes without crushing, leaving ½-inch headspace. Ladle additional hot syrup over grapes, if needed, leaving ½-inch headspace. Remove air bubbles. Clean jar rim. Center lid on jar and adjust band to fingertip-tight. Place jar on the rack elevated over simmering water (180°F) in boiling-water canner. Repeat until all jars are filled.

PROCESS Lower the rack into simmering water. Water must cover jars by 1 inch. Adjust heat to medium-high, cover canner and bring water to a rolling boil. Process pint jars 15 minutes or quart jars 20 minutes. Turn off heat and remove cover. Let jars cool 5 minutes. Remove jars from canner; do not retighten bands if loose. Cool 12 hours. Test seals. Label and store jars.

Grapes – Underripe

Yield: about 6 pint or 3 quart jars

6 pounds underripe grapes

1 batch Syrup for Canning, see page 16

PREP Wash underripe grapes under cold running water; drain. Stem grapes.

COOK Prepare Syrup for Canning in a medium saucepan. Bring mixture to a boil over medium-high heat. Reduce heat to a simmer (180°F).

FILL Ladle ½ cup hot syrup into a hot jar. Fill jar with grapes using a non-metallic utensil to gently pack grapes without crushing, leaving ½-inch headspace. Ladle additional hot syrup over grapes, if needed, leaving ½-inch headspace. Remove air bubbles. Clean jar rim. Center lid on jar and adjust band to fingertip-tight. Place jar on the rack elevated over simmering water (180°F) in boiling-water canner. Repeat until all jars are filled.

PROCESS Lower the rack into simmering water. Water must cover jars by 1 inch. Adjust heat to medium-high, cover canner and bring water to a rolling boil. Process pint or quart jars 20 minutes. Turn off heat and remove cover. Let jars cool 5 minutes. Remove jars from canner; do not retighten bands if loose. Cool 12 hours. Test seals. Label and store jars.

Grapes for Baking: Use only grapes with tender seeds. Heat the grapes in water or extra-light syrup until hot throughout. Process this recipe as for Grapes – Underripe.

Grapes, Pineapple, and Peaches in White Grape Juice No sugar added

Yield: about 6 pint or 3 quart jars

1½ pounds grapes

1½ pounds pineapple (about ½ medium)

1½ pounds peaches (about 5 medium)

Ball Fruit-Fresh Produce Protector

5 cups unsweetened white grape juice

PREP Wash grapes, pineapple, and peaches under cold running water; drain. Stem grapes. Leave grapes whole. Remove top and bottom ends of pineapple; core and peel. Cut pineapple into 1-inch cubes. To peel peaches, blanch in boiling water 30 to 60 seconds. Immediately transfer to cold water. Cut off peel. Cut in half lengthwise and remove pit and fibrous flesh. Cut peaches into 1-inch cubes. Treat peaches with Fruit-Fresh to prevent darkening (see page 16).

COOK Drain peaches. Cook grapes, pineapple, and peaches in a small amount of water, over medium heat, until hot throughout. Heat white grape juice just to a boil.

FILL Pack hot fruit into a hot jar, leaving ½-inch headspace. Ladle hot juice over fruit, leaving ½-inch headspace. Remove air bubbles. Clean jar rim. Center lid on jar and adjust band to fingertip-tight. Place the filled jar on elevated rack over simmering water (180°F) in boiling-water canner. Repeat until all jars are filled.

PROCESS Lower the rack into simmering water. Water must cover jars by 1 inch. Adjust heat to medium-high, cover canner and bring water to a rolling boil. Process pint jars 20 minutes or quart jars 25 minutes. Turn off heat and remove cover. Let jars cool 5 minutes. Remove jars from canner; do not retighten bands if loose. Cool 12 hours. Test seals. Label and store jars.

Guavas

Yield: about 6 pint or 3 quart jars

6 pounds guavas (about 12 to 18 medium)

1 batch Syrup for Canning, see page 16

PREP Wash guavas under cold running water; drain. Cut guavas in half lengthwise. Remove seeds and peel.

COOK Prepare Syrup for Canning in a large saucepan. Bring mixture to a boil over medium-high heat. Remove from heat. Add guavas to syrup and let stand 30 minutes. Transfer guavas to a large bowl. Return syrup to a boil. Reduce heat to a simmer (180°F).

FILL Pack guavas into a hot jar, leaving ½-inch headspace. Ladle hot syrup over guavas, leaving ½-inch headspace. Remove air bubbles. Clean jar rim. Center lid on jar and adjust band to fingertip-tight. Place jar on the rack elevated over simmering water (180°F) in boiling-water canner. Repeat until all jars are filled.

PROCESS Lower the rack into simmering water. Water must cover jars by 1 inch. Adjust heat to medium-high, cover canner and bring water to a rolling boil. Process pint jars 15 minutes or quart jars 20 minutes. Turn off heat and remove cover. Let jars cool 5 minutes. Remove jars from canner; do not retighten bands if loose. Cool 12 hours. Test seals. Label and store jars.

Loquats

Yield: about 6 pint or 3 quart jars

6 to 7½ pounds loquats (about 72 to 90 medium)

1 batch Syrup for Canning, see page 16

Ball Citric Acid or bottled lemon juice

Salt (optional)

PREP Wash loquats under cold running water; drain. Remove stem and blossom ends. Cut loquats in half lengthwise and remove seeds.

COOK Prepare Syrup for Canning in a large saucepan. Bring mixture to a boil over medium-high heat. Cook loquats in syrup until hot throughout.

FILL Add ¼ teaspoon citric acid or 1 tablespoon bottled lemon juice to a hot pint jar or ½ teaspoon citric acid or 2 tablespoons bottled lemon juice to a hot quart jar. Add ½ teaspoon salt to a pint jar 1 teaspoon salt to a quart jar, if desired. Pack hot loquats into a hot jar, leaving ½-inch headspace. Ladle hot syrup over loquats, leaving ½-inch headspace. Remove air bubbles. Clean jar rim. Center lid on jar and adjust band to fingertip-tight. Place jar on the rack elevated over simmering water (180°F) in boiling-water canner. Repeat until all jars are filled.

PROCESS Lower the rack into simmering water. Water must cover jars by 1 inch. Adjust heat to medium-high, cover canner and bring water to a rolling boil. Process pint jars 15 minutes or quart jars 20 minutes. Turn off heat and remove cover. Let jars

cool 5 minutes. Remove jars from canner; do not retighten bands if loose. Cool 12 hours. Test seals. Label and store jars.

Mangoes – Green

Yield: about 6 pint or 3 quart jars

9 to 10½ pounds green mangoes (about 7 to 9 medium)

1 batch Syrup for Canning, see page 16

PREP Wash mangoes under cold running water; drain. Cut each mango lengthwise into two large pieces, starting at the top and cutting downward to the bottom. Make cuts about ⅓ inch from the center of the fruit to avoid the pit and fibrous flesh. Peel mango pieces and cut into ¼-inch slices.

COOK Prepare Syrup for Canning in a large saucepan. Bring mixture to a boil over medium-high heat. Cook mango slices in syrup for 2 minutes.

FILL Pack hot mango slices into a hot jar, leaving ½-inch headspace. Ladle hot syrup over mango, leaving ½-inch headspace. Remove air bubbles. Clean jar rim. Center lid on jar and adjust band to fingertip-tight. Place jar on the rack elevated over simmering water (180°F) in boiling-water canner. Repeat until all jars are filled.

PROCESS Lower the rack into simmering water. Water must cover jars by 1 inch. Adjust heat to medium-high, cover canner and bring water to a rolling boil. Process pint jars 15 minutes or quart jars 20 minutes. Turn off heat and remove cover. Let jars cool 5 minutes. Remove jars from canner; do not retighten bands if loose. Cool 12 hours. Test seals. Label and store jars.

Note: Green mangoes can irritate the skin of some individuals, similar to poison ivy. Wear rubber gloves to avoid an irritating reaction.

 A mango splitter will easily pit mangoes while cutting them into two equal pieces.

Mixed Fruits

Apricots, Cherries, Grapefruit, Peaches, Pears, Pineapple, Plums, White Grapes, etc.

Yield: about 6 pint or 3 quart jars

6 to 9 pounds mixed fruits

1 batch Syrup for Canning, see page 16

PREP Use three or more varieties of fruit. Wash fruit under cold running water; drain. Peel fruit as instructed in recipe for individual fruit type. Cut fruit into ½-inch cubes.

COOK Prepare Syrup for Canning in a large saucepan. Bring mixture to a boil over medium-high heat. Cook fruit in syrup until hot throughout.

FILL Pack hot fruit into a hot jar, leaving ½-inch headspace. Ladle hot syrup over fruit, leaving ½-inch headspace. Remove air bubbles. Clean jar rim. Center lid on jar and adjust band to fingertip-tight. Place jar on the rack elevated over simmering water (180°F) in boiling-water canner. Repeat until all jars are filled.

PROCESS Lower the rack into simmering water. Water must cover jars by 1 inch. Adjust heat to medium-high, cover canner and bring water to a rolling boil. Process pint jars 20 minutes or quart jars 25 minutes. Turn off heat and remove cover. Let jars cool 5 minutes. Remove jars from canner; do not retighten bands if loose. Cool 12 hours. Test seals. Label and store jars.

 Cut fruit into larger pieces if it is to be used for dessert or salad.

Nectarines

Yield: 6 pint or 3 quart jars

6 to 7½ pounds nectarines
(about 18 to 23 medium)

Ball Fruit-Fresh Produce
Protector

1 batch Syrup for Canning,
see page 16

PREP Wash nectarines under cold running water; drain. Cut nectarines in half and remove pits and fibrous flesh. Do not peel. Treat with Fruit-Fresh to prevent darkening (see page 16).

COOK

RAW PACK—Prepare Syrup for Canning in a medium saucepan. Bring mixture to a boil. Reduce heat to a simmer (180°F). Drain nectarines.

HOT PACK—Drain nectarines. Cook nectarines in syrup one layer at a time until hot throughout.

FILL

RAW PACK—Pack nectarines, cavity side down and layers overlapping, into a hot jar, leaving ½-inch headspace. Ladle hot syrup over nectarines, leaving ½-inch headspace.

HOT PACK—Pack hot nectarines, cavity side down and layers overlapping, into a hot jar, leaving ½-inch headspace. Ladle hot cooking syrup over nectarines, leaving ½-inch headspace.

Remove air bubbles. Clean jar rim. Center lid on jar and adjust band to fingertip-tight. Place jar on the rack elevated over simmering water (180°F) in boiling-water canner. Repeat until all jars are filled.

PROCESS Lower the rack into simmering water. Water must cover jars by 1 inch. Adjust heat to medium-high, cover canner and bring water to a rolling boil. Process RAW PACK pint jars 25 minutes or quart jars 30 minutes. Process HOT PACK pint jars 20 minutes or quart jars 25 minutes. Turn off heat and remove cover. Let jars cool 5 minutes. Remove jars from canner; do not retighten bands if loose. Cool 12 hours. Test seals. Label and store jars.

Orange Slices in Honey Syrup

Yield: about 3 half-pint jars

2½ pounds oranges
(about 4 large)

1¼ cups sugar

1¼ cups honey

1 lemon, juiced

3 sticks cinnamon

1½ teaspoons whole cloves

1½ teaspoons whole allspice

PREP Wash oranges under cold running water; drain. Cut oranges crosswise into ¼-inch slices. Remove seeds. Cut orange slices in half. Tie whole spices in a spice bag.

COOK Put orange slices in a small saucepan, add enough water to cover, and simmer (180°F) until peel is tender. Combine sugar, honey, and lemon juice in a medium saucepan. Bring mixture to a boil over medium-high heat, stirring until sugar dissolves. Reduce heat to a simmer (180°F). Add orange slices and spice bag to syrup; simmer 30 minutes. Remove spice bag.

FILL Pack hot orange slices into a hot jar, leaving ½-inch headspace. Ladle hot syrup over oranges, leaving ½-inch headspace. Remove air bubbles. Clean jar rim. Center lid on jar and adjust band to fingertip-tight. Place jar on the rack elevated over simmering water (180°F) in boiling-water canner. Repeat until all jars are filled.

PROCESS Lower the rack into simmering water. Water must cover jars by 1 inch. Adjust heat to medium-high, cover canner and bring water to a rolling boil. Process half-pint jars 10 minutes. Turn off heat and remove cover. Let jars cool 5 minutes. Remove jars from canner; do not retighten bands if loose. Cool 12 hours. Test seals. Label and store jars.

 Our Tip Use Orange Slices in Honey Syrup to flavor hot or cold tea, serve with hot cereal, or use to glaze ham or duck.

Papayas

Yield: about 6 pint or 3 quart jars

9 to 10½ pounds papayas
(about 3 to 4 medium)

Bottled lemon juice

1 batch Syrup for Canning,
see page 16

PREP Wash papayas under cold running water; drain. Cut papayas in half lengthwise, remove seeds, and peel. Cut papayas into ½- to 1-inch cubes.

COOK Prepare Syrup for Canning in a large saucepan. Bring mixture to a boil over medium-high heat. Reduce heat to a simmer (180°F). Cook papaya cubes in syrup for 2 to 3 minutes.

FILL Add 1½ teaspoons bottled lemon juice to a hot pint jar or 1 tablespoon bottled lemon juice to a hot quart jar. Pack hot papaya cubes into jar, leaving ½-inch headspace. Ladle hot syrup over papaya, leaving ½-inch headspace. Remove air bubbles. Clean jar rim. Center lid on jar and adjust band to fingertip-tight. Place jar on the rack elevated over simmering water (180°F) in boiling-water canner. Repeat until all jars are filled.

PROCESS Lower the rack into simmering water. Water must cover jars by 1 inch. Adjust heat to medium-high, cover canner and bring water to a rolling boil. Process pint jars 15 minutes or quart jars 20 minutes. Turn off heat and remove cover. Let jars cool 5 minutes. Remove jars from canner; do not retighten bands if loose. Cool 12 hours. Test seals. Label and store jars.

Peaches

Yield: 6 pint or 3 quart jars

6 to 9 pounds peaches
(about 18 to 27 medium)

Ball Fruit-Fresh Produce
Protector

1 batch Syrup for Canning,
see page 16

PREP Wash peaches under cold running water; drain. To peel peaches, blanch in boiling water for 30 to 60 seconds. Immediately transfer to cold water. Cut off peel. Cut peaches in half lengthwise; remove pits and fibrous flesh. Treat with Fruit-Fresh to prevent darkening (see page 16).

COOK

RAW PACK—Prepare Syrup for Canning in a medium saucepan. Bring mixture to a boil. Reduce heat to a simmer (180°F). Drain peaches.

HOT PACK—Prepare Syrup for Canning in a large saucepan. Drain peaches. Cook peaches in syrup one layer at time until hot throughout.

FILL

RAW PACK—Pack peaches, cavity side down and layers overlapping, into a hot jar, leaving ½-inch headspace. Ladle hot syrup over peaches, leaving ½-inch headspace.

HOT PACK—Pack hot peaches, cavity side down and layers overlapping, into a hot jar, leaving ½-inch headspace. Ladle hot cooking syrup over peaches, leaving ½-inch headspace.

Remove air bubbles. Clean jar rim. Center lid on jar and adjust band to fingertip-tight. Place jar on the rack elevated over simmering water (180°F) in boiling-water canner. Repeat until all jars are filled.

PROCESS Lower the rack into simmering water. Water must cover jars by 1 inch. Adjust heat to medium-high, cover canner and bring water to a rolling boil. Process RAW PACK pint jars 25 minutes or quart jars 30 minutes. Process HOT PACK pint jars 20 minutes or quart jars 25 minutes. Turn off heat and remove cover. Let jars cool 5 minutes. Remove jars from canner; do not retighten bands if loose. Cool 12 hours. Test seals. Label and store jars.

 Our Tip Use a pitting spoon for easy removal of pit and fibrous flesh. If you don't have a pitting spoon, try a grapefruit spoon or the tip of a knife.

Peaches in Apple Juice No sugar added

Yield: about 6 pint or 3 quart jars

- 6 to 9 pounds peaches (about 18 to 27 medium)
- Ball Fruit-Fresh Produce Protector
- 5 cups unsweetened apple juice, fresh or bottled

PREP Wash peaches under cold running water; drain. To peel peaches, blanch in boiling water 30 to 60 seconds. Immediately transfer to cold water. Cut off peel. Cut peaches in half lengthwise; remove pits and fibrous flesh. Treat with Fruit-Fresh to prevent darkening (see page 16).

COOK Drain peaches. Cook peaches in water, one layer at a time, over medium heat until peaches are hot throughout. Heat apple juice just to a boil.

FILL Pack hot peaches, cavity side down and layers overlapping, into a hot jar, leaving ½-inch headspace. Ladle hot juice over peaches, leaving ½-inch headspace. Remove air bubbles. Clean jar rim. Center lid on jar and adjust band to fingertip-tight. Place the filled jar on elevated rack over simmering water (180°F) in boiling-water canner. Repeat until all jars are filled.

PROCESS Lower the rack into simmering water. Water must cover jars by 1 inch. Adjust heat to medium-high, cover canner and bring water to a rolling boil. Process pint jars 20 minutes or quart jars 25 minutes. Turn off heat and remove cover. Let jars cool 5 minutes. Remove jars from canner; do not retighten bands if loose. Cool 12 hours. Test seals. Label and store jars.

Honey-Spiced Peaches

Yield: about 6 pint or 3 quart jars

- 8 pounds peaches (about 32 small)
- Ball Fruit-Fresh Produce Protector
- 1 cup sugar
- 4 cups water
- 2 cups honey
- 3 sticks cinnamon
- 1½ teaspoons whole allspice
- ¾ teaspoon whole cloves

PREP Wash peaches under cold running water; drain. To peel peaches, blanch in boiling water for 30 to 60 seconds. Immediately transfer to cold water. Cut off peel. Leave peaches whole. Treat peaches with Fruit-Fresh to prevent darkening (see page 16).

COOK Combine sugar, water, and honey in a large saucepan. Bring mixture to a boil over medium-high heat, stirring to dissolve sugar. Reduce heat to maintain a gentle boil. Drain peaches. Cook peaches, one layer at a time, in syrup 3 minutes or until hot throughout. Remove peaches to a bowl; keep hot. Repeat until all peaches are cooked.

FILL Pack hot peaches into a hot jar, leaving ½-inch headspace. Add ½ cinnamon stick, ¼ teaspoon whole allspice, and ⅛ teaspoon whole cloves to pint jar; 1 cinnamon stick, ½ teaspoon whole allspice, and ¼ teaspoon whole cloves to quart jar. Ladle hot syrup over peaches, leaving ½-inch headspace. Remove air bubbles. Clean jar rim. Center lid on jar and adjust band to fingertip-tight. Place jar on the rack elevated over simmering water (180°F) in boiling-water canner. Repeat until all jars are filled.

PROCESS Lower the rack into simmering water. Water must cover jars by 1 inch. Adjust heat to medium-high, cover canner and bring water to a rolling boil. Process pint or quart jars 25 minutes. Turn off heat and remove cover. Let jars cool 5 minutes. Remove jars from canner; do not retighten bands if loose. Cool 12 hours. Test seals. Label and store jars.

Pears

Yield: 6 pint or 3 quart jars

- 6 to 9 pounds pears (about 18 to 27 medium)
- Ball Fruit-Fresh Produce Protector
- 1 batch Syrup for Canning, see page 16

PREP Wash pears under cold running water; drain. Cut in half lengthwise, core, and peel. Treat with Fruit-Fresh to prevent darkening (see page 16).

COOK Prepare Syrup for Canning in a large saucepan. Bring mixture to a boil. Reduce heat to a simmer (180°F). Drain pears. Cook pears in syrup, one layer at a time, over medium heat until hot throughout.

FILL Pack hot pears, cavity side down and layers overlapping, into a hot jar, leaving ½-inch headspace. Ladle hot syrup over pears, leaving ½-inch headspace. Remove air bubbles. Clean jar rim. Center lid on jar and adjust band to fingertip-tight. Place jar on the rack elevated over simmering water (180°F) in boiling-water canner. Repeat until all jars are filled.

PROCESS Lower the rack into simmering water. Water must cover jars by 1 inch. Adjust heat to medium-high, cover canner and bring water to a rolling boil. Process pint jars 20 minutes or quart jars 25 minutes. Turn off heat and remove cover. Let jars cool 5 minutes. Remove jars from canner; do not retighten bands if loose. Cool 12 hours. Test seals. Label and store jars.

Note: Pears should be harvested at full growth and stored between 60°F and 65°F until ripe but not soft. Bartlett pears are considered best for canning. Kieffer pears and similar varieties are satisfactory if properly ripened and cooked until almost tender.

 Our Tip A pear corer makes quick work of removing the stem and core. You can find pear corers in specialty kitchen stores.

Pear Mincemeat

Yield: about 9 pint jars

7 pounds Bartlett pears (about 21 medium)	1 tablespoon cloves
1 lemon	1 tablespoon cinnamon
2 pounds golden or dark raisins	1 tablespoon nutmeg
6¾ cups sugar	1 tablespoon allspice
	1 teaspoon ginger
	1 cup vinegar, 5% acidity

PREP Wash pears and lemon under cold running water; drain. Cut pears in half lengthwise and core. Coarsely chop pears. Cut lemon into quarters and remove seeds. Finely chop lemon, including peel, using a food processor or food grinder.

COOK Combine all ingredients in a large saucepan. Bring mixture to a boil over medium heat, stirring to prevent sticking. Reduce heat and simmer 30 minutes.

FILL Ladle hot mincemeat into a hot jar, leaving ½-inch headspace. Remove air bubbles. Clean jar rim. Center lid on jar and adjust band to fingertip-tight. Place jar on the rack elevated over simmering water (180°F) in boiling-water canner. Repeat until all jars are filled.

PROCESS Lower the rack into simmering water. Water must cover jars by 1 inch. Adjust heat to medium-high, cover canner and bring water to a rolling boil. Process pint jars 25 minutes. Turn off heat and remove cover. Let jars cool 5 minutes. Remove jars from canner; do not retighten bands if loose. Cool 12 hours. Test seals. Label and store jars.

Our Tip: Serve Pear Mincemeat as an accompaniment to roast pork or beef. Or, try this side dish: Put a generous dollop of Pear Mincemeat into the cavity of halved acorn squash during the last 15 minutes of baking. Drizzle warm honey over acorn squash before serving.

Pears and Nectarines in White Grape Juice No sugar added

Yield: about 6 pint or 3 quart jars

3 to 4½ pounds pears (about 9 to 14 medium)	Ball Fruit-Fresh Produce Protector
3 to 4½ pounds nectarines (about 9 to 14 medium)	5 cups unsweetened white grape juice, fresh or bottled

PREP Wash pears and nectarines under cold running water; drain. Cut pears and nectarines in half lengthwise, core or pit, and peel. Treat with Fruit-Fresh to prevent darkening (see page 16).

COOK Drain pears and nectarines. Cook fruit in water, one layer at a time, over medium heat until fruit is hot throughout. Heat white grape juice just to a boil.

FILL Pack hot pears and nectarines, cavity side down and layers overlapping, into a hot jar, leaving ½-inch headspace. Ladle hot juice over fruit, leaving ½-inch headspace. Remove air bubbles. Clean jar rim. Center lid on jar and adjust band to fingertip-tight. Place the filled jar on elevated rack over simmering water (180°F) in boiling-water canner. Repeat until all jars are filled.

PROCESS Lower the rack into simmering water. Water must cover jars by 1 inch. Adjust heat to medium-high, cover canner and bring water to a rolling boil. Process pint jars 20 minutes or quart jars 25 minutes. Turn off heat and remove cover. Let jars cool 5 minutes. Remove jars from canner; do not retighten bands if loose. Cool 12 hours. Test seals. Label and store jars.

Pineapple

Yield: about 6 pint or 3 quart jars

12 pounds fresh pineapple (about 3 medium)	1 batch Syrup for Canning, see page 16

PREP Wash pineapple under cold running water; drain. Cut off top and bottom ends of pineapples; core and peel. Cut pineapple crosswise into ½-inch slices. Pineapple may also be cut lengthwise into wedges or into 1-inch cubes.

COOK Prepare Syrup for Canning in a large saucepan. Bring mixture to a boil over medium-high heat. Simmer pineapple in syrup until hot throughout.

FILL Pack hot pineapple into a hot jar, leaving ½-inch headspace. Ladle hot syrup over pineapple, leaving ½-inch headspace. Remove air bubbles. Clean jar rim. Center lid on jar and adjust band to fingertip-tight. Place jar on the rack elevated over simmering water (180°F) in boiling-water canner. Repeat until all jars are filled.

PROCESS Lower the rack into simmering water. Water must cover jars by 1 inch. Adjust heat to medium-high, cover canner and bring water to a rolling boil. Process pint jars 15 minutes or quart jars 20 minutes. Turn off heat and let jars cool 5 minutes. Remove jars from canner; do not retighten bands if loose. Cool 12 hours. Test seals. Label and store jars.

Spiced Pineapple in Pineapple Juice No sugar added

Yield: about 6 pint or 3 quart jars

12 pounds fresh pineapple (about 3 medium)	5 cups unsweetened pineapple juice, fresh or bottled
3 sticks cinnamon	

PREP Wash pineapples under cold running water; drain. Cut off top and bottom ends of pineapples; core and peel. Cut pineapples crosswise into ½-inch slices or cut into 1-inch cubes.

COOK Heat pineapple in a small amount of water until hot throughout, stirring to prevent sticking. Heat the pineapple juice just to a boil.

FILL Pack hot pineapple into a hot jar, leaving ½-inch headspace. Put one cinnamon stick into jar. Ladle hot pineapple juice over pineapple, leaving ½-inch headspace. Remove air bubbles. Clean jar rim. Center lid on jar and adjust band to fingertip-tight. Place jar on the rack elevated over simmering water (180°F) in boiling-water canner. Repeat until all jars are filled.

PROCESS Lower the rack into simmering water. Water must cover jars by 1 inch. Adjust heat to medium-high, cover canner and bring water to a rolling boil. Process pint jars 15 minutes or quart jars 20 minutes. Turn off heat and let jars cool 5 minutes. Remove jars from canner; do not retighten bands if loose. Cool 12 hours. Test seals. Label and store jars.

Plums or Fresh Prunes

Yield: 6 pint or 3 quart jars

4½ to 7½ pounds plums or prunes (about 9 to 15 medium plums or 45 to 75 medium prune plums)	1 batch Syrup for Canning, see page 16

PREP Wash plums under cold running water; drain. Prick whole plums in several places using a thin metal skewer to help prevent peel from bursting open, although peel may crack when cooked.

COOK

RAW PACK—Prepare Syrup for Canning in a medium saucepan. Bring mixture to a boil. Reduce heat to a simmer (180°F).

HOT PACK—Prepare Syrup for Canning in a large saucepan. Bring mixture to a boil. Reduce heat to a simmer (180°F); simmer 5 minutes. Cook plums in syrup, one layer at a time, until hot throughout, transferring plums to a bowl after cooking. Remove saucepan from heat. Return all plums to saucepan, cover, and let stand 30 minutes. Bring mixture to a boil; reduce heat to a simmer (180° F).

FILL

RAW PACK—Pack plums firmly but without crushing into a hot jar, leaving 1/2-inch headspace. Ladle hot syrup over plums, leaving 1/2-inch headspace.

HOT PACK—Pack hot plums firmly but without crushing into a hot jar, leaving 1/2-inch headspace. Ladle hot cooking syrup over plums, leaving 1/2-inch headspace.

Remove air bubbles. Clean jar rim. Center lid on jar and adjust band to fingertip-tight. Place jar on the rack elevated over simmering water (180°F) in boiling-water canner. Repeat until all jars are filled.

PROCESS Lower the rack into simmering water. Water must cover jars by 1 inch. Adjust heat to medium-high, cover canner and bring water to a rolling boil. Process pint jars 20 minutes or quart jars 25 minutes. Turn off heat and remove cover. Let jars cool 5 minutes. Remove jars from canner; do not retighten bands if loose. Cool 12 hours. Test seals. Label and store jars.

 Plums may be peeled but are typically canned with the peel. Plums may be canned whole or halved with pit removed.

 Green Gage and other meaty plums are better for canning over juicy varieties. A ripe plum will be fragrant and yield to a gentle squeeze, yet will feel firm.

Rhubarb

Yield: about 6 pint or 3 quart jars

4 1/2 to 6 pounds rhubarb   Sugar
  (about 27 to 36 stalks)

PREP Wash rhubarb under cold running water; drain. Remove leafy tops and root ends. Cut stalks into 1-inch pieces; measure rhubarb. For each quart of rhubarb, measure 1/2 cup to 1 cup sugar. Combine rhubarb and sugar in a large saucepan, stirring to coat rhubarb with sugar. Let stand in refrigerator 3 to 4 hours.

COOK Bring rhubarb slowly to a boil over medium heat, stirring to prevent sticking. Cook 1 minute.

FILL Pack hot rhubarb and juice into a hot jar, leaving 1/2-inch headspace. Remove air bubbles. Clean jar rim. Center lid on jar and adjust band to fingertip-tight. Place jar on the rack elevated over simmering water (180°F) in boiling-water canner. Repeat until all jars are filled.

PROCESS Lower the rack into simmering water. Water must cover jars by 1 inch. Adjust heat to medium-high, cover canner and bring water to a rolling boil. Process pint or quart jars 15 minutes. Turn off heat and remove cover. Let jars cool 5 minutes. Remove jars from canner; do not retighten bands if loose. Cool 12 hours. Test seals. Label and store jars.

Strawberries

Yield: about 6 pint or 3 quart jars

7 1/2 to 9 pounds strawberries   Sugar

PREP Wash strawberries under cold running water; drain. Remove stems and caps. Leave strawberries whole; measure strawberries. For each quart of strawberries, measure 1/2 to 3/4 cup sugar. Combine strawberries and sugar in a large saucepan, stirring to coat strawberries with sugar. Let stand in refrigerator 5 to 6 hours.

COOK Heat strawberry mixture slowly over medium heat, stirring to prevent sticking, until sugar dissolves and strawberries are hot throughout.

FILL Pack hot strawberries and juice into a hot jar, leaving 1/2-inch headspace. Remove air bubbles. Clean jar rim. Center lid on jar and adjust band to fingertip-tight. Place jar on the rack elevated over simmering water (180°F) in boiling-water canner. Repeat until all jars are filled.

PROCESS Lower the rack into simmering water. Water must cover jars by 1 inch. Adjust heat to medium-high, cover canner and bring water to a rolling boil. Process pint jars 10 minutes or quart jars 15 minutes. Turn off heat and remove cover. Let jars cool 5 minutes. Remove jars from canner; do not retighten bands if loose. Cool 12 hours. Test seals. Label and store jars.

Zucchini in Pineapple Juice

Yield: about 8 pint jars

4 quarts 1/2-inch cubed or   46 ounces bottled
  shredded zucchini   unsweetened
  (about 32 small)   pineapple juice

3 cups sugar   1 1/2 cups bottled lemon juice

PREP Wash zucchini under cold running water; drain. Remove stem and blossom ends. Peel zucchini and cut in half lengthwise. Remove seeds. Cut zucchini into 1/2-inch cubes or shred using a food grater.

COOK Combine zucchini, sugar, pineapple juice, and lemon juice in a large saucepan. Bring mixture to a boil, stirring until sugar dissolves. Reduce heat to a simmer (180°F). Simmer 20 minutes, stirring to prevent sticking.

FILL Pack hot zucchini and juice into a hot jar, leaving 1/2-inch headspace. Remove air bubbles. Clean jar rim. Center lid on jar and adjust band to fingertip-tight. Place jar on the rack elevated over simmering water (180°F) in boiling-water canner. Repeat until all jars are filled.

PROCESS Lower the rack into simmering water; water must cover jars by 1 inch. Adjust heat to medium-high, cover canner and bring water to a rolling boil. Process pint jars 15 minutes. Turn off heat and remove cover. Let jars cool 5 minutes. Remove jars from canner; do not retighten bands if loose. Cool 12 hours. Test seals. Label and store jars.

Note: Use only commercial bottled pineapple juice and bottled lemon juice in this recipe to achieve the correct pH level (acidity) for safe processing in a boiling-water canner.

 This recipe is used in Zucchini-Pineapple Doughnuts (see page 173). Try it in your favorite zucchini bread recipe!

 Select small zucchini with few seeds, about 1-inch x 6-inch. Use a melon baller or pear corer to scoop out the seeds if needed.

Fruit Juices,
NECTARS, & PURÉES

Apple Juice

Yield: about 6 pint or 3 quart jars

| 12 pounds apples (about 36 medium) | 1 quart water |

PREP Wash apples under cold running water; drain. Remove stems and blossom ends. Coarsely chop apples.

COOK Combine apples and water in a large saucepan. Cook until apples are tender, stirring to prevent sticking. Strain apples through a damp jelly bag or several layers of cheesecloth to extract juice. Heat juice for 5 minutes at 190°F. Do not boil juice.

FILL Ladle hot apple juice into a hot jar, leaving ¼-inch headspace. Clean jar rim. Center lid on jar and adjust band to fingertip-tight. Place jar on the rack elevated over simmering water (180°F) in boiling-water canner. Repeat until all jars are filled.

PROCESS Lower the rack into simmering water. Water must cover jars by 1 inch. Adjust heat to medium-high, cover canner and bring water to a rolling boil. Process pint or quart jars 10 minutes. Turn off heat and remove cover. Let jars cool 5 minutes. Remove jars from canner; do not retighten bands if loose. Cool 12 hours. Test seals. Label and store jars.

Apple Juice Canned in Half-Gallon Jars: Prepare apple juice and fill jars according to recipe. Process half-gallon jars 10 minutes.

Berry Juice

Boysenberry, Loganberry, Raspberry, etc.

| Berries | Sugar (optional) |
| Water | |

PREP Wash berries under cold running water; drain. Discard crushed, bruised, or diseased berries. Coarsely crush berries.

COOK Combine berries and water in a large saucepan. Simmer berries until soft, stirring to prevent sticking. Strain berries through a damp jelly bag or several layers of cheesecloth to extract juice. Measure juice. Add ¼ to ½ cup sugar for each quart of juice, if desired. Heat juice for 5 minutes at 190°F. Do not boil juice.

FILL Ladle hot berry juice into a hot jar, leaving ¼-inch headspace. Clean jar rim. Center lid on jar and adjust band to fingertip-tight. Place jar on the rack elevated over simmering water (180°F) in boiling-water canner. Repeat until all jars are filled.

PROCESS Lower the rack into simmering water. Water must cover jars by 1 inch. Adjust heat to medium-high, cover canner and bring water to a rolling boil. Process pint or quart jars 15 minutes. Turn off heat and remove cover. Let jars cool 5 minutes. Remove jars from canner; do not retighten bands if loose. Cool 12 hours. Test seals. Label and store jars.

Cranberry Juice

Yield: about 4 pint or 2 quart jars

| 2 quarts cranberries (about 2 to 2½ pounds) | 2 quarts water |
| | Sugar (optional) |

PREP Wash cranberries under cold running water; drain. Discard crushed, bruised, or diseased cranberries.

COOK Combine cranberries and water in a large saucepan. Cook over medium-high heat until cranberries burst open. Strain mixture through a damp jelly bag or several layers of cheesecloth to extract juice. Let juice stand in refrigerator 24 hours. Ladle juice from pan, being careful not to disturb sediment on the bottom of the pan. Strain juice again. Measure juice. Add ¼ to ½ cup sugar for each quart of juice, if desired. Heat juice for 5 minutes at 190°F. Do not boil juice.

FILL Ladle hot cranberry juice into a hot jar, leaving ¼-inch headspace. Clean jar rim. Center lid on jar and adjust band to fingertip-tight. Place jar on the rack elevated over simmering water (180°F) in boiling-water canner. Repeat until all jars are filled.

PROCESS Lower the rack into simmering water. Water must cover jars by 1 inch. Adjust heat to medium-high, cover canner and bring water to a rolling boil. Process pint or quart jars 15 minutes. Turn off heat and remove cover. Let jars cool 5 minutes. Remove jars from canner; do not retighten bands if loose. Cool 12 hours. Test seals. Label and store jars.

Fruit Purée or Nectar

Peaches, Apples, Nectarines, Plums, etc.

Yield: about 6 pint or 3 quart jars

| 12 to 18 pounds fruit (about 36 to 54 medium) | Water |
| | Sugar (optional) |

PREP Wash fruit under cold running water; drain. Peel, pit or core, and coarsely chop fruit. Measure fruit.

COOK Combine fruit and 1 cup of water for each quart of fruit in a large saucepan. Cook over medium heat until fruit is soft. Purée fruit mixture using an electric food strainer or food mill. Return fruit purée to saucepan. Add sugar to taste, if desired. Bring purée to a boil, stirring to prevent sticking.

FILL Ladle hot fruit purée into a hot jar, leaving ¼-inch headspace. Remove air bubbles. Clean jar rim. Center lid on jar and adjust band to fingertip-tight. Place jar on the rack elevated over simmering water (180°F) in boiling-water canner. Repeat until all jars are filled.

PROCESS Lower the rack into simmering water. Water must cover jars by 1 inch. Adjust heat to medium-high, cover canner and bring water to a rolling boil. Process pint or quart jars 15 minutes. Turn off heat and remove cover. Let jars cool 5 minutes. Remove jars from canner; do not retighten bands if loose. Cool 12 hours. Test seals. Label and store jars.

Note: When canning fig purée, measure purée before returning it to the saucepan. Add 2 tablespoons bottled lemon juice or ½ teaspoon Ball Citric Acid to each quart of puréed figs.

 Our Tip Ball 4-ounce Jelly Jars are the perfect size for individual servings. Process 4-ounce jars 15 minutes.

Golden Nectar

Yield: about 6 pint or 3 quart jars

2 quarts sliced peaches (about 4 pounds)	7 cups fresh orange juice (about 2 to 3 pounds)
Ball Fruit-Fresh Produce Protector	1½ cups honey
6 cups cubed cantaloupe (about 6 pounds)	1 cup pineapple juice, fresh or bottled
1 quart water	½ cup lemon juice, fresh or bottled

PREP Wash peaches, cantaloupe, and oranges under cold running water; drain. To peel peaches, blanch in boiling water for 30 to 60 seconds. Immediately transfer to cold water. Cut off peel. Cut peaches in half lengthwise; remove pits and fibrous flesh. Slice peaches. Treat with Fruit-Fresh to prevent darkening (see page 16). Cut cantaloupe in half and remove seeds. Peel cantaloupe. Cut into 1-inch cubes. Cut oranges in half and remove seeds. Juice oranges. Measure 7 cups orange juice.

COOK Combine peaches, cantaloupe, and water in a large saucepan. Cook over medium heat until fruit is soft. Purée mixture using an electric food strainer or food mill. Return purée to saucepan. Add remaining ingredients. Bring nectar to a boil, stirring to prevent sticking.

FILL Ladle hot nectar into a hot jar, leaving ¼-inch headspace. Clean jar rim. Center lid on jar and adjust band to fingertip-tight. Place jar on the rack elevated over simmering water (180°F) in boiling-water canner. Repeat until all jars are filled.

PROCESS Lower the rack into simmering water. Water must cover jars by 1 inch. Adjust heat to medium-high, cover canner and bring water to a rolling boil. Process pint or quart jars 20 minutes. Turn off heat and remove cover. Let jars cool 5 minutes. Remove jars from canner; do not retighten bands if loose. Cool 12 hours. Test seals. Label and store jars.

Grape Juice

Yield: about 12 pint or 6 quart jars

21 pounds grapes	Sugar (optional)
Water	

PREP Wash grapes under cold running water; drain. Stem and crush grapes. Measure crushed grapes. Add ¼ cup water to each quart of crushed grapes.

COOK Heat juice for 10 minutes at 190°F. Do not boil juice. Strain juice through a damp jelly bag or several layers of cheesecloth. Let juice stand in refrigerator 24 hours. Ladle juice from pan, being careful not to disturb sediment on the bottom of the pan. Strain juice again. Measure juice. Add ¼ to ½ cup of sugar to each quart of juice. Reheat juice for 5 minutes at 190°F. Do not boil juice.

FILL Ladle hot grape juice into a hot jar, leaving ¼-inch headspace. Clean jar rim. Center lid on jar and adjust band to fingertip-tight. Place jar on the rack elevated over simmering water (180°F) in boiling-water canner. Repeat until all jars are filled.

PROCESS Lower the rack into simmering water. Water must cover jars by 1 inch. Adjust heat to medium-high, cover canner and bring water to a rolling boil. Process pint or quart jars 15 minutes. Turn off heat and remove cover. Let jars cool 5 minutes. Remove jars from canner; do not retighten bands if loose. Cool 12 hours. Test seals. Label and store jars.

Grape Juice Canned in Half-Gallon Jars: Prepare grape juice and fill jars according to recipe. Process half-gallon jars 15 minutes.

Grapefruit Juice

Grapefruit	Sugar (optional)

PREP Wash grapefruit under cold running water; drain. Cut grapefruit in half crosswise. Remove seeds. Extract juice using a juice reamer. Strain juice through a damp jelly bag or several layers of cheesecloth to remove pulp, if desired.

COOK Combine grapefruit juice and sugar to taste, if desired, in a large saucepan. Heat juice for 5 minutes at 190°F. Do not boil juice.

FILL Ladle hot grapefruit juice into a hot jar, leaving ¼-inch headspace. Clean jar rim. Center lid on jar and adjust band to fingertip-tight. Place jar on the rack elevated over simmering water (180°F) in boiling-water canner. Repeat until all jars are filled.

PROCESS Lower the rack into simmering water. Water must cover jars by 1 inch. Adjust heat to medium-high, cover canner and bring water to a rolling boil. Process pint or quart jars 15 minutes. Turn off heat and remove cover. Let jars cool 5 minutes. Remove jars from canner; do not retighten bands if loose. Cool 12 hours. Test seals. Label and store jars.

Strawberry-Grapefruit Juice

Yield: about 5 quart jars

4 quarts strawberries	1½ to 2 cups sugar
6 medium pink grapefruit	1 quart water

PREP Wash strawberries and grapefruits under cold running water; drain. Remove stems and caps from strawberries. Crush strawberries using a potato masher. Cut grapefruit in half crosswise. Remove seeds. Extract juice using a juice reamer.

COOK Combine crushed strawberries, grapefruit juice, sugar, and water in a large saucepan. Heat juice for 5 minutes at 190°F, stirring until sugar dissolves. Do not boil juice. Strain juice through a damp jelly bag or several layers of cheesecloth.

FILL Ladle hot strawberry-grapefruit juice into a hot jar, leaving ¼-inch headspace. Clean jar rim. Center lid on jar and adjust band to fingertip-tight. Place jar on the rack elevated over simmering water (180°F) in boiling-water canner. Repeat until all jars are filled.

PROCESS Lower the rack into simmering water. Water must cover jars by 1 inch. Adjust heat to medium-high, cover canner and bring water to a rolling boil. Process pint or quart jars 15 minutes. Turn off heat and remove cover. Let jars cool 5 minutes. Remove jars from canner; do not retighten bands if loose. Cool 12 hours. Test seals. Label and store jars.

Tomatoes

Tomatoes are the ultimate summer's bounty and the requisite pantry staple for any home cook. Naturally, they make the perfect subject for canning. Few other fruits have the range of tomatoes—easily transitioning from savory to sweet; from simple to extravagant. With the renaissance of heirloom varieties, there is no better way to make use of the great tomato tastes of summer than canning and preserving them for year-round use.

In this chapter, we'll show you how to preserve and amplify your summer tomatoes alongside recipes for creating the perfect bases for your favorite soups, sauces, stews, and salsas for the rest of the year.

Getting Started

Canning, like baking, depends on chemistry to produce successful results. We've thoroughly tested all the recipes you'll find here for safety and longevity. Measuring ingredients precisely and following all of the steps exactly will ensure successful canning free of any spoilers—molds, yeasts, and enzymes.

Get the right pH every time

There are as many varieties of tomatoes as there are desirable tomato attributes—juicy, meaty, pink, yellow, mellow, and bright. Not all tomatoes are acidic enough to be canned alone. Pay close attention to each recipe's call for lemon juice or Ball® Citric Acid.

Learn the rules for combining foods

The recipes you find here have tomato and vegetable combinations that we've scientifically determined to have the acidity that ensures shelf-stable results for you. Each kind of vegetable has a specific acidity level, so only these vegetable combinations in these measurements can be safely processed using the boiling water method.

Let salt be a matter of taste

You'll see that salt is an ingredient in most of our tomato recipes. A hint of salt enhances flavor, especially when other herbs and spices are not used, but how much is a matter of taste. If you prefer not to add salt, it can be omitted without changing any of the recipe steps or processing times.

Understand how altitude affects canning

Just as in baking, processing times are affected by altitude. The processing times given for our recipes apply when canning at 0 to 1,000 feet above sea level. If you're canning at a higher elevation, refer to the Boiling-Water Canner Altitude Adjustments (see page 9).

Featured Recipe | **Vine-Fresh Tomato Soup** page 35

Pictured Above | **Whole Tomatoes** page 32 | **Tomatillo Salsa** page 37 | **Vine-Fresh Tomato Soup** page 35

Good Things to Know

Tomatoes

Harvest or purchase only the best-quality tomatoes when at their peak for ripeness, flavor, and color. Fortunately, tomatoes have a long harvest season, so you can purchase just the amount that is easily used in a short time. Tomatoes typically store well at room temperature, out of direct sunlight, for a few days. Rotate tomatoes from side to side to help ensure that they don't bruise and that they continue to ripen evenly while being stored. Do not use tomatoes from dead vines or vines that have frosted over. Cut away bruised, cracked, or green portions before preparing your recipe. Green tomatoes are more acidic than fully ripened tomatoes, so they may be used in any of the recipes in this book.

Citric Acid or Bottled Lemon Juice

Due to the varying levels of acid found in tomatoes and their position on the acidity-alkalinity (pH) scale, additional acid is needed when canning tomatoes and tomato-based recipes. The most common form of acid used for this purpose is citric acid, or a blend of ascorbic and citric acids. The recipes in this book give you the option to use Ball® Citric Acid or bottled lemon juice, which is added to each jar of tomatoes, tomato sauce, or tomato juice and some other tomato-based recipes. This will ensure these recipes have a safe acid level regardless of the method used for processing—boiling-water or pressure. If lemon juice is preferred, use only bottled lemon juice for the correct acid value every time. Each recipe will give the exact amount to use.

Vinegar of 5% acidity may also be used to acidify tomatoes; however, vinegar can impart an undesirable flavor. Refer to the chart below when using vinegar to acidify tomato recipes.

Figure 8 | **Acidifying Tomatoes**

Acidulant	Pint Jar	Quart Jar
Ball Citric Acid	¼ Teaspoon	½ Teaspoon
Bottled Lemon Juice	1 Tablespoon	2 Tablespoons
Vinegar, 5% Acidity	2 Tablespoons	4 Tablespoons

Note: Add a little sugar to each jar of tomatoes or tomato product to offset the acid taste, if desired.

Spices and Flavorings

Spices and herbs add character and uniqueness to tomato recipes. Tomatoes can be transformed into regional specialties simply by changing the combination of spices and herbs. Ground spices are used unless otherwise specified in the recipe. Use whole or crushed spices and herbs only when listed. For some recipes, just the essence of flavoring is needed, so whole spices and herbs are tied in a spice bag or several layers of cheesecloth, which is added to the recipe during cooking, then removed before filling jars.

Tomatoes – Packed in Water
Whole, Halved, or Quartered

Yield: about 6 pint or 3 quart jars

7½ to 10½ pounds tomatoes (about 23 to 32 medium)	Ball Citric Acid or bottled lemon juice
1 to 1½ quarts water	Salt (optional)

PREP Wash tomatoes under cold running water; drain. To peel tomatoes, blanch 30 to 60 seconds in boiling water. Immediately transfer to cold water. Cut off peel. Core tomatoes. Leave tomatoes whole, cut in half, or quarter.

COOK

RAW PACK—Bring water to a boil; reduce heat to a simmer (180°F). Keep water hot.

HOT PACK—Place tomatoes into a large saucepan. Add just enough water to cover tomatoes. Bring mixture to a boil over medium-high heat. Boil gently 5 minutes, stirring to prevent sticking.

FILL

Add ¼ teaspoon citric acid or 1 tablespoon bottled lemon juice to a hot pint jar; ½ teaspoon citric acid or 2 tablespoons bottled lemon juice to a hot quart jar. Add ½ teaspoon salt to pint jar; 1 teaspoon salt to quart jar, if desired.

RAW PACK—Pack raw tomatoes into jar, leaving ½-inch headspace. Ladle hot water over tomatoes, leaving ½-inch headspace.

HOT PACK—Pack cooked tomatoes into jar, leaving ½-inch headspace. Ladle hot cooking liquid over tomatoes, leaving ½-inch headspace.

Remove air bubbles. Clean jar rim. Center lid on jar and adjust band to fingertip-tight. Place jar on the rack elevated over simmering water (180°F) in boiling-water canner. Repeat until all jars are filled.

PROCESS Lower the rack into simmering water. Water must cover jars by 1 inch. Adjust heat to medium-high, cover canner and bring water to a rolling boil. Process pint jars 40 minutes or quart jars 45 minutes. Turn off heat and remove cover. Let jars cool 5 minutes. Remove jars from canner; do not retighten bands if loose. Cool 12 hours. Test seals. Label and store jars.

Tomatoes – Packed in Own Juice
Whole, Halved, or Quartered

Yield: about 6 pint or 3 quart jars

7 1/2 to 10 1/2 pounds tomatoes (about 23 to 32 medium)	Ball Citric Acid or bottled lemon juice
	Salt (optional)

PREP Wash tomatoes under cold running water; drain. To peel tomatoes, blanch 30 to 60 seconds in boiling water. Immediately transfer to cold water. Cut off peel. Core tomatoes. Leave tomatoes whole, cut in half, or quarter.

COOK When using the natural juice of the tomatoes as the liquid in the jar, cooking is not required. However, the processing time is longer and must not be reduced.

FILL Add 1/4 teaspoon citric acid or 1 tablespoon bottled lemon juice to a hot pint jar; 1/2 teaspoon citric acid or 2 tablespoons bottled lemon juice to a hot quart jar. Add 1/2 teaspoon salt to pint jar; 1 teaspoon salt to quart jar, if desired. Pack raw tomatoes into jar, pressing gently on tomatoes until the natural juice fills the spaces between tomatoes, leaving 1/2-inch headspace. Remove air bubbles. Clean jar rim. Center lid on jar and adjust band to fingertip-tight. Place jar on the rack elevated over simmering water (180°F) in boiling-water canner. Repeat until all jars are filled.

PROCESS Lower the rack into simmering water. Water must cover jars by 1 inch. Adjust heat to medium-high, cover canner and bring water to a rolling boil. Process pint or quart jars 1 hour and 25 minutes. Turn off heat and remove cover. Let jars cool 5 minutes. Remove jars from canner; do not retighten bands if loose. Cool 12 hours. Test seals. Label and store jars.

Basil-Garlic Tomato Sauce

Yield: about 7 pint or 3 quart jars

20 pounds tomatoes (about 60 medium)	1/4 cup finely minced fresh basil
1 cup chopped onion (about 1 large)	Ball Citric Acid or bottled lemon juice
8 cloves garlic, minced	
1 tablespoon extra-virgin olive oil	

PREP Wash tomatoes and basil under cold running water; drain. Remove core and blossom ends from tomatoes. Cut tomatoes into quarters. Peel onion. Chop onion; measure 1 cup chopped onion. Peel garlic and mince. Finely mince basil, discarding stems; measure 1/4 cup finely minced basil.

COOK Sauté onion and garlic in olive oil, in a large saucepan, until onion is transparent. Add tomatoes and simmer 20 minutes, stirring occasionally. Purée tomato mixture using an electric food strainer or food mill to remove peels and seeds. Return purée to saucepan. Stir in basil. Cook purée, uncovered, over medium-high heat until reduced by one-half, stirring to prevent sticking.

FILL Add 1/4 teaspoon citric acid or 1 tablespoon bottled lemon juice to a hot pint jar; 1/2 teaspoon citric acid or 2 tablespoons bottled lemon juice to a hot quart jar. Ladle hot sauce into jar, leaving 1/2-inch headspace. Remove air bubbles. Clean jar rim. Center lid on jar and adjust band to fingertip-tight. Place jar on the rack elevated over simmering water (180°F) in boiling-water canner. Repeat until all jars are filled.

PROCESS Lower the rack into simmering water. Water must cover jars by 1 inch. Adjust heat to medium-high, cover canner and bring water to a rolling boil. Process pint jars 35 minutes or quart jars 40 minutes. Turn off heat and remove cover. Let jars cool 5 minutes. Remove jars from canner; do not retighten bands if loose. Cool 12 hours. Test seals. Label and store jars.

Roasted Garlic Roma Tomato Sauce

Yield: about 3 quart jars

9-10 pounds Roma style tomatoes, rinsed	2 tablespoon fresh basil, minced
3 small whole heads of garlic	1 teaspoon salt
2 medium onions, small diced (about 1 cup)	1/2 teaspoon coarsely ground black pepper
1 teaspoon olive oil	Ball Citric Acid or bottled lemon juice
1 tablespoon fresh oregano, minced	

PREP Wash tomatoes under cold running water; drain. Dry the tomatoes. Peel and dice onions.

COOK Roast tomatoes on a grill or under a broiler until skins begin to wrinkle and become lightly blackened in spots, turning to roast evenly on all sides. Remove from heat. Place roasted tomatoes in a paper bag and close. Cool until tomatoes are easy to handle, about 15 minutes. Peel and core tomatoes. Cut tomatoes in half crosswise and remove seeds. Cut tomatoes into 1/2-inch chunks; set aside. Place garlic on aluminum foil and drizzle olive oil over garlic. Wrap foil around garlic, sealing edges tightly. Roast garlic at 350°F until tender, about 30 minutes. Cool until garlic is easy to handle. Separate cloves of garlic and peel. Combine tomatoes, garlic, and remaining ingredients in a large saucepan. Cook over medium heat until hot throughout, about 30 minutes.

FILL Add 1/2 teaspoon citric acid or 2 tablespoons lemon juice to a hot jar; ladle hot sauce into a hot jar leaving a 1/2 inch headspace. Remove air bubbles. Pack tomato mixture into jar, leaving 1/2-inch headspace. Remove air bubbles. Clean jar rim. Center lid on jar and adjust band to fingertip-tight. Place jar on rack elevated over simmering water (180°F) in boiling-water canner. Repeat until all jars are filled.

PROCESS Lower the rack into simmering water. Water must cover jars by 1 inch. Adjust heat to medium-high, cover canner and bring water to a rolling boil. Process quart jars 1 hour and 25 minutes. Turn off heat and remove cover. Let jars cool 5 minutes. Remove jars from canner; do not retighten bands if loose. Cool 12 hours. Test seals. Label and store jars.

 Our Tip Roasted Garlic Roma Tomato Sauce is wonderful on top of pasta. For a light meal, substitute pasta with spaghetti squash.

Seasoned Tomato Sauce

Yield: about 14 pint or 7 quart jars

45 pounds tomatoes (about 125 to 135 medium)	1 tablespoon black pepper
6 cups chopped onions (about 5 to 6 large)	1 1/2 tablespoons sugar
12 cloves garlic, minced	1/4 cup salt (optional)
1/2 cup extra-virgin olive oil	2 teaspoons crushed red pepper flakes (optional)
2 tablespoons oregano	Ball Citric Acid or bottled lemon juice
6 bay leaves	

PREP Wash tomatoes under cold running water; drain. Remove core and blossom ends from tomatoes. Cut tomatoes into quarters. Peel onions. Chop onions; measure 6 cups chopped onions. Peel garlic and mince.

COOK Sauté onion and garlic in olive oil in a large saucepan. Add tomatoes, oregano, bay leaves, black pepper, and sugar. Stir in salt and crushed red pepper, if desired. Simmer 20 minutes, stirring occasionally. Remove bay leaves. Purée tomato mixture using an electric food strainer or food mill to remove peels and seeds. Return purée to saucepan. Cook purée, uncovered, over medium-high heat until purée thickens, stirring to prevent sticking. Cook until volume is reduced by one-half.

FILL Add ¼ teaspoon citric acid or 1 tablespoon bottled lemon juice to a hot pint jar; ½ teaspoon citric acid or 2 tablespoons bottled lemon juice to a hot quart jar. Ladle hot sauce into jar, leaving ½-inch headspace. Remove air bubbles. Clean jar rim. Center lid on jar and adjust band to fingertip-tight. Place jar on the rack elevated over simmering water (180°F) in boiling-water canner. Repeat until all jars are filled.

PROCESS Lower the rack into simmering water. Water must cover jars by 1 inch. Adjust heat to medium-high, cover canner and bring water to a rolling boil. Process pint jars 35 minutes or quart jars 40 minutes. Turn off heat and remove cover. Let jars cool 5 minutes. Remove jars from canner; do not retighten bands if loose. Cool 12 hours. Test seals. Label and store jars.

The type and amount of dried herbs and spices may be changed to your taste, but do not increase the measurement for fresh onions, garlic, or olive oil.

Tomato Garden Juice Blend

Yield: about 14 pint or 7 quart jars

22 pounds tomatoes (about 66 medium)	½ cup chopped onion, (about 1 medium)
¾ cup diced carrots (about 2 medium)	¼ cup chopped parsley
¾ cup chopped celery (about 2 stalks)	1 tablespoon salt (optional)
¾ cup chopped green bell pepper (about 1 medium)	Ball Citric Acid or bottled lemon juice

PREP Wash tomatoes, carrots, celery, and bell pepper under cold running water; drain. Remove core and blossom ends from tomatoes. Cut tomatoes into quarters. Remove stem ends from carrots and peel. Dice carrots; measure ¾ cup diced carrots. Remove leafy tops and root ends from celery. Chop celery; measure ¾ cup chopped celery. Remove stem and seeds from bell pepper. Chop bell pepper; measure ¾ cup chopped pepper. Peel onion. Chop onion; measure ½ cup chopped onion. Chop parsley, discarding stems; measure ¼ cup chopped parsley.

COOK Combine tomatoes and vegetables in a large saucepan. Bring tomato mixture to a simmer (180°F); simmer 20 minutes, stirring to prevent sticking. Juice the tomato mixture using an electric food strainer or food mill to remove peels and seeds. Return juice to saucepan. Add salt, if desired. Heat the juice for 5 minutes at 190°F. Do not boil juice.

FILL Add ¼ teaspoon citric acid or 1 tablespoon bottled lemon juice to a hot pint jar; ½ teaspoon citric acid or 2 tablespoons bottled lemon juice to a hot quart jar. Ladle hot juice into jar, leaving ¼-inch headspace. Clean jar rim. Center lid on jar and adjust band to fingertip-tight. Place jar on the rack elevated over simmering water (180°F) in boiling-water canner. Repeat until all jars are filled.

PROCESS Lower the rack into simmering water. Water must cover jars by 1 inch. Adjust heat to medium-high, cover canner and bring water to a rolling boil. Process pint jars 35 minutes or quart jars 40 minutes. Turn off heat and remove cover. Let jars cool 5 minutes. Remove jars from canner; do not retighten bands if loose. Cool 12 hours. Test seals. Label and store jars.

Note: The measurement for vegetables in this recipe may be decreased, but do not increase the amount of vegetables.

Tomato Juice

Yield: about 6 pint or 3 quart jars

9 to 10½ pounds tomatoes (about 27 to 32 medium)	Ball Citric Acid or bottled lemon juice
	Salt (optional)

PREP Wash tomatoes under cold running water; drain. Remove core and blossom ends. Cut tomatoes into quarters.

COOK Simmer tomatoes in a large saucepan until they are soft, stirring to prevent sticking. Juice tomatoes using an electric food strainer or food mill to remove peels and seeds. Return juice to saucepan; heat juice for 5 minutes at 190°F. Do not boil juice.

FILL Add ¼ teaspoon citric acid or 1 tablespoon bottled lemon juice to a hot pint jar; ½ teaspoon citric acid or 2 tablespoons bottled lemon juice to a hot quart jar. Add ½ teaspoon salt to pint jar; 1 teaspoon salt to quart jar, if desired. Ladle hot juice into jar, leaving ¼-inch headspace. Clean jar rim. Center lid on jar and adjust band to fingertip-tight. Place jar on the rack elevated over simmering water (180°F) in boiling-water canner. Repeat until all jars are filled.

PROCESS Lower the rack into simmering water. Water must cover jars by 1 inch. Adjust heat to medium-high, cover canner and bring water to a rolling boil. Process pint jars 35 minutes or quart jars 40 minutes. Turn off heat and remove cover. Let jars cool 5 minutes. Remove jars from canner; do not retighten bands if loose. Cool 12 hours. Test seals. Label and store jars.

Add one or two sprigs of fresh herbs like dill, cilantro, or parsley to juice during cooking. Remove herbs before canning. Herbs may be canned in the juice, but they will develop a strong flavor over time. Tomato juice may also be seasoned to taste with sugar, spices, or hot sauce.

Tomato Paste

Yield: about 8 half-pint jars

14 pounds plum tomatoes (about 48 large)	2 cloves garlic (optional)
1 teaspoon salt (optional)	1 teaspoon Ball Citric Acid or 4½ tablespoons bottled lemon juice
2 sprigs basil (optional)	

PREP Wash tomatoes under cold running water; drain. Remove core and blossom ends from tomatoes. Coarsely chop tomatoes. Measure 8 quarts chopped tomatoes. Leave sprigs of basil intact, if used. Peel garlic, if used.

COOK Combine tomatoes and salt, if desired, in a large saucepan. Cook over medium heat for 1 hour; stirring to prevent sticking. Puree tomato mixture using an electric food strainer or food mill to remove peels and seeds. Return puree to saucepan. Add basil and garlic, if desired. Stir in citric acid or bottled lemon juice. Continue cooking over medium heat, stirring frequently, until mixture is thick enough to mound on a spoon, about 2½ hours. Remove basil and garlic.

FILL Ladle hot paste into jar, leaving ½-inch headspace. Remove air bubbles. Clean jar rim. Center lid on jar and adjust band to fingertip-tight. Place jar on the rack elevated over simmering water (180° F) in boiling-water canner. Repeat until all jars are filled.

PROCESS Lower the rack into simmering water. Water must cover jars by 1 inch. Adjust heat to medium-high, cover canner and bring water to a rolling boil. Process half-pint jars 45 minutes. Turn off heat and remove cover. Let jars cool 5 minutes. Remove jars from canner; do not retighten bands if loose. Cool 12 hours. Test seals. Label and store jars.

Tomato Sauce

Yield: about 14 pint or 7 quart jars

45 pounds tomatoes (about 125 to 135 medium)	Ball Citric Acid or bottled lemon juice

PREP Wash tomatoes under cold running water; drain. Remove core and blossom ends from tomatoes. Cut tomatoes into quarters.

COOK Simmer tomatoes in a large saucepan until they are soft, stirring to prevent sticking. Purée tomatoes using an electric food strainer or food mill to remove peels and seeds. Return purée to saucepan. Cook purée, uncovered, over medium-high heat until purée thickens, stirring to prevent sticking. Cook until volume is reduced by one-half.

FILL Add ¼ teaspoon citric acid or 1 tablespoon bottled lemon juice to a hot pint jar; ½ teaspoon citric acid or 2 tablespoons bottled lemon juice to a hot quart jar. Ladle hot sauce into hot jar, leaving ½-inch headspace. Remove air bubbles. Clean jar rim. Center lid on jar and adjust band to fingertip-tight. Place jar on the rack elevated over simmering water (180°F) in boiling-water canner. Repeat until all jars are filled.

PROCESS Lower the rack into simmering water. Water must cover jars by 1 inch. Adjust heat to medium-high, cover canner and bring water to a rolling boil. Process pint jars 35 minutes or quart jars 40 minutes. Turn off heat and remove cover. Let jars cool 5 minutes. Remove jars from canner; do not retighten bands if loose. Cool 12 hours. Test seals. Label and store jars.

Vine-Fresh Tomato Soup

Yield: about 4 quart jars

12 to 14 pounds red, orange, or yellow tomatoes (about 36 to 42 medium)	¼ cup tomato paste
1 medium red bell pepper	1 tablespoon sugar
1 medium yellow onion	1 tablespoon salt
2 cloves garlic, minced	1 teaspoon ground black pepper
2 tablespoons extra-virgin olive oil	Ball Citric Acid or bottled lemon juice

PREP Wash tomatoes under cold running water; drain. Remove core and blossom ends from tomatoes. Cut tomatoes into quarters. Remove stem and seeds from bell pepper. Coarsely chop bell pepper. Peel and coarsely chop onion. Peel and mince garlic.

COOK Sauté onion and garlic in olive oil, in a large saucepan, until onion is transparent. Add tomatoes, bell pepper, tomato paste, and sugar. Bring mixture to a boil over medium-high heat. Reduce heat to a simmer (180°F). Cook tomato mixture, covered, until tomatoes are cooked down and begin to thicken, about 30 minutes. Purée tomato mixture using an electric food strainer or food mill to remove peels and seeds. Return purée to a large saucepan. Add salt and pepper. Simmer about 15 minutes, stirring to prevent sticking.

FILL Add ½ teaspoon citric acid or 2 tablespoons bottled lemon juice to a hot quart jar. Ladle tomato soup into jar, leaving ½-inch headspace. Clean jar rim. Center lid on jar and adjust band to fingertip-tight. Place jar on the rack elevated over simmering water (180°F) in boiling-water canner. Repeat until all jars are filled.

PROCESS Lower the rack into simmering water. Water must cover jars by 1 inch. Adjust heat to medium-high, cover canner and bring water to a rolling boil. Process quart jars 40 minutes. Turn off heat and remove cover. Let jars cool 5 minutes. Remove jars from canner; do not retighten bands if loose. Cool 12 hours. Test seals. Label and store jars.

 Our Tip! Vegetables may be omitted to suit your taste, but do not increase the measurement of vegetables or change the type of vegetables used in this recipe.

Spice Blends
for SEASONING TOMATOES, TOMATO SAUCE, & TOMATO JUICE

Add versatility and convenience to meal planning using these spice blends when canning basic tomatoes, tomato sauce, or tomato juice. Prepare chosen tomato recipe as instructed, then add spice blend to each jar before filling.

Cajun Spice Blend

Makes enough to season 6 pint jars

3 teaspoons chili powder	1½ teaspoons ground allspice
2 teaspoons paprika	1½ teaspoons dried thyme
1½ teaspoons onion flakes	1 teaspoon cayenne pepper
1½ teaspoons garlic powder	

Combine herbs and spices in a small bowl; set aside. Prepare unseasoned tomatoes, tomato sauce, or tomato juice according to canning recipe. After citric acid or bottled lemon juice is added to a hot jar according to canning recipe, add 2 teaspoons of spice blend. Continue to fill jar and process following instructions for canning recipe.

Italian Spice Blend

Makes enough to season 6 pint jars

4 teaspoons dried basil	1½ teaspoons dried sage
2 teaspoons dried thyme	1 teaspoon garlic powder
2½ teaspoons dried oregano	1 teaspoon hot pepper flakes
1½ teaspoons dried rosemary	

Combine herbs and spices in a small bowl; set aside. Prepare unseasoned tomatoes, tomato sauce, or tomato juice according to canning recipe. After citric acid or bottled lemon juice is added to a hot jar according to canning recipe, add 2¼ teaspoons of spice blend. Continue to fill jar and process following instructions for canning recipe.

Mexican Spice Blend

Makes enough to season 6 pint jars

6 teaspoons chili powder

2 teaspoons ground cumin

2 teaspoons dried oregano

2 teaspoons garlic powder

2 teaspoons ground coriander

1½ teaspoons seasoned salt

Combine herbs and spices in a small bowl; set aside. Prepare unseasoned tomatoes, tomato sauce, or tomato juice according to canning recipe. After citric acid or bottled lemon juice is added to a hot jar according to canning recipe, add 2½ teaspoons of spice blend. Continue to fill jar and process following instructions for canning recipe.

Salsas

Fiesta Salsa

Yield: about 4 pint jars

7 cups chopped tomatoes (about 7 to 8 medium)

2 cups chopped cucumbers (about 1 medium)

2 cups chopped banana peppers (about 4 to 5)

1 cup sliced green onions (about 25 to 30)

½ cup chopped Anaheim peppers (about 2 to 3 medium)

½ cup chopped jalapeño peppers (about 2 to 3 medium)

¼ cup minced cilantro

3 cloves garlic, minced

1 tablespoon minced fresh marjoram

1 teaspoon salt (optional)

½ cup vinegar, 5% acidity

2 tablespoons lime juice

PREP Wash tomatoes, cucumbers, peppers, and onions under cold running water; drain. To peel tomatoes, blanch 30 to 60 seconds in boiling water. Immediately transfer to cold water. Cut off peel. Cut tomatoes in half, core, and remove seeds. Chop tomatoes; measure 7 cups chopped tomatoes. Peel cucumbers. Cut cucumbers in half lengthwise and remove seeds. Chop cucumbers; measure 2 cups chopped cucumbers. Remove stems and seeds from banana peppers, Anaheim peppers, and jalapeño peppers. Chop peppers; measure 2 cups banana peppers, ½ cup chopped Anaheim peppers, and ½ cup jalapeño peppers. Peel green onions; remove root ends and dark green leaves. Thinly slice green onions; measure 1 cup sliced green onions.

COOK Combine all ingredients in a large saucepan. Bring mixture to a boil over medium-high heat. Reduce heat to a simmer (180°F); simmer 10 minutes.

FILL Ladle hot salsa into a hot jar, leaving ½-inch headspace. Remove air bubbles. Clean jar rim. Center lid on jar and adjust band to fingertip-tight. Place jar on the rack elevated over simmering water (180°F) in boiling-water canner. Repeat until all jars are filled.

PROCESS Lower the rack into simmering water. Water must cover jars by 1 inch. Adjust heat to medium-high, cover canner and bring water to a rolling boil. Process pint jars 15 minutes. Turn off heat and remove cover. Let jars cool 5 minutes. Remove jars from canner; do not retighten bands if loose. Cool 12 hours. Test seals. Label and store jars.

Note: When cutting or seeding hot peppers, wear rubber gloves to prevent hands from being burned.

 Our Tip For "hot" salsa, do not remove seeds and veins from peppers.

Jalapeño Salsa

Yield: about 3 pint jars

3 cups chopped tomatoes (about 3 medium)

3 cups chopped jalapeño peppers (about 12 to 18 medium)

1 cup chopped onion (about 1 large)

6 cloves garlic, minced

2 tablespoons minced cilantro

2 teaspoons oregano

1½ teaspoons salt

½ teaspoon cumin

½ cup cider vinegar, 5% acidity

PREP Wash tomatoes and peppers under cold running water; drain. To peel tomatoes, blanch 30 to 60 seconds in boiling water. Immediately transfer to cold water. Cut off peel. Cut tomatoes in half, core, and remove seeds. Chop tomatoes; measure 3 cups chopped tomatoes. Remove stems and seeds from jalapeño peppers. Chop peppers; measure 3 cups chopped jalapeño peppers. Peel onion. Chop onion; measure 1 cup chopped onion.

COOK Combine all ingredients in a large saucepan. Bring mixture to a boil over medium-high heat. Reduce heat to a simmer (180°F); simmer 10 minutes.

FILL Ladle hot salsa into a hot jar, leaving ½-inch headspace. Remove air bubbles. Clean jar rim. Center lid on jar and adjust band to fingertip-tight. Place jar on the rack elevated over simmering water (180°F) in boiling-water canner. Repeat until all jars are filled.

PROCESS Lower the rack into simmering water. Water must cover jars by 1 inch. Adjust heat to medium-high, cover canner and bring water to a rolling boil. Process pint jars 15 minutes. Turn off heat and remove cover. Let jars cool 5 minutes. Remove jars from canner; do not retighten bands if loose. Cool 12 hours. Test seals. Label and store jars.

Note: When cutting or seeding hot peppers, wear rubber gloves to prevent hands from being burned.

Salsa Verde

Yield: about 6 half-pint or 3 pint jars

7 cups chopped green tomatoes (8 to 9 medium)

5 to 10 jalapeño, habañero, or Scotch bonnet peppers, finely chopped

2 cups finely chopped red onions (about 3 to 4 medium)

2 cloves garlic, finely chopped

½ cup lime juice

½ cup loosely packed cilantro

2 teaspoons cumin

1 teaspoon oregano

1 teaspoon salt

1 teaspoon freshly ground black pepper

PREP Wash tomatoes, peppers, and cilantro under cold running water; drain. To peel tomatoes, blanch 30 to 60 seconds in boiling water. Immediately transfer to cold water. Cut off peel. Core tomatoes and chop. Measure 7 cups chopped tomatoes. Remove stems and seeds from peppers. Finely chop peppers. Peel and chop onions. Measure 2 cups chopped onions. Peel and finely chop garlic. Mince cilantro.

COOK Combine tomatoes, peppers, onions, garlic, and lime juice in a large saucepan. Bring mixture to a boil over medium-high heat, stirring constantly. Stir in cilantro, cumin, oregano, salt, and pepper. Reduce heat to a gentle boil. Boil 3 minutes, stirring frequently.

FILL Ladle hot salsa into a hot jar, leaving 1/2–inch headspace. Remove air bubbles. Clean jar rim. Center lid on jar and adjust band to fingertip-tight. Place jar on the rack elevated over simmering water (180°F) in boiling-water canner. Repeat until all jars are filled.

PROCESS Lower the rack into simmering water. Water must cover jars by 1 inch. Adjust heat to medium-high, cover canner and bring water to a rolling boil. Process half-pint or pint jars 20 minutes. Turn off heat and remove cover. Let jars cool 5 minutes. Remove jars from canner; do not retighten bands if loose. Cool 12 hours. Test seals. Label and store jars.

Note: When cutting or seeding hot peppers, wear rubber gloves to prevent hands from being burned.

You Choose

You decide on the level of heat you want. Habañero and Scotch bonnet peppers are among the hottest chili peppers. Jalapeño is a milder chili pepper. To regulate the heat, use a few of each type of pepper. To dial up the heat, don't remove the seeds and veins from peppers.

Spicy Tomato Salsa

Yield: about 6 pint jars

- 6 pounds tomatoes (about 12 large)
- 6 jalapeño peppers
- 9 dried hot chili peppers
- 3 cups diced red onion (about 2 medium)
- 1 1/2 cups chopped cilantro, tightly packed
- 15 cloves garlic, minced
- 1 tablespoon salt
- 3/4 teaspoon crushed red pepper
- 3/4 cup red wine vinegar

PREP Wash tomatoes and jalapeño peppers under cold running water; drain. To peel tomatoes, blanch 30 to 60 seconds in boiling water. Immediately transfer to cold water. Cut off peel. Cut tomatoes in half, core, and remove seeds. Dice tomatoes into 1/4-inch pieces. Remove stems and seeds from jalapeño peppers. Dice jalapeño peppers. Peel red onions. Dice onions; measure 3 cups diced red onions. Remove seeds from dried chili peppers. Put dried chili peppers in a small bowl. Pour boiling water over chili peppers just to cover. Secure plastic wrap over bowl and let peppers steep for 15 minutes. Drain off one half of the water. Purée chili peppers and remaining water in a food processor or blender until smooth, about 1 minute.

COOK Combine all ingredients in a large saucepan. Bring mixture to a boil over medium-high heat. Reduce heat to a simmer (180°F); simmer 10 minutes or until thickened.

FILL Ladle hot salsa into a hot jar, leaving 1/2-inch headspace. Remove air bubbles. Clean jar rim. Center lid on jar and adjust band to fingertip-tight. Place jar on the rack elevated over simmering water (180°F) in boiling-water canner. Repeat until all jars are filled.

PROCESS Lower the rack into simmering water. Water must cover jars by 1 inch. Adjust heat to medium-high, cover canner and bring water to a rolling boil. Process pint jars 15 minutes. Turn off heat and remove cover. Let jars cool 5 minutes. Remove jars from canner; do not retighten bands if loose. Cool 12 hours. Test seals. Label and store jars.

Note: When cutting or seeding hot peppers, wear rubber gloves to prevent hands from being burned.

Tomatillo Salsa

Yield: about 3 pint jars

- 5 1/2 cups chopped tomatillos (about 2 pounds)
- 1 cup chopped green chili peppers (about 2 to 3)
- 1 cup chopped onion (about 1 large)
- 4 cloves garlic, minced
- 2 tablespoons minced cilantro
- 2 teaspoons cumin
- 1/2 teaspoon salt
- 1/2 teaspoon red pepper
- 1/2 cup vinegar, 5% acidity
- 1/4 cup lime juice

PREP Remove papery husk from tomatillos. Wash tomatillos and peppers under cold running water; drain. Core and chop tomatillos. Measure 5 1/2 cups chopped tomatillos. Peel and chop onion. Measure 1 cup chopped onion. Remove stems and seeds from green chili peppers. Chop chili peppers; measure 1 cup chopped green chili peppers.

COOK Combine all ingredients in a large saucepan. Bring mixture to a boil over medium-high heat. Reduce heat to a simmer (180°F); simmer 10 minutes.

FILL Ladle hot salsa into a hot jar, leaving 1/2-inch headspace. Remove air bubbles. Clean jar rim. Center lid on jar and adjust band to fingertip-tight. Place jar on the rack elevated over simmering water (180°F) in boiling-water canner. Repeat until all jars are filled.

PROCESS Lower the rack into simmering water. Water must cover jars by 1 inch. Adjust heat to medium-high, cover canner and bring water to a rolling boil. Process pint jars 15 minutes. Turn off heat and remove cover. Let jars cool 5 minutes. Remove jars from canner; do not retighten bands if loose. Cool 12 hours. Test seals. Label and store jars.

Note: When cutting or seeding hot peppers, wear rubber gloves to prevent hands from being burned.

You Choose

If you like your salsa hot, hot, hot, leave in the green chili pepper seeds and veins, or add more crushed red pepper to up the heat.

Our Tip

Here is a quick and easy party dip that's ready to serve in just 5 minutes! Combine 1 1/2 cups salsa and 16-ounces softened cream cheese or cubed processed cheese. Heat in a microwave oven for 5 minutes, stirring well after 3 minutes. Serve hot with tortilla chips or toasted pita chips.

Canning High-Acid Foods Step-By-Step

Using A Boiling-Water Canner

Experience the goodness of flavors ranging from sweet to tart and mellow to bold with home canned fruits, tomatoes, jams, jellies, and pickles lining your pantry shelf. Foods naturally high in acid and foods that are acidified, having a pH value of 4.6 or lower, are classified as high-acid foods. Acid plays a favorable role when it comes to preserving food in jars. Because bacteria does not thrive in an acidic environment and molds, yeasts, and enzymes are easily destroyed at 212°F, high-acid foods can be safely processed using a boiling-water canner.

Prep

Read your recipe completely through, then select the freshest produce from your garden or local market, gather other essential ingredients, and assemble your canning equipment—now you can get started! Wash the size and number of jars, lids, and bands needed for your recipe in hot, soapy water. Rinse in hot water. Dry bands and lids and set them aside to use later. Submerge jars in a saucepan filled with simmering (180°F) water; simmer jars 10 minutes. Keep jars warm in simmering water until they are needed. Remember, preheating jars is just as important when using the RAW PACK method as it is for the HOT PACK method.

Recipes in this book will guide you through each step for preparing ingredients. Wash fresh fruits, vegetables, and herbs under cold running water to remove grit and to reduce the number of microorganisms. Prepare your produce by blanching, peeling, pitting, crushing, straining, and measuring as the recipe instructs. Plan your time carefully when preparing a recipe requiring multiple steps, or fermenting, brining, juicing, or steeping to ensure you have the allotted time needed to complete the recipe.

Cooking

Follow your selected recipe for the correct cooking technique to use. Blanching or steaming helps control enzyme activity for most fruits until they are processed. Tomatoes and some fruits are easier to peel if they are first blanched. Cooking some ingredients for a short time makes them easier to purée, strain, or crush. Soft spreads have a specific sequence for combining ingredients, which is usually determined by the type of pectin used to achieve a gel. Recipes like sauces and chutneys develop a balanced flavor and desired consistency when ingredients are cooked together for a long time over low heat. Some recipes let you choose either the RAW PACK or HOT PACK method to fill jars. These recipes will use either hot syrup, hot juice, or hot water to cover the food.

Filling

❶ Using a jar lifter, remove one jar from the simmering water. Carefully empty excess water from the jar. Stand it upright on a dry towel or cutting board. ❷ Place a jar funnel onto the jar. Fill the jar with your prepared tomatoes, leaving ½-inch headspace. Pack tomatoes closely without crushing. Ingredients like salt, herbs, or whole spices can be added at this time, following recipe instructions. Ladle hot water into the jar, leaving ½-inch headspace. ❸ Use the notched end of the bubble remover/headspace tool to accurately measure headspace. ❹ Slide the narrow end of the tool (or other non-metallic utensil) inside the jar, placing it between the jar and the food. Gently move the food away from the side of the jar to release trapped air. Repeat 2 or 3 times around the inside perimeter of the jar. ❺ Clean the jar rim and threads with a clean, damp cloth to remove food particles, seeds, or other residue that may prevent the jar from sealing. ❻ Center a lid onto the jar rim. Adjust the band onto the jar just until fingertip-tight.

Processing

❼ As each jar is filled, place it onto the rack elevated over simmering water (180°F) in the boiling-water canner. Repeat until all jars are filled. Carefully lower the rack into the canner. Check the water level in the canner. The water must cover the jars by 1 inch. Add boiling water to the canner if needed. ❽ Adjust the heat to medium-high; place the lid on the canner. After the water comes to a rolling boil, set your timer for the exact processing time given in the recipe.

Turn off the heat after the processing period is complete; remove the canner lid. Let jars stand in the canner for 5 minutes. ❾ Remove the jars from the canner using a jar lifter. Set jars upright 1 to 2 inches apart on a dry towel or cutting board. Do not retighten bands if they come loose during processing. Let jars cool undisturbed for 12 hours.

After the jars are cooled, the lid will appear to be concave. Gently press the center of the lid with your fingertip, if the lid does not move, the jar is vacuum sealed. Remove the band; wipe the lid and jar using a clean, damp cloth to remove food particles or other residue. Jars can be stored with or without the bands. Label jars with the name of the recipe and the date it was processed. Store home-canned foods in a cool (50° to 70°F), dry, dark place. For the best quality and nutritional value, use home-canned foods within 1 year.

1 Remove one hot jar from simmering water.

2 Fill hot jar with tomatoes, then add hot water.

3 Measure headspace for accuracy.

4 Remove trapped air bubbles from jar.

5 Wipe jar rim with a clean, damp cloth.

6 Center lid onto jar and adjust band until fingertip-tight.

7 Place filled jar onto canner rack; repeat until all jars are filled; lower rack into canner.

8 Place lid on canner; bring water to a rolling boil; time processing period.

9 Let jars cool 12 hours. Test jars for a vacuum seal.

Jams, Jellies & Fruit Spreads

Soft spreads are some of the most iconic and versatile of canned goods—they are as elegant as they are simple. Their easy grace comes from the simplicity of their ingredients, as each one is made from just four ingredients: fruit, sugar, acid, and pectin. Fruit provides the flavor and color, pectin is the gelling agent that the acid helps set, and sugar develops a framework for the gel and preserves the taste and color of the fruit. Together, these four ingredients form a luscious spread with endless uses.

Getting Started

Creating delicious spreads is as simple as measuring accurately, cooking to the correct temperature, and preserving using the boiling water method. The combination of ingredients and cooking techniques used to prepare each soft spread contributes to its unique consistency, ranging from soft honey-like preserves to firm, spreadable jelly. This is no time to skimp on quality. Select only the best in-season fruits, vegetables, and fresh herbs and spices. If commercial pectin is needed, be certain the "Best By" date is current.

Preparation makes the difference

Always wash fruits or vegetables under cold running water rather than soaking them. This is especially important when cleaning fresh berries and delicate fruits that have a tendency to absorb moisture. Cut, crush, or juice produce exactly as stated in the recipe to help maintain the correct balance between ingredients. Measure the full amount of sugar listed in the recipe. If a less sweet spread is desired, try a recipe specifically developed for less sugar, like those using Ball® RealFruit Low or No-Sugar Needed Pectin. When using commercial juice from a concentrate or bottle, use only unsweetened, no-calcium-added juice unless otherwise stated in the recipe.

Balance is the key to success

Because you're trying to develop a gel structure while cooking soft spreads, it's important to maintain the balance between ingredients. Use a wide-diameter saucepan with a flat, heavy bottom that has tall sides to prevent boil-over during cooking. Giving the soft spread more surface area helps evaporate water so the fruit will gel. Doubling recipes would throw off that balance—so prepare only a single batch at a time. Overcooking or undercooking will adversely affect the set. Traditional or long-cooking recipes are cooked to the gelling point (see page 43). Recipes that use commercial pectin are boiled for a specific time as stated in the recipe.

Simple cooking and preserving tips

Foam will form on top of soft spreads during cooking. To reduce the foam, add ½ teaspoon butter or margarine after removing the saucepan from the heat.

Jar size is important. The jar helps to keep the pectin molecules in close proximity to each other so that the pectin gels, so don't increase jar size.

To preserve your soft spreads in 4-ounce jars or 12-ounce jars, use the same processing time as given for 8-ounce jars.

Good Things to Know

Fruit

Fruit provides the distinguishing flavor, color, and texture for which soft spreads are enjoyed. It also contributes all or part of the pectin and acid necessary to develop a gel formation. Pectin and acid are found naturally in all fruit at varying levels. Traditional or long-cook soft spread recipes rely on the pectin and acid present in the fruit to help develop the gel structure. Therefore, these recipes benefit from using a small amount of slightly underripe fruit for its increased pectin and acid levels. Use no more than 25% (¼) underripe fruit. Select fully-ripe fruit for the remaining measure for heightened flavor and color.

Fruit that does not contain enough natural pectin and acid to produce the gel structure requires the addition of commercial pectin. Commercial pectin contains the pectin and acid necessary to balance the ingredients required to achieve a gel. Recipes using added pectin are referred to as quick-cook recipes.

Pectin

Pectin is a gelling agent found naturally in fruits, vegetables, and plants. Commercial pectin for making soft spreads is extracted from apples and citrus fruits, because they have naturally high levels of pectin. Pectin is one of four essential ingredients necessary for soft spreads to gel. Recipes that incorporate commercial pectin like Ball® Classic Pectin, Ball® Liquid Pectin, and Ball® Low or No-Sugar Needed Pectin require much less cooking time than soft spreads made without added pectin. Ball® Instant Pectin is used to prepare no-cook jam for refrigerator or freezer storage. Each pectin type has unique characteristics. Because of these unique characteristics, the different varieties of pectin are not interchangeable. Recipes in this book give complete instructions for the type of pectin to use. Commercial pectin should not be added to recipes that do not list it as an ingredient.

The firmness of a soft spread may vary depending on the level of natural pectin in the fruit or combination of fruits used to prepare the recipe, the size of the saucepan, the cooking temperature, and the type of commercial pectin used. Pectin in the liquid form tends to have a softer gel compared to pectin in the powdered form. Spreads prepared using pectin that does not require the addition of sugar are spreadable and similar in texture to that of fruit butters. Whether you are using a long-cook or a quick-cook recipe, the firmness of a soft spread cannot be determined until it cools to room temperature. Most soft spreads are gelled after 24 hours, but some soft spreads may take longer to gel—sometimes up to two weeks. Soft spreads that do not achieve the desired set may be recooked in order to get a firmer gel; refer to page 69 for remake instructions.

When preparing jams, jellies, and other soft spreads following a recipe from the Ball Fresh Preserving Kitchen that lists a box of pectin (1.75 ounces), refer to How to Measure Ball RealFruit Classic Pectin (see figure 9) for conversion measurements. Store unused containers of powdered pectin like Ball Classic and Ball Low or No-Sugar Needed Pectin at a temperature between 50° and 70°F.

Figure 9 | **How To Measure Ball® RealFruit Pectin**

Measurement		Package Size
6 tablespoons Ball RealFruit Classic Pectin	=	1 (1.75 oz) box Ball Original Pectin
2 (3 oz) pouches Ball RealFruit Liquid Pectin	=	2 (3 oz) pouches Ball Liquid Pectin
3 tablespoons Ball RealFruit Low or No-Sugar Needed Pectin	=	1 (1.75 oz) box Ball No-Sugar Needed Pectin
5 tablespoons Ball RealFruit Instant Pectin	=	1 (1.59 oz) box Ball Freezer Jam Pectin

Acid

Acid is one of four essential ingredients required to form a gel or set in all soft spreads. Fruit contains varying amounts of natural acid that contributes to gel formation and enhances the overall flavor of the soft spread. Recipes using fruits that contain a high level of natural acid may not require the addition of acid in another form. But fruits that have little natural acid rely on additional acid, such as lemon juice, to aid in gel formation. Each recipe will indicate whether additional acid is needed and the amount to add. Lemon juice is most often used to acidify soft spread recipes. Orange juice, lime juice, and grapefruit juice also contribute acid and offer interesting flavor variations. Vinegar (5% acidity) may be used in savory recipes.

Sugar

Soft spreads rely on sugar for gel structure, enhanced flavor, color retention, and preserving qualities. Granulated sugar is used in all recipes in this book unless another type of sweetener is listed. Cane and beet sugars work equally well in their granulated form. Do not reduce the amount of sugar listed in the recipe. Use standard measuring cups and level measures of sugar. If a low or no-sugar spread is desired, follow a recipe specifically developed to use less sugar or non-sugar sweetener.

Sometimes a combination of sweeteners is used to add interest to the flavor profile. Light corn syrup may be used to replace part of the sugar in soft spread recipes. In traditional or long-cook recipes, those that do not use commercial pectin, light corn syrup may replace 25% (¼) of the sugar. When commercial pectin is used in the recipe, 50% (½) of the sugar can be replaced with light corn syrup. Therefore, one cup of sugar omitted should be replaced with one cup of light corn syrup.

Honey can also be used to replace some of the sugar in soft spread recipes. A light-flavored honey is generally best to use, so that it does not mask the fruit flavor. When preparing recipes without the addition of commercial pectin, honey can replace 25% (¼) of the sugar. For recipes that require commercial pectin, two cups of honey can replace two cups of sugar if the recipe yields seven half-pint jars or greater. For recipes that yield six half-pint jars or less, honey can replace up to one cup of sugar. An equal measure of honey replaces the amount of sugar that is omitted.

Other Ingredients

Combinations of fruits, nuts, spices, herbs, extracts, liqueurs, and wines bring unique flavors and interesting textures to soft spreads. A general rule to follow, unless otherwise instructed by the recipe, is to add nuts in the last 5 minutes of cooking. Herbs and whole spices may be tied in a spice bag and added to the mixture during cooking to impart an essence of flavor. The spice bag is removed before filling jars. Liqueurs, wines, or other alcohol blends are added at varying times during preparation and cooking. Recipes using these ingredients will instruct you when to added them for best results. Alcohol may be omitted from recipes using 1 cup or less of liqueur, wine, or other alcohol blends. This amount is used only for its flavoring attributes. Replace the alcohol with the same measure of fruit juice using a flavor that will complement the soft spread.

Gelling Test

One of four tests is used to determine when a traditional or long-cook soft spread (no commercial pectin added) is done cooking. Butters and conserves are two of the easiest spreads to test for doneness. They are cooked until the pulp and juice do not separate and the mixture mounds on a spoon. Use the plate test to ensure the pulp and juice do not separate. Jellies are tested using the sheet test or temperature test to determine doneness. The plate test or temperature test is used to determine the gelling point

for jams and marmalades. Remove the saucepan from the burner while conducting the sheet test and plate test so that the spread does not continue to cook.

Sheet Test—Dip a cold metal spoon into boiling jelly; remove a spoonful (see figure 10). Hold the spoon over a plate and tilt it on its side so the jelly will drop. Jelly droplets that are light and syrupy indicate more cooking is needed. The jelly will form thick drops and begin sheeting off a cold metal spoon after additional cooking. The gelling point is reached when the jelly sheets or flakes off the spoon.

Plate Test—Place a small amount of hot spread on a chilled plate. Set the plate in the freezer until the spread cools to room temperature. Gently run a finger through the spread. If it separates, then slowly returns to its original form, the spread is at the gelling point.

Temperature Test—The gelling point is 8°F above the boiling point of water. At zero to 1,000 feet above sea level, the gelling point is 220°F. Clip a candy/jelly thermometer, in a vertical position, to the side of the saucepan. Be careful not to touch the side or bottom of the saucepan with the thermometer. When the soft spread is at a rolling boil that cannot be stirred down, read the thermometer to determine if the spread is at the gelling point.

It is important to note: Soft spreads that use commercial pectin to aid in developing the gel structure are cooked at a rolling boil for a specific time as instructed in the recipe. It is not necessary to test the gel before filling the jars to process.

Figure 10 | **Sheeting Test For Gelling Point Without Added Pectin**

At first, jelly drops are light and syrupy

Then they become larger and show signs of sheeting

When the gelling point is reached, jelly breaks from spoon in a sheet or flake

Soft Spreads

There are four simple steps to follow when making all varieties of soft spreads: prepare ingredients, cook recipe, fill jars, and process jars in a boiling-water canner. Begin by washing fruits or vegetables under cold running water. Do not soak produce in water, as this may redeposit residue you're trying to remove, and may cause soft fruits, like berries and peaches, to absorb water. Drain and gently pat the produce dry to remove all excess moisture.

Each recipe will give specific instructions for coring, peeling, chopping, crushing, or juicing fruits and vegetables. Follow the instructions carefully to ensure that the correct measure of produce is incorporated into the recipe for correct balance of ingredients. Juice from concentrate or bottled juice may be an option listed in some recipes. Unsweetened juice without added calcium is recommended unless otherwise stated in the recipe.

Measure all ingredients accurately and don't omit or substitute ingredients. Use the full amount of sugar given in the recipe. If you prefer less sugar in your soft spread, try a recipe made with Ball Low or No-Sugar Needed Pectin for greater versatility. Ball Low or No-Sugar Needed Pectin may be prepared without sugar, using 1 to 3 cups of sugar, or using a non-sugar sweetener. Follow the pectin label instructions for adding sweetener.

Combine and cook recipe ingredients following instructions for cooking temperature and testing for doneness. To help reduce foam after cooking, add 1/2 teaspoon butter or margarine to mixture, stirring to blend well. Jar sizes and processing times will vary depending on recipe ingredients and type of soft spread you selected, so follow each recipe carefully. To use 4-ounce jars or 12-ounce jars for soft spreads, follow the same processing time as given for 8-ounce jars.

Butters

Fruit butter is a thick, smooth spread rich with concentrated flavor. Slow-cooking fruit pulp and sugar over medium heat melds these basic ingredients together in perfect balance, creating a spreadable texture that yields to the most delicate breads and pastries. Spices or a second fruit or fruit juice may be added to layer on flavor. Fruit butters are cooked until they mound on a spoon. To test for doneness, put a small dollop of fruit butter onto a plate. If there is no separation of liquid from the fruit pulp, it's ready.

Apple Butter

Yield: about 6 half-pint or 3 pint jars

4 pounds apples (about 12 to 16 medium)	4 cups sugar
2 cups water	2 teaspoons cinnamon
	1/4 teaspoon cloves

PREP Wash apples under cold running water; drain. Core and peel apples. Cut apples into quarters.

COOK Combine apples and water in a large saucepan. Cook apples at a simmer (180°F) until soft. Purée mixture using an electric food strainer or food mill. Measure 2 quarts of apple pulp; return apple pulp to saucepan. Add sugar and spices, stirring until sugar dissolves. Cook at a gentle boil over medium heat until apple mixture is thick enough to mound on a spoon, stirring frequently to prevent sticking. If mixture becomes too thick, add a small amount of water or apple juice for desired consistency. Remove from heat.

FILL Ladle hot butter into a hot jar, leaving 1/4-inch headspace. Remove air bubbles. Clean jar rim. Center lid on jar and adjust band to fingertip-tight. Place jar on the rack elevated over simmering water (180°F) in boiling-water canner. Repeat until all jars are filled.

PROCESS Lower the rack into simmering water. Water must cover jars by 1 inch. Adjust heat to medium-high, cover canner and bring water to a rolling boil. Process half-pint or pint jars 10 minutes. Turn off heat and remove cover. Let jars cool 5 minutes. Remove jars from canner; do not retighten bands if loose. Cool 12 hours. Check seals. Label and store jars.

 You Choose Do you have a fondness for robust flavors? If so, substitute a portion of white granulated sugar with light or dark brown granulated sugar to impart a little taste of molasses.

Sweet Cider Apple Butter

Yield: about 8 half-pint or 4 pint jars

6 pounds apples (about 18 to 24 medium)	3 cups sugar
2 cups sweet apple cider	1 1/2 teaspoons cinnamon
	1/2 teaspoon cloves

PREP Wash apples under cold running water; drain. Core and peel apples. Cut apples into quarters.

COOK Combine apples and sweet cider in a large saucepan. Cook apples at a simmer (180°F) until soft. Purée mixture in an electric food strainer or food mill. Measure 3 quarts of apple pulp; return apple pulp to saucepan. Add sugar and spices, stirring until sugar dissolves. Cook at a gentle boil over medium heat until apple mixture is thick enough to mound on a spoon, stirring frequently to prevent sticking. If mixture becomes too thick, add a small amount of sweet apple cider for desired consistency. Remove from heat.

FILL Ladle hot butter into a hot jar, leaving 1/4-inch headspace. Remove air bubbles. Clean jar rim. Center lid on jar and adjust band to fingertip-tight. Place jar on the rack elevated over simmering water (180°F) in boiling-water canner. Repeat until all jars are filled.

PROCESS Lower the rack into simmering water. Water must cover jars by 1 inch. Adjust heat to medium-high, cover canner and bring water to a rolling boil. Process half-pint or pint jars 15 minutes. Turn off heat and remove cover. Let jars cool 5 minutes. Remove jars from canner; do not retighten bands if loose. Cool 12 hours. Check seals. Label and store jars.

Apricot Butter

Yield: about 6 half-pint or 3 pint jars

2 pounds apricots (about 16 to 24 medium)	3 cups sugar
1/2 cup water	2 tablespoons lemon juice, fresh or bottled

PREP Wash apricots under cold running water; drain. To peel apricots, blanch in boiling water 30 to 60 seconds. Immediately transfer to cold water. Cut off peel. Cut apricots in half lengthwise; remove pits and fibrous flesh.

COOK Combine apricots and water in a large saucepan. Cook apricots at a simmer (180°F) until soft. Purée mixture using an electric food strainer or food mill. Measure 1 1/2 quarts of apricot pulp; return apricot pulp to saucepan. Add sugar and lemon juice, stirring until sugar dissolves. Cook at a gentle boil over medium heat until apricot mixture is thick enough to mound on a spoon, stirring frequently to prevent sticking. Remove from heat.

FILL Ladle hot butter into a hot jar, leaving 1/4-inch headspace. Remove air bubbles. Clean jar rim. Center lid on jar and adjust band to fingertip-tight. Place jar on the rack elevated over simmering water (180°F) in boiling-water canner. Repeat until all jars are filled.

PROCESS Lower the rack into simmering water. Water must cover jars by 1 inch. Adjust heat to medium-high, cover canner and bring water to a rolling boil. Process half-pint or pint jars 10 minutes. Turn off heat and remove cover. Let jars cool 5 minutes. Remove jars from canner; do not retighten bands if loose. Cool 12 hours. Check seals. Label and store jars.

Cranapple Butter

Yield: about 6 pint jars

6 pounds apples (about 18 to 24 medium)	4 cups sugar
	2 teaspoons cinnamon
2 quarts bottled cranberry juice cocktail (64 ounces)	1/2 teaspoon nutmeg

PREP Wash apples under cold running water; drain. Core and peel apples. Cut apples lengthwise into eighths.

COOK Combine apples and cranberry juice cocktail in a large saucepan. Cook apples at a simmer (180°F) until soft. Purée mixture using an electric food strainer or food mill. Return apple pulp to saucepan. Add sugar and spices, stirring until sugar dissolves. Cook at a gentle boil over medium heat until apple mixture is thick enough to mound on a spoon, stirring frequently to prevent sticking. Remove from heat.

FILL Ladle hot butter into a hot jar, leaving 1/4-inch headspace. Remove air bubbles. Clean jar rim. Center lid on jar and adjust band to fingertip-tight. Place jar on the rack elevated over simmering water (180°F) in boiling-water canner. Repeat until all jars are filled.

PROCESS Lower the rack into simmering water. Water must cover jars by 1 inch. Adjust heat to medium-high, cover canner and bring water to a rolling boil. Process pint jars 10 minutes. Turn off heat and remove cover. Let jars cool 5 minutes. Remove jars from canner; do not retighten bands if loose. Cool 12 hours. Check seals. Label and store jars.

Bump up the taste and texture of this butter recipe by using 1 pound fresh cranberries and 5 pounds fresh apples. Cook cranberries, apples, and cranberry juice cocktail until fruit is soft, then purée mixture. Refer to recipe instructions for cooking and processing Cranapple Butter.

Honeyed Yellow Tomato Butter

Yield: about 3 half-pint jars

5 pounds yellow tomatoes (about 15 to 20 medium)	1 1-inch piece fresh ginger, peeled
2 cups sugar	1 tablespoon whole allspice
1 cup honey	2 sticks cinnamon

PREP Wash tomatoes under cold running water; drain. To peel tomatoes, blanch in boiling water 30 to 60 seconds. Immediately transfer to cold water. Peel and core tomatoes. Cut tomatoes into quarters and remove seeds. Tie ginger and spices in a spice bag.

COOK Heat tomatoes at a simmer (180°F), in a large saucepan until soft. Purée mixture using an electric food strainer or food mill. Measure 2 quarts of tomato pulp; return tomato pulp to saucepan. Add sugar and honey, stirring until sugar dissolves. Add spice bag. Cook at a gentle boil over medium heat until tomato mixture is thick enough to mound on a spoon, stirring frequently to prevent sticking. Remove from heat. Remove spice bag.

FILL Ladle hot butter into a hot jar, leaving 1/4-inch headspace. Remove air bubbles. Clean jar rim. Center lid on jar and adjust band to fingertip-tight. Place jar on the rack elevated over simmering water (180°F) in boiling-water canner. Repeat until all jars are filled.

PROCESS Lower the rack into simmering water. Water must cover jars by 1 inch. Adjust heat to medium-high, cover canner and bring water to a rolling boil. Process half-pint jars 10 minutes. Turn off heat and remove cover. Let jars cool 5 minutes. Remove jars from canner; do not retighten bands if loose. Cool 12 hours. Check seals. Label and store jars.

Peach Butter

Yield: about 8 half-pint or 4 pint jars

4 to 41/2 pounds peaches (about 14 to 18 medium)	1/2 cup water
	4 cups sugar

PREP Wash peaches under cold running water; drain. To peel peaches, blanch in boiling water 30 to 60 seconds. Immediately transfer to cold water. Cut off peel. Cut peaches in half lengthwise; remove pits and fibrous flesh.

COOK Combine peaches and water in a large saucepan. Cook peaches at a simmer (180°F) until soft. Purée mixture in an electric food strainer or food mill. Measure 2 quarts of peach pulp; return peach pulp to saucepan. Add sugar, stirring until sugar dissolves. Cook at a gentle boil over medium heat until peach mixture is thick enough to mound on a spoon, stirring frequently to prevent sticking. Remove from heat.

FILL Ladle hot butter into a hot jar, leaving 1/4-inch headspace. Remove air bubbles. Clean jar rim. Center lid on jar and adjust band to fingertip-tight. Place jar on the rack elevated over simmering water (180°F) in boiling-water canner. Repeat until all jars are filled.

PROCESS Lower the rack into simmering water. Water must cover jars by 1 inch. Adjust heat to medium-high, cover canner and bring water to a rolling boil. Process half-pint or pint jars 10 minutes. Turn off heat and remove cover. Let jars cool 5 minutes. Remove jars from canner; do not retighten bands if loose. Cool 12 hours. Check seals. Label and store jars.

Add 1/2 to 1 teaspoon each of ginger, nutmeg, and cinnamon or any combination of spices when adding sugar for spiced peach butter.

Pear Butter

Yield: about 8 half-pint or 4 pint jars

6 pounds pears (about 18 to 24 medium)	1 teaspoon grated orange peel (about 1/2 medium)
1/2 cup water	1/2 teaspoon nutmeg
4 cups sugar	1/3 cup orange juice (about 1/2 medium)

PREP Wash pears and orange under cold running water; drain. Cut pears in half lengthwise; core and peel. Cut pears into eighths. Grate orange peel; measure 1 teaspoon grated orange peel. Cut orange in half and remove seeds. Juice orange; measure 1/3 cup orange juice.

COOK Combine pears and water in a large saucepan. Cook pears at a simmer (180°F) until soft. Purée mixture using an electric food strainer or food mill. Measure 2 quarts of pear pulp; return pear pulp to saucepan. Add sugar, stirring until sugar dissolves. Stir in remaining ingredients. Cook at a gentle boil over medium heat until pear mixture is thick enough to mound on a spoon, stirring frequently to prevent sticking. Remove from heat.

FILL Ladle hot butter into a hot jar, leaving 1/4-inch headspace. Remove air bubbles. Clean jar rim. Center lid on jar and adjust band to fingertip-tight. Place jar on the rack elevated over simmering water (180°F) in boiling-water canner. Repeat until all jars are filled.

PROCESS Lower the rack into simmering water. Water must cover jars by 1 inch. Adjust heat to medium-high, cover canner and bring water to a rolling boil. Process half-pint or pint jars 10 minutes. Turn off heat and remove cover. Let jars cool 5 minutes. Remove jars from canner; do not retighten bands if loose. Cool 12 hours. Check seals. Label and store jars.

Conserves

Conserves are a combination of two or more fruits cooked to a thick consistency. Dried fruits, nuts, coconut, or raisins add rich flavors and unique textures to this spread. Most conserve recipes rely on the pectin in the fruit and a long cooking time to develop their spreadable consistency. Conserves are cooked to, or almost to, the gelling point. Check for doneness using the plate test or temperature method.

Ambrosia Conserve

Yield: about 6 half-pint jars

1 large pineapple (about 5 pounds)	5 cups sugar
1/3 cup grated orange peel (about 2 medium)	1 cup shredded coconut
1 cup orange juice (about 2 medium)	1 cup chopped maraschino cherries
	1/2 cup slivered almonds

PREP Wash pineapple and oranges under cold running water; drain. Cut off leaves and bottom end from pineapple. Peel and core pineapple. Coarsely chop pineapple; measure 5 cups chopped pineapple. Grate orange peel; measure 1/3 cup grated orange peel. Cut oranges in half and remove seeds. Juice oranges; measure 1 cup of orange juice.

COOK Combine pineapple, orange peel, and orange juice in a large saucepan. Cook pineapple mixture at a simmer (180°F) for 10 minutes. Add sugar, stirring until sugar dissolves. Bring mixture to a boil over medium-high heat. Cook rapidly almost to the gelling point (220°F), stirring to prevent sticking. Stir in remaining ingredients during the last 5 minutes of cooking. Remove from heat.

FILL Ladle hot conserve into a hot jar, leaving 1/4-inch headspace. Remove air bubbles. Clean jar rim. Center lid on jar and adjust band to fingertip-tight. Place jar on the rack elevated over simmering water (180°F) in boiling-water canner. Repeat until all jars are filled.

PROCESS Lower the rack into simmering water. Water must cover jars by 1 inch. Adjust heat to medium-high, cover canner and bring water to a rolling boil. Process half-pint jars 15 minutes. Turn off heat and remove cover. Let jars cool 5 minutes. Remove jars from canner; do not retighten bands if loose. Cool 12 hours. Check seals. Label and store jars.

Apricot-Orange Conserve

Yield: about 6 half-pint jars

3 1/2 cups chopped apricots (about 12 to 15 medium)	2 tablespoons lemon juice, fresh or bottled
2 tablespoons finely grated orange peel (about 1/2 medium)	3 1/2 cups sugar
	1/2 cup chopped walnuts
1 1/2 cups orange juice (about 3 medium)	

PREP Wash apricots and oranges under cold running water; drain. To peel apricots, blanch in boiling water 30 to 60 seconds. Immediately transfer to cold water. Cut off peel. Cut apricots in half lengthwise; remove pits and fibrous flesh. Chop apricots; measure 3 1/2 cups chopped apricots. Grate orange peel; measure

2 tablespoons grated orange peel. Cut oranges in half and remove seeds. Juice orange; measure 1 1/2 cups orange juice.

COOK Combine chopped apricots, orange peel, orange juice, and lemon juice in a large saucepan. Cook apricot mixture at a simmer (180°F) for 10 minutes. Add sugar, stirring until sugar dissolves. Bring mixture to a boil over medium-high heat. Cook rapidly almost to the gelling point (220°F), stirring to prevent sticking. Stir in walnuts during the last 5 minutes of cooking. Remove from heat.

FILL Ladle hot conserve into a hot jar, leaving 1/4-inch headspace. Remove air bubbles. Clean jar rim. Center lid on jar and adjust band to fingertip-tight. Place jar on the rack elevated over simmering water (180°F) in boiling-water canner. Repeat until all jars are filled.

PROCESS Lower the rack into simmering water. Water must cover jars by 1 inch. Adjust heat to medium-high, cover canner and bring water to a rolling boil. Process half-pint jars 10 minutes. Turn off heat and remove cover. Let jars cool 5 minutes. Remove jars from canner; do not retighten bands if they are loose. Cool 12 hours. Check seals. Label and store jars.

 Make a second batch of Apricot-Orange Conserve using this recipe variation: add 2 tablespoons minced crystallized ginger and 2 tablespoons minced candied citron, then switch out the walnuts for pecans.

Blueberry Conserve

Yield: about 4 half-pint jars

1 quart blueberries (about 1 1/2 pounds)	1 small lemon, thinly sliced
4 cups sugar	1 small orange, thinly sliced
1/2 cup raisins	2 cups water

PREP Wash blueberries, lemon, and orange under cold running water; drain. Cut lemon and orange in half and remove seeds. Thinly slice lemon and orange, discarding ends.

COOK Combine all ingredients, except blueberries, in a large saucepan. Cook mixture at a simmer (180°F) for 10 minutes, stirring until sugar dissolves. Add blueberries. Bring mixture to a boil over medium-high heat. Cook rapidly almost to the gelling point (220°F), stirring to prevent sticking. Remove from heat.

FILL Ladle hot conserve into a hot jar, leaving 1/4-inch headspace. Remove air bubbles. Clean jar rim. Center lid on jar and adjust band to fingertip-tight. Place jar on the rack elevated over simmering water (180°F) in boiling-water canner. Repeat until all jars are filled.

PROCESS Lower the rack into simmering water. Water must cover jars by 1 inch. Adjust heat to medium-high, cover canner and bring water to a rolling boil. Process half-pint jars 15 minutes. Turn off heat and remove cover. Let jars cool 5 minutes. Remove jars from canner; do not retighten bands if loose. Cool 12 hours. Check seals. Label and store jars.

Cherry-Raspberry Conserve

Yield: about 4 half-pint jars

- 3 cups pitted sweet cherries (about 1½ pounds)
- 3 cups red raspberry pulp (about 1½ pounds)
- 4 cups sugar

PREP Wash cherries and red raspberries under cold running water; drain. Stem and pit cherries. Measure 3 cups pitted cherries. Coarsely crush raspberries one layer at a time using a potato masher. Strain crushed raspberries through a fine sieve or food mill to remove seeds. Measure 3 cups of raspberry pulp.

COOK Heat cherries at a simmer (180°F), in a large saucepan, until tender. Add raspberry pulp and sugar, stirring until sugar dissolves. Bring mixture to a boil over medium-high heat. Cook rapidly almost to the gelling point (220°F), stirring to prevent sticking. Remove from heat.

FILL Ladle hot conserve into a hot jar, leaving ¼-inch headspace. Remove air bubbles. Clean jar rim. Center lid on jar and adjust band to fingertip-tight. Place jar on the rack elevated over simmering water (180°F) in boiling-water canner. Repeat until all jars are filled.

PROCESS Lower the rack into simmering water. Water must cover jars by 1 inch. Adjust heat to medium-high, cover canner and bring water to a rolling boil. Process half-pint jars 15 minutes. Turn off heat and remove cover. Let jars cool 5 minutes. Remove jars from canner; do not retighten bands if loose. Cool 12 hours. Check seals. Label and store jars.

Cranberry Conserve

Yield: about 4 half-pint jars

- 1 quart cranberries (about 1 pound)
- ¾ cup chopped orange (about 1 medium)
- 2 cups water
- ½ cup raisins
- 3 cups sugar
- ½ cup chopped walnuts

PREP Wash cranberries and orange under cold running water; drain. Cut orange in half and remove seeds. Coarsely chop orange, including peel, using a food processor or knife. Measure ¾ cup of chopped orange.

COOK Combine chopped orange and water in a large saucepan. Cook over medium heat until peel is tender. Add cranberries, raisins, and sugar, stirring until sugar dissolves. Bring mixture to a boil over medium-high heat. Cook rapidly almost to the gelling point (220°F), stirring to prevent sticking. Add walnuts during the last 5 minutes of cooking. Remove from heat.

FILL Ladle hot conserve into a hot jar, leaving ¼-inch headspace. Remove air bubbles. Clean jar rim. Center lid on jar and adjust band to fingertip-tight. Place jar on the rack elevated over simmering water (180°F) in boiling-water canner. Repeat until all jars are filled.

PROCESS Lower the rack into simmering water. Water must cover jars by 1 inch. Adjust heat to medium-high, cover canner and bring water to a rolling boil. Process half-pint jars 15 minutes. Turn off heat and remove cover. Let jars cool 5 minutes. Remove jars from canner; do not retighten bands if loose. Cool 12 hours. Check seals. Label and store jars.

Our Tip Are you looking for an alternative to traditional cranberry sauce for your holiday meals? This is it! Cranberry Conserve blends traditional flavors in a new way. Serve it with turkey, poultry, or pork. To add another layer of flavor, toast walnuts in a saucepan or oven for 3 to 4 minutes.

Peach-Pineapple Conserve

Yield: about 6 half-pint jars

- 2 cups dried peaches
- 1 cup water
- 3½ cups sugar
- 1½ cups canned unsweetened crushed pineapple
- ⅔ cup chopped orange pulp (about 1 medium)
- 2 tablespoons lemon juice, fresh or bottled

PREP Wash orange under cold running water; drain. Cut orange in half and remove seeds. Remove orange pulp from each section. Coarsely chop orange pulp using a food processor or knife. Measure ⅔ cup chopped orange pulp.

COOK Combine dried peaches and water in a small saucepan. Simmer until dried peaches are tender. Drain, reserving liquid. Coarsely chop dried peaches using a food processor or knife. Combine chopped peaches and reserved cooking liquid, sugar, crushed pineapple, orange pulp, and lemon juice in a large saucepan. Bring mixture to a boil over medium-high heat, stirring until sugar dissolves. Cook rapidly almost to the gelling point (220°F), stirring to prevent sticking. Remove from heat.

FILL Ladle hot conserve into a hot jar, leaving ¼-inch headspace. Remove air bubbles. Clean jar rim. Center lid on jar and adjust band to fingertip-tight. Place jar on the rack elevated over simmering water (180°F) in boiling-water canner. Repeat until all jars are filled.

PROCESS Lower the rack into simmering water. Water must cover jars by 1 inch. Adjust heat to medium-high, cover canner and bring water to a rolling boil. Process half-pint jars 10 minutes. Turn off heat and remove cover. Let jars cool 5 minutes. Remove jars from canner; do not retighten bands if loose. Cool 12 hours. Check seals. Label and store jars.

Pineapple-Apricot Conserve No sugar added

Yield: about 5 half-pint jars

- 2 cups dried apricots
- 2 cups water
- 4 cups canned unsweetened crushed pineapple, drained
- 1 cup golden raisins
- 1 teaspoon ginger
- 4 teaspoons lemon juice, fresh or bottled

PREP Drain juice from crushed pineapple using a fine sieve.

COOK Combine dried apricots and water in a small saucepan. Simmer dried apricots until tender. Purée mixture using an electric food strainer or food mill. Combine apricot purée, crushed pineapple, golden raisins, ginger, and lemon juice in a large saucepan. Bring mixture to a boil over medium-high heat. Cook rapidly almost to the gelling point (220°F), stirring to prevent sticking. Remove from heat.

FILL Ladle hot conserve into a hot jar, leaving ¼-inch headspace. Remove air bubbles. Clean jar rim. Center lid on jar and adjust band to fingertip-tight. Place jar on the rack elevated over simmering water (180°F) in boiling-water canner. Repeat until all jars are filled.

PROCESS Lower the rack into simmering water. Water must cover jars by 1 inch. Adjust heat to medium-high, cover canner and bring water to a rolling boil. Process half-pint jars 10 minutes. Turn off heat and remove cover. Let jars cool 5 minutes. Remove jars from canner; do not retighten bands if loose. Cool 12 hours. Check seals. Label and store jars.

Plum Conserve

Yield: about 5 half-pint jars

2 pounds plums (about 10 to 12 medium)	1 cup raisins
1 large orange	1/3 cup thinly sliced orange peel
3 cups sugar	1 cup chopped pecans

PREP Wash plums and orange under cold running water; drain. Cut plums in half and remove pits. Coarsely chop plums; measure 5 cups chopped plums. Peel orange, reserving peel. Cut orange in half and remove seeds. Remove orange pulp from each section. Coarsely chop orange pulp; measure 1 cup chopped orange pulp. Cut orange peel into thin slivers; measure 1/3 cup slivered orange peel.

COOK Combine all ingredients, except pecans, in a large saucepan. Bring mixture to a boil over medium-high heat, stirring until sugar dissolves. Cook rapidly almost to the gelling point (220°F), stirring to prevent sticking. Add pecans during the last 5 minutes of cooking. Remove from heat.

FILL Ladle hot conserve into a hot jar, leaving 1/4-inch headspace. Remove air bubbles. Clean jar rim. Center lid on jar and adjust band to fingertip-tight. Place jar on the rack elevated over simmering water (180°F) in boiling-water canner. Repeat until all jars are filled.

PROCESS Lower the rack into simmering water. Water must cover jars by 1 inch. Adjust heat to medium-high, cover canner and bring water to a rolling boil. Process half-pint jars 15 minutes. Turn off heat and remove cover. Let jars cool 5 minutes. Remove jars from canner; do not retighten bands if loose. Cool 12 hours. Check seals. Label and store jars.

 Our Tip Pair this sweet conserve with an assortment of cheeses like Gouda, Manchego, Asiago, or Sharp Cheddar.

Rhubarb Conserve

Yield: about 7 half-pint jars

2 pounds rhubarb (about 8 to 16 stalks)	1 cup raisins
1/4 cup water	1 1/4 teaspoons mace
5 cups sugar	2 3-ounce pouches Ball Liquid Pectin
2 medium oranges	1/2 cup chopped walnuts
1 medium lemon	

PREP Wash rhubarb, oranges, and lemon under cold running water; drain. Remove green leafy tops and root ends from rhubarb. Dice rhubarb into 1/4-inch pieces. Cut oranges and lemon in half and remove seeds. Finely chop oranges and lemon, including peels, using a food processor or knife.

COOK Combine rhubarb and water in a large saucepan. Cook at a simmer (180°F) for 2 minutes. Add sugar, orange, lemon, raisins, and mace, stirring until sugar dissolves. Bring mixture to a boil over medium-high heat. Stir in pectin. Bring mixture to a rolling boil that cannot be stirred down. Boil hard for 1 minute, stirring constantly. Remove from heat. Stir in walnuts.

FILL Ladle hot conserve into a hot jar, leaving 1/4-inch headspace. Remove air bubbles. Clean jar rim. Center lid on jar and adjust band to fingertip-tight. Place jar on the rack elevated over simmering water (180°F) in boiling-water canner. Repeat until all jars are filled.

PROCESS Lower the rack into simmering water. Water must cover jars by 1 inch. Adjust heat to medium-high, cover canner and bring water to a rolling boil. Process half-pint jars 10 minutes. Turn off heat and remove cover. Let jars cool 5 minutes. Remove jars from canner; do not retighten bands if loose. Cool 12 hours. Check seals. Label and store jars.

Spring Conserve

Yield: about 7 half-pint jars

1 1/2 cups crushed pineapple (about 1/2 small)	1 tablespoon grated lemon peel (about 1/2 medium)
1 1/2 cups crushed strawberries (about 1 pound)	2 tablespoons lemon juice (about 1 medium)
1 1/4 cups diced rhubarb (about 2 to 4 stalks)	6 1/2 cups sugar
6 tablespoons Ball Classic Pectin	1/2 cup chopped pecans
	1/2 cup golden raisins

PREP Wash pineapple, strawberries, rhubarb, and lemon under cold running water; drain. Cut off leaves and bottom end from pineapple. Peel and core pineapple. Crush pineapple using a food processor; measure 1 1/2 cups of crushed pineapple. Remove stems and caps from strawberries. Coarsely crush strawberries one layer at a time using a potato masher. Measure 1 1/2 cups of crushed strawberries. Remove leafy tops and root ends from rhubarb. Dice rhubarb into 1/4-inch pieces; measure 1 1/4 cups of diced rhubarb. Cut lemon in half and remove seeds. Juice lemon, reserving 2 tablespoons lemon juice. Grate lemon peel; measure 1 tablespoon grated lemon peel.

COOK Combine pineapple, strawberries, rhubarb, pectin, lemon peel, and lemon juice in a large saucepan, stirring to blend in pectin. Bring mixture to a boil over medium-high heat. Add sugar, stirring until sugar dissolves. Bring to a rolling boil that cannot be stirred down. Boil hard for 1 minute, stirring constantly. Remove from heat. Stir in walnuts and raisins.

FILL Ladle hot conserve into a hot jar, leaving 1/4-inch headspace. Remove air bubbles. Clean jar rim. Center lid on jar and adjust band to fingertip-tight. Place jar on the rack elevated over simmering water (180°F) in boiling-water canner. Repeat until all jars are filled.

PROCESS Lower the rack into simmering water. Water must cover jars by 1 inch. Adjust heat to medium-high, cover canner and bring water to a rolling boil. Process half-pint jars 15 minutes. Turn off heat and remove cover. Let jars cool 5 minutes. Remove jars from canner; do not retighten bands if loose. Cool 12 hours. Check seals. Label and store jars.

Jams

Traditional long-cook jams, those made without added pectin, are thick, firm spreads made by cooking crushed or chopped fruit and sugar to the gelling point. Long-cooking recipes yield a sweet concentration of fruit and sugar that is dark in color and bursting with fruit flavor. Jams prepared using added pectin have a short cooking time. Quick-cook jams present a bright fruit color and sweet, crisp fruit flavor. Whichever cooking method is used, jams are firm without being stiff. A dollop of jam on a plate will slowly spread.

Apricot Jam

Yield: about 5 pint jars

2 quarts crushed, peeled, pitted apricots (about 4 pounds)

1/4 cup lemon juice (about 1 large)

6 cups sugar

PREP Wash apricots under cold running water; drain. To peel apricots, blanch in boiling water 30 to 60 seconds. Immediately transfer to cold water. Cut off peel. Cut apricots in half lengthwise; remove pits and fibrous flesh. Coarsely chop apricots, then crush using a potato masher. Measure 2 quarts crushed apricots.

COOK Combine crushed apricots, lemon juice, and sugar in a large saucepan. Bring mixture slowly to a boil, stirring until sugar dissolves. Increase heat to medium-high and cook rapidly to gelling point (220°F), stirring to prevent sticking. Remove from heat. Skim off foam if necessary.

FILL Ladle hot jam into a hot jar, leaving 1/4-inch headspace. Remove air bubbles. Clean jar rim. Center lid on jar and adjust band to fingertip-tight. Place jar on the rack elevated over simmering water (180°F) in boiling-water canner. Repeat until all jars are filled.

PROCESS Lower the rack into simmering water. Water must cover jars by 1 inch. Adjust heat to medium-high, cover canner and bring water to a rolling boil. Process pint jars 15 minutes. Turn off heat and remove cover. Let jars cool 5 minutes. Remove jars from canner; do not retighten bands if loose. Cool 12 hours. Check seals. Label and store jars.

Berry Jam

Blackberry, Blueberry, Boysenberry, Dewberry, Gooseberry, Loganberry, Raspberry, Youngberry

Yield: about 6 half-pint or 3 pint jars

9 cups crushed berries (about 4 to 5 pounds)

6 cups sugar

PREP Wash berries under cold running water; drain. Coarsely crush berries one layer at a time using a potato masher. Measure 9 cups of crushed berries.

COOK Combine crushed berries and sugar in a large saucepan. Bring mixture slowly to a boil, stirring until sugar dissolves. Increase heat to medium-high and cook rapidly to gelling point (220°F), stirring to prevent sticking. Remove from heat. Skim off foam if necessary.

FILL Ladle hot jam into a hot jar, leaving 1/4-inch headspace. Remove air bubbles. Clean jar rim. Center lid on jar and adjust band to fingertip-tight. Place jar on the rack elevated over simmering water (180°F) in boiling-water canner. Repeat until all jars are filled.

PROCESS Lower the rack into simmering water. Water must cover jars by 1 inch. Adjust heat to medium-high, cover canner and bring water to a rolling boil. Process half-pint or pint jars 15 minutes. Turn off heat and remove cover. Let jars cool 5 minutes. Remove jars from canner; do not retighten bands if loose. Cool 12 hours. Check seals. Label and store jars.

 Take full advantage of the versatility this recipe offers. Prepare a batch of berry jam using your very favorite berry, then prepare a batch of jam combining two or three berries. Whichever variation you choose, use only 9 cups of crushed berries.

 If seedless jam is preferred, crushed berries may be heated until soft and pressed through a sieve or food mill; measure pulp and proceed with recipe.

Berry-Cherry Jam Low or no sugar added

Yield: about 6 half-pint jars

1 quart strawberries (about 2 1/2 to 3 pounds)

2 cups chopped and pitted sweet cherries (about 1 1/2 to 2 pounds)

2 cups blackberries (about 1 1/2 to 2 pounds)

1 cup water

3 tablespoons Ball Low or No-Sugar Needed Pectin

Sweetener, if desired

PREP Wash strawberries, cherries, and blackberries under cold running water; drain. Remove stems and caps from strawberries. Crush strawberries one layer at a time using a potato masher; measure 1 quart crushed strawberries. Stem and pit cherries. Coarsely chop cherries; measure 2 cups chopped cherries.

COOK Combine strawberries, cherries, blackberries, water, and pectin in a large saucepan, stirring to blend in pectin. Bring mixture to a boil over high heat, stirring constantly. Add sweetener according to label instructions, if desired. Return mixture to a boil that cannot be stirred down. Boil hard for 1 minute, stirring constantly. Remove mixture from heat if gel begins to form before 1-minute boil is completed. Skim off foam if necessary.

FILL Ladle hot jam into a hot jar, leaving 1/4-inch headspace. Remove air bubbles. Clean jar rim. Center lid on jar and adjust band to fingertip-tight. Place jar on the rack elevated over simmering water (180°F) in boiling-water canner. Repeat until all jars are filled.

PROCESS Lower the rack into simmering water. Water must cover jars by 1 inch. Adjust heat to medium-high, cover canner and bring water to a rolling boil. Process half-pint jars 10 minutes. Turn off heat and remove cover. Let jars cool 5 minutes. Remove jars from canner; do not retighten bands if loose. Cool 12 hours. Check seals. Label and store jars.

Bing Cherry Jam

Yield: about 6 half-pint jars

1 quart chopped, pitted Bing cherries (about 2 pounds)

6 tablespoons Ball Classic Pectin

1/2 teaspoon cinnamon

1/2 teaspoon cloves

1/4 cup lemon juice

1/4 cup almond liqueur

4 1/2 cups sugar

PREP Wash cherries under cold running water; drain. Stem and pit cherries. Coarsely chop cherries. Measure 1 quart chopped cherries.

COOK Combine cherries, pectin, cinnamon, cloves, lemon juice, and almond liqueur in a large saucepan, stirring to blend in pectin. Bring mixture slowly to a boil over medium-high heat. Add sugar, stirring until sugar dissolves. Bring mixture to a rolling boil that cannot be stirred down. Boil hard for 1 minute, stirring constantly. Remove from heat. Skim off foam if necessary.

FILL Ladle hot jam into a hot jar, leaving 1/4-inch headspace. Remove air bubbles. Clean jar rim. Center lid on jar and adjust band to fingertip-tight. Place jar on the rack elevated over simmering water (180°F) in boiling-water canner. Repeat until all jars are filled.

PROCESS Lower the rack into simmering water. Water must cover jars by 1 inch. Adjust heat to medium-high, cover canner and bring water to a rolling boil. Process half-pint jars 10 minutes. Turn off heat and remove cover. Let jars cool 5 minutes. Remove jars from canner; do not retighten bands if loose. Cool 12 hours. Check seals. Label and store jars.

Blueberry-Lemon Jam

Yield: about 8 half-pint jars

4½ cups blueberries (about 1½ pounds)

⅓ cup lemon juice

2 teaspoons grated lemon peel

6½ cups sugar

2 3-ounce pouches Ball Liquid Pectin

PREP Wash blueberries and lemon under cold running water; drain. Crush blueberries one layer at a time using a potato masher. Grate lemon peel; measure 2 teaspoons grated lemon peel. Cut lemon in half crosswise and remove seeds. Juice lemon; measure ⅓ cup lemon juice.

COOK Combine crushed blueberries, grated lemon peel, and lemon juice in a large saucepan. Bring mixture to a boil over medium-high heat. Add sugar, stirring until sugar dissolves. Bring mixture to a rolling boil that cannot be stirred down. Stir in pectin. Boil hard for 1 minute, stirring constantly. Remove from heat. Skim off foam if necessary.

FILL Ladle hot jam into a hot jar, leaving ¼-inch headspace. Remove air bubbles. Clean jar rim. Center lid on jar and adjust band to fingertip-tight. Place jar on the rack elevated over simmering water (180°F) in boiling-water canner. Repeat until all jars are filled.

PROCESS Lower the rack into simmering water. Water must cover jars by 1 inch. Adjust heat to medium-high, cover canner and bring water to a rolling boil. Process half-pint jars 10 minutes. Turn off heat and remove cover. Let jars cool 5 minutes. Remove jars from canner; do not retighten bands if loose. Cool 12 hours. Check seals. Label and store jars.

Blueberry-Lime Jam

Yield: about 6 half-pint jars

4½ cups blueberries (about 1½ pounds)

6 tablespoons Ball Classic Pectin

5 cups sugar

1 tablespoon grated lime peel (about 1 large)

⅓ cup lime juice

PREP Wash blueberries and lime under cold running water; drain. Crush blueberries one layer at a time using a potato masher. Grate lime peel; measure 1 tablespoon grated lime peel. Cut lime in half crosswise and remove seeds. Juice lime; measure ⅓ cup lime juice.

COOK Combine crushed blueberries and pectin in a large saucepan, stirring to blend in pectin. Bring mixture to a boil over medium-high heat. Add sugar, stirring until sugar dissolves. Stir in grated lime peel and lime juice. Bring mixture to a rolling boil that cannot be stirred down. Boil hard for 1 minute, stirring constantly. Remove from heat. Skim off foam if necessary.

FILL Ladle hot jam into a hot jar, leaving ¼-inch headspace. Remove air bubbles. Clean jar rim. Center lid on jar and adjust band to fingertip-tight. Place jar on the rack elevated over simmering water (180°F) in boiling-water canner. Repeat until all jars are filled.

PROCESS Lower the rack into simmering water. Water must cover jars by 1 inch. Adjust heat to medium-high, cover canner and bring water to a rolling boil. Process half-pint jars 10 minutes. Turn off heat and remove cover. Let jars cool 5 minutes. Remove jars from canner; do not retighten bands if loose. Cool 12 hours. Check seals. Label and store jars.

Cherry Jam

Yield: about 8 half-pint jars

1 quart chopped, pitted sweet or sour cherries (about 2 pounds)

6¼ cups sugar

2 tablespoons lemon juice, fresh or bottled (use only with sweet cherries)

2 3-ounce pouches Ball Liquid Pectin

PREP Wash cherries under cold running water; drain. Remove stems and pits. Coarsely chop cherries. Measure 1 quart chopped cherries.

COOK Combine chopped cherries, sugar, and lemon juice (if needed) in a large saucepan. Bring mixture slowly to a boil over medium-high heat, stirring until sugar dissolves. Stir in pectin. Bring mixture to a rolling boil that cannot be stirred down. Boil hard for 1 minute, stirring constantly. Remove from heat. Skim off foam if necessary.

FILL Ladle hot jam into a hot jar, leaving ¼-inch headspace. Remove air bubbles. Clean jar rim. Center lid on jar and adjust band to fingertip-tight. Place jar on the rack elevated over simmering water (180°F) in boiling-water canner. Repeat until all jars are filled.

PROCESS Lower the rack into simmering water. Water must cover jars by 1 inch. Adjust heat to medium-high, cover canner and bring water to a rolling boil. Process half-pint jars 15 minutes. Turn off heat and remove cover. Let jars cool 5 minutes. Remove jars from canner; do not retighten bands if loose. Cool 12 hours. Check seals. Label and store jars.

 Popular sweet cherries you'll want to try include Rainier, Royal Ann, Sweetheart, Lambert, and Bing. If you favor a sour cherry, select from Early Richmond, Montmorency, and Morello.

Damson Plum Jam

Yield: about 6 half-pint or 3 pint jars

5 cups coarsely chopped Damson plums (about 2 pounds)

3 cups sugar

¾ cup water

PREP Wash plums under cold running water; drain. Cut plums in half and remove pits. Coarsely chop plums. Measure 5 cups chopped plums.

COOK Combine chopped plums, sugar, and water in a large saucepan. Bring mixture slowly to a boil, stirring until sugar dissolves. Increase heat to medium-high and cook rapidly to gelling point (220°F), stirring to prevent sticking. Remove from heat. Skim off foam if necessary.

FILL Ladle hot jam into a hot jar, leaving ¼-inch headspace. Remove air bubbles. Clean jar rim. Center lid on jar and adjust band to fingertip-tight. Place jar on the rack elevated over simmering water (180°F) in boiling-water canner. Repeat until all jars are filled.

PROCESS Lower the rack into simmering water. Water must cover jars by 1 inch. Adjust heat to medium-high, cover canner and bring water to a rolling boil. Process half-pint or pint jars 15 minutes. Turn off heat and remove cover. Let jars cool 5 minutes. Remove jars from canner; do not retighten bands if loose. Cool 12 hours. Check seals. Label and store jars.

Elderberry Jam

Yield: about 6 half-pint or 3 pint jars

2 quarts crushed elderberries (about 3 to 4 pounds)

6 cups sugar

1/4 cup vinegar, 5% acidity

PREP Wash elderberries under cold running water; drain. Lightly crush elderberries one layer at a time using a potato masher. Measure 2 quarts crushed elderberries.

COOK Combine crushed elderberries, sugar, and vinegar in a large saucepan. Bring mixture slowly to a boil, stirring until sugar dissolves. Increase heat to medium-high and cook rapidly to gelling point (220°F), stirring to prevent sticking. Remove from heat. Skim off foam if necessary.

FILL Ladle hot jam into a hot jar, leaving 1/4-inch headspace. Remove air bubbles. Clean jar rim. Center lid on jar and adjust band to fingertip-tight. Place jar on the rack elevated over simmering water (180°F) in boiling-water canner. Repeat until all jars are filled.

PROCESS Lower the rack into simmering water. Water must cover jars by 1 inch. Adjust heat to medium-high, cover canner and bring water to a rolling boil. Process half-pint or pint jars 15 minutes. Turn off heat and remove cover. Let jars cool 5 minutes. Remove jars from canner; do not retighten bands if loose. Cool 12 hours. Check seals. Label and store jars.

Fig Jam

Yield: about 10 half-pint or 5 pint jars

5 pounds figs (about 45 medium)

6 cups sugar

3/4 cup water

1/4 cup bottled lemon juice

PREP Wash figs under cold running water; drain. Remove stems. Cover figs with boiling water; let stand 10 minutes; drain. Chop figs; measure 2 quarts chopped figs.

COOK Combine chopped figs, sugar, and water in a large saucepan. Bring mixture slowly to a boil, stirring until sugar dissolves. Increase heat to medium-high and cook rapidly to gelling point (220°F), stirring to prevent sticking. Add lemon juice and cook 1 minute longer. Remove from heat. Skim off foam if necessary.

FILL Ladle hot jam into a hot jar, leaving 1/4-inch headspace. Remove air bubbles. Clean jar rim. Center lid on jar and adjust band to fingertip-tight. Place jar on the rack elevated over simmering water (180°F) in boiling-water canner. Repeat until all jars are filled.

PROCESS Lower the rack into simmering water. Water must cover jars by 1 inch. Adjust heat to medium-high, cover canner and bring water to a rolling boil. Process half-pint or pint jars 15 minutes. Turn off heat and remove cover. Let jars cool 5 minutes. Remove jars from canner; do not retighten bands if loose. Cool 12 hours. Check seals. Label and store jars.

 Fig Jam is truly versatile. Use this jam in breakfast pastries and cookies, layer it with goat cheese on a toasted crostini, or combine it with chopped fruit and nuts as a stuffing for rolled pork loin.

Grape Jam

Concord, Muscadine, Scuppernong

Yield: about 6 half-pint or 3 pint jars

2 quarts grapes (about 4 pounds)

1/2 cup water

6 cups sugar

PREP Wash grapes under cold running water; drain. Stem grapes. Separate grape pulp from skins. Coarsely chop skins, if desired. Cook skins in water 15 to 20 minutes. Cook grape pulp without water until soft. Strain grape pulp through a fine sieve or food mill to remove seeds.

COOK Combine grape pulp, grape skins, and sugar in a large saucepan. Bring mixture slowly to a boil, stirring until sugar dissolves. Increase heat to medium-high and cook rapidly to gelling point (220°F), stirring to prevent sticking. Remove from heat. Skim off foam if necessary.

FILL Ladle hot jam into a hot jar, leaving 1/4-inch headspace. Remove air bubbles. Clean jar rim. Center lid on jar and adjust band to fingertip-tight. Place jar on the rack elevated over simmering water (180°F) in boiling-water canner. Repeat until all jars are filled.

PROCESS Lower the rack into simmering water. Water must cover jars by 1 inch. Adjust heat to medium-high, cover canner and bring water to a rolling boil. Process half-pint or pint jars 15 minutes. Turn off heat and remove cover. Let jars cool 5 minutes. Remove jars from canner; do not retighten bands if loose. Cool 12 hours. Check seals. Label and store jars.

 Concord, Muscadine, and Scuppernong grapes are most often used to make jam. However, other grape varieties may be used. Remember that grapes do not improve or ripen after harvesting, so select fruit that is fully sweet, has plump globes, and has the correct color for mature fruit.

Kiwi Jam

Yield: about 4 half-pint jars

3 cups chopped, peeled kiwi (about 9 to 12 medium)

6 tablespoons Ball Classic Pectin

1 cup bottled unsweetened pineapple juice

4 cups sugar

PREP Peel kiwi. Coarsely chop kiwi; measure 3 cups of chopped kiwi.

COOK Combine chopped kiwi, pectin, and pineapple juice in a large saucepan, stirring to blend in pectin. Bring mixture to a boil over medium-high heat. Add sugar, stirring until sugar dissolves. Bring mixture to a rolling boil that cannot be stirred down. Boil hard for 1 minute, stirring constantly. Remove from heat. Skim foam if necessary.

FILL Ladle hot jam into a hot jar, leaving 1/4-inch headspace. Remove air bubbles. Clean jar rim. Center lid on jar and adjust band to fingertip-tight. Place jar on the rack elevated over simmering water (180°F) in boiling-water canner. Repeat until all jars are filled.

PROCESS Lower the rack into simmering water. Water must cover jars by 1 inch. Adjust heat to medium-high, cover canner and bring water to a rolling boil. Process half-pint jars 10 minutes. Turn off heat and remove cover. Let jars cool 5 minutes. Remove jars from canner; do not retighten bands if loose. Cool 12 hours. Check seals. Label and store jars.

Mango-Raspberry Jam

Yield: about 7 half-pint jars

3 pounds mangoes (about 4 to 5 medium)	2 tablespoons lemon juice, fresh or bottled
1½ cups crushed red raspberries (about 1 pound)	6 tablespoons Ball Classic Pectin
	5½ cups sugar

PREP Wash mangoes and red raspberries under cold running water; drain. Cut mango lengthwise into two large pieces starting at the top and cutting down to the bottom. Make cuts about ⅓ inch from the center of the fruit to avoid the pit and fibrous flesh. Peel mango pieces and finely chop; measure 3 cups chopped mango. Lightly crush red raspberries one layer at a time using a potato masher; measure 1½ cups crushed red raspberries.

COOK Combine chopped mango, crushed red raspberries, lemon juice, and pectin in a large saucepan, stirring to blend in pectin. Bring mixture to a boil over medium-high heat. Add sugar, stirring until sugar dissolves. Bring mixture to a rolling boil that cannot be stirred down. Boil hard for 1 minute, stirring constantly. Remove from heat. Skim off foam if necessary.

FILL Ladle hot jam into a hot jar, leaving ¼-inch headspace. Remove air bubbles. Clean jar rim. Center lid on jar and adjust band to fingertip-tight. Place jar on the rack elevated over simmering water (180°F) in boiling-water canner. Repeat until all jars are filled.

PROCESS Lower the rack into simmering water. Water must cover jars by 1 inch. Adjust heat to medium-high, cover canner and bring water to a rolling boil. Process half-pint jars 10 minutes. Turn off heat and remove cover. Let jars cool 5 minutes. Remove jars from canner; do not retighten bands if loose. Cool 12 hours, Check seals. Label and store jars.

Peach Jam Low or no sugar added

Yield: about 6 half-pint jars

6 cups chopped, peeled, pitted peaches (about 8 to 10 medium)	3 tablespoons lemon juice, fresh or bottled
1 cup unsweetened white grape juice, fresh or bottled	4½ tablespoons Ball Low or No-Sugar Needed Pectin
	Sweetener, if desired

PREP Wash peaches under cold running water; drain. To peel peaches, blanch in boiling water 30 to 60 seconds. Immediately transfer to cold water. Cut off peel. Cut peaches in half; remove pit and fibrous flesh. Finely chop peaches, using a food processor or knife. Measure 5 cups chopped peaches.

COOK Combine chopped peaches, white grape juice, lemon juice, and pectin in a large saucepan, stirring to blend in pectin. Bring mixture to a boil over medium-high heat, stirring constantly. Add sweetener according to label instructions, if desired. Bring mixture to a boil; boil hard for 1 minute, stirring constantly. Remove mixture from heat if gel begins to form before 1-minute boil is completed. Skim off foam if necessary.

FILL Ladle hot jam into a hot jar, leaving ¼-inch headspace. Remove air bubbles. Clean jar rim. Center lid on jar and adjust band to fingertip-tight. Place jar on the rack elevated over simmering water (180°F) in boiling-water canner. Repeat until all jars are filled.

PROCESS Lower the rack into simmering water. Water must cover jars by 1 inch. Adjust heat to medium-high, cover canner and bring water to a rolling boil. Process half-pint jars 10 minutes. Turn off heat and remove cover. Let jars cool 5 minutes. Remove jars from canner; do not retighten bands if loose. Cool 12 hours. Check seals. Label and store jars.

Peach Jam

Yield: about 7 half-pint jars

1 quart finely chopped, peeled, pitted peaches (about 3 pounds)	⅓ cup lemon juice (about 1 large)
7½ cups sugar	2 3-ounce pouches Ball Liquid Pectin

PREP Wash peaches and lemon under cold running water; drain. To peel peaches, blanch in boiling water 30 to 60 seconds. Immediately transfer to cold water. Cut off peel. Cut peaches in half; remove pit and fibrous flesh. Chop peaches using a food processor or knife. Cut lemon in half and remove seeds. Juice lemon; measure ¼ cup lemon juice.

COOK Combine chopped peaches, sugar, and lemon juice in a large saucepan. Bring mixture to a boil over medium-high heat, stirring until sugar dissolves. Stir in liquid pectin. Bring mixture to a rolling boil that cannot be stirred down. Boil hard for 1 minute, stirring constantly. Remove from heat. Skim off foam if necessary.

FILL Ladle hot jam into a hot jar, leaving ¼-inch headspace. Remove air bubbles. Clean jar rim. Center lid on jar and adjust band to fingertip-tight. Place jar on the rack elevated over simmering water (180°F) in boiling-water canner. Repeat until all jars are filled.

PROCESS Lower the rack into simmering water. Water must cover jars by 1 inch. Adjust heat to medium-high, cover canner and bring water to a rolling boil. Process half-pint jars 10 minutes. Turn off heat and remove cover. Let jars cool 5 minutes. Remove jars from canner; do not retighten bands if loose. Cool 12 hours. Check seals. Label and store jars.

Pear Jam

Yield: about 8 half-pint jars

1 quart finely chopped, peeled, cored pears (about 2 to 3 pounds)	¼ cup lemon juice (about 1 large)
7½ cups sugar	1 3-ounce pouch Ball Liquid Pectin

PREP Wash pears and lemon under cold running water; drain. Cut pears in half lengthwise, peel, and core. Chop pears; measure 1 quart chopped pears. Cut lemon in half and remove seeds. Juice lemon; measure ¼ cup lemon juice.

COOK Combine chopped pears, sugar, and lemon juice in a large saucepan. Bring mixture to a boil over medium-high heat, stirring until sugar dissolves. Stir in pectin. Bring mixture to a rolling boil that cannot be stirred down. Boil hard for 1 minute, stirring constantly. Remove from heat. Skim off foam if necessary.

FILL Ladle hot jam into a hot jar, leaving ¼-inch headspace. Remove air bubbles. Clean jar rim. Center lid on jar and adjust band to fingertip-tight. Place jar on the rack elevated over simmering water (180°F) in boiling-water canner. Repeat until all jars are filled.

PROCESS Lower the rack into simmering water. Water must cover jars by 1 inch. Adjust heat to medium-high, cover canner and bring water to a rolling boil. Process half-pint jars 10 minutes. Turn off heat and remove cover. Let jars cool 5 minutes. Remove jars from canner; do not retighten bands if loose. Cool 12 hours. Check seals. Label and store jars.

Pineapple Jam

Yield: about 3 half-pint jars

1 large pineapple (about 5 pounds)	½ lemon, thinly sliced
2½ cups sugar	1 cup water

PREP Wash pineapple and lemon under cold running water; drain. Cut off leaves and bottom end of pineapple. Peel and core pineapple. Chop pineapple; measure 1 quart chopped pineapple. Cut lemon in half and remove seeds. Thinly slice ½ lemon, discarding end.

COOK Combine all ingredients in a large saucepan. Bring mixture slowly to a boil, stirring until sugar dissolves. Increase heat to medium-high and cook rapidly to gelling point (220°F), stirring to prevent sticking. Remove from heat. Skim off foam if necessary.

FILL Ladle hot jam into a hot jar, leaving ¼-inch headspace. Remove air bubbles. Clean jar rim. Center lid on jar and adjust band to fingertip-tight. Place jar on the rack elevated over simmering water (180°F) in boiling-water canner. Repeat until all jars are filled.

PROCESS Lower the rack into simmering water. Water must cover jars by 1 inch. Adjust heat to medium-high, cover canner and bring water to a rolling boil. Process half-pint jars 15 minutes. Turn off heat and remove cover. Let jars cool 5 minutes. Remove jars from canner; do not retighten bands if loose. Cool 12 hours. Check seals. Label and store jars.

Raspberry-Currant Jam

Yield: about 4 half-pint or 2 pint jars

2 cups red currant pulp (about 1 pound)	2 cups crushed red raspberries (about 1 to 1½ pounds)
¼ cup water	3 cups sugar

PREP Wash currants and red raspberries under cold running water; drain. Stem currants. Cook currants in water until soft. Strain currants and liquid through a fine sieve or food mill. Measure 2 cups of currant pulp. Gently crush red raspberries one layer at a time using a potato masher. Measure 2 cups crushed red raspberries.

COOK Combine currant pulp, crushed red raspberries, and sugar in a large saucepan. Bring mixture slowly to a boil, stirring until sugar dissolves. Increase heat to medium-high and cook rapidly to gelling point (220°F), stirring to prevent sticking. Remove from heat. Skim off foam if necessary.

FILL Ladle hot jam into a hot jar, leaving ¼-inch headspace. Remove air bubbles. Clean jar rim. Center lid on jar and adjust band to fingertip-tight. Place jar on the rack elevated over simmering water (180°F) in boiling-water canner. Repeat until all jars are filled.

PROCESS Lower the rack into simmering water. Water must cover jars by 1 inch. Adjust heat to medium-high, cover canner and bring water to a rolling boil. Process half-pint or pint jars 15 minutes. Turn off heat and remove cover. Let jars cool 5 minutes. Remove jars from canner; do not retighten bands if loose. Cool 12 hours. Check seals. Label and store jars.

Raspberry Jam

Yield: about 8 half-pint jars

1 quart crushed red raspberries (about 2 to 2½ pounds)	6½ cups sugar
	1 3-ounce pouch Ball Liquid Pectin

PREP Wash red raspberries under cold running water; drain. Gently crush red raspberries one layer at a time using a potato masher.

COOK Combine red raspberries and sugar in a large saucepan. Bring mixture to a boil over medium-high heat, stirring until sugar dissolves. Stir in pectin. Bring mixture to a rolling boil that cannot be stirred down. Boil hard for 1 minute, stirring constantly. Remove from heat. Skim off foam if necessary.

FILL Ladle hot jam into a hot jar, leaving ¼-inch headspace. Remove air bubbles. Clean jar rim. Center lid on jar and adjust band to fingertip-tight. Place jar on the rack elevated over simmering water (180°F) in boiling-water canner. Repeat until all jars are filled.

PROCESS Lower the rack into simmering water. Water must cover jars by 1 inch. Adjust heat to medium-high, cover canner and bring water to a rolling boil. Process half-pint jars 10 minutes. Turn off heat and remove cover. Let jars cool 5 minutes. Remove jars from canner; do not retighten bands if loose. Cool 12 hours. Check seals. Label and store jars.

Raspberry Jam Low or no sugar added

Yield: about 6 half-pint jars

2½ quarts red raspberries (about 5 to 6 pounds)	3 tablespoons Ball Low or No-Sugar Needed Pectin
1 cup water	Sweetener, if desired

PREP Wash red raspberries under cold running water; drain. Gently crush red raspberries one layer at a time using a potato masher. Measure 5 cups crushed red raspberries.

COOK Combine crushed red raspberries, water, and pectin in a large saucepan, stirring to blend in pectin. Bring mixture to a boil over medium-high heat, stirring constantly. Add sweetener according to label instructions, if desired. Bring mixture to a boil; boil hard for 1 minute, stirring constantly. Remove mixture from heat if a gel begins to form before 1-minute boil is completed. Skim off foam if necessary.

FILL Ladle hot jam into a hot jar, leaving ¼-inch headspace. Remove air bubbles. Clean jar rim. Center lid on jar and adjust band to fingertip-tight. Place jar on the rack elevated over simmering water (180°F) in boiling-water canner. Repeat until all jars are filled.

PROCESS Lower the rack into simmering water. Water must cover jars by 1 inch. Adjust heat to medium-high, cover canner and bring water to a rolling boil. Process half-pint jars 10 minutes. Turn off heat and remove cover. Let jars cool 5 minutes. Remove jars from canner; do not retighten bands if loose. Cool 12 hours. Check seals. Label and store jars.

Red Tomato Jam

Yield: about 5 half-pint jars

6 pounds red tomatoes (about 18 medium)

6 tablespoons Ball Classic Pectin

1 teaspoon grated lemon peel (about 1/2 medium)

1/2 teaspoon salt

2 teaspoons lemon juice (about 1/2 medium)

3 1/2 cups sugar

PREP Wash red tomatoes and lemon under cold running water; drain. Remove stem and blossom ends from tomatoes. Cut tomatoes into quarters. Cook tomatoes until soft. Puree mixture using an electric food strainer or food mill to remove peels and seeds. Grate lemon peel; measure 1 teaspoon grated peel. Juice lemon; measure 2 teaspoons lemon juice.

COOK Gently boil tomato pulp in a large saucepan over medium-high heat to reduce by half, stirring frequently to prevent sticking. Add pectin, lemon peel, salt, and lemon juice, stirring to blend in pectin. Bring mixture to a boil over medium-high heat, stirring constantly. Add sugar, stirring until sugar dissolves. Bring mixture to a rolling boil that cannot be stirred down. Boil hard for 1 minute, stirring constantly. Remove from heat. Skim foam if necessary.

FILL Ladle hot jam into a hot jar, leaving 1/4-inch headspace. Remove air bubbles. Clean jar rim. Center lid on jar and adjust band to fingertip-tight. Place jar on the rack elevated over simmering water (180°F) in boiling-water canner. Repeat until all jars are filled.

PROCESS Lower the rack into simmering water. Water must cover jars by 1 inch. Adjust heat to medium-high, cover canner and bring water to a rolling boil. Process half-pint jars 10 minutes. Turn off heat and remove cover. Let jars cool 5 minutes. Remove jars from canner; do not retighten bands if loose. Cool 12 hours. Check seals. Label and store jars.

Rhubarb-Orange Jam

Yield: about 7 half-pint jars

2 1/2 pounds rhubarb (about 10 to 18 stalks)

2 medium oranges

6 tablespoons Ball Classic Pectin

6 cups sugar

PREP Wash rhubarb and oranges under cold running water; drain. Remove leafy tops and root ends from rhubarb. Chop rhubarb into 1/2-inch pieces. Cut oranges in half and remove seeds. Juice oranges; measure 1 cup of orange juice. Using the peel from half of one orange, remove pith. Cut peel into thin slivers.

COOK Combine chopped rhubarb, orange juice, and orange peel in a large saucepan. Simmer rhubarb mixture, covered, about 3 minutes or until rhubarb is tender. Add pectin, stirring to blend in pectin. Bring mixture to a boil over medium-high heat. Add sugar, stirring until sugar dissolves. Bring mixture to a rolling boil that cannot be stirred down. Boil hard for 1 minute, stirring constantly. Remove from heat. Skim off foam if necessary.

FILL Ladle hot jam into a hot jar, leaving 1/4-inch headspace. Remove air bubbles. Clean jar rim. Center lid on jar and adjust band to fingertip-tight. Place jar on the rack elevated over simmering water (180°F) in boiling-water canner. Repeat until all jars are filled.

PROCESS Lower the rack into simmering water. Water must cover jars by 1 inch. Adjust heat to medium-high, cover canner and bring water to a rolling boil. Process half-pint jars 10 minutes. Turn off heat and remove cover. Let jars cool 5 minutes. Remove jars from canner; do not retighten bands if loose. Cool 12 hours. Check seals. Label and store jars.

Strawberry Jam

Yield: about 8 half-pint or 4 pint jars

2 quarts strawberries (about 4 to 5 pounds)

6 cups sugar

PREP Wash strawberries under cold running water; drain. Remove stems and caps from strawberries. Crush strawberries one layer at a time using a potato masher. Measure 2 quarts crushed strawberries.

COOK Combine crushed strawberries and sugar in a large saucepan. Bring mixture to a boil, stirring until sugar dissolves. Cook rapidly over medium-high heat to gelling point (220°F), stirring to prevent sticking. Remove from heat. Skim off foam if necessary.

FILL Ladle hot jam into a hot jar, leaving 1/4-inch headspace. Remove air bubbles. Clean jar rim. Center lid on jar and adjust band to fingertip-tight. Place jar on the rack elevated over simmering water (180°F) in boiling-water canner. Repeat until all jars are filled.

PROCESS Lower the rack into simmering water. Water must cover jars by 1 inch. Adjust heat to medium-high, cover canner and bring water to a rolling boil. Process half-pint or pint jars 15 minutes. Turn off heat and remove cover. Let jars cool 5 minutes. Remove jars from canner; do not retighten bands if loose. Cool 12 hours. Check seals. Label and store jars.

Strawberry Jam

Yield: about 8 half-pint jars

2 quarts strawberries (about 4 to 5 pounds)

6 tablespoons Ball Classic Pectin

1/4 cup lemon juice, fresh or bottled

7 cups sugar

PREP Wash strawberries under cold running water; drain. Remove stems and caps from strawberries. Crush strawberries one layer at a time using a potato masher.

COOK Combine strawberries, pectin, and lemon juice in a large saucepan, stirring to blend in pectin. Bring mixture to a boil over medium-high heat. Add sugar, stirring until sugar dissolves. Bring mixture to a rolling boil that cannot be stirred down. Boil hard for 1 minute, stirring constantly. Remove from heat. Skim off foam if necessary.

FILL Ladle hot jam into a hot jar, leaving 1/4-inch headspace. Remove air bubbles. Clean jar rim. Center lid on jar and adjust band to fingertip-tight. Place jar on the rack elevated over simmering water (180°F) in boiling-water canner. Repeat until all jars are filled.

PROCESS Lower the rack into simmering water. Water must cover jars by 1 inch. Adjust heat to medium-high, cover canner and bring water to a rolling boil. Process half-pint jars 10 minutes. Turn off heat and remove cover. Let jars cool 5 minutes. Remove jars from canner; do not retighten bands if loose. Cool 12 hours. Check seals. Label and store jars.

Strawberry Jam Low or no sugar added

Yield: about 6 half-pint jars

2 quarts strawberries (about 4 to 5 pounds)	3 tablespoons Ball Low or No-Sugar Needed Pectin
1 cup water	Sweetener, if desired

PREP Wash strawberries under cold running water; drain. Remove stems and caps from strawberries. Crush strawberries one layer at a time using a potato masher.

COOK Combine strawberries, water, and pectin in a large saucepan, stirring to blend in pectin. Bring mixture to a boil over high heat, stirring constantly. Add sweetener according to pectin instructions, if desired. Return mixture to a boil; boil hard for 1 minute, stirring constantly. Remove mixture from heat if a gel begins to form before 1-minute boil is completed. Skim off foam if necessary.

FILL Ladle hot jam into a hot jar, leaving 1/4-inch headspace. Remove air bubbles. Clean jar rim. Center lid on jar and adjust band to fingertip-tight. Place jar on the rack elevated over simmering water (180°F) in boiling-water canner. Repeat until all jars are filled.

PROCESS Lower the rack into simmering water. Water must cover jars by 1 inch. Adjust heat to medium-high, cover canner and bring water to a rolling boil. Process half-pint jars 10 minutes. Turn off heat and remove cover. Let jars cool 5 minutes. Remove jars from canner; do not retighten bands if loose. Cool 12 hours. Check seals. Label and store jars.

Strawberry-Rhubarb Jam

Yield: about 6 half-pint jars

2 cups crushed strawberries (about 1 1/2 to 2 pounds)	6 tablespoons Ball Classic Pectin
2 cups chopped rhubarb (about 3 to 6 stalks)	1/4 cup lemon juice, fresh or bottled
	5 1/2 cups sugar

PREP Wash strawberries and rhubarb under cold running water; drain. Remove stems and caps from strawberries. Crush strawberries one layer at a time using a potato masher. Measure 2 cups crushed strawberries. Remove leafy tops and root ends from rhubarb. Chop rhubarb into 1/2-inch pieces. Measure 2 cups chopped rhubarb.

COOK Combine strawberries, rhubarb, pectin, and lemon juice in a large saucepan, stirring to blend in pectin. Bring mixture to a boil over medium-high heat. Add sugar, stirring until sugar dissolves. Return mixture to a rolling boil that cannot be stirred down. Boil hard for 1 minute, stirring constantly. Remove from heat. Skim off foam if necessary.

FILL Ladle hot jam into a hot jar, leaving 1/4-inch headspace. Remove air bubbles. Clean jar rim. Center lid on jar and adjust band to fingertip-tight. Place jar on the rack elevated over simmering water (180°F) in boiling-water canner. Repeat until all jars are filled.

PROCESS Lower the rack into simmering water. Water must cover jars by 1 inch. Adjust heat to medium-high, cover canner and bring water to a rolling boil. Process half-pint jars 10 minutes. Turn off heat and remove cover. Let jars cool 5 minutes. Remove jars from canner; do not retighten bands if loose. Cool 12 hours. Check seals. Label and store jars.

Sweet Cherry-Loganberry Jam

Yield: about 6 half-pint jars

2 cups chopped, pitted dark sweet cherries (about 1 pound)	6 tablespoons Ball Classic Pectin
2 cups crushed loganberries (about 1 to 1 1/4 pounds)	5 cups sugar

PREP Wash cherries and loganberries under cold running water; drain. Stem and pit cherries. Chop cherries; measure 2 cups chopped cherries. Crush loganberries one layer at a time using a potato masher. Measure 2 cups crushed loganberries.

COOK Combine chopped cherries, crushed loganberries, and pectin in a large saucepan, stirring to blend in pectin. Bring mixture to a boil over medium-high heat. Add sugar, stirring until sugar dissolves. Return mixture to a rolling boil that cannot be stirred down. Boil hard for 1 minute, stirring constantly. Remove from heat. Skim off foam if necessary.

FILL Ladle hot jam into a hot jar, leaving 1/4-inch headspace. Remove air bubbles. Clean jar rim. Center lid on jar and adjust band to fingertip-tight. Place jar on the rack elevated over simmering water (180°F) in boiling-water canner. Repeat until all jars are filled.

PROCESS Lower the rack into simmering water. Water must cover jars by 1 inch. Adjust heat to medium-high, cover canner and bring water to a rolling boil. Process half-pint jars 10 minutes. Turn off heat and remove cover. Let jars cool 5 minutes. Remove jars from canner; do not retighten bands if loose. Cool 12 hours. Check seals. Label and store jars.

Sweet-Tart Gooseberry Jam

Yield: about 7 half-pint jars

2 1/2 cups crushed tart gooseberries (about 1 to 1 1/2 pounds)	6 tablespoons Ball Classic Pectin
2 1/2 cups crushed sweet gooseberries (about 1 to 1 1/2 pounds)	2 tablespoons vinegar, 5% acidity
	6 cups sugar

PREP Wash sweet and tart gooseberries under cold running water; drain. Remove stems and blossom ends from gooseberries. Crush sweet and tart gooseberries one layer at a time using a potato masher. Measure 2 1/2 cups each of sweet and tart gooseberries.

COOK Combine crushed gooseberries, pectin, and vinegar in a large saucepan, stirring to blend in pectin. Bring mixture to a boil over medium-high heat. Add sugar, stirring until sugar dissolves. Bring mixture to a rolling boil that cannot be stirred down. Boil for 1 minute, stirring constantly. Remove from heat. Skim off foam if necessary.

FILL Ladle hot jam into a hot jar, leaving 1/4-inch headspace. Remove air bubbles. Clean jar rim. Center lid on jar and adjust band to fingertip-tight. Place jar on the rack elevated over simmering water (180°F) in boiling-water canner. Repeat until all jars are filled.

PROCESS Lower the rack into simmering water. Water must cover jars by 1 inch. Adjust heat to medium-high, cover canner and bring water to a rolling boil. Process half-pint jars 10 minutes. Turn off heat and remove cover. Let jars cool 5 minutes. Remove jars from canner; do not retighten bands if loose. Cool 12 hours. Check seals. Label and store jars.

Jellies are shimmery, translucent spreads that have unique qualities not matched by other soft spreads. Jellies are firm in texture, allowing them to hold their shape when spooned from the jar, yet they are tender enough to spread easily. Jellies are made using juice extracted from fruits or vegetables, as well as juice made from concentrate and bottled juice. Prepare jellies using only the type of juice and type of pectin (if needed) that is listed in the recipe. For jelly made without added pectin, the sheet test or temperature method is used to determine when to turn off the heat (see page 43).

How to Prepare Juice for Jelly

Follow these general guidelines for preparing juice for making jelly unless otherwise instructed in the individual recipe. Juice is prepared in a way that keeps it crystal clear. Follow the instructions carefully for a clear, shimmering juice. If the juice cannot be used immediately, it may be canned or frozen to use later. If juice is canned, follow the recipe for canning apple juice (see page 28). If juice is frozen, follow the recipe for freezing fruit juices (see page 145).

Hard Fruits—These include apples, pears, nectarines, and similar types of fruit. Select top-quality fruit at its peak of ripeness. Wash under cold running water; drain. Remove stems and blossom ends as needed. Do not peel or core. Chop or quarter the fruit; measure fruit. Put prepared fruit in a large saucepan. Add 1 cup of water for each slightly heaped quart of fruit. Cover saucepan and simmer fruit over medium heat until soft, about 20 minutes. Strain fruit and liquid through a damp jelly bag or several layers of cheesecloth to extract juice.

Soft Fruits—These include grapes, cherries, berries, and similar types of fruit. Select top-quality fruit at its peak of ripeness. Wash fruit under cold running water; drain. Remove stems, pits, and seeds as needed. Lightly crush fruit one layer at a time using a potato masher; measure fruit. Combine fruit and 1/4- to 1/2-cup of water for each quart of fruit in a large saucepan. Cover saucepan and simmer fruit over medium-low heat until soft, about 10 minutes. Strain fruit and liquid through a damp jelly bag or several layers of cheesecloth to extract juice.

For a clear juice, do not press or squeeze the jelly bag in an attempt to extract the last few drops of juice. Put the juice in a deep container and let it stand overnight in the refrigerator. When you're ready to prepare jelly, ladle the juice from the container, being careful not to disturb any sediment or pulp that may have settled to the bottom.

Apple Jelly

Yield: about 4 half-pint jars

4 cups apple juice (about 3 to 4 pounds)	2 tablespoons lemon juice, fresh or bottled (optional)
	3 cups sugar

PREP Follow instructions for preparing, How to Prepare Juice for Jelly, see this page.

COOK Combine apple juice, lemon juice (if desired), and sugar in a large saucepan, stirring until sugar dissolves. Bring mixture to a boil over high heat. Cook rapidly to gelling point (220°F), stirring constantly. Remove from heat. Skim off foam if necessary.

FILL Ladle hot jelly into a hot jar, leaving 1/4-inch headspace. Clean jar rim. Center lid on jar and adjust band to fingertip-tight.

Place jar on the rack elevated over simmering water (180°F) in boiling-water canner. Repeat until all jars are filled.

PROCESS Lower the rack into simmering water. Water must cover jars by 1 inch. Adjust heat to medium-high, cover canner and bring water to a rolling boil. Process half-pint jars 10 minutes. Turn off heat and remove cover. Let jars cool 5 minutes. Remove jars from canner; do not retighten bands if loose. Cool 12 hours. Check seals. Label and store jars.

 To make apple jelly your way, tie whole spices such as cloves, allspice, or cinnamon sticks in a spice bag. Add spice bag while apples are cooking. Remove spice bag before straining juice.

Apple Jelly Low or no sugar added

Yield: about 4 half-pint jars

4 pounds apples (about 12 medium)	3 tablespoons Ball Low or No-Sugar Needed Pectin
4 cups water	Sweetener, if desired

PREP Follow instructions for preparing, How to Prepare Juice for Jelly, see this page.

COOK Combine apple juice and pectin in a large saucepan, stirring to blend in pectin. Bring mixture to a boil over high heat, stirring constantly. Add sweetener according to pectin label, if desired. Return mixture to a boil; boil 1 minute, stirring constantly. Remove mixture from heat if a gel begins to form before 1-minute boil is completed. Skim off foam if necessary.

FILL Ladle hot jelly into a hot jar, leaving 1/4-inch headspace. Clean jar rim. Center lid on jar and adjust band to fingertip-tight. Place jar on the rack elevated over simmering water (180°F) in boiling-water canner. Repeat until all jars are filled.

PROCESS Lower the rack into simmering water. Water must cover jars by 1 inch. Adjust heat to medium-high, cover canner and bring water to a rolling boil. Process half-pint jars 10 minutes. Turn off heat and remove cover. Let jars cool 5 minutes. Remove jars from canner; do not retighten bands if loose. Cool 12 hours. Check seals. Label and store jars.

Berry Jelly

Blackberry, Blueberry, Boysenberry, Dewberry, Gooseberry, Loganberry, Raspberry, Youngberry

Yield: about 5 half-pint jars

3 1/4 cups berry juice (about 3 to 4 pounds)	6 tablespoons Ball Classic Pectin
2 tablespoons lemon juice, fresh or bottled (optional)	5 cups sugar

PREP Follow instructions for preparing, How to Prepare Juice for Jelly, see this page.

COOK Combine berry juice, lemon juice (if desired), and pectin in a large saucepan. Bring mixture to a boil over medium-high heat, stirring to blend in pectin. Add sugar, stirring until sugar dissolves. Bring mixture to a rolling boil that cannot be stirred down. Boil hard for 1 minute, stirring constantly. Remove from heat. Skim off foam if necessary.

FILL Ladle hot jelly into a hot jar, leaving 1/4-inch headspace. Clean jar rim. Center lid on jar and adjust band to fingertip-tight. Place jar on the rack elevated over simmering water (180°F) in boiling-water canner. Repeat until all jars are filled.

PROCESS Lower the rack into simmering water. Water must cover jars by 1 inch. Adjust heat to medium-high, cover canner and bring water to a rolling boil. Process half-pint jars 10 minutes. Turn off heat and remove cover. Let jars cool 5 minutes. Remove jars from canner; do not retighten bands if loose. Cool 12 hours. Check seals. Label and store jars.

Blackberry Jelly

Yield: about 8 half-pint jars

4 cups blackberry juice (about 4 to 5 pounds)

2 3-ounce pouches Ball Liquid Pectin

7½ cups sugar

PREP Follow instructions for preparing, How to Prepare Juice for Jelly, page 56.

COOK Combine blackberry juice and sugar in a large saucepan, stirring until sugar dissolves. Bring mixture to a boil over high heat, stirring constantly. Add pectin. Bring mixture to a rolling boil that cannot be stirred down. Boil hard for 1 minute, stirring constantly. Remove from heat. Skim off foam if necessary.

FILL Ladle hot jelly into a hot jar, leaving ¼-inch headspace. Clean jar rim. Center lid on jar and adjust band to fingertip-tight. Place jar on the rack elevated over simmering water (180°F) in boiling-water canner. Repeat until all jars are filled.

PROCESS Lower the rack into simmering water. Water must cover jars by 1 inch. Adjust heat to medium-high, cover canner and bring water to a rolling boil. Process half-pint jars 10 minutes. Turn off heat and remove cover. Let jars cool 5 minutes. Remove jars from canner; do not retighten bands if loose. Cool 12 hours. Check seals. Label and store jars.

 Intensify the flavor of this jelly by adding 1 tablespoon lime juice, fresh or bottled. Or, if you prefer a hint of mint, add 1 tablespoon freshly made mint extract (see page 59).

Crabapple Jelly

Yield: about 6 half-pint jars

4 cups crabapple juice (about 3 pounds)

4 cups sugar

PREP Follow instructions for preparing, How to Prepare Juice for Jelly, page 56.

COOK Combine crabapple juice and sugar in a large saucepan, stirring until sugar dissolves. Bring mixture to a boil over high heat, stirring constantly. Cook rapidly over high heat to gelling point (220°F), stirring constantly. Remove from heat. Skim off foam if necessary.

FILL Ladle hot jelly into a hot jar, leaving ¼-inch headspace. Clean jar rim. Center lid on jar and adjust band to fingertip-tight. Place jar on the rack elevated over simmering water (180°F) in boiling-water canner. Repeat until all jars are filled.

PROCESS Lower the rack into simmering water. Water must cover jars by 1 inch. Adjust heat to medium-high, cover canner and bring water to a rolling boil. Process half-pint jars 10 minutes. Turn off heat and remove cover. Let jars cool 5 minutes. Remove jars from canner; do not retighten bands if loose. Cool 12 hours. Check seals. Label and store jars.

Currant Jelly

Yield: about 8 half-pint jars

5 cups red currant juice (about 5 pounds)

1 3-ounce pouch Ball Liquid Pectin

7 cups sugar

PREP Follow instructions for preparing, How to Prepare Juice for Jelly, page 56.

COOK Combine currant juice and sugar in a large saucepan, stirring until sugar dissolves. Bring mixture to a boil over high heat, stirring constantly. Add pectin. Bring mixture to a rolling boil that cannot be stirred down. Boil hard for 1 minute, stirring constantly. Remove from heat. Skim off foam if necessary.

FILL Ladle hot jelly into a hot jar, leaving ¼-inch headspace. Clean jar rim. Center lid on jar and adjust band to fingertip-tight. Place jar on the rack elevated over simmering water (180°F) in boiling-water canner. Repeat until all jars are filled.

PROCESS Lower the rack into simmering water. Water must cover jars by 1 inch. Adjust heat to medium-high, cover canner and bring water to a rolling boil. Process half-pint jars 10 minutes. Turn off heat and remove cover. Let jars cool 5 minutes. Remove jars from canner; do not retighten bands if loose. Cool 12 hours. Check seals. Label and store jars.

 Red currants are milder and sweeter than the black variety. Black currants are quite tart. Either variety can be used to prepare this recipe. Currant jelly complements game, poultry, pork, beef, and venison.

Grape Jelly

Yield: about 4 half-pint jars

4 cups Concord grape juice (about 3½ pounds)

3 cups sugar

PREP Follow instructions for preparing, How to Prepare Juice for Jelly, page 56.

COOK Combine Concord grape juice and sugar in a large saucepan, stirring until sugar dissolves. Bring mixture to a boil over high heat, stirring constantly. Cook rapidly over high heat to gelling point (220°F), stirring to prevent sticking. Remove from heat. Skim off foam if necessary.

FILL Ladle hot jelly into a hot jar, leaving ¼-inch headspace. Clean jar rim. Center lid on jar and adjust band to fingertip-tight. Place jar on the rack elevated over simmering water (180°F) in boiling-water canner. Repeat until all jars are filled.

PROCESS Lower the rack into simmering water. Water must cover jars by 1 inch. Adjust heat to medium-high, cover canner and bring water to a rolling boil. Process half-pint jars 10 minutes. Turn off heat and remove cover. Let jars cool 5 minutes. Remove jars from canner; do not retighten bands if loose. Cool 12 hours. Check seals. Label and store jars.

Grape Jelly

Yield: about 7 half-pint jars

4 cups Concord grape juice (about 3½ pounds)

6¾ cups sugar

1 3-ounce pouch Ball Liquid Pectin

PREP Follow instructions for preparing, How to Prepare Juice for Jelly, page 56.

COOK Combine Concord grape juice and sugar in a large saucepan, stirring until sugar dissolves. Bring mixture to a boil over high heat, stirring constantly. Add pectin. Return mixture to a rolling boil that cannot be stirred down. Boil hard for 1 minute, stirring constantly. Remove from heat. Skim off foam if necessary.

FILL Ladle hot jelly into a hot jar, leaving ¼-inch headspace. Clean jar rim. Center lid on jar and adjust band to fingertip-tight. Place jar on the rack elevated over simmering water (180°F) in boiling-water canner. Repeat until all jars are filled.

PROCESS Lower the rack into simmering water. Water must cover jars by 1 inch. Adjust heat to medium-high, cover canner and bring water to a rolling boil. Process half-pint jars 10 minutes. Turn off heat and remove cover. Let jars cool 5 minutes. Remove jars from canner; do not retighten bands if loose. Cool 12 hours. Check seals. Label and store jars.

Grape Jelly Low or no sugar added
Green, Purple, Red

Yield: about 4 half-pint jars

3 pounds grapes

1 cup water

3 tablespoons Ball Low or No-Sugar Needed Pectin

Sweetener, if desired

PREP Follow instructions for preparing, How to Prepare Juice for Jelly, page 56.

COOK Combine grape juice and pectin in a large saucepan, stirring to blend in pectin. Bring mixture to a boil over high heat, stirring constantly. Add sweetener according to pectin label, if desired. Return mixture to a rolling boil that cannot be stirred down. Boil hard for 1 minute, stirring constantly. Remove mixture from heat if gel begins to form before 1-minute boil is completed. Skim off foam if necessary.

FILL Ladle hot jelly into a hot jar, leaving ¼-inch headspace. Clean jar rim. Center lid on jar and adjust band to fingertip-tight. Place jar on the rack elevated over simmering water (180°F) in boiling-water canner. Repeat until all jars are filled.

PROCESS Lower the rack into simmering water. Water must cover jars by 1 inch. Adjust heat to medium-high, cover canner and bring water to a rolling boil. Process half-pint jars 10 minutes. Turn off heat and remove cover. Let jars cool 5 minutes. Remove jars from canner; do not retighten bands if loose. Cool 12 hours. Check seals. Label and store jars.

Quick Grape Jelly

Yield: about 5 half-pint jars

3 cups bottled unsweetened grape juice, without added calcium (24 ounces)

6 tablespoons Ball Classic Pectin

4½ cups sugar

PREP Use grape juice that is at room temperature.

COOK Combine grape juice and pectin in a large saucepan. Bring mixture to a boil over high heat, stirring to blend in pectin. Add sugar, stirring until sugar dissolves. Bring mixture to a rolling boil that cannot be stirred down. Boil hard for 1 minute, stirring constantly. Remove from heat. Skim off foam if necessary.

FILL Ladle hot jelly into a hot jar, leaving ¼-inch headspace. Clean jar rim. Center lid on jar and adjust band to fingertip-tight. Place jar on the rack elevated over simmering water (180°F) in boiling-water canner. Repeat until all jars are filled.

PROCESS Lower the rack into simmering water. Water must cover jars by 1 inch. Adjust heat to medium-high, cover canner and bring water to a rolling boil. Process half-pint jars 10 minutes. Turn off heat and remove cover. Let jars cool 5 minutes. Remove jars from canner; do not retighten bands if loose. Cool 12 hours. Check seals. Label and store jars.

Green Pepper Jelly

Yield: about 6 half-pint jars

7 green bell peppers

1 jalapeño pepper (optional)

1½ cups cider vinegar, 5% acidity, divided

1½ cups bottled apple juice

6 tablespoons Ball Classic Pectin

½ teaspoon salt

5 cups sugar

Green food coloring (optional)

PREP Wash peppers under cold running water; drain. Remove stems and seeds from peppers. Cut peppers into ½-inch pieces. Purée half the peppers with ¾-cup vinegar in a food processor or blender; set aside. Purée remaining peppers and vinegar. Combine purée and apple juice in a large bowl. Cover and refrigerate overnight. Strain puréed mixture through a damp jelly bag or several layers of cheesecloth. Measure 4 cups of juice. Add additional apple juice to make 4 cups if necessary.

COOK Combine pepper and apple juice mixture, pectin, and salt in a large saucepan, stirring to blend in pectin. Bring mixture to a boil over high heat, stirring constantly. Add sugar, stirring until sugar dissolves. Return mixture to a rolling boil that cannot be stirred down. Boil hard for 1 minute, stirring constantly. Remove from heat. Skim off foam if necessary. Stir in a few drops of green food coloring, if desired.

FILL Ladle hot jelly into a hot jar, leaving ¼-inch headspace. Clean jar rim. Center lid on jar and adjust band to fingertip-tight. Place jar on the rack elevated over simmering water (180°F) in boiling-water canner. Repeat until all jars are filled.

PROCESS Lower the rack into simmering water. Water must cover jars by 1 inch. Adjust heat to medium-high, cover canner and bring water to a rolling boil. Process half-pint jars 10 minutes. Turn off heat and remove cover. Let jars cool 5 minutes. Remove jars from canner; do not retighten bands if loose. Cool 12 hours. Check seals. Label and store jars.

Note: When cutting or seeding hot peppers, wear rubber gloves to prevent hands from being burned.

Jalapeño Jelly

Yield: about 5 half-pint jars

3/4 pound jalapeño peppers	2 3-ounce pouches Ball Liquid Pectin
2 cups cider vinegar, 5% acidity, divided	Green food coloring (optional)
6 cups sugar	

PREP Wash peppers under cold running water; drain. Remove stems and seeds. Purée peppers with 1 cup cider vinegar in a food processor or blender.

COOK Combine pepper purée, 1 cup cider vinegar, and sugar in a large saucepan. Bring mixture to a boil over high heat, stirring until sugar dissolves. Boil 10 minutes, stirring constantly. Add pectin. Bring mixture to a rolling boil that cannot be stirred down. Boil hard for 1 minute, stirring constantly. Remove from heat. Skim off foam if necessary.

FILL Ladle hot jelly into a hot jar, leaving 1/4-inch headspace. Clean jar rim. Center lid on jar and adjust band to fingertip-tight. Place jar on the rack elevated over simmering water (180°F) in boiling-water canner. Repeat until all jars are filled.

PROCESS Lower the rack into simmering water. Water must cover jars by 1 inch. Adjust heat to medium-high, cover canner and bring water to a rolling boil. Process half-pint jars 10 minutes. Turn off heat and remove cover. Let jars cool 5 minutes. Remove jars from canner; do not retighten bands if loose. Cool 12 hours. Check seals. Label and store jars.

Note: When cutting or seeding hot peppers, wear rubber gloves to prevent hands from being burned.

Mint Jelly

Yield: about 4 half-pint jars

4 cups apple juice (about 3 pounds)	2 tablespoons lemon juice, fresh or bottled (optional)
1 cup firmly packed mint leaves	3 cups sugar
1 cup boiling water	Green food coloring (optional)

PREP Follow instructions for preparing, How to Prepare Juice for Jelly, page 56. Put mint leaves in a bowl, add boiling water, and let stand 1 hour. Strain mint leaves, pressing to extract juice. Measure 1/2-cup mint extract.

COOK Combine apple juice, mint extract, lemon juice (if desired), and sugar in a large saucepan, stirring until sugar dissolves. Bring mixture to a boil over high heat, stirring constantly. Cook rapidly over high heat to gelling point (220°F), stirring constantly. Remove from heat. Skim off foam if necessary. Stir in a few drops of green food coloring, if desired.

FILL Ladle hot jelly into a hot jar, leaving 1/4-inch headspace. Clean jar rim. Center lid on jar and adjust band to fingertip-tight. Place jar on the rack elevated over simmering water (180°F) in boiling-water canner. Repeat until all jars are filled.

PROCESS Lower the rack into simmering water. Water must cover jars by 1 inch. Adjust heat to medium-high, cover canner and bring water to a rolling boil. Process half-pint jars 10 minutes. Turn off heat and remove cover. Let jars cool 5 minutes. Remove jars from canner; do not retighten bands if loose. Cool 12 hours. Check seals. Label and store jars.

Peach Jelly

Yield: about 7 half-pint jars

3 1/2 cups peach juice (about 3 to 4 pounds)	2 3-ounce pouches Ball Liquid Pectin
4 tablespoons lemon juice, fresh or bottled	7 1/2 cups sugar

PREP Follow instructions for preparing, How to Prepare Juice for Jelly, page 56.

COOK Combine peach juice and pectin in a large saucepan. Bring mixture to a boil over high heat, stirring to blend in pectin. Add sugar, stirring until sugar dissolves. Bring mixture to a rolling boil that cannot be stirred down. Boil hard for 1 minute, stirring constantly. Remove from heat. Skim off foam if necessary.

FILL Ladle hot jelly into a hot jar, leaving 1/4-inch headspace. Clean jar rim. Center lid on jar and adjust band to fingertip-tight. Place jar on the rack elevated over simmering water (180°F) in boiling-water canner. Repeat until all jars are filled.

PROCESS Lower the rack into simmering water. Water must cover jars by 1 inch. Adjust heat to medium-high, cover canner and bring water to a rolling boil. Process half-pint jars 10 minutes. Turn off heat and remove cover. Let jars cool 5 minutes. Remove jars from canner; do not retighten bands if loose. Cool 12 hours. Check seals. Label and store jars.

Plum Jelly

Yield: about 8 half-pint jars

5 1/2 cups plum juice (about 5 pounds)	6 tablespoons Ball Classic Pectin
	7 1/2 cups sugar

PREP Follow instructions for preparing, How to Prepare Juice for Jelly, page 56.

COOK Combine plum juice and pectin in a large saucepan. Bring mixture to a boil over high heat, stirring to blend in pectin. Add sugar, stirring until sugar dissolves. Bring mixture to a rolling boil that cannot be stirred down. Boil hard for 1 minute, stirring constantly. Remove from heat. Skim off foam if necessary.

FILL Ladle hot jelly into a hot jar, leaving 1/4-inch headspace. Clean jar rim. Center lid on jar and adjust band to fingertip-tight. Place jar on the rack elevated over simmering water (180°F) in boiling-water canner. Repeat until all jars are filled.

PROCESS Lower the rack into simmering water. Water must cover jars by 1 inch. Adjust heat to medium-high, cover canner and bring water to a rolling boil. Process half-pint jars 10 minutes. Turn off heat and remove cover. Let jars cool 5 minutes. Remove jars from canner; do not retighten bands if loose. Cool 12 hours. Check seals. Label and store jars.

Pomegranate Jelly

Yield: about 6 half-pint jars

3½ cups pomegranate juice (7 to 10 large)

5 cups sugar

6 tablespoons Ball Classic Pectin

PREP Wash pomegranates under cold running water; drain. Remove the cap from each pomegranate by cutting a circle around the cap, about ½ inch from the center. Lift off the cap. You will see that the pomegranate is divided into sections. Score the skin of the pomegranate lengthwise into quarters, using the section breaks as a guide. Fill a medium bowl with water. Hold the pomegranate under water and break the sections apart. While holding one of the sections under water, place your thumb between the seeds and skin of the pomegranate and guide your thumb down the length of the section to release the seeds. Repeat until all pomegranates are seeded. Remove all fibrous peel and drain seeds. Extract juice using an electric juice extractor or food strainer. Strain juice through a damp jelly bag or several layers of cheesecloth. Measure 3½ cups of pomegranate juice.

COOK Combine pomegranate juice and pectin in a large saucepan. Bring mixture to a boil over high heat, stirring to blend in pectin. Add sugar, stirring until sugar dissolves. Bring mixture to a rolling boil that cannot be stirred down. Boil hard for 1 minute, stirring constantly. Remove from heat. Skim off foam if necessary.

FILL Ladle hot jelly into a hot jar, leaving ¼-inch headspace. Clean jar rim. Center lid on jar and adjust band to fingertip-tight. Place jar on the rack elevated over simmering water (180°F) in boiling-water canner. Repeat until all jars are filled.

PROCESS Lower the rack into simmering water. Water must cover jars by 1 inch. Adjust heat to medium-high, cover canner and bring water to a rolling boil. Process half-pint jars 10 minutes. Turn off heat and remove cover. Let jars cool 5 minutes. Remove jars from canner; do not retighten bands if loose. Cool 12 hours. Check seals. Label and store jars.

Tomato Jelly

Yield: about 4 half-pint jars

3 pounds tomatoes (about 9 medium)

½ teaspoon salt

6 tablespoons Ball Classic Pectin

2 tablespoons bottled lemon juice

1 tablespoon minced crystallized ginger

½ teaspoon hot pepper sauce

4 cups sugar

PREP Wash tomatoes under cold running water; drain. Remove core and blossom ends from tomatoes. Cut tomatoes into quarters. Simmer tomatoes until they are soft and lose their shape. Strain tomatoes and liquid through a damp jelly bag or several layers of cheesecloth. Measure 2 cups of tomato juice.

COOK Combine tomato juice, pectin, crystallized ginger, salt, lemon juice, and hot pepper sauce in a large saucepan. Bring mixture to a boil over high heat, stirring to blend in pectin. Add sugar, stirring until sugar dissolves. Bring mixture to a rolling boil that cannot be stirred down. Boil hard for 1 minute, stirring constantly. Remove from heat. Skim off foam if necessary.

FILL Ladle hot jelly into a hot jar, leaving ¼-inch headspace. Clean jar rim. Center lid on jar and adjust band to fingertip-tight. Place jar on the rack elevated over simmering water (180°F) in boiling-water canner. Repeat until all jars are filled.

PROCESS Lower the rack into simmering water. Water must cover jars by 1 inch. Adjust heat to medium-high, cover canner and bring water to a rolling boil. Process half-pint jars 10 minutes. Turn off heat and remove cover. Let jars cool 5 minutes. Remove jars from canner; do not retighten bands if loose. Cool 12 hours. Check seals. Label and store jars.

Marmalades

Marmalades are delicious, sweet-tart spreads containing small pieces of fruit and peel evenly suspended in a transparent jelly. They are commonly associated with citrus fruits like oranges, lemons, limes, and grapefruits. Citrus fruits make interesting marmalades all on their own or paired with other fruits and vegetables. Marmalades have a similar structure to jams, which is achieved by preparing small batches and rapidly cooking the mixture almost to the gelling point. Use the plate test or temperature method to help determine when cooking is done (see page 43).

Carrot-Pineapple-Orange Marmalade

Yield: about 4 half-pint jars

2 medium lemons

3 cups sugar

3 medium oranges

½ teaspoon allspice

1 cup finely chopped fresh pineapple (about ½ small)

¼ teaspoon nutmeg

1 3-ounce pouch Ball Liquid Pectin

1 cup shredded carrots (about 2 to 3 medium)

PREP Wash lemons, oranges, pineapple, and carrots under cold running water; drain. Peel lemons. Cut off white pith from peel. Slice yellow peel into thin strips. Cut lemons in half crosswise and remove seeds. Extract juice from lemons; measure ⅓ cup of lemon juice. Cut oranges in half crosswise and remove seeds. Remove orange pulp from each half; measure 2 cups orange pulp. Remove leaves and bottom end of pineapple. Peel and core pineapple. Finely chop pineapple using a food processor or knife. Drain pineapple. Measure 1 cup finely chopped pineapple. Remove stem ends from carrots and peel. Shred carrots; measure 1 cup shredded carrots.

COOK Combine lemon peel, lemon juice, orange pulp, pineapple, and carrots into a large saucepan. Add sugar, allspice, and nutmeg, stirring until sugar dissolves. Bring mixture to a boil over high heat, stirring constantly. Add pectin. Return mixture to a rolling boil that cannot be stirred down. Boil hard 1 minute, stirring constantly. Remove from heat. Skim off foam if necessary.

FILL Ladle hot marmalade into a hot jar, leaving ¼-inch headspace. Remove air bubbles. Clean jar rim. Center lid on jar and adjust band to fingertip-tight. Place jar on the rack elevated over simmering water (180°F) in boiling-water canner. Repeat until all jars are filled.

PROCESS Lower the rack into simmering water. Water must cover jars by 1 inch. Adjust heat to medium-high, cover canner and bring water to a rolling boil. Process half-pint jars 10 minutes. Turn off heat and remove cover. Let jars cool 5 minutes. Remove jars from canner; do not retighten bands if loose. Cool 12 hours. Check seals. Label and store jars.

Cherry Marmalade

Yield: about 4 half-pint jars

1 quart pitted
   sweet cherries
   (about 1½ to 2 pounds)

⅔ cup chopped orange
   (about 1 medium)

3½ cups sugar

¼ cup lemon juice,
   fresh or bottled

PREP Wash cherries and orange under cold running water; drain. Remove stems and pits from cherries. Measure 1 quart of pitted cherries. Cut oranges in half crosswise and remove seeds. Finely chop orange pulp and peel using a food processor or knife. Measure ⅔ cup chopped orange pulp.

COOK Combine cherries, chopped orange, sugar, and lemon juice in a large saucepan, stirring until sugar dissolves. Bring mixture to a boil over medium-high heat, stirring constantly. Cook rapidly over medium-high heat to gelling point (220°F), stirring constantly. Remove from heat. Skim off foam if necessary.

FILL Ladle hot marmalade into a hot jar, leaving ¼-inch headspace. Remove air bubbles. Clean jar rim. Center lid on jar and adjust band to fingertip-tight. Place jar on the rack elevated over simmering water (180°F) in boiling-water canner. Repeat until all jars are filled.

PROCESS Lower the rack into simmering water. Water must cover jars by 1 inch. Adjust heat to medium-high, cover canner and bring water to a rolling boil. Process half-pint jars 15 minutes. Turn off heat and remove cover. Let jars cool 5 minutes. Remove jars from canner; do not retighten bands if loose. Cool 12 hours. Check seals. Label and store jars.

Grapefruit Marmalade

Yield: about 3 half-pint jars

⅔ cup thinly sliced
   grapefruit peel
   (about 1 medium)

1⅓ cups chopped grapefruit
   pulp (about 1 medium)

6 cups water, divided

Sugar

PREP Wash grapefruit under cold running water; drain. Cut grapefruit in half crosswise and remove seeds. Remove pulp from each half of grapefruit, reserving peel; measure 1⅓ cups of grapefruit pulp. Remove white pith from grapefruit peel and thinly slice; measure ⅔ cup sliced peel.

COOK Combine sliced grapefruit peel and 2 cups water in a large saucepan. Boil peel 10 minutes; drain. Return cooked peel to saucepan. Add grapefruit pulp and 4 cups water. Boil mixture 10 minutes; remove from heat. Cover and let stand in refrigerator for 12 to 18 hours. Measure the fruit and liquid together. Add 1 cup sugar for each cup fruit mixture, stirring until sugar dissolves. Bring mixture to a boil over medium-high heat, stirring constantly. Cook rapidly over medium-high heat almost to the gelling point (220°F), stirring constantly. Remove from heat. Skim off foam if necessary.

FILL Ladle hot marmalade into a hot jar, leaving ¼-inch headspace. Remove air bubbles. Clean jar rim. Center lid on jar and adjust band to fingertip-tight. Place jar on the rack elevated over simmering water (180°F) in boiling-water canner. Repeat until all jars are filled.

PROCESS Lower the rack into simmering water. Water must cover jars by 1 inch. Adjust heat to medium-high, cover canner and bring water to a rolling boil. Process half-pint jars 10 minutes. Turn off heat and remove cover. Let jars cool 5 minutes. Remove jars from canner; do not retighten bands if loose. Cool 12 hours. Check seals. Label and store jars.

Herbed Garden Marmalade

Yield: about 5 half-pint jars

1½ pounds tomatoes
   (about 3 to 5 medium)

2 teaspoons slivered lemon
   peel (about ½ medium)

1 clove garlic, minced

1 tablespoon minced
   fresh basil

1 tablespoon minced
   fresh oregano

6 tablespoons
   Ball Classic Pectin

¼ cup lemon juice,
   fresh or bottled

4½ cups sugar

PREP Wash tomatoes and lemon under cold running water; drain. To peel tomatoes, blanch 30 to 60 seconds in boiling water. Immediately transfer to cold water. Cut off peel. Core and seed the tomatoes. Chop tomatoes into ¼- to ½-inch pieces. Measure 3 cups chopped tomatoes.

COOK Simmer tomatoes in a large saucepan for 10 minutes. Measure 3 cups cooked tomatoes. Return 3 cups cooked tomatoes to saucepan and add lemon peel, garlic, herbs, pectin, and lemon juice, stirring to blend in pectin. Bring mixture to a boil, stirring constantly. Add sugar, stirring until sugar dissolves. Return mixture to a rolling boil that cannot be stirred down. Boil hard for 1 minute, stirring constantly. Remove from heat. Skim off foam if necessary.

FILL Ladle hot marmalade into a hot jar, leaving ¼-inch headspace. Remove air bubbles. Clean jar rim. Center lid on jar and adjust band to fingertip-tight. Place jar on the rack elevated over simmering water (180°F) in boiling-water canner. Repeat until all jars are filled.

PROCESS Lower the rack into simmering water. Water must cover jars by 1 inch. Adjust heat to medium-high, cover canner and bring water to a rolling boil. Process half-pint jars 10 minutes. Turn off heat and remove cover. Let jars cool 5 minutes. Remove jars from canner; do not retighten bands if loose. Cool 12 hours. Check seals. Label and store jars.

Kumquat Marmalade

Yield: about 8 half-pint jars

2 cups thinly sliced kumquats (about 24 medium)	1/3 cup lemon juice, fresh or bottled
1 1/2 cups chopped orange pulp (about 2 medium)	1 1/2 quarts water
1 1/2 cups sliced orange peel (about 2 medium)	Sugar

PREP Wash kumquats and oranges under cold running water; drain. Thinly slice kumquats crosswise. Cut oranges in half crosswise and remove seeds. Remove pulp from each orange half, reserving peel. Chop orange pulp; measure 1 1/2 cups of chopped orange pulp. Remove white pith from orange peel. Thinly slice orange peel into 1/2-inch pieces; measure 1 1/2 cups sliced peel.

COOK Combine all ingredients, except sugar, in a large saucepan. Boil gently for 5 minutes; remove from heat. Cover and let stand in refrigerator for 12 to 18 hours. Cook rapidly until peel is tender. Measure the fruit and liquid together. Add 1 cup sugar for each cup fruit mixture, stirring until sugar dissolves. Bring mixture to a boil over medium-high heat, stirring constantly. Cook rapidly over medium-high heat almost to the gelling point (220°F), stirring constantly. Remove from heat. Skim off foam if necessary.

FILL Ladle hot marmalade into a hot jar, leaving 1/4-inch headspace. Remove air bubbles. Clean jar rim. Center lid on jar and adjust band to fingertip-tight. Place jar on the rack elevated over simmering water (180°F) in boiling-water canner. Repeat until all jars are filled.

PROCESS Lower the rack into simmering water. Water must cover jars by 1 inch. Adjust heat to medium-high, cover canner and bring water to a rolling boil. Process half-pint jars 10 minutes. Turn off heat and remove cover. Let jars cool 5 minutes. Remove jars from canner; do not retighten bands if loose. Cool 12 hours. Check seals. Label and store jars.

Orange Marmalade

Yield: about 7 half-pint jars

2 cups thinly sliced orange peel (about 10 medium)	1 cup thinly sliced lemon (about 2 medium)
1 quart chopped orange pulp (about 8 to 10 medium)	1 1/2 quarts water
	Sugar

PREP Wash oranges and lemons under cold running water; drain. Cut oranges in half crosswise and remove seeds. Remove pulp from each orange half, reserving peel. Chop orange pulp; measure 1 quart of chopped orange pulp. Remove white pith from orange peel. Thinly slice orange peel; measure 2 cups sliced peel. Thinly slice lemons crosswise; remove seeds and discard ends. Measure 1 cup sliced lemons.

COOK Combine all ingredients, except sugar, in a large saucepan. Boil gently for 5 minutes; remove from heat. Cover and let stand in refrigerator for 12 to 18 hours. Cook rapidly until peel is tender. Measure the fruit and liquid mixture. Add 1 cup sugar for each cup fruit mixture, stirring until sugar dissolves. Bring mixture to a boil over medium-high heat, stirring constantly. Cook rapidly over high medium-heat almost to the gelling point (220°F), stirring constantly. Remove from heat. Skim off foam if necessary.

Prickly Pear Marmalade

Yield: about 6 half-pint jars

3 cups chopped orange pulp (about 6 to 8 medium)	1 quart water
1 cup thinly sliced lemon (about 2 medium)	6 cups sugar
1 quart chopped, peeled prickly pears (about 8 to 10 medium)	

PREP Wash oranges, lemons, and prickly pears under cold running water; drain. Cut oranges in half crosswise and remove seeds. Remove pulp from each orange half, reserving peel. Chop orange pulp; measure 3 cups of chopped orange pulp. Thinly slice lemons crosswise; remove seeds and discard ends. Measure 1 cup sliced lemons. Peel and seed the prickly pears. Chop prickly pears; measure 1 quart chopped prickly pears.

COOK Combine orange pulp, lemon slices, and water in a large saucepan. Boil gently for 5 minutes; remove from heat. Cover and let stand in refrigerator 12 to 18 hours. Cook rapidly until peel is tender. Add prickly pears and sugar, stirring until sugar dissolves. Bring mixture to a boil over medium-high heat, stirring constantly. Cook rapidly over medium-high heat almost to the gelling point (220°F), stirring constantly. Remove from heat. Skim off foam if necessary.

FILL Ladle hot marmalade into a hot jar, leaving 1/4-inch headspace. Remove air bubbles. Clean jar rim. Center lid on jar and adjust band to fingertip-tight. Place jar on the rack elevated over simmering water (180°F) in boiling-water canner. Repeat until all jars are filled.

PROCESS Lower the rack into simmering water. Water must cover jars by 1 inch. Adjust heat to medium-high, cover canner and bring water to a rolling boil. Process half-pint jars 15 minutes. Turn off heat and remove cover. Let jars cool 5 minutes. Remove jars from canner; do not retighten bands if loose. Cool 12 hours. Check seals. Label and store jars.

Red Onion Marmalade

Yield: about 5 half-pint jars

1 1/2 cups thinly sliced red onions (about 1 to 1 1/2 pounds)	6 tablespoons Ball Classic Pectin
1/2 cup finely chopped dried cranberries (about 1/2 pound)	2 teaspoons grated orange peel (about 1/2 small)
1/4 cup light brown sugar	3 cups bottled unsweetened apple juice
1/4 cup cider vinegar, 5% acidity	4 cups granulated sugar

PREP Wash orange under cold running water; drain. Grate orange peel; measure 2 teaspoons grated orange peel. Peel and thinly slice red onions crosswise. Measure 1 1/2 cups of sliced red onions. Finely chop dried cranberries using a food processor or knife. Measure 1/2 cup chopped dried cranberries.

COOK Sauté onions, dried cranberries, brown sugar, and cider vinegar in a skillet until onions are transparent. Combine onion mixture, pectin, orange peel, and apple juice in a large saucepan. Bring mixture to a boil over medium-high heat, stirring constantly. Add granulated sugar, stirring until sugar dissolves. Return mixture to a rolling boil that cannot be stirred down. Boil hard for 1 minute, stirring constantly. Remove from heat. Skim off foam if necessary.

FILL Ladle hot marmalade into a hot jar, leaving 1/4-inch headspace. Remove air bubbles. Clean jar rim. Center lid on jar and adjust band to fingertip-tight. Place jar on the rack elevated over simmering water (180°F) in boiling-water canner. Repeat until all jars are filled.

PROCESS Lower the rack into simmering water. Water must cover jars by 1 inch. Adjust heat to medium-high, cover canner and bring water to a rolling boil. Process half-pint jars 15 minutes. Turn off heat and remove cover. Let jars cool 5 minutes. Remove jars from canner; do not retighten bands if loose. Cool 12 hours. Check seals. Label and store jars.

Strawberry-Lemon Marmalade

Yield: about 7 half-pint jars

1/4 cup thinly sliced lemon peel (about 1 medium)	6 tablespoons Ball Classic Pectin
4 cups crushed strawberries (about 2 to 3 pounds)	1 tablespoon lemon juice
	6 cups sugar

PREP Wash lemon and strawberries under cold running water; drain. Cut off yellow layer of lemon peel. Thinly slice lemon peel; measure 1/4 cup sliced lemon peel. Cut lemon in half and remove seeds. Extract juice from lemon; measure 1 tablespoon lemon juice. Remove stems and caps from strawberries. Crush strawberries one layer at a time using a potato masher. Measure 4 cups crushed strawberries.

COOK Combine sliced lemon peel and enough water to cover in a small saucepan. Gently boil 5 minutes; drain. Combine lemon peel, strawberries, pectin, and lemon juice in a large saucepan. Bring mixture to a boil over medium-high heat, stirring constantly. Add sugar, stirring until sugar dissolves. Return mixture to a rolling boil that cannot be stirred down. Boil hard for 1 minute, stirring constantly. Remove from heat. Skim off foam if necessary.

FILL Ladle hot marmalade into a hot jar, leaving 1/4-inch headspace. Remove air bubbles. Clean jar rim. Center lid on jar

and adjust band to fingertip-tight. Place jar on the rack elevated over simmering water (180°F) in boiling-water canner. Repeat until all jars are filled.

PROCESS Lower the rack into simmering water. Water must cover jars by 1 inch. Adjust heat to medium-high, cover canner and bring water to a rolling boil. Process half-pint jars 10 minutes. Turn off heat and remove cover. Let jars cool 5 minutes. Remove jars from canner; do not retighten bands if loose. Cool 12 hours. Check seals. Label and store jars.

Preserves

Preserves are unlike all other soft spreads in that preserves vary in texture from thick, honey-like syrup to a very soft jelly. True preserves do not retain their shape when spooned from the jar. Small whole fruits or large uniform pieces of fruit are cooked with sugar long enough for the fruit to become tender and plump and develop a glossy, transparent appearance. Preserves can be made with or without added pectin. Those made without pectin may take longer to prepare, but the highly saturated fruit flavor is well worth the wait.

Apple Preserves

Yield: about 6 half-pint jars

6 cups sliced apples (about 6 to 7 large)	1/2 thinly sliced lemon (about 1/2 large)
1 cup water	4 cups sugar
1 tablespoon lemon juice (about 1/2 large)	2 teaspoons nutmeg
6 tablespoons Ball Classic Pectin	

PREP Wash the apples and lemon under cold running water; drain. Core and peel apples. Cut apples into 1/4- to 1/3-inch slices. Measure 6 cups sliced apples. Cut lemon in half and remove seeds. Extract juice from half of lemon; measure 1 tablespoon lemon juice. Thinly slice remaining half of lemon, discarding end.

COOK Combine apples, water, and lemon juice in a large saucepan. Cover; simmer apples 10 minutes. Add pectin, stirring to blend in pectin. Bring mixture to a boil over medium-high heat, stirring constantly. Add lemon slices, sugar, and nutmeg, stirring until sugar dissolves. Bring mixture to a rolling boil that cannot be stirred down. Boil hard for 1 minute, stirring constantly. Remove from heat. Skim off foam if necessary.

FILL Ladle hot preserves into a hot jar, leaving 1/4-inch headspace. Remove air bubbles. Clean jar rim. Center lid on jar and adjust band to fingertip-tight. Place jar on the rack elevated over simmering water (180°F) in boiling-water canner. Repeat until all jars are filled.

PROCESS Lower the rack into simmering water. Water must cover jars by 1 inch. Adjust heat to medium-high, cover canner and bring water to a rolling boil. Process half-pint jars 10 minutes. Turn off heat and remove cover. Let jars cool 5 minutes. Remove jars from canner; do not retighten bands if loose. Cool 12 hours. Check seals. Label and store jars.

 Our Tip Not everyone has the same fondness for nutmeg. In its place, try cinnamon or pumpkin pie spice, adding just the measure that suits your taste.

Apricot Preserves

Yield: about 4 half-pint jars

5 cups halved, peeled, pitted, apricots (about 2 pounds)	4 cups sugar
	¼ cup lemon juice, fresh or bottled

PREP Wash whole apricots under cold running water; drain. To peel apricots, blanch in boiling water 30 to 60 seconds. Immediately transfer to cold water. Cut off peel. Cut apricots in half lengthwise; remove pits and fibrous flesh. Measure 5 cups apricot halves.

COOK Combine apricots, sugar, and lemon juice in a large saucepan. Cover and let stand in refrigerator for 4 to 5 hours. Bring mixture to a boil, stirring until sugar dissolves. Cook rapidly over high heat almost to gelling point (220°F), stirring constantly. Remove from heat. Skim off foam if necessary.

FILL Ladle hot preserves into a hot jar, leaving ¼-inch headspace. Remove air bubbles. Clean jar rim. Center lid on jar and adjust band to fingertip-tight. Place jar on the rack elevated over simmering water (180°F) in boiling-water canner. Repeat until all jars are filled.

PROCESS Lower the rack into simmering water. Water must cover jars by 1 inch. Adjust heat to medium-high, cover canner and bring water to a rolling boil. Process half-pint jars 15 minutes. Turn off heat and remove cover. Let jars cool 5 minutes. Remove jars from canner; do not retighten bands if loose. Cool 12 hours. Check seals. Label and store jars.

Bar-le-Duc (Currant) Preserves

Yield: about 5 half-pint jars

2 quarts currants, divided (about 2 pounds)	7 cups sugar, divided

PREP Wash currants under cold running water; drain. Stem currants. Use just enough currants to make 1 cup of juice, reserving remaining currants for preserves. Follow instructions for How to Prepare Juice for Jelly, page 56.

COOK Combine currants and currant juice in a large saucepan. Add 4 cups sugar, stirring until sugar dissolves. Gently boil 5 minutes. Cover and let stand in refrigerator for 12 to 18 hours. Add 3 cups sugar. Bring mixture to a rolling boil that cannot be stirred down. Cook rapidly over high heat almost to gelling point (220°F), stirring constantly. Remove from heat. Skim off foam if necessary.

FILL Ladle hot preserves into a hot jar, leaving ¼-inch headspace. Remove air bubbles. Clean jar rim. Center lid on jar and adjust band to fingertip-tight. Place jar on the rack elevated over simmering water (180°F) in boiling-water canner. Repeat until all jars are filled.

PROCESS Lower the rack into simmering water. Water must cover jars by 1 inch. Adjust heat to medium-high, cover canner and bring water to a rolling boil. Process half-pint jars 15 minutes. Turn off heat and remove cover. Let jars cool 5 minutes. Remove jars from canner; do not retighten bands if loose. Cool 12 hours. Check seals. Label and store jars.

Berry Preserves

Blackberry, Black Raspberry, Red Raspberry, Loganberry

Yield: about 4 half-pint jars

2 pounds berries	4 cups sugar

PREP Wash berries under cold running water; drain.

COOK Combine berries and sugar in a large saucepan. Let mixture stand until juices begin to flow, about 10 minutes. Bring mixture to a boil, stirring until sugar dissolves. Cook rapidly over high heat almost to gelling point (220°F), stirring constantly. Remove from heat. Skim off foam if necessary.

FILL Ladle hot preserves into a hot jar, leaving ¼-inch headspace. Remove air bubbles. Clean jar rim. Center lid on jar and adjust band to fingertip-tight. Place jar on the rack elevated over simmering water (180°F) in boiling-water canner. Repeat until all jars are filled.

PROCESS Lower the rack into simmering water. Water must cover jars by 1 inch. Adjust heat to medium-high, cover canner and bring water to a rolling boil. Process half-pint jars 15 minutes. Turn off heat and let jars cool 5 minutes. Remove jars from canner; do not retighten bands if loose. Cool 12 hours. Check seals. Label and store jars.

Cherry Preserves

Yield: about 4 half-pint jars

2 pounds cherries	4 cups sugar

PREP Wash cherries under cold running water; drain. Remove stems and pits from cherries over a bowl to retain all juice. Set pitted cherries aside.

COOK Combine cherry juice and sugar in a large saucepan. Bring mixture to a boil, stirring until sugar dissolves. Add a small amount of water if there is not enough juice to dissolve sugar. Add cherries. Boil over high heat until cherries become glossy. Cover and let stand in refrigerator 12 to 18 hours. Bring mixture to a rolling boil that cannot be stirred down. Cook rapidly over high heat almost to gelling point (220°F), stirring constantly. Remove from heat. Skim off foam if necessary.

FILL Ladle hot preserves into a hot jar, leaving ¼-inch headspace. Remove air bubbles. Clean jar rim. Center lid on jar and adjust band to fingertip-tight. Place jar on the rack elevated over simmering water (180°F) in boiling-water canner. Repeat until all jars are filled.

PROCESS Lower the rack into simmering water. Water must cover jars by 1 inch. Adjust heat to medium-high, cover canner and bring water to a rolling boil. Process half-pint jars 15 minutes. Turn off heat and remove cover. Let jars cool 5 minutes. Remove jars from canner; do not retighten bands if loose. Cool 12 hours. Check seals. Label and store jars.

Citron Melon Preserves

Yield: about 3 half-pint jars

1½ quarts citron melon (about 2 pounds)	1 quart water
4 cups sugar, divided	½ cup thinly sliced lemon (about 1 medium)

PREP The outer portion of citron melon is superior for preserves. The inner flesh may be used, although it should be prepared separately from the outer portion. Wash melon under cold running water; drain. Cut melon crosswise into ½-inch slices; trim off green peel, and remove seeds. Cut rind away from flesh. Cut rind and flesh separately into 1-inch pieces.

COOK Combine 2 cups sugar and water in a large saucepan. Bring mixture to a boil over high heat, stirring until sugar dissolves. Add citron melon and cook rapidly until tender. Cover and let stand in refrigerator 12 to 18 hours. Add 2 cups sugar and lemon slices to citron melon mixture. Boil gently until melon is transparent and syrup is thick. Remove from heat. Skim off foam if necessary.

FILL Ladle hot preserves into a hot jar, leaving ¼-inch headspace. Remove air bubbles. Clean jar rim. Center lid on jar and adjust band to fingertip-tight. Place jar on the rack elevated over simmering water (180°F) in boiling-water canner. Repeat until all jars are filled.

PROCESS Lower the rack into simmering water. Water must cover jars by 1 inch. Adjust heat to medium-high, cover canner and bring water to a rolling boil. Process half-pint jars 15 minutes. Turn off heat and remove cover. Let jars cool 5 minutes. Remove jars from canner; do not retighten bands if loose. Cool 12 hours. Check seals. Label and store jars.

Note: If the syrup becomes too thick, add a small amount of boiling water. If syrup is too thin, remove fully cooked citron melon; set aside. Boil syrup to desired thickness. Return citron melon to syrup and cook until hot throughout.

Cranberry-Apple Preserves

Yield: about 9 half-pint jars

2 pounds cranberries	3 cups sugar
3 green apples	2 cups water
1 orange	½ cup honey

PREP Wash cranberries, apples, and orange under cold running water; drain. Core and peel apples. Chop apples into 1-inch pieces. Cut orange in half crosswise and remove seeds. Finely chop orange, including peel, using a food processor or knife.

COOK Combine all ingredients in a large saucepan. Bring mixture to a boil, stirring until sugar dissolves. Cook rapidly almost to gelling point (220°F), stirring constantly. Remove from heat. Skim off foam if necessary.

FILL Ladle hot preserves into a hot jar, leaving ¼-inch headspace. Remove air bubbles. Clean jar rim. Center lid on jar and adjust band to fingertip-tight. Place jar on the rack elevated over simmering water (180°F) in boiling-water canner. Repeat until all jars are filled.

PROCESS Lower the rack into simmering water. Water must cover jars by 1 inch. Adjust heat to medium-high, cover canner and bring water to a rolling boil. Process half-pint jars 15 minutes. Turn off heat and remove cover. Let jars cool 5 minutes. Remove jars from canner; do not retighten bands if loose. Cool 12 hours. Check seals. Label and store jars.

Fig Preserves

Yield: about 6 half-pint jars

2 quarts figs	1 quart water
2 quarts boiling water	1 lemon
2⅔ cups sugar	

PREP Wash figs and lemon under cold running water; drain. Pour 2 quarts boiling water over figs. Let stand 15 minutes; drain. Rinse figs under cold water; drain. Cut lemon crosswise into thin slices; remove seeds and discard ends.

COOK Combine sugar, lemon slices, and 1 quart water in a large saucepan. Bring mixture to a boil, stirring until sugar dissolves. Boil 10 minutes. Skim syrup to remove foam if necessary. Remove lemon slices. Cook figs in syrup one layer at a time over high heat until they are transparent. Remove figs and place in a shallow pan. Boil syrup until it is thick. Pour syrup over figs and let stand in refrigerator 6 to 8 hours. Reheat figs and syrup to a boil. Remove from heat. Skim off foam if necessary.

FILL Ladle hot preserves into a hot jar, leaving ¼-inch headspace. Remove air bubbles. Clean jar rim. Center lid on jar and adjust band to fingertip-tight. Place jar on the rack elevated over simmering water (180°F) in boiling-water canner. Repeat until all jars are filled.

PROCESS Lower the rack into simmering water. Water must cover jars by 1 inch. Adjust heat to medium-high, cover canner and bring water to a rolling boil. Process half-pint jars 10 minutes. Turn off heat and remove cover. Let jars cool 5 minutes. Remove jars from canner; do not retighten bands if loose. Cool 12 hours. Check seals. Label and store jars.

Our Tip Here's a serving suggestion that works equally well at the start or close of a memorable dinner. Spread a thick layer of creamy mascarpone cheese over the bottom of a baked puff pastry shell. Drain Fig Preserves, reserving syrup. Cut figs in half lengthwise. Arrange figs over cheese. Sprinkle toasted walnuts over figs. Combine fig syrup and a splash of brandy. Drizzle syrup over figs.

Kiwi Preserves

Yield: about 3 half-pint jars

4 large kiwi	¼ cup lime juice, fresh or bottled
3 cups sugar	
¾ cup unsweetened pineapple juice	1 3-ounce pouch Ball Liquid Pectin

PREP Peel kiwi and slice crosswise into ⅛-inch slices.

COOK Combine kiwi, sugar, pineapple juice, and lime juice in a large saucepan. Bring mixture to a boil, stirring until sugar dissolves. Add pectin. Bring mixture to a rolling boil that cannot be stirred down. Boil hard for 1 minute, stirring constantly. Remove from heat. Skim off foam if necessary.

FILL Ladle hot preserves into a hot jar, leaving ¼-inch headspace. Remove air bubbles. Clean jar rim. Center lid on jar and adjust band to fingertip-tight. Place jar on the rack elevated over simmering water (180°F) in boiling-water canner. Repeat until all jars are filled.

PROCESS Lower the rack into simmering water. Water must cover jars by 1 inch. Adjust heat to medium-high, cover canner and bring water to a rolling boil. Process half-pint jars 10 minutes. Turn off heat and remove cover. Let jars cool 5 minutes. Remove jars from canner; do not retighten bands if loose. Cool 12 hours. Check seals. Label and store jars.

Peach Preserves

Yield: about 9 half-pint jars

4 cups sliced, pitted, peeled peaches (about 2 to 3 pounds)

6 tablespoons Ball Classic Pectin

2 tablespoons lemon juice, fresh or bottled

7 cups sugar

PREP Wash peaches under cold running water; drain. To peel peaches, blanch in boiling water for 30 to 60 seconds. Immediately transfer to cold water. Cut off peel. Cut peaches in half lengthwise; remove pits and fibrous flesh. Cut peaches into 1/8-inch slices.

COOK Combine sliced peaches, pectin, and lemon juice in a large saucepan. Bring mixture to a boil, stirring to blend in pectin. Add sugar, stirring until sugar dissolves. Bring mixture to a rolling boil that cannot be stirred down. Boil hard for 1 minute, stirring constantly. Remove from heat. Skim off foam if necessary.

FILL Ladle hot preserves into a hot jar, leaving 1/4-inch headspace. Remove air bubbles. Clean jar rim. Center lid on jar and adjust band to fingertip-tight. Place jar on the rack elevated over simmering water (180°F) in boiling-water canner. Repeat until all jars are filled.

PROCESS Lower the rack into simmering water. Water must cover jars by 1 inch. Adjust heat to medium-high, cover canner and bring water to a rolling boil. Process half-pint jars 10 minutes. Turn off heat and remove cover. Let jars cool 5 minutes. Remove jars from canner; do not retighten bands if loose. Cool 12 hours. Check seals. Label and store jars.

Pear Preserves

Yield: about 5 half-pint jars

6 medium pears (about 2 pounds)

1 medium lemon

3 cups sugar, divided

3 cups water

PREP Wash pears and lemon under cold running water; drain. Cut pears in half lengthwise. Stem and core pears. Pears may be canned in halves, quarters, or eighths. Cut lemon crosswise into thin slices; remove seeds and discard ends. Measure 1/2 cup lemon slices.

COOK Combine 1 1/2 cups sugar and water in a large saucepan. Boil mixture for 2 minutes, stirring until sugar dissolves. Add pears; boil gently 15 minutes. Add 1 1/2 cups sugar and lemon slices, stirring until sugar dissolves. Cook rapidly until pears are transparent. Cover and let stand in refrigerator 12 to 24 hours. Reheat pears and syrup to a boil. Remove pears from syrup, keep hot. Cook syrup 5 minutes to thicken. Remove from heat. Skim off foam if necessary.

FILL Pack hot pears into a hot jar, leaving 1/4-inch headspace. Ladle hot syrup over pears, leaving 1/4-inch headspace. Remove air bubbles. Clean jar rim. Center lid on jar and adjust band to fingertip-tight. Place jar on the rack elevated over simmering water (180°F) in boiling-water canner. Repeat until all jars are filled.

PROCESS Lower the rack into simmering water. Water must cover jars by 1 inch. Adjust heat to medium-high, cover canner and bring water to a rolling boil. Process half-pint jars 20 minutes. Turn off heat and remove cover. Let jars cool 5 minutes. Remove jars from canner; do not retighten bands if loose. Cool 12 hours. Check seals. Label and store jars.

 Our Tip If Seckel pears are used, preserve whole with stem intact. Kieffer pears should be stored in a cool, dry place 3 to 5 weeks before preserving.

Plum Preserves

Yield: about 5 half-pint jars

2 1/2 pounds tart plums (about 10 to 12 medium)

4 cups sugar

1 cup water

PREP Wash plums under cold running water; drain. Cut plums in half lengthwise; remove pits and fibrous flesh. Do not peel plums. Measure 5 cups halved plums.

COOK Combine plums, sugar, and water in a large saucepan. Bring mixture to a boil, stirring until sugar dissolves. Cook rapidly over high heat almost to gelling point (220°F), stirring constantly. Remove from heat. Skim off foam if necessary.

FILL Ladle hot preserves into a hot jar, leaving 1/4-inch headspace. Remove air bubbles. Clean jar rim. Center lid on jar and adjust band to fingertip-tight. Place jar on the rack elevated over simmering water (180°F) in boiling-water canner. Repeat until all jars are filled.

PROCESS Lower the rack into simmering water. Water must cover jars by 1 inch. Adjust heat to medium-high, cover canner and bring water to a rolling boil. Process half-pint jars 15 minutes. Turn off heat and remove cover. Let jars cool 5 minutes. Remove jars from canner; do not retighten bands if loose. Cool 12 hours. Check seals. Label and store jars.

Quince Preserves

Yield: about 4 half-pint jars

3 pounds quince (about 9 to 12 medium)

3 cups sugar

2 quarts water

PREP Wash quince under cold running water; drain. Peel and core quince; discard all gritty portions. Cut quince into quarters; measure 7 cups quartered quince.

COOK Combine sugar and water in a large saucepan. Bring mixture to a boil, stirring until sugar dissolves. Boil 5 minutes. Add quince; cook until fruit is transparent. Cook rapidly over high heat almost to gelling point (220°F), stirring constantly. Remove from heat. Skim off foam if necessary.

FILL Ladle hot preserves into a hot jar, leaving 1/4-inch headspace. Remove air bubbles. Clean jar rim. Center lid on jar and adjust band to fingertip-tight. Place jar on the rack elevated over simmering water (180°F) in boiling-water canner. Repeat until all jars are filled.

PROCESS Lower the rack into simmering water. Water must cover jars by 1 inch. Adjust heat to medium-high, cover canner and bring water to a rolling boil. Process half-pint jars 15 minutes. Turn off heat and remove cover. Let jars cool 5 minutes. Remove jars from canner; do not retighten bands if loose. Cool 12 hours. Check seals. Label and store jars.

 You Choose A piece of candied ginger, sprig of rosemary, or a cinnamon stick may be added to each jar.

Red Raspberry-Currant Preserves

Yield: about 7 half-pint jars

3 cups red raspberries (about 1 to 1½ pounds)

1 cup red currant juice (about 1½ to 2 pounds)

¼ cup raspberry liqueur

6½ cups sugar

1 3-ounce pouch Ball Liquid Pectin

PREP Wash red raspberries and red currants under cold running water; drain. To prepare red currant juice, follow instructions for How to Prepare Juice for Jelly, page 56. Measure 1 cup red currant juice.

COOK Combine red raspberries, red currant juice, raspberry liqueur, and sugar in a large saucepan. Bring mixture to a boil, stirring until sugar dissolves. Add pectin. Bring mixture to a rolling boil that cannot be stirred down. Boil hard for 1 minute, stirring constantly. Remove from heat. Skim off foam if necessary.

FILL Ladle hot preserves into a hot jar, leaving ¼-inch headspace. Remove air bubbles. Clean jar rim. Center lid on jar and adjust band to fingertip-tight. Place jar on the rack elevated over simmering water (180°F) in boiling-water canner. Repeat until all jars are filled.

PROCESS Lower the rack into simmering water. Water must cover jars by 1 inch. Adjust heat to medium-high, cover canner and bring water to a rolling boil. Process half-pint jars 15 minutes. Turn off heat and remove cover. Let jars cool 5 minutes. Remove jars from canner; do not retighten bands if loose. Cool 12 hours. Check seals. Label and store jars.

 If you prefer not to use raspberry liqueur, omit the liqueur and increase the red currant juice to 1¼ cups.

 Red Raspberry-Currant Preserves are unbelievable when paired with something chocolate. Spread a generous amount between layers of a very rich, very dense chocolate cake, or pipe it into the center of chocolate cupcakes. Yummy!

Sour Cherry Preserves

Yield: about 6 half-pint jars

3 pounds red sour cherries

6 tablespoons Ball Classic Pectin

5 cups sugar

PREP Wash red sour cherries under cold running water; drain. Remove stems and pits from sour cherries.

COOK Combine red sour cherries and pectin in a large saucepan. Bring mixture to a boil, stirring constantly. Add sugar, stirring until sugar dissolves. Return mixture to a rolling boil that cannot be stirred down. Boil hard 1 minute, stirring constantly. Remove from heat. Skim off foam if necessary.

FILL Ladle hot preserves into a hot jar, leaving ¼-inch headspace. Remove air bubbles. Clean jar rim. Center lid on jar and adjust band to fingertip-tight. Place jar on the rack elevated over simmering water (180°F) in boiling-water canner. Repeat until all jars are filled.

PROCESS Lower the rack into simmering water. Water must cover jars by 1 inch. Adjust heat to medium-high, cover canner and bring water to a rolling boil. Process half-pint jars 15 minutes. Turn off heat and remove cover. Let jars cool 5 minutes. Remove jars from canner; do not retighten bands if loose. Cool 12 hours. Check seals. Label and store jars.

Strawberry Preserves

Yield: about 7 half-pint jars

2 quarts strawberries (about 3 pounds)

6 tablespoons Ball Classic Pectin

¼ cup finely chopped lemon (about 1 medium)

¼ cup water

6½ cups sugar

PREP Wash strawberries and lemon under cold running water; drain. Remove stems and caps from strawberries. Cut lemon in half and remove seeds. Finely chop lemon, including peel, using a food processor or knife.

COOK Combine strawberries, pectin, chopped lemon, and water in a large saucepan. Bring mixture to a boil, stirring constantly. Add sugar, stirring until sugar dissolves. Bring mixture to a rolling boil that cannot be stirred down. Boil hard for 1 minute, stirring constantly. Remove from heat. Skim off foam if necessary.

FILL Ladle hot preserves into a hot jar, leaving ¼-inch headspace. Remove air bubbles. Clean jar rim. Center lid on jar and adjust band to fingertip-tight. Place jar on the rack elevated over simmering water (180°F) in boiling-water canner. Repeat until all jars are filled.

PROCESS Lower the rack into simmering water. Water must cover jars by 1 inch. Adjust heat to medium-high, cover canner and bring water to a rolling boil. Process half-pint jars 15 minutes. Turn off heat and remove cover. Let jars cool 5 minutes. Remove jars from canner; do not retighten bands if loose. Cool 12 hours. Check seals. Label and store jars.

Heirloom Strawberry Preserves

Yield: about 4 half-pint jars

1½ quarts strawberries (about 1½ to 2 pounds)

5 cups sugar

⅓ cup lemon juice, fresh or bottled

PREP Wash strawberries under cold running water; drain. Remove stems and caps from strawberries.

COOK Combine strawberries and sugar in a large saucepan. Let stand in refrigerator 3 to 4 hours. Bring mixture to a boil, stirring until sugar dissolves. Add lemon juice. Boil over high heat until strawberries are transparent and syrup is thick. Ladle preserves into a shallow pan. Let preserves stand in refrigerator 12 to 24 hours. Stir occasionally to distribute strawberries throughout syrup. Cook strawberries and syrup in a large saucepan until hot throughout. Remove from heat. Skim off foam if necessary.

FILL Ladle hot preserves into a hot jar, leaving ¼-inch headspace. Remove air bubbles. Clean jar rim. Center lid on jar and adjust band to fingertip-tight. Place jar on the rack elevated over simmering water (180°F) in boiling-water canner. Repeat until all jars are filled.

PROCESS Lower the rack into simmering water. Water must cover jars by 1 inch. Adjust heat to medium-high, cover canner and bring water to a rolling boil. Process half-pint jars 20 minutes. Turn off heat and remove cover. Let jars cool 5 minutes. Remove jars from canner; do not retighten bands if loose. Cool 12 hours. Check seals. Label and store jars.

 This traditional recipe is for the purist. You take the next step and grow or purchase heirloom strawberries. Look for locally grown varieties when in season, selecting small fully red berries.

 For a portable dessert, try our version of strawberry shortcake. Spoon Heirloom Strawberry Preserves over ladyfinger cookies, then add a squiggle of whipped cream.

Tomato Preserves

Yield: about 6 half-pint jars

1½ quarts small yellow, green, or red tomatoes (about 2 pounds)

1 tablespoon Ball Mixed Pickling Spice

1 piece fresh ginger, about ½ inch thick

4 cups sugar

1 cup thinly sliced lemon (about 2 medium)

¾ cup water

PREP Wash tomatoes and lemon under cold running water; drain. To peel tomatoes, blanch 30 to 60 seconds in boiling water. Immediately transfer to cold water. Cut off peel. Do not core tomatoes. Tie spices and fresh ginger in a spice bag.

COOK Combine spice bag, sugar, lemon, and water in a large saucepan. Simmer mixture 15 minutes, stirring until sugar dissolves. Add tomatoes. Boil mixture over high heat until tomatoes are transparent, stirring frequently. Remove from heat. Cover and let stand in refrigerator 12 to 18 hours. Reheat tomatoes and syrup to a boil. Remove spice bag. Remove tomatoes and lemon slices; keep hot. Boil syrup to thicken, about 3 minutes. Return tomatoes and lemon to syrup; boil 1 minute. Remove from heat. Skim off foam if necessary.

FILL Ladle hot preserves into a hot jar, leaving ¼-inch headspace. Remove air bubbles. Clean jar rim. Center lid on jar and adjust band to fingertip-tight. Place jar on the rack elevated over simmering water (180°F) in boiling-water canner. Repeat until all jars are filled.

PROCESS Lower the rack into simmering water. Water must cover jars by 1 inch. Adjust heat to medium-high, cover canner and bring water to a rolling boil. Process half-pint jars 20 minutes. Turn off heat and remove cover. Let jars cool 5 minutes. Remove jars from canner; do not retighten bands if loose. Cool 12 hours. Check seals. Label and store jars.

Watermelon Rind Preserves

Yield: about 6 half-pint jars

1½ quarts prepared watermelon rind

4 tablespoons salt

3½ quarts water, divided

1 tablespoon ginger

4 cups sugar

¼ cup lemon juice

½ cup thinly sliced lemon (about 1 medium)

PREP Wash watermelon and lemon under cold running water; drain. Trim green peel and pink flesh from thick watermelon rind. Cut rind into 1-inch pieces. Dissolve salt in 2 quarts water. Pour salted water over rind. Let stand 5 to 6 hours. Drain; rinse; drain again. Cover rind with cold water and let stand 30 minutes. Drain. Put rind in a large saucepan. Sprinkle ginger over rind. Add just enough water to cover rind. Cook mixture over medium-high heat until rind is tender. Drain.

COOK Combine sugar, lemon juice, and 1½ quarts water in a large saucepan. Boil mixture 5 minutes. Add watermelon rind. Boil gently over high heat until watermelon rind is transparent and syrup thickens. Add sliced lemon and cook 5 minutes. Remove from heat. Skim off foam if necessary.

FILL Ladle hot preserves into a hot jar, leaving ¼-inch headspace. Remove air bubbles. Clean jar rim. Center lid on jar and adjust band to fingertip-tight. Place jar on the rack elevated over simmering water (180°F) in boiling-water canner. Repeat until all jars are filled.

PROCESS Lower the rack into simmering water. Water must cover jars by 1 inch. Adjust heat to medium-high, cover canner and bring water to a rolling boil. Process half-pint jars 20 minutes. Turn off heat and remove cover. Let jars cool 5 minutes. Remove jars from canner; do not retighten bands if loose. Cool 12 hours. Check seals. Label and store jars.

Western Special Preserves

Yield: about 5 half-pint jars

1 cup red currants (about 1 pound)

1 cup water

5 cups sugar

2 cups loganberries (about 1 pound)

2 cups red raspberries (about ½ pound)

2 cups pitted sweet cherries (about 1 pound)

PREP Wash red currants, loganberries, red raspberries, and sweet cherries under cold running water; drain. Follow instructions for How to Prepare Juice for Jelly, page 56, to prepare red currant juice. Remove stems and pits from cherries; measure 2 cups pitted cherries.

COOK Combine currant juice and sugar in a large saucepan, stirring until sugar dissolves. Boil mixture 5 minutes over high heat. Add remaining ingredients. Cook rapidly over high heat almost to the gelling point (220°F), stirring constantly. Remove from heat. Skim off foam if necessary.

FILL Ladle hot preserves into a hot jar, leaving ¼-inch headspace. Remove air bubbles. Clean jar rim. Center lid on jar and adjust band to fingertip-tight. Place jar on the rack elevated over simmering water (180°F) in boiling-water canner. Repeat until all jars are filled.

PROCESS Lower the rack into simmering water. Water must cover jars by 1 inch. Adjust heat to medium-high, cover canner and bring water to a rolling boil. Process half-pint jars 15 minutes. Turn off heat and remove cover. Let jars cool 5 minutes. Remove jars from canner; do not retighten bands if loose. Cool 12 hours. Check seals. Label and store jars.

How to Remake Cooked Soft Spreads

As in cooking soft spreads, time and temperature are important factors to monitor when cooling soft spreads. The soft spread will not be gelled upon removing jars from the canner. It requires a cooling period of approximately 24 hours to gel. Some recipes may even take as long as two weeks before the gel structure is set. After the processing time is completed, remove jars from the canner and set them upright on a towel or cutting board to cool. Never invert or shake the jars during cooling, as this may prevent the jar from sealing, or it may break down the gel structure that is beginning to form. If the soft spread in question is vacuum sealed and processed following a tested recipe in this book, it is safe to wait up to two weeks for the soft spread to set. If the soft spread did not set, or the gel is too soft, it can be recooked in order to develop a firmer set. Select the correlating remake instructions from the following options for the type of soft spread to be recooked.

Ball RealFruit Classic Pectin

Recook no more than 2 quarts (8 cups) of unset soft spread at one time. Measure the soft spread. For each cup of soft spread to be recooked, measure 1½ teaspoons pectin, 1 tablespoon water, and 2 tablespoons sugar. Combine pectin and water in a large saucepan, stirring to blend in pectin. Bring the mixture to a boil over medium-high heat, stirring constantly to prevent sticking. Add the soft spread and sugar, stirring until sugar dissolves. Bring mixture to a rolling boil; boil hard 30 seconds, stirring constantly. Remove from heat. Skim off foam if necessary. Ladle hot soft spread into a hot jar, leaving ¼-inch headspace. Center a new lid on jar rim. Adjust band to fingertip-tight. Place jar in boiling-water canner. Repeat until all jars are filled. Process soft spread for the full length of time indicated in the original recipe. Allow jars to cool 24 hours before evaluating the set.

Ball RealFruit Liquid Pectin

Recook no more than 2 quarts (8 cups) of unset soft spread at one time. Measure the soft spread. For each cup of soft spread to be recooked, measure 3 tablespoons sugar, 1½ teaspoons lemon juice, and 1½ teaspoons pectin. Bring soft spread to a boil over medium-high heat in a large saucepan, stirring to prevent sticking. Add sugar, lemon juice, and pectin, stirring until sugar dissolves. Bring mixture to a rolling boil; boil hard for 1 minute, stirring constantly. Remove from heat. Skim off foam if necessary. Ladle hot soft spread into a hot jar, leaving ¼-inch headspace. Center a new lid on jar rim. Adjust band to fingertip-tight. Place jar in boiling-water canner. Repeat until all jars are filled. Process soft spread for the full length of time indicated in the original recipe. Allow jars to cool 24 hours before evaluating the set.

Ball RealFruit Low or No-Sugar Needed Pectin

Recook only 1 quart (4 cups) of unset soft spread at one time. Measure the soft spread. For each quart of soft spread, measure 4 teaspoons pectin and ¼ cup water. Combine pectin and water in a medium saucepan, stirring to blend in pectin. Bring mixture to a boil over medium-high heat, stirring constantly. Add soft spread, stirring to blend evenly. Boil mixture hard 30 seconds, stirring constantly. Remove from heat. Skim off foam if necessary. Ladle hot soft spread into a hot jar, leaving ¼-inch headspace. Center a new lid on jar rim. Adjust band to fingertip-tight. Place jar in boiling-water canner. Repeat until all jars are filled. Process soft spread for the full length of time indicated in the original recipe. Allow jars to cool 24 hours before evaluating the set.

No Added Pectin

Recook only 1 batch of unset soft spread at one time. Cook soft spread over medium-high heat in a large saucepan, stirring to prevent sticking. Cook soft spread until it reaches the temperature indicated in the original recipe, or to the gelling point if a temperature is not given (see page 43). Ladle hot soft spread into hot jar, leaving ¼-inch headspace. Center a new lid on jar rim. Adjust band fingertip-tight. Place jar in boiling-water canner. Repeat until all jars are filled. Process soft spread for the full length of time indicated in the original recipe. Allow jars to cool 24 hours before evaluating the set.

Chutneys, Pickles & Relishes

Pickles, with their crunch and bright tartness, transform simply-prepared meals into culinary adventures. Because of their versatility, pickles, chutneys, and relishes are the perfect condiments to have at your fingertips. And we're not just talking pickled cucumbers—zucchini, carrots, onions, peppers and hot peppers, and even fruits are perfect for pickling. These unconventional pickles are perfect to bring an elevated note to cheeseboards, sandwiches, salads, and any savory dish you can think of.

Getting Started

Pickled foods are either fermented in brine (salt or salt and water solution) or packed in a pickling liquid that is acidified to aid in preservation. Brining or fermenting cucumbers (or other produce) in a large container can take between 3 to 6 weeks or longer to complete. Pickles preserved using a pickling liquid are called fresh pack pickles and can be prepared in as little as one hour.

Balance and proportion are everything

Successful brining or fermenting pickles requires quality ingredients, accurate measurements, daily maintenance, and temperature control to achieve the best results. Your ingredients and procedures may be right, but if the correct proportions of sugar, salt, vinegar, and spices are not maintained, the quality and safety of your pickles can be jeopardized.

Protect against spoilers

After brining or fermenting pickles, the pickles can be combined with spices, sugar, or herbs to add flavor. Processing is required for brined and fresh pack pickles to destroy microorganisms and deactivate enzymes that may adversely affect flavor, color, and texture.

Quality ingredients make a difference

Pickling cucumbers make the best whole, spear, or sliced pickles. They are highly perishable, so be prepared to use them the same day they are harvested or purchased. Store unused pickling cucumbers in the refrigerator for one or two days. Spices and dried herbs have a long shelf life if stored correctly. You can extend the shelf life and quality of your seasonings by storing them out of direct light and away from heat. Purchase 5% acidity vinegar for pickling. Do not use homemade vinegar.

Featured Recipe | **Arugula and Pickled Butternut Squash Salad** page 174

Pictured Above | **Pickled Butternut Squash** page 93 | **Kosher-Style Pickles** page 78 | **Bread & Butter Pickles** page 78

Good Things to Know

Fruits and Vegetables

Ideally, fruits and vegetables should be harvested no more than 24 hours before pickling. If preparation is delayed, the produce should be refrigerated until ready for use. Pickling cucumbers, especially, deteriorate rapidly at room temperature.

Unlike recipes in other areas of canning, some pickling recipes may specifically call for slightly underripe fruits and vegetables, such as pears, peaches, and green tomatoes. Produce should be of ideal size and uniform shape for the recipe selected.

Select pickling cucumbers for their quality, size, flavor. and ripeness. Use only pickling cucumber varieties for whole, spear. and sliced pickles. Other varieties may be a suitable choice for relish or chutney. Do not use waxed cucumbers since the brine cannot penetrate the wax coating. Discard diseased, shriveled, miss-shapen, or hollow cucumbers.

Whole fruits and vegetables must be washed thoroughly under cold running water before being cut or peeled. Using a soft produce brush is helpful in removing soil that may cling to produce. However, do not scrub vigorously, as this may cause bacteria to penetrate the peel. Enzymes are prevalent around the blossom end of cucumbers, and could soften the cucumbers during fermentation, so cut off 1/16 inch from the blossom end. Remove stem end, if desired.

Salt

Salt acts as a preservative and adds flavor and crispness to pickles. Use pure granulated salt for brined and fresh pack pickles. Pure granulated salt like Ball® Salt for Pickling and Preserving does not contain iodine or anti-caking additives that may cause pickles to darken or soften, or cause the brine to become cloudy. Do not substitute pure granulated salt with flake, rock, Kosher, or sea salt. Different forms of salt do not measure the same as granulated salt; thus, substitutions will compromise the balance of ingredients needed to preserve pickled food.

Vinegar

Vinegar gives pickles a tart taste and acts as a preservative. All recipes in this book use high-grade cider or white distilled vinegar of 5% (50 grain) acidity. Vinegar of unknown acidity must not be used since its preservative ability will also be unknown. Cider vinegar imparts a mellow acid flavor while white vinegar gives pickled foods a sharp pungent acidic taste. Since cider vinegar may discolor produce, use white vinegar when color retention is important. Vinegar must not be diluted unless specified in the recipe. Never decrease the amount of vinegar or increase the amount of water, as doing so will change the pH (acidity) level and compromise the balance of ingredients needed to safely preserve pickled food.

Sugar

Granulated cane or beet sugar is used for all pickled recipes in this book unless the recipe specifically designates another sweetener. Brown sugar, honey, and maple syrup are sometimes used in a recipe. Recipes in this book have not been tested using non-sugar substitutes; thus, their preservative qualities and integrity when exposed to heat is unknown.

Spices, Herbs, and Crisping Agents

Fresh ground or whole spices and fresh or dried herbs add immeasurably to the unique flavor of pickled foods. Whole spices and herbs are often tied in a spice bag or several layers of cheesecloth for easy removal after they have flavored the pickling liquid. Substituting ground spices and herbs for their whole version will cause the pickling liquid to be cloudy, and too heavily seasoned.

Ball® Pickle Crisp™ is an easy way to add extra crunch to fresh pack pickles and pickled vegetables. Measure the granules into each jar following the recipe and product label instructions. Pre-soaking the cucumbers or vegetables to be pickled in a solution of Pickle Crisp before processing is not required.

Water

Soft water must be used to make pickling brine. Minerals in hard water will have a negative effect on the quality of pickles. If soft tap water is not available, water can be softened by being boiled for 15 minutes, then allowed to stand for 24 hours. A scum will likely appear on the top of the water; remove the scum before using. Ladle water from the container, being careful not to disturb any sediment that settled to the bottom. Distilled water can also be used for pickling.

Pickling Methods

Fresh Pack Method

Fresh-pack describes a method of pickling vegetables in a very short period of time. Some fresh pack recipes are brined for as short as one hour, or as long as overnight. Fresh-pack pickles are put into the jar either raw or hot—the recipe will guide you on which method to use. The pickling liquid is prepared by combining vinegar (5% acidity), water, salt, sugar (if listed), herbs, and spices, then cooking the mixture to a boil. For the hot-pack method, the vegetables to be pickled are cooked in the pickling liquid before filling the jar. After the jar is filled with either raw or hot pickles, hot pickling liquid is ladled over them. Filled jars are processed in a boiling-water canner. Fresh-pack pickles may be eaten immediately; however, curing the pickles for 3 to 6 weeks aids in blending flavors and increases acid. Fresh-pack pickles are crunchy, range from sweet to sour, and keep longer than raw vegetables.

Brined Method

Brining (also known as fermenting) is a traditional method of pickling vegetables over a period of several weeks. Vegetables are submerged in a salt and water brine. Microbes that grow in the brine produce acid, which preserves the vegetables. Whole cucumbers and cabbage are the most commonly fermented vegetables. The key to successful fermentation is maintaining the brine strength, storing the container in a cool place (70° to 75°F), and removing scum and/or mold daily. Fermented pickles are pleasingly sour, slightly crunchy, and aromatic. Fermented pickles may be canned as sour pickles, or herbs, spices, and sugar may be added for variety.

Brining Cucumbers

1. Weigh cucumbers; keep a record of the starting weight. Wash cucumbers under cold running water; drain. Cut off 1/16-inch from the blossom end of the cucumbers. Put cucumbers in a clean pickling container. Make a 10% brine by dissolving 1 cup pickling salt in 2 quarts water. Pour brine over cucumbers.

   Cucumbers must be submerged under the brine at all times during fermentation. Place a plate, slightly smaller in diameter than the container, directly on the cucumbers. Put a sealed glass jar filled with water on the plate as a weight to hold the cucumbers under the brine. As an alternative to the plate and jar, fill a clean food-grade plastic bag with brine, 1½ tablespoons salt to 1 quart water, and secure it closed. Place this plastic bag inside a second clean food-grade plastic bag and secure it closed. Adjust the amount of brine in the plastic bag to create just the right pressure to hold the cucumbers under the brine, if necessary. Not only does the brine-filled bag serve as a weight, but it also seals out air and prevents the growth of film, yeasts, and molds.

2. Maintaining the 10% brine is critical to the fermentation process. This is achieved by adding salt to the brine following a set schedule. On the second day, add 1 cup pickling or canning salt for each 5 pounds of cucumbers. With the plate holding the cucumbers under the brine, gradually add salt onto the plate. The salt will dissolve in the brine that covers the plate without coming in contact with the cucumbers. To add salt when using a plastic bag as the weight, slowly add salt to the brine so that it dissolves instantly without coming in contact with the cucumbers.

3. At the end of the first week, add 1/4 cup pickling or canning salt for each 5 pounds of cucumbers. Repeat adding 1/4 cup pickling or canning salt for each 5 pounds of cucumbers one time each week for the next 4 weeks.

4. Fermentation seen as scum (bubble formation) on the surface of the brine should continue for approximately 4 weeks. Remove scum and/or mold daily. Scum will appear as light-colored foam or residue. Mold is dark or black in color. If scum or mold is not completely removed each day, it can contaminate and spoil the entire batch of pickles. Scum and/or mold may not form when using a brine-filled plastic bag as a weight; however, check the container each day to ensure there is no formation of scum or mold.

5. Bubbles that rise to the surface of the brine indicates the cucumbers are fermenting. To determine when fermentation is done, test for bubbles by tapping on the side of the container with your hand. If bubbles do not rise to the surface of the brine, fermentation is complete. As a second test, cut a cucumber in half to evaluate the color of the pulp. An even, consistent color throughout indicates the cucumbers are fermented. Noticeable white spots or rings signify additional fermentation is required.

Desalting Cucumbers

Salt absorbed during fermentation causes brined cucumbers to be very salty. While it is safe to eat these cucumbers, most people prefer a pickle with less salt. Desalting brined cucumbers reduces the level of salt, but does not remove all of the salt.

1. Remove cucumbers from brine. Measure the volume of cucumbers. Submerge cucumbers in hot (180°F) water; using at least 3 times the amount of water as cucumbers. Let stand about 4 hours in the refrigerator, stirring occasionally. Lift cucumbers out of the water. Discard water; rinse container. Repeat 2 times.

2. Lift cucumbers from third soak. Prick cucumbers in several places using a thin metal skewer. Pricking the cucumbers aids in the absorption of pickling liquid, which helps to prevent shriveling.

3. Put cucumbers in a solution of 1 part water to 3 parts vinegar and let stand for 12 hours in the refrigerator. Taste the cucumbers to determine if a sufficient amount of salt is removed; if not, let stand 12 hours longer. When desalting is complete, cucumbers are ready to be used in a pickling recipe.

Note: As an alternative method of desalting, brined cucumbers can be soaked in cold water. Use 3 times the amount of water as cucumbers. Change the water every 8 hours, stirring cucumbers occasionally. The salt should be removed within a 24 hour period.

Brined
PICKLED VEGETABLES

Brined (or fermented) pickles are typically made using pickling cucumbers, although other types of vegetables make equally delicious fermented foods. Cucumbers are submerged in a salt and water brine for an extended period of time (see Brining Cucumbers). During fermentation, the salt draws out juices and sugar from the cucumbers to form lactic acid. Lactic acid acts to preserve the cucumbers. Dill, garlic, and other herbs and spices may be added for flavor during fermentation, or later to flavor the pickling liquid used for processing. Fermenting yields favorable changes to color, texture, and flavor.

To reduce the cooked flavor and loss of crispness for fermented cucumbers and fresh pack dills, bring the water in the canner to a rolling boil before lowering jars into the canner. Start counting processing time as soon as the filled jars are submerged in the boiling water; process following the same time specified by the tested recipe. Brined and fermented pickles will benefit from being cured in the jars for 3 to 6 weeks after processing.

For all other pickle types, jars are submerged in simmering water, and processing time begins when the water in the canner comes to a rolling boil.

Brined Dill Pickles

Yield: about 6 quart jars

10 pounds 4- to 6-inch cucumbers	1½ cups Ball Salt for Pickling & Preserving
¾ cup Ball Mixed Pickling Spice, divided	8 quarts cold water
2 to 3 bunches fresh or dried dill, divided	2 cups vinegar, 5% acidity
	6 cloves garlic (optional)

PREP Wash cucumbers under cold running water; drain. Remove ¹/₁₆ inch from blossom end of cucumbers. Place half the mixed pickling spice and one layer of dill in a pickling container. Add cucumbers to within 4 inches from top. Combine salt, water, and vinegar, stirring until salt dissolves. Pour brine over cucumbers. Place a layer of dill and remaining mixed pickling spice over top. Add garlic, if desired. Weight cucumbers under brine; store container at 70° to 75°F. Let cucumbers ferment until they have an even color throughout and are well flavored.

COOK Remove pickles from brine. Strain brine, discarding spices, garlic, and dill. Bring brine to a boil in a large saucepan.

FILL Pack pickles into a hot jar, leaving ½-inch headspace. Ladle hot brine over pickles, leaving ½-inch headspace. Remove air bubbles. Clean jar rim. Center lid on jar and adjust band to fingertip-tight. Place jar on the rack elevated over simmering water (180°F) in boiling-water canner. Repeat until all jars are filled.

PROCESS Lower the rack into simmering water. Water must cover jars by 1 inch. Adjust heat to medium-high, cover canner and bring water to a rolling boil. Process quart jars 15 minutes. Turn off heat and remove cover. Let jars cool 5 minutes. Remove jars from canner; do not retighten bands if loose. Cool 12 hours. Check seals. Label and store jars.

Cucumber Chips

Yield: about 3 pint jars

6 pounds 4- to 5-inch cucumbers, cut into ¼-inch slices	2 cups granulated sugar
	2 sticks cinnamon
½ cup Ball Salt for Pickling & Preserving	1 ¼ inch x 1 inch piece fresh ginger
1 tablespoon turmeric	1 tablespoon mustard seed
1 quart plus 3 cups vinegar, 5% acidity, divided	1 teaspoon whole cloves
	2 cups brown sugar
1 quart plus 1 cup water, divided	

PREP Wash cucumbers under cold running water; drain. Remove stem and ¹/₁₆ inch from blossom ends of cucumbers. Cut cucumbers crosswise into ¼-inch slices. Put cucumber slices in a large bowl, sprinkle with salt, and stir to evenly coat cucumber slices. Let stand 3 hours. Drain cucumber slices. Rinse under cold running water; drain.

COOK Combine turmeric, 3 cups vinegar, and 1 quart water in a saucepan. Bring mixture to a boil. Pour hot brine over cucumber slices. Let stand until mixture returns to room temperature; drain. If cucumber slices taste too salty, rinse with cold running water; drain. Combine granulated sugar, 1 quart vinegar, and 1 cup water in a large saucepan. Tie spices in a spice bag. Add spice bag to pickling liquid. Bring pickling liquid to a simmer (180°F); simmer 15 minutes. Pour hot pickling liquid over cucumber slices. Let stand in refrigerator for 12 to 24 hours. Remove spice bag and discard. Remove cucumber slices; set aside. Combine pickling liquid and brown sugar in a large saucepan. Bring pickling liquid to a boil.

FILL Pack pickles into a hot jar, leaving ½-inch headspace. Ladle hot pickling liquid over pickles, leaving ½-inch headspace. Remove air bubbles. Clean jar rim. Center lid on jar and adjust band to fingertip-tight. Place jar on the rack elevated over simmering water (180°F) in boiling-water canner. Repeat until all jars are filled.

PROCESS Lower the rack into simmering water. Water must cover jars by 1 inch. Adjust heat to medium-high, cover canner and bring water to a rolling boil. Process pint jars 10 minutes. Turn off heat and remove cover. Let jars cool 5 minutes. Remove jars from canner; do not retighten bands if loose. Cool 12 hours. Check seals. Label and store jars.

 Our Tip Deep fry a stack of these Cucumber Chips for the best appetizer ever! Begin with your favorite batter for deep frying, a jar of your famous Cucumber Chips, and 1 quart of vegetable oil for frying. Drain pickles and pat dry. Drench pickles in the batter, then deep fry in oil at 350°F. Pickles will float to the top when done. Serve crispy fried pickles with your favorite dipping sauce.

Cucumber Chunks

Yield: about 8 pint jars

5 pounds 3- to 4-inch cucumbers, cut into 1-inch chunks	2 quarts plus 1 cup vinegar, 5% acidity, divided
1½ cups Ball Salt for Pickling & Preserving	4 to 5 cups sugar, divided
4 quarts plus 3 cups water, divided	2 tablespoons Ball Mixed Pickling Spice

PREP Wash cucumbers under cold running water; drain. Remove stem and ¹/₁₆ inch from blossom end of cucumbers.

Cut cucumbers into 1-inch chunks. Place cucumber chunks in a pickling container. Dissolve salt in 4 quarts of water; pour brine over cucumber chunks. Weight cucumber chunks under brine; cover container. Store container at 70° to 75°F for 36 hours. Drain, discarding brine. Rinse cucumbers under cold running water; drain. Tie spices in a spice bag.

COOK Combine cucumbers and 1 quart vinegar in a large saucepan. Add enough water for liquid to cover cucumbers. Bring mixture to a simmer (180°F); simmer 10 minutes. Drain, discarding liquid. Combine spice bag, 2 cups sugar, 5 cups vinegar, and 3 cups water in a large saucepan. Bring mixture to a simmer (180°F); simmer 10 minutes. Pour hot pickling liquid over cucumber chunks; cover container. Store container at 70° to 75°F for 24 hours. Drain, reserving pickling liquid. Combine pickling liquid and remaining 2 to 3 cups sugar (to taste) in a large saucepan. Bring pickling liquid to a boil. Pour hot pickling liquid over cucumber chunks. Cover container; let stand 24 hours at 70° to 75°F. Remove spice bag. Drain pickling liquid into a large saucepan. Bring pickling liquid to a boil.

FILL Pack pickles into a hot jar, leaving ½-inch headspace. Ladle hot pickling liquid over pickles, leaving ½-inch headspace. Remove air bubbles. Clean jar rim. Center lid on jar and adjust band to fingertip-tight. Place jar on the rack elevated over simmering water (180°F) in boiling-water canner. Repeat until all jars are filled.

PROCESS Lower the rack into simmering water. Water must cover jars by 1 inch. Adjust heat to medium-high, cover canner and bring water to a rolling boil. Process pint jars 15 minutes. Turn off heat and remove cover. Let jars cool 5 minutes. Remove jars from canner; do not retighten bands if loose. Cool 12 hours. Check seals. Label and store jars.

Cucumber Rings

Yield: about 6 pint jars

3 pounds brined cucumbers, desalted	3 sticks cinnamon
2 cups water	1½ teaspoons whole cloves
2 cups vinegar, 5% acidity, divided	1 ¼ inch x 1 inch piece fresh ginger, peeled
2 cups sugar	1 medium lemon, thinly sliced

PREP Wash lemon under cold running water; drain. Thinly slice lemon. Measure 3 pounds desalted, brined cucumbers (see page 73). Cut cucumbers into ¼-inch slices. Place cucumber slices into a large bowl. Combine water and 1 cup vinegar; pour over cucumber slices. Let stand 2 hours in refrigerator. Add remaining 1 cup vinegar. Let stand 2 hours in refrigerator. Drain; reserving pickling liquid. Tie spices in a spice bag.

COOK Combine pickling liquid, sugar, spice bag, and lemon slices in a large saucepan. Add cucumber slices and cook over medium heat until cucumbers are transparent. Put mixture in a shallow pan and refrigerate 24 hours. Remove spice bag and lemon slices; discard. Drain cucumber slices, reserving pickling liquid. Strain liquid. Bring pickling liquid to a boil.

FILL Pack pickles into a hot jar, leaving ½-inch headspace. Ladle hot pickling liquid over pickles, leaving ½-inch headspace. Remove air bubbles. Clean jar rim. Center lid on jar and adjust band to fingertip-tight. Place jar on the rack elevated over simmering water (180°F) in boiling-water canner. Repeat until all jars are filled.

PROCESS Lower the rack into simmering water. Water must cover jars by 1 inch. Adjust heat to medium-high, cover canner and bring water to a rolling boil. Process pint jars 15 minutes. Turn off heat and remove cover. Let jars cool 5 minutes. Remove jars from canner; do not retighten bands if loose. Cool 12 hours, Check seals. Label and store jars.

Note: Brined cucumbers may be cut into rings, spears, or chunks. The yield may vary depending on how the cucumbers are cut.

Cucumber Sandwich Pickles

Yield: about 3 pint jars

2 pounds 3- to 4-inch cucumbers, cut into ¼-inch slices	1 cup brown sugar
½ cup Ball Salt for Pickling & Preserving	1 cup granulated sugar
3 quarts water, divided	½ teaspoon celery seed
1 quart plus 1 cup vinegar, 5% acidity, divided	½ teaspoon mustard seed
	½ teaspoon turmeric

PREP Wash cucumbers under cold running water; drain. Remove stem and 1/16 inch from blossom ends of cucumbers. Cut cucumbers crosswise into ¼-inch slices. Place cucumber slices in a large bowl. Combine salt and 2 quarts water, stirring until salt dissolves. Pour salted water over cucumber slices. Let stand 2 to 3 hours in refrigerator. Drain cucumber slices. Rinse cucumber slices under cold running water; drain.

COOK Combine 3 cups vinegar and 3 cups water in a large saucepan. Bring mixture to a boil. Reduce heat to a simmer (180°F); add cucumber slices and simmer 5 minutes. Drain, discarding liquid. Combine 2 cups vinegar, 1 cup water, brown sugar, granulated sugar, and spices in a large saucepan. Simmer mixture 10 minutes. Add cucumber slices and bring mixture to a boil.

FILL Ladle hot pickles and pickling liquid into a hot jar, leaving ½-inch headspace. Remove air bubbles. Clean jar rim. Center lid on jar and adjust band to fingertip-tight. Place jar on the rack elevated over simmering water (180°F) in boiling-water canner. Repeat until all jars are filled.

PROCESS Lower the rack into simmering water. Water must cover jars by 1 inch. Adjust heat to medium-high, cover canner and bring water to a rolling boil. Process pint jars 10 minutes. Turn off heat and remove cover. Let jars cool 5 minutes. Remove jars from canner; do not retighten bands if loose. Cool 12 hours. Check seals. Label and store jars.

Our Tip Make an unforgettable grilled cheese sandwich using Cucumber Sandwich Pickles. Start with two generous slices of marbled rye bread. Spread butter on one side of bread for grilling and spicy mustard on the opposite side for flavor; set one slice of bread aside. Place one bread slice on plate with spicy mustard side up; layer on a thick cut of smoked Gouda cheese, red onion, and a handful of pickles. Top with second slice of bread, butter side up. Grill sandwich until cheese begins to melt and bread is toasted. Enjoy!

Sauerkraut

Yield: about 12 pint or 6 quart jars

25 pounds cabbage (about 5 large heads)

¾ cup Ball Salt for Pickling & Preserving

PREP Wash cabbage under cold running water; drain. Remove outer leaves and discard. Cut into halves or quarters and remove core. Cut cabbage into thin shreds 1/16 inch thick, using a food processor or knife. Combine 3 tablespoons salt and 5 pounds shredded cabbage in a large bowl; mix to evenly coat cabbage. Let salted cabbage stand for a few minutes to wilt. Transfer salted cabbage to a pickling container. Pack firmly, pressing with a tamper or hands until juice comes to the surface. Repeat until all cabbage is salted and packed into pickling container, allowing 3 to 4 inches from top of pickling container. If juice does not cover cabbage, add brine (see Note). Place a plate directly on the cabbage. Put a sealed jar filled with water on the plate as a weight to hold cabbage under the brine. Store container at 65° to 70°F for 3 to 6 weeks. Formation of gas bubbles indicates fermentation is taking place. Remove and discard scum formation each day.

COOK Put sauerkraut and liquid in a large saucepan. Bring mixture to a simmer (180°F). Do not boil.

FILL Pack hot sauerkraut into a hot jar, leaving ½-inch headspace. Ladle hot liquid over sauerkraut, leaving ½-inch headspace. Remove air bubbles. Clean jar rim. Center lid on jar and adjust band to fingertip-tight. Place jar on the rack elevated over simmering water (180°F) in boiling-water canner. Repeat until all jars are filled.

PROCESS Lower the rack into simmering water. Water must cover jars by 1 inch. Adjust heat to medium-high, cover canner and bring water to a rolling boil. Process pint jars 15 minutes and quart jars 20 minutes. Turn off heat and remove cover. Let jars cool 5 minutes. Remove jars from canner; do not retighten bands if they are loose. Cool 12 hours. Check seals. Label and store jars.

Note: To make brine, combine 1 quart water and 1½ tablespoons salt in a saucepan, stirring until salt dissolves. Bring brine to a boil. Remove from heat and cool to room temperature before using.

Sweet Cucumber Pickles

Yield: about 5 pint jars

3 pounds brined cucumbers, desalted

3⅓ cups sugar

1 quart vinegar, 5% acidity

2 sticks cinnamon

1 tablespoon slivered fresh ginger

1 tablespoon whole cloves

1 tablespoon whole mace

PREP Measure 3 pounds brined, desalted cucumbers (see page 73). Tie spices in a spice bag.

COOK Combine sugar and vinegar in a large saucepan. Bring mixture to a boil, stirring until sugar dissolves. Add spice bag and cucumbers. Boil mixture 3 minutes. Transfer cucumbers and brine to a pickling container; cover container. Store container at 65° to 70°F for 3 days. Each day, drain off brine; bring brine to a boil; pour over cucumbers. Remove and discard spice bag after the third day. Drain cucumbers, reserving brine. Bring brine to a boil.

FILL Pack pickles into a hot jar, leaving ½-inch headspace. Ladle hot brine over pickles, leaving ½-inch headspace. Remove air bubbles. Clean jar rim. Center lid on jar and adjust band to fingertip-tight. Place jar on the rack elevated over simmering water (180°F) in boiling-water canner. Repeat until all jars are filled.

PROCESS Lower the rack into simmering water. Water must cover jars by 1 inch. Adjust heat to medium-high, cover canner and bring water to a rolling boil. Process pint jars 15 minutes. Turn off heat and remove cover. Let jars cool 5 minutes. Remove jars from canner; do not retighten bands if loose. Cool 12 hours. Check seals. Label and store jars.

 To make Sour Cucumber Pickles, omit part or all of sugar.

Sweet Cucumber Rings

Yield: about 7 quart jars

10 pounds 5- to 6-inch pickling cucumbers

Water

Ice cubes

1 quart plus ½ cup cider vinegar, 5% acidity, divided

1 small bottle red food coloring

12 cups sugar, divided

1 cup red hot cinnamon candies

8 sticks cinnamon

Ball Pickle Crisp (optional)

PREP Wash cucumbers under cold running water; drain. Remove stem and 1/16 inch from blossom end of cucumbers. Cut cucumbers crosswise in half. Remove seeds from cucumbers using an apple corer. Slice cucumbers into ½-inch slices. Put cucumbers into a pickling container. Cover with ice and let stand in refrigerator for 3 hours, adding more ice as it melts. Drain water. Remove cucumber rings. Wash pickling container.

COOK
Combine cucumber rings, 1 cup vinegar and red food coloring in a large saucepan. Add cold water just to cover. Bring mixture to a boil. Reduce heat and boil gently for 2 hours or until cucumbers are red throughout. Drain. Return cucumbers to pickling container. Combine 3½ cups water, 3½ cups cider vinegar, 10 cups sugar, red hot cinnamon candies, and cinnamon sticks in a large saucepan. Bring mixture to a boil, stirring until sugar dissolves and red hot candies melt. Pour pickling liquid over cucumber rings; cover pickling container with plastic wrap. Store container at 70° to 75°F for 8 to 12 hours.

Day 2 and Day 3—Drain cucumber rings, reserving pickling liquid. Return cucumber rings to pickling container. Combine pickling liquid and 1 cup sugar in a large saucepan. Bring mixture to a boil, stirring until sugar dissolves. Pour pickling liquid over cucumber rings; cover container with plastic wrap. Store container at 70° to 75°F for 24 hours. Repeat on Day 3.

Day 4—Remove cinnamon sticks and discard. Transfer cucumber rings and pickling liquid to a large saucepan. Bring mixture to a boil.

FILL Pack hot pickles into a hot jar, leaving ½-inch headspace. Ladle hot brine over pickles, leaving ½-inch headspace. Add ¼ teaspoon Pickle Crisp to quart jar, if desired. Remove air bubbles. Clean jar rim. Center lid on jar and adjust band to fingertip-tight. Place jar on the rack elevated over simmering water (180°F) in boiling-water canner. Repeat until all jars are filled.

PROCESS Lower the rack into simmering water. Water must cover jars by 1 inch. Adjust heat to medium-high, cover canner and bring water to a rolling boil. Process quart jars 10 minutes. Turn off heat and remove cover. Let jars cool 5 minutes. Remove jars from canner; do not retighten bands if loose. Cool 12 hours. Check seals. Label and store jars.

Sweet Gherkin Pickles

Yield: about 7 pint jars

8 pounds 1½-inch to 2½-inch cucumbers	½ teaspoon turmeric
½ cup Ball Salt for Pickling & Preserving, divided	2 teaspoons celery seed
8 cups sugar, divided	2 teaspoons Ball Mixed Pickling Spice
1 quart plus 2 cups vinegar, 5% acidity, divided	2 sticks cinnamon
	½ teaspoon whole allspice

PREP Wash cucumbers under cold running water; drain. Remove stem and 1/16 inch from blossom end of cucumbers. Tie celery seed, mixed pickling spice, cinnamon sticks, and whole allspice in a spice bag.

COOK

Put cucumbers in a pickling container. Combine 6 quarts boiling water and ¼ cup salt, stirring until salt dissolves. Pour brine over cucumbers; cover pickling container. Store container at 70° to 75°F for 6 to 8 hours.

Day 2—Drain cucumbers. Combine 6 quarts boiling water and ¼ cup salt, stirring until salt dissolves. Pour brine over cucumbers; cover pickling container. Store container at 70° to 75°F for 6 to 8 hours.

Day 3—Drain cucumbers. Prick cucumbers all over using a thin metal skewer. Combine 3 cups sugar, 3 cups vinegar, turmeric, and spice bag in a large saucepan. Bring mixture to a boil, stirring until sugar dissolves. Pour brine over cucumbers; cover pickling container. Store container at 70° to 75°F for 6 to 8 hours.

Day 4—Drain cucumbers, reserving brine. Add 2 cups sugar and 2 cups vinegar to brine. Bring mixture to a boil, stirring until sugar dissolves. Pour brine over cucumbers; cover container. Store container at 70° to 75°F for 6 to 8 hours.

Day 5—Drain cucumbers, reserving brine. Add 2 cups sugar and 1 cup vinegar to brine. Bring mixture to a boil, stirring until sugar dissolves. Pour brine over cucumbers; cover pickling container. Store container at 70° to 75°F for 6 to 8 hours.

Day 6—Remove spice bag; discard. Drain cucumbers, reserving brine. Add 1 cup sugar to brine. Bring mixture to a boil, stirring until sugar dissolves.

FILL Pack pickles into a hot jar, leaving ½-inch headspace. Ladle hot pickling liquid over pickles, leaving ½-inch headspace. Remove air bubbles. Clean jar rim. Center lid on jar and adjust band to fingertip-tight. Place jar on the rack elevated over simmering water (180°F) in boiling-water canner. Repeat until all jars are filled.

PROCESS Lower the rack into simmering water. Water must cover jars by 1 inch. Adjust heat to medium-high, cover canner and bring water to a rolling boil. Process pint jars 10 minutes. Turn off heat and remove cover. Let jars cool 5 minutes. Remove jars from canner; do not retighten bands if loose. Cool 12 hours. Check seals. Label and store jars.

Our Tip The gherkin is a nubby little cucumber of small stature, about 1 to 3 inches long. It is frequently brined, then flavored for the savory palate; however, gherkins take on a whole new life when cured in a spicy sweet syrup. Gherkins quickly lose their tangy flavor when cooked, so use them in your favorite salad or slaw, on a cold meat sandwich, or presented on a relish platter.

Sweet Icicle Pickles

Yield: about 6 pint or 3 quart jars

4 pounds 4-inch to 6-inch cucumbers	1½ tablespoons Ball Mixed Pickling Spice
1 cup Ball Salt for Pickling & Preserving	5 cups sugar
2 quarts water	1 quart plus 1 cup vinegar, 5% acidity

PREP Wash cucumbers under cold running water; drain. Remove stem and 1/16 inch from blossom ends. Cut cucumbers lengthwise into quarters. Put cucumbers in a pickling container. Tie mixed pickling spice in a spice bag.

COOK Combine salt and water in a large saucepan. Bring brine to a boil, stirring until salt dissolves. Pour brine over cucumbers. Weight cucumbers under brine; cover pickling container. Store container at 70° to 75°F for 7 days. Drain, discarding brine. Rinse cucumbers under cold running water; drain. Return cucumbers to pickling container. Cover cucumbers with boiling water; cover pickling container. Store container at 70° to 75°F for 24 hours. Drain, discarding water. Combine spice bag, sugar, and vinegar in a large saucepan. Bring mixture to a boil. Pour pickling liquid over cucumbers; cover pickling container. Store container at 70° to 75°F for 24 hours. Once each day for the next 4 days, drain and reheat pickling liquid. Pour pickling liquid over cucumbers; cover pickling container. Store at 70° to 75°F for 24 hours. Remove spice bag; discard. Drain cucumbers, reserving brine. Bring brine to a boil in a large saucepan.

FILL Pack pickles into a hot jar, leaving ½-inch headspace. Ladle hot pickling liquid over pickles, leaving ½-inch headspace. Remove air bubbles. Clean jar rim. Center lid on jar and adjust band to fingertip-tight. Place jar on the rack elevated over simmering water (180°F) in boiling-water canner. Repeat until all jars are filled.

PROCESS Lower the rack into simmering water. Water must cover jars by 1 inch. Adjust heat to medium-high, cover canner and bring water to a rolling boil. Process pint or quart jars 10 minutes. Turn off heat and remove cover. Let jars cool 5 minutes. Remove jars from canner; do not retighten bands if loose. Cool 12 hours. Check seals. Label and store jars.

Fresh Pack
PICKLED FOODS

Fresh pack pickles are made by covering vegetables or fruits with a hot pickling liquid prepared using various combinations of vinegar, water, sugar, herbs, and spices. Sometimes the vegetables or fruits are first brined in a salt water solution for 1 hour to 24 hours, after which the brine is drained and the vegetables or fruits are rinsed. Fresh pack pickles develop a uniform flavor if allowed to stand for 3 to 6 weeks after processing in jars.

Cucumber &
VEGETABLE PICKLES

Bread and Butter Pickles

Yield: about 7 pint jars

4 pounds 4- to 6-inch cucumbers	2 teaspoons turmeric
2 pounds onions, thinly sliced	2 teaspoons celery seed
1/3 cup Ball Salt for Pickling & Preserving	1 teaspoon ginger
2 cups sugar	1 teaspoon peppercorn
2 tablespoons mustard seed	3 cups vinegar, 5% acidity
	Ball Pickle Crisp (optional)

PREP Wash cucumbers under cold running water; drain. Remove stem and 1/16 inch from blossom end of cucumbers. Cut cucumbers crosswise into 1/4-inch slices. Cut onions crosswise into thin slices. Put cucumbers and onions in a large bowl, layering with salt. Cover with ice cubes. Let stand 1 1/2 hours. Drain cucumbers and onion. Rinse cucumbers and onions under cold running water; drain.

COOK Combine sugar, spices, and vinegar in a large saucepan. Bring mixture to a boil, stirring until sugar dissolves. Add cucumbers and onions. Bring mixture to a boil.

FILL Pack hot pickles and liquid into a hot jar, leaving 1/2-inch headspace. Add 1/8 teaspoon Pickle Crisp to pint jar, if desired. Remove air bubbles. Clean jar rim. Center lid on jar and adjust band to fingertip-tight. Place jar on the rack elevated over simmering water (180°F) in boiling-water canner. Repeat until all jars are filled.

PROCESS Lower the rack into simmering water. Water must cover jars by 1 inch. Adjust heat to medium-high, cover canner and bring water to a rolling boil. Process pint jars 10 minutes. Turn off heat and remove cover. Let jars cool 5 minutes. Remove jars from canner; do not retighten bands if loose. Cool 12 hours. Check seals. Label and store jars.

Dill Pickles

Yield: about 7 pint or 3 quart jars

8 pounds 4- to 6-inch cucumbers	1 quart water
3/4 cup sugar	3 tablespoons Ball Mixed Pickling Spice
1/2 cup Ball Salt for Pickling & Preserving	Green or dry dill (1 head per jar)
1 quart vinegar, 5% acidity	Ball Pickle Crisp (optional)

PREP Wash cucumbers under cold running water; drain. Remove stem and 1/16 inch from blossom end of cucumbers. Cut cucumbers in half lengthwise. Tie spices in a spice bag.

COOK Combine sugar, salt, vinegar, and water in a large saucepan. Add spice bag. Bring mixture to a boil, stirring until sugar dissolves. Reduce heat to a simmer (180°F); simmer 15 minutes.

FILL Pack cucumbers into a hot jar, leaving 1/2-inch headspace. Put one head of dill in jar. Add 1/8 teaspoon Pickle Crisp to pint jar or 1/4 teaspoon Pickle Crisp to quart jar, if desired. Ladle hot pickling liquid over cucumbers, leaving 1/2-inch headspace. Remove air bubbles. Clean jar rim. Center lid on jar and adjust band to fingertip-tight. Place jar on the rack elevated over simmering water (180°F) in boiling-water canner. Repeat until all jars are filled.

PROCESS Lower the rack into simmering water. Water must cover jars by 1 inch. Adjust heat to medium-high, cover canner and bring water to a rolling boil. Process pint or quart jars 15 minutes. Turn off heat and remove cover. Let jars cool 5 minutes. Remove jars from canner; do not retighten bands if loose. Cool 12 hours. Check seals. Label and store jars.

Kosher-Style Pickles

Yield: about 7 pint or 3 quart jars

8 pounds 4- to 6-inch cucumbers	3 or 3 1/2 teaspoons mustard seed
3/4 cup sugar	3 or 7 green or dry heads of dill
1/2 cup Ball Salt for Pickling & Preserving	3 or 7 bay leaves
1 quart vinegar, 5% acidity	3 or 7 cloves garlic
1 quart water	3 or 7 hot red peppers
3 tablespoons Ball Mixed Pickling Spice	Ball Pickle Crisp (optional)

PREP Wash cucumbers and hot red peppers under cold running water; drain. Remove stem and 1/16 inch from blossom end of cucumbers. Cut cucumbers in half lengthwise. Tie mixed pickling spice in a spice bag. Peel garlic.

COOK Combine sugar, salt, vinegar, and water in a large saucepan. Add spice bag. Bring mixture to a boil, stirring until sugar dissolves. Reduce heat to a simmer (180°F); simmer 15 minutes. Remove spice bag.

FILL Pack cucumbers into a hot jar, leaving 1/2-inch headspace. Put 1/2 teaspoon mustard seed, one head dill, 1 bay leaf, 1 clove garlic, and 1 hot red pepper in pint or quart jar. Add 1/8 teaspoon Pickle Crisp to pint jar or 1/4 teaspoon Pickle Crisp to quart jar, if desired. Ladle hot pickling liquid over cucumbers, leaving 1/2-inch headspace. Remove air bubbles. Clean jar rim. Center lid on jar and adjust band to fingertip-tight. Place jar on the rack elevated over simmering water (180°F) in boiling-water canner. Repeat until all jars are filled.

PROCESS Lower the rack into simmering water. Water must cover jars by 1 inch. Adjust heat to medium-high, cover canner and bring water to a rolling boil. Process pint or quart jars 15 minutes. Turn off heat and remove cover. Let jars cool 5 minutes. Remove jars from canner; do not retighten bands if loose. Cool 12 hours. Check seals. Label and store jars.

Note: When cutting or seeding hot peppers, wear rubber gloves to prevent hands from being burned.

End-of-the-Garden Pickles

Yield: about 5 pint jars

- 1 pound zucchini (about 3 medium)
- 1 pound green beans
- 1/2 pound carrots (about 3 medium)
- 1/2 pound pearl onions
- 1 pound green bell peppers (about 2 large)
- 1/2 pound red bell pepper (about 1 large)
- 1 cup granulated sugar
- 1 cup brown sugar
- 2 tablespoons dry mustard
- 2 tablespoons mustard seed
- 1 1/2 tablespoons Ball Salt for Pickling & Preserving
- 1 teaspoon cinnamon
- 1 teaspoon ginger
- 3 cups cider vinegar, 5% acidity
- Ball Pickle Crisp (optional)

PREP Wash zucchini, green beans, carrots, and green and red peppers under cold running water; drain. Remove stem and blossom ends from zucchini. Cut zucchini crosswise into 1/4-inch slices. Remove ends from green beans. Remove stems from carrots; peel. Cut carrots crosswise into 1/4-inch slices. To peel pearl onions, cover with boiling water and let stand 2 minutes; drain. Quickly rinse under cold running water. Cut off peels. Remove stems and seeds from green and red peppers. Cut peppers lengthwise into 1/2-inch strips.

COOK Combine sugars, spices, and vinegar in a large saucepan. Bring mixture to a boil, stirring until sugar dissolves. Add vegetables; stir. Bring mixture to a boil. Reduce heat to a simmer (180°F); simmer 15 minutes.

FILL Pack hot vegetables and pickling liquid into a hot jar, leaving 1/2-inch headspace. Add 1/8 teaspoon Pickle Crisp to pint jar, if desired. Remove air bubbles. Clean jar rim. Center lid on jar and adjust band to fingertip-tight. Place jar on the rack elevated over simmering water (180°F) in boiling-water canner. Repeat until all jars are filled.

PROCESS Lower the rack into simmering water. Water must cover jars by 1 inch. Adjust heat to medium-high, cover canner and bring water to a rolling boil. Process pint jars 15 minutes. Turn off heat and remove cover. Let jars cool 5 minutes. Remove jars from canner; do not retighten bands if loose. Cool 12 hours. Check seals. Label and store jars.

Hamburger Dills

Yield: about 7 pint jars

- 4 pounds 4- to 6-inch cucumbers
- 6 tablespoons Ball Salt for Pickling & Preserving
- 1 quart plus 1/2 cup water
- 1 quart vinegar, 5% acidity
- 14 heads fresh dill
- 3 1/2 teaspoons mustard seed
- 14 peppercorns
- Ball Pickle Crisp (optional)

PREP Wash cucumbers under cold running water; drain. Remove stem and 1/16 inch from blossom ends of cucumbers. Cut cucumbers crosswise or lengthwise into 1/4-inch slices.

COOK Combine salt, water, and vinegar in a large saucepan. Bring mixture to a boil. Reduce heat to a simmer (180°F); simmer 10 minutes.

FILL Pack cucumbers into a hot jar, leaving 1/2-inch headspace. Put 2 heads of dill, 1/2 teaspoon mustard seed, and 2 peppercorns in jar. Add 1/8 teaspoon Pickle Crisp to pint jar, if desired. Ladle hot pickling liquid over cucumbers, leaving 1/2-inch headspace. Remove air bubbles. Clean jar rim. Center lid on jar and adjust band to fingertip-tight. Place jar on the rack elevated over simmering water (180°F) in boiling-water canner. Repeat until all jars are filled.

PROCESS Lower the rack into simmering water. Water must cover jars by 1 inch. Adjust heat to medium-high, cover canner and bring water to a rolling boil. Process pint jars 15 minutes. Turn off heat and remove cover. Let jars cool 5 minutes. Remove jars from canner; do not retighten bands if loose. Cool 12 hours. Check seals. Label and store jars.

Hot Pickle Mix

Yield: about 7 pint jars

- 1 1/2 quarts 1/2-inch sliced pickling cucumbers
- 1 1/2 quarts 1/2-inch sliced long red or green peppers (Anaheim, banana, etc.)
- 2 medium green bell peppers
- 2 medium red bell peppers
- 1 1/2 cups sliced carrots (about 3 medium)
- 3 cups cauliflowerets (about 1 small head)
- 1 cup pearl onions
- 1 1/2 cups Ball Salt for Pickling & Preserving
- 4 quarts plus 2 cups water, divided
- 3 or 4 jalapeño peppers
- 1/4 cup sugar
- 2 tablespoons prepared horseradish
- 2 cloves garlic
- 2 quarts plus 2 cups vinegar, 5% acidity
- Ball Pickle Crisp (optional)

PREP Wash cucumbers, peppers, carrots, and cauliflower under cold running water; drain. Remove stem and 1/16 inch from blossom ends of cucumbers. Cut cucumbers crosswise into 1/2-inch slices; measure 1 1/2 quarts sliced cucumbers. Cut long peppers crosswise into 1/2-inch slices; measure 1 1/2 quarts sliced peppers. Remove stems and seeds from red and green bell peppers. Cut bell peppers lengthwise into 1/2-inch strips. Cut cauliflower into individual cauliflowerets; measure 3 cups cauliflowerets. To peel pearl onions, cover with boiling water and let stand 2 minutes; drain. Quickly rinse under cold running water. Cut off peel. Measure 1 cup peeled pearl onions. Cut jalapeño peppers in half; set aside.

COOK Combine vegetables, except jalapeño peppers, in a large bowl. Dissolve salt in 4 quarts water. Pour salted water over vegetables; let stand 1 hour. Combine remaining ingredients, except jalapeño peppers and Pickle Crisp, in a large saucepan. Bring mixture to a boil. Reduce heat to a simmer (180°F); simmer 15 minutes. Remove garlic. Drain vegetables. Rinse vegetables under cold water; drain.

FILL Pack vegetables, except jalapeño peppers, into a hot jar, leaving 1/2-inch headspace. Add 1 piece jalapeño pepper to jar. Add 1/8 teaspoon Pickle Crisp to pint jar, if desired. Ladle hot liquid over vegetables, leaving 1/2-inch headspace. Clean jar rim. Center lid on jar and adjust band to fingertip-tight. Place jar on the rack elevated over simmering water (180°F) in boiling-water canner. Repeat until all jars are filled.

PROCESS Lower the rack into simmering water. Water must cover jars by 1 inch. Adjust heat to medium-high, cover canner and bring water to a rolling boil. Process pint jars 10 minutes. Turn off heat and remove cover. Let jars cool 5 minutes. Remove jars from canner; do not retighten bands if loose. Cool 12 hours. Check seals. Label and store jars.

Note: When cutting or seeding hot peppers, wear rubber gloves to prevent hands from being burned.

Mixed Pickles

Yield: about 6 pint jars

1¼ pounds 3- to 4-inch cucumbers

2 cups 1½-inch sliced carrots (about 3 medium)

2 cups 1½-inch sliced celery (about 4 stalks)

2 cups pearl onions

2 red bell peppers

3 cups cauliflowerets (about 1 small head)

2 hot red peppers

1 cup Ball Salt for Pickling & Preserving

4 quarts water

2 cups sugar

¼ cup mustard seed

2 tablespoons celery seed

1 quart plus 2½ cups vinegar, 5% acidity

Ball Pickle Crisp (optional)

PREP Wash cucumbers, carrots, celery, peppers, and cauliflower under cold running water; drain. Remove stem and 1/16 inch from blossom ends of cucumbers. Cut cucumbers crosswise into 1-inch slices. Remove stem ends from carrots and peel. Cut carrots crosswise into 1½-inch slices; measure 2 cups sliced carrots. Remove leafy tops and root ends from celery. Cut celery crosswise into 1½-inch slices. To peel pearl onions, cover with boiling water and let stand 2 minutes; drain. Quickly rinse under cold running water. Cut off peel; measure 2 cups pearl onions. Remove stem and seeds from red bell peppers. Cut bell peppers lengthwise into ½-inch strips. Cut cauliflower into individual cauliflowerets; measure 3 cups cauliflowerets. Remove stem end from hot red peppers. Cut hot red peppers into ½-inch rings.

COOK Put vegetables in a large bowl. Combine salt and water, stirring until salt dissolves. Pour salted water over vegetables. Let vegetables stand 12 hours in refrigerator. Combine remaining ingredients, except Pickle Crisp, in a large saucepan. Bring mixture to a boil; boil 5 minutes. Reduce heat to a simmer (180°F). Drain vegetables. Rinse vegetables under cold running water; drain. Add vegetables to pickling liquid and simmer 5 minutes.

FILL Pack vegetables and liquid into a hot jar, leaving ½-inch headspace. Add ⅛ teaspoon Pickle Crisp to pint jar, if desired. Remove air bubbles. Clean jar rim. Center lid on jar and adjust band to fingertip-tight. Place jar on the rack elevated over simmering water (180°F) in boiling-water canner. Repeat until all jars are filled.

PROCESS Lower the rack into simmering water. Water must cover jars by 1 inch. Adjust heat to medium-high, cover canner and bring water to a rolling boil. Process pint jars 15 minutes. Turn off heat and remove cover. Let jars cool 5 minutes. Remove jars from canner; do not retighten bands if loose. Cool 12 hours. Check seals. Label and store jars.

Note: When cutting or seeding hot peppers, wear rubber gloves to prevent hands from being burned.

 Turn this wonderful blend of vegetables into a tasty vegetable pasta salad. Simply toss drained vegetables with chilled cooked pasta, such as farfalle or penne, stir in Italian dressing, and top with grated Parmesan cheese.

Mustard Pickles

Yield: about 8 pint or 4 quart jars

1½ pounds 3- to 4-inch cucumbers

1 quart green tomato wedges (about 6 medium)

3 cups cauliflowerets (about 1 small head)

3 cups chopped green bell peppers (about 3 medium)

3 cups chopped red bell peppers (about 3 medium)

2 cups pearl onions

1 cup Ball Salt for Pickling & Preserving

4 quarts plus ½ cup water, divided

1½ cups sugar

½ cup flour

1 tablespoon turmeric

½ cup prepared mustard

1 quart plus 1 cup vinegar, 5% acidity

Ball Pickle Crisp (optional)

PREP Wash cucumbers, green tomatoes, cauliflower, and green and red bell peppers under cold running water; drain. Remove stem and 1/16 inch from blossom ends of cucumbers. Cut cucumbers crosswise into ½-inch slices. Core green tomatoes and cut into thick wedges. Measure 1 quart green tomato wedges. Cut cauliflower into individual cauliflowerets; measure 3 cups cauliflowerets. Remove stem and seeds from green and red bell peppers. Chop peppers; measure 3 cups each green and red bell peppers. To peel pearl onions, cover with boiling water and let stand 2 minutes; drain. Quickly rinse under cold running water. Cut off peel; measure 2 cups pearl onions.

COOK Put vegetables in a large bowl. Combine salt and 4 quarts of water, stirring until salt dissolves. Pour salted water over vegetables. Let vegetables stand 12 hours in refrigerator. Drain vegetables. Rinse vegetables under cold running water; drain. Combine sugar, flour, and turmeric in a large saucepan. Gradually add ½ cup water, stirring until smooth. Stir in mustard and vinegar. Cook over medium-high heat until sauce coats a spoon. Reduce heat to a simmer (180°F); add vegetables and simmer 15 minutes.

FILL Pack vegetables and liquid into a hot jar, leaving ½-inch headspace. Add ⅛ teaspoon Pickle Crisp to pint jar or ¼ teaspoon Pickle Crisp to quart jar, if desired. Remove air bubbles. Clean jar rim. Center lid on jar and adjust band to fingertip-tight. Place jar on the rack elevated over simmering water (180°F) in boiling-water canner. Repeat until all jars are filled.

PROCESS Lower the rack into simmering water. Water must cover jars by 1 inch. Adjust heat to medium-high, cover canner and bring water to a rolling boil. Process pint or quart jars 10 minutes. Turn off heat and remove cover. Let jars cool 5 minutes. Remove jars from canner; do not retighten bands if loose. Cool 12 hours. Check seals. Label and store jars.

Reduced-Salt Dill Pickles

Yield: about 6 pint jars

4 pounds 3- to 5-inch cucumbers

3 cups sugar

2 tablespoons Ball Salt for Pickling & Preserving

1 quart plus 2 cups vinegar, 5% acidity

2 tablespoons Ball Mixed Pickling Spice

Green or dry dill (1 head per jar)

Ball Pickle Crisp (optional)

PREP Wash cucumbers under cold running water; drain. Remove stem and 1/16 inch from blossom end of cucumbers. Cut cucumbers crosswise into 1/4-inch slices. Tie spices in a spice bag.

COOK Combine sugar, salt, and vinegar in a large saucepan. Add spice bag. Bring mixture to a boil, stirring until sugar dissolves. Reduce heat to a simmer (180°F); simmer 15 minutes. Remove spice bag.

FILL Pack cucumbers into a hot jar, leaving 1/2-inch headspace. Put one head of dill in jar. Add 1/8 teaspoon Pickle Crisp to pint jar, if desired. Ladle hot pickling liquid over cucumbers, leaving 1/2-inch headspace. Remove air bubbles. Clean jar rim. Center lid on jar and adjust band to fingertip-tight. Place jar on the rack elevated over simmering water (180°F) in boiling-water canner. Repeat until all jars are filled.

PROCESS Lower the rack into simmering water. Water must cover jars by 1 inch. Adjust heat to medium-high, cover canner and bring water to a rolling boil. Process pint jars 15 minutes. Turn off heat and remove cover. Let jars cool 5 minutes. Remove jars from canner; do not retighten bands if loose. Cool 12 hours. Check seals. Label and store jars.

Reduced-Salt Sweet Pickles

Yield: about 4 pint jars

4 pounds 3- to 4-inch cucumbers

1 tablespoon Ball Salt for Pickling & Preserving

3 1/2 cups sugar, divided

1 quart plus 1 2/3 cups vinegar, 5% acidity, divided

1 tablespoon whole allspice

1 tablespoon celery seed

2 teaspoons mustard seed

Ball Pickle Crisp (optional)

PREP Wash cucumbers under cold running water; drain. Remove stem and 1/16 inch from blossom end of cucumbers. Cut cucumbers crosswise into 1/4-inch slices.

COOK Combine salt, 1/2 cup sugar, and 4 cups vinegar in a large saucepan. Bring mixture to a boil, stirring until sugar dissolves. Reduce heat to a simmer (180°F); add cucumber slices and simmer 5 minutes. Drain. Keep cucumber slices warm. Combine 3 cups sugar, 1 2/3 cups vinegar, whole allspice, celery seed, and mustard seed in a large saucepan. Bring mixture to a boil, stirring to dissolve sugar. Reduce heat to a simmer; simmer 15 minutes.

FILL Pack cucumber slices into a hot jar, leaving 1/2-inch headspace. Add 1/8 teaspoon Pickle Crisp to pint jar, if desired. Ladle hot pickling liquid over cucumber slices, leaving 1/2-inch headspace. Remove air bubbles. Clean jar rim. Center lid on jar and adjust band to fingertip-tight. Place jar on the rack elevated over simmering water (180°F) in boiling-water canner. Repeat until all jars are filled.

PROCESS Lower the rack into simmering water. Water must cover jars by 1 inch. Adjust heat to medium-high, cover canner and bring water to a rolling boil. Process pint jars 10 minutes. Turn off heat and remove cover. Let jars cool 5 minutes. Remove jars from canner; do not retighten bands if loose. Cool 12 hours. Check seals. Label and store jars.

Sweet Pickle Spears

Yield: about 10 half-pint jars

4 pounds 3- to 4-inch cucumbers

4 cups sugar

3 3/4 cups vinegar, 5% acidity

3 tablespoons Ball Salt for Pickling & Preserving

4 teaspoons celery seed

4 teaspoons turmeric

1 1/2 teaspoons mustard seed

Ball Pickle Crisp (optional)

PREP Wash cucumbers under cold running water; drain. Remove stem and 1/16 inch from blossom ends of cucumbers. Cut cucumbers lengthwise into spears.

COOK Cover cucumbers with boiling water; let stand 2 hours. Drain. Combine remaining ingredients, except Pickle Crisp, in a large saucepan. Bring mixture to a boil. Reduce heat to a simmer (180°F); simmer 5 minutes.

FILL Pack cucumbers into a hot jar, leaving 1/2-inch headspace. Add 1/16 teaspoon Pickle Crisp to half-pint jar, if desired. Ladle hot pickling liquid over cucumbers, leaving 1/2-inch headspace. Remove air bubbles. Clean jar rim. Center lid on jar and adjust band to fingertip-tight. Place jar on the rack elevated over simmering water (180°F) in boiling-water canner. Repeat until all jars are filled.

PROCESS Lower the rack into simmering water. Water must cover jars by 1 inch. Adjust heat to medium-high, cover canner and bring water to a rolling boil. Process half-pint jars 10 minutes. Turn off heat and remove cover. Let jars cool 5 minutes. Remove jars from canner; do not retighten bands if loose. Cool 12 hours. Check seals. Label and store jars.

Chutneys

Chutney is a flavorful combination of vegetables and/or fruits that imparts sweet and sour notes from the pairing of sugar and vinegar. Long, slow cooking deepens the spice flavors while developing a rich, thick consistency that mounds on a spoon. Use as an accompaniment for entrees or to enliven side dishes.

Curried Apple Chutney

Yield: about 5 pint jars

1 quart chopped apples (about 8 medium)	1 tablespoon ginger
1 pound dark raisins	1 teaspoon allspice
2 cups brown sugar	1 teaspoon curry powder
1/2 cup chopped onion (about 1 medium)	1 teaspoon Ball Salt for Pickling & Preserving
1/2 cup chopped red bell pepper (about 1 large)	1 hot red pepper, chopped
1 1/2 tablespoons mustard seed	1 clove garlic, minced
	2 cups vinegar, 5% acidity

PREP Wash apples, red bell pepper, and hot red pepper under cold running water; drain. Core and peel apples. Coarsely chop apples; measure 1 quart chopped apples. Remove stems and seeds from red bell pepper. Chop bell pepper; measure 1/2 cup chopped bell pepper. Peel and chop onion; measure 1/2 cup chopped onion. Remove stem from hot red pepper. Finely chop hot red pepper. Peel garlic and finely mince.

COOK Combine all ingredients in a large saucepan. Bring mixture to a boil. Reduce heat to a simmer (180°F); simmer mixture, uncovered, until thick, stirring to prevent sticking.

FILL Pack hot chutney into a hot jar, leaving 1/2-inch headspace. Remove air bubbles. Clean jar rim. Center lid on jar and adjust band to fingertip-tight. Place jar on the rack elevated over simmering water (180°F) in boiling-water canner. Repeat until all jars are filled.

PROCESS Lower the rack into simmering water. Water must cover jars by 1 inch. Adjust heat to medium-high, cover canner and bring water to a rolling boil. Process pint jars 10 minutes. Turn off heat and remove cover. Let jars cool 5 minutes. Remove jars from canner; do not retighten bands if loose. Cool 12 hours. Check seals. Label and store jars.

Note: When cutting or seeding hot peppers, wear rubber gloves to prevent hands from being burned.

Nectarine Chutney

Yield: about 3 pint jars

2 quarts sliced nectarines (about 12 large)	2 tablespoons crystallized ginger
2 teaspoons Ball Salt for Pickling & Preserving	1/4 teaspoon cloves
2 1/2 cups brown sugar	1/4 teaspoon cinnamon
1 1/2 cups red wine vinegar	2 cloves garlic, minced
1/4 cup Worcestershire sauce	1 chili pepper, finely chopped
1 cup finely chopped onion (about 1 large)	3/4 cup lime juice

PREP Wash nectarines and chili pepper under cold running water; drain. Peel nectarines. Cut in half lengthwise and remove pits. Cut nectarines into 1/4-inch slices. Measure 2 quarts sliced nectarines. Peel and chop onion. Measure 1 cup chopped onion. Finely mince crystallized ginger. Peel garlic and finely mince. Remove stem from chili pepper. Finely chop chili pepper.

COOK Put sliced nectarines in a large bowl. Sprinkle salt over sliced nectarines. Stir to evenly coat nectarine slices with salt. Let stand 20 minutes. Combine sugar, red wine vinegar, and Worcestershire sauce in a large saucepan. Bring mixture to a boil. Stir in sliced nectarines and cook until transparent. Remove nectarines; set aside. Reduce heat to a simmer (180°F). Add remaining ingredients to saucepan and cook until onions are tender. Return sliced nectarines to syrup and continue cooking until mixture is thick, stirring to prevent sticking.

FILL Pack hot chutney into a hot jar, leaving 1/2-inch headspace. Remove air bubbles. Clean jar rim. Center lid on jar and adjust band to fingertip-tight. Place jar on the rack elevated over simmering water (180°F) in boiling-water canner. Repeat until all jars are filled.

PROCESS Lower the rack into simmering water. Water must cover jars by 1 inch. Adjust heat to medium-high, cover canner and bring water to a rolling boil. Process pint jars 10 minutes. Turn off heat and remove cover. Let jars cool 5 minutes. Remove jars from canner; do not retighten bands if loose. Cool 12 hours. Check seals. Label and store jars.

Note: When cutting or seeding hot peppers, wear rubber gloves to prevent hands from being burned.

Peach or Pear Chutney

Yield: about 7 pint jars

4 quarts finely chopped peaches or pears (about 20 medium)	2 tablespoons ginger
2 to 3 cups brown sugar	2 teaspoons Ball Salt for Pickling & Preserving
1 cup light raisins	1 clove garlic (optional)
1 cup chopped onion (about 1 medium)	1 hot red pepper, finely chopped
1/4 cup mustard seed	1 quart plus 1 cup vinegar, 5% acidity

PREP Wash peaches or pears and hot red pepper under cold running water; drain. To peel peaches, blanch in boiling water for 30 to 60 seconds. Immediately transfer to cold water. Slip off peel. Cut peaches in half lengthwise and remove pits and fibrous flesh. If making pear chutney, peel pears, then cut pears in half lengthwise and remove cores. Finely chop peaches or pears. Measure 4 quarts chopped peaches or pears. Peel onion and chop. Peel garlic and mince, if desired. Remove stem from hot red pepper. Finely chop hot red pepper.

COOK Combine all ingredients in a large saucepan. Bring mixture to a simmer (180°F); simmer until thick, stirring to prevent sticking.

FILL Pack hot chutney into a hot jar, leaving 1/2-inch headspace. Remove air bubbles. Clean jar rim. Center lid on jar and adjust band to fingertip-tight. Place jar on the rack elevated over simmering water (180°F) in boiling-water canner. Repeat until all jars are filled.

PROCESS Lower the rack into simmering water. Water must cover jars by 1 inch. Adjust heat to medium-high, cover canner and bring water to a rolling boil. Process pint jars 10 minutes. Turn off heat and remove cover. Let jars cool 5 minutes. Remove jars from canner; do not retighten bands if loose. Cool 12 hours. Check seals. Label and store jars.

Note: When cutting or seeding hot peppers, wear rubber gloves to prevent hands from being burned.

 For mild chutney, remove seeds and veins from hot pepper.

Plum Chutney

Yield: about 6 pint jars

- 4 quarts chopped plums (about 95 to 100 medium)
- 3 cups brown sugar
- 2 cups dark raisins
- 1 cup chopped onion (about 1 large)
- 2 tablespoons mustard seed
- 2 teaspoons ginger
- 1 teaspoon Ball Salt for Pickling & Preserving
- 3 cups vinegar, 5% acidity

PREP Wash plums under cold running water; drain. Cut plums in half lengthwise and remove pits. Coarsely chop plums; measure 4 quarts chopped plums. Peel onion. Chop onion; measure 1 cup chopped onion.

COOK Combine all ingredients in a large saucepan. Bring mixture to a boil. Reduce heat to a simmer (180°F); simmer until thick, stirring to prevent sticking

FILL Pack hot chutney into a hot jar, leaving 1/2-inch headspace. Remove air bubbles. Clean jar rim. Center lid on jar and adjust band to fingertip-tight. Place jar on the rack elevated over simmering water (180°F) in boiling-water canner. Repeat until all jars are filled.

PROCESS Lower the rack into simmering water. Water must cover jars by 1 inch. Adjust heat to medium-high, cover canner and bring water to a rolling boil. Process pint jars 10 minutes. Turn off heat and remove cover. Let jars cool 5 minutes. Remove jars from canner; do not retighten bands if loose. Cool 12 hours. Check seals. Label and store jars.

Sweet Yellow Tomato Chutney

Yield: about 7 pint jars

- 6 pounds yellow tomatoes (about 18 medium)
- 3 pounds Granny Smith apples (about 10 medium)
- 1 pound onions (about 2 medium)
- 1 pound golden raisins
- 1 1/2 cups granulated sugar
- 1 cup brown sugar
- 1/4 cup mustard seed
- 1 tablespoon minced fresh ginger
- 1 1/2 teaspoons cinnamon
- 1 teaspoon Ball Salt for Pickling & Preserving
- 3 hot peppers
- 2 cloves garlic, minced
- 1 quart cider vinegar, 5% acidity

PREP Wash tomatoes, apples, and hot peppers under cold running water; drain. To peel tomatoes, blanch 30 to 60 seconds in boiling water. Immediately transfer to cold water. Cut off peel. Core and chop tomatoes. Core and chop apples. Peel and chop onions. Remove stem and seeds from hot peppers. Finely chop hot peppers.

COOK Combine all ingredients in a large saucepan. Bring mixture to a boil. Reduce heat to a simmer (180°F); simmer until thick, stirring to prevent sticking.

FILL Pack hot chutney into a hot jar, leaving 1/2-inch headspace. Remove air bubbles. Clean jar rim. Center lid on jar and adjust

band to fingertip-tight. Place jar on the rack elevated over simmering water (180°F) in boiling-water canner. Repeat until all jars are filled.

PROCESS Lower the rack into simmering water. Water must cover jars by 1 inch. Adjust heat to medium-high, cover canner and bring water to a rolling boil. Process pint jars 10 minutes. Turn off heat and remove cover. Let jars cool 5 minutes. Remove jars from canner; do not retighten bands if loose. Cool 12 hours. Check seals. Label and store jars.

Note: When cutting or seeding hot peppers, wear rubber gloves to prevent hands from being burned.

Tomato-Apple Chutney

Yield: about 6 pint jars

- 2 1/2 quarts chopped tomatoes (about 12 large)
- 1 quart chopped apples (about 5 medium)
- 3 cups brown sugar
- 2 cups chopped cucumber (about 1 large)
- 1 1/2 cups chopped onions (about 1 1/2 medium)
- 1 1/2 cups chopped red bell peppers (about 2 medium)
- 1 hot red pepper
- 1 cup dark raisins
- 1 clove garlic
- 1 tablespoon ginger
- 1 teaspoon Ball Salt for Pickling & Preserving
- 1 teaspoon cinnamon
- 3 cups vinegar, 5% acidity

PREP Wash tomatoes, apples, cucumber, red bell peppers, and hot red pepper under cold running water; drain. To peel tomatoes, blanch 30 to 60 seconds in boiling water. Immediately transfer to cold water. Cut off peel. Core and chop tomatoes; measure 2 1/2 quarts chopped tomatoes. Core and chop apples; measure 1 quart chopped apples. Peel and chop cucumber; measure 2 cups chopped cucumbers. Peel and chop onions; measure 1 1/2 cups chopped onions. Remove stems and seeds from red bell peppers and hot red pepper. Chop red bell peppers. Finely chop hot red pepper.

COOK Combine all ingredients in a large saucepan. Bring mixture to a boil. Reduce heat to a simmer (180°F); simmer until thick, stirring to prevent sticking.

FILL Pack hot chutney into a hot jar, leaving 1/2-inch headspace. Remove air bubbles. Clean jar rim. Center lid on jar and adjust band to fingertip-tight. Place jar on the rack elevated over simmering water (180°F) in boiling-water canner. Repeat until all jars are filled.

PROCESS Lower the rack into simmering water. Water must cover jars by 1 inch. Adjust heat to medium-high, cover canner and bring water to a rolling boil. Process pint jars 15 minutes. Turn off heat and remove cover. Let jars cool 5 minutes. Remove jars from canner; do not retighten bands if loose. Cool 12 hours. Check seals. Label and store jars.

Note: When cutting or seeding hot peppers, wear rubber gloves to prevent hands from being burned.

 Serve this chutney right from the jar with soft or semi-soft cheese and crackers or apple slices. Consider serving it with Baby Swiss, Havarti, Jarlsberg, Boursin, or Colby.

Fruit Pickles

Fruit pickles deliver some of the most surprising flavors and amazing colors of all pickled foods. Whole or halved fruits work equally well for pickling. Fruit is simmered in spicy sweet-and-sour syrup until it's tender and transparent. Then the syrup is boiled to the thickness of honey.

Fig Pickles

Yield: about 8 pint or 4 quart jars

- 4 quarts firm ripe figs (about 30 medium)
- 5 cups sugar, divided
- 2 quarts water
- 3 cups vinegar, 5% acidity
- 2 sticks cinnamon
- 1 tablespoon whole allspice
- 1 tablespoon whole cloves

PREP Wash figs under cold running water; drain. Peel figs. Tie spices in a spice bag.

COOK Combine 3 cups sugar and water in a large saucepan. Bring mixture to a simmer (180°F), stirring until sugar dissolves. Add figs and cook 30 minutes. Add 2 cups sugar and vinegar, stirring until sugar dissolves. Add spice bag. Continue cooking figs until they are transparent. Remove from heat. Cover; let stand 12 to 24 hours in refrigerator. Bring figs to a simmer and cook until hot throughout. Remove spice bag.

FILL Pack figs and pickling liquid into a hot jar, leaving 1/2-inch headspace. Remove air bubbles. Clean jar rim. Center lid on jar and adjust band to fingertip-tight. Place jar on the rack elevated over simmering water (180°F) in boiling-water canner. Repeat until all jars are filled.

PROCESS Lower the rack into simmering water. Water must cover jars by 1 inch. Adjust heat to medium-high, cover canner and bring water to a rolling boil. Process pint or quart jars 15 minutes. Turn off heat and remove cover. Let jars cool 5 minutes. Remove jars from canner; do not retighten bands if loose. Cool 12 hours. Check seals. Label and store jars.

 Balance sweet or savory with pickled figs. These figs pair well with rich triple cream cheeses, grilled or roasted meats, panna cotta, or vanilla ice cream; sprinkle with a pinch of sea salt.

Peach Pickles

Yield: about 3 quart jars

- 8 pounds small peaches (about 40 to 48 small)
- Ball Fruit-Fresh Produce Protector
- 4 sticks cinnamon
- 2 tablespoons whole cloves
- 1 tablespoon grated fresh ginger
- 6 cups sugar
- 1 quart vinegar, 5% acidity

PREP Wash peaches under cold running water; drain. To peel peaches, blanch 30 to 60 seconds in boiling water. Immediately transfer to cold water. Cut off peel. Treat with Fruit-Fresh to prevent darkening (see page 16). Tie spices in a spice bag.

COOK Combine spice bag, sugar, and vinegar in a large saucepan. Bring mixture to a boil over medium-high heat; boil 5 minutes. Reduce heat to medium. Drain peaches. Gently boil peaches in syrup until they give slightly when pierced with a fork. Remove from heat. Cover; let stand 12 to 24 hours in refrigerator. Bring peaches to a simmer and cook until hot throughout. Remove spice bag.

FILL Pack peaches into a hot jar, leaving 1/2-inch headspace. Ladle syrup over peaches, leaving 1/2-inch headspace. Remove air bubbles. Clean jar rim. Center lid on jar and adjust band to fingertip-tight. Place jar on the rack elevated over simmering water (180°F) in boiling-water canner. Repeat until all jars are filled.

PROCESS Lower the rack into simmering water. Water must cover jars by 1 inch. Adjust heat to medium-high, cover canner and bring water to a rolling boil. Process quart jars 20 minutes. Turn off heat and remove cover. Let jars cool 5 minutes. Remove jars from canner; do not retighten bands if loose. Cool 12 hours. Check seals. Label and store jars.

Pear Pickles

Yield: about 8 pint or 4 quart jars

- 8 pounds Seckel pears (about 40 to 48 small)
- Ball Fruit-Fresh Produce Protector
- 1 tablespoon Ball Mixed Pickling Spice
- 1 teaspoon whole cloves
- 1 1/4 x 1 inch piece fresh ginger
- 4 cups sugar
- 1/2 cup thinly sliced lemon (about 1/2 medium)
- 2 1/2 cups water
- 2 1/2 cups vinegar, 5% acidity

PREP Wash pears under cold running water; drain. Peel pears, leaving whole with stem intact. Treat with Fruit-Fresh to prevent darkening (see page 16). Tie spices in a spice bag.

COOK Combine spice bag, sugar, lemon, water, and vinegar in a large saucepan. Bring mixture to a simmer (180°F), stirring until sugar dissolves. Simmer 5 minutes. Add pears, one layer at a time, and simmer until they give slightly when pierced with a fork. Transfer pears to a bowl. Repeat until all pears are cooked. Return pears to saucepan. Cover; let stand 12 to 18 hours in refrigerator. Bring pears to a simmer (180°F); simmer until pears are hot throughout. Remove pears; set aside. Bring pickling liquid to a boil. Remove spice bag.

FILL Pack pears into a hot jar, leaving 1/2-inch headspace. Ladle hot pickling liquid over pears, leaving 1/2-inch headspace. Remove air bubbles. Clean jar rim. Center lid on jar and adjust band to fingertip-tight. Place jar on the rack elevated over simmering water (180°F) in boiling-water canner. Repeat until all jars are filled.

PROCESS Lower the rack into simmering water. Water must cover jars by 1 inch. Adjust heat to medium-high, cover canner and bring water to a rolling boil. Process pint or quart jars 20 minutes. Turn off heat and remove cover. Let jars cool 5 minutes. Remove jars from canner; do not retighten bands if loose. Cool 12 hours. Check seals. Label and store jars.

Note: Other small firm ripe pears may be used. If Kieffer or Sand pears are used, they should be cored, covered with hot water, simmered 10 to 15 minutes, and drained before adding to pickling liquid.

 Delicate and delicious, Pear Pickles add interest to a light dinner salad. Fill your salad plate with mixed spring greens; add thinly sliced cold roast beef, thin slices of red onion, and two or three pickled pears. Whisk together 2 tablespoons oil and 3 tablespoons pickled pear juice; drizzle over salad. Garnish with coarsely chopped walnuts.

Spicy Melon Pickles

Yield: about 7 half-pint jars

- 3 quarts plus 1 cup 1-inch cube or ball cantaloupe (about 7 to 8 pounds)
- 3 cups vinegar, 5% acidity
- 2 cups water
- 2 sticks cinnamon
- 2 teaspoons whole cloves
- 1 teaspoon whole allspice
- 1 teaspoon slivered, whole nutmeg
- 4 1/2 cups sugar

PREP Wash cantaloupe under cold running water; drain. Cut cantaloupe in half and remove seeds. Using a 1-inch melon ball tool, scoop out melon balls. Or, cut each half into 1-inch sections. Peel cantaloupe sections. Cut into 1-inch cubes. Measure 3 quarts plus 1 cup melon balls. Tie spices in a spice bag.

COOK Combine spice bag, vinegar, and water in a large saucepan. Bring mixture to a boil. Reduce heat to a simmer (180°F); simmer 5 minutes. Remove from heat. Add cantaloupe and let stand 1 1/2 to 2 hours. Add sugar. Bring mixture to a boil, stirring until sugar dissolves. Reduce heat to a simmer. Simmer cantaloupe until it becomes slightly transparent.

FILL Pack hot melon balls into a hot jar, leaving 1/2-inch headspace. Ladle hot pickling liquid over melon balls, leaving 1/2-inch headspace. Remove air bubbles. Clean jar rim. Center lid on jar and adjust band to fingertip-tight. Place jar on the rack elevated over simmering water (180°F) in boiling-water canner. Repeat until all jars are filled.

PROCESS Lower the rack into simmering water. Water must cover jars by 1 inch. Adjust heat to medium-high, cover canner and bring water to a rolling boil. Process half-pint jars 10 minutes. Turn off heat and remove cover. Let jars cool 5 minutes. Remove jars from canner; do not retighten bands if loose. Cool 12 hours. Check seals. Label and store jars.

Watermelon Rind Pickles

Yield: about 6 pint jars

- 4 quarts 1-inch cubed watermelon rind (about 8 pounds)
- 1 cup Ball Salt for Pickling & Preserving
- 8 quarts water, divided
- 3 sticks cinnamon
- 1 tablespoon whole cloves
- 1 tablespoon whole allspice
- 1/4 teaspoon mustard seed
- 7 cups sugar
- 1/2 cup thinly sliced lemon (about 1 medium)
- 2 cups vinegar, 5% acidity

PREP Wash watermelon under cold running water; drain. Cut watermelon into quarters. Cut each section into 1-inch slices. Remove dark green peel from watermelon but do not cut away white rind; discard peel. Cut off pink flesh and use for another purpose. Cut white watermelon rind into 1-inch cubes. Put 4 quarts water in a large saucepan. Add salt, stirring until salt dissolves. Add cubed watermelon rind. Let stand in the refrigerator 12 hours or overnight. Drain and rinse watermelon rind under cold running water. Tie spices in a spice bag.

COOK Combine watermelon rind and 1 gallon water in a large saucepan. Cook over medium-high heat until rind is tender. Drain and set aside. Combine spice bag, sugar, lemon slices, and vinegar in a large saucepan. Bring mixture to a boil. Reduce heat to a simmer; simmer 10 minutes. Add watermelon rind. Simmer watermelon rind until it is transparent. Remove spice bag.

FILL Pack hot watermelon rind into a hot jar, leaving 1/2-inch headspace. Ladle hot pickling liquid over watermelon rind, leaving 1/2-inch headspace. Remove air bubbles. Clean jar rim. Center lid on jar and adjust band to fingertip-tight. Place jar on the rack elevated over simmering water (180°F) in boiling-water canner. Repeat until all jars are filled.

PROCESS Lower the rack into simmering water. Water must cover jars by 1 inch. Adjust heat to medium-high, cover canner and bring water to a rolling boil. Process pint jars 10 minutes. Turn off heat and remove cover. Let jars cool 5 minutes. Remove jars from canner; do not retighten bands if loose. Cool 12 hours. Check seals. Label and store jars.

Relishes

Relish is prepared using chopped vegetables and/or fruits cooked in a spicy vinegar pickling liquid. The addition of sugar for sweetness, hot peppers for heat, and whole or ground spices for flavor offers endless flavor combinations. Relish is a favorite atop a sandwich, mixed with mayo for spreading or dipping, and served alongside a choice fillet of beef, pork, or salmon.

Artichoke Relish

Yield: about 10 half-pint jars

- 2 pounds Jerusalem artichokes
- 1 cup plus 1/4 teaspoon Ball Salt for Pickling & Preserving, divided
- 4 quarts water, divided
- 2 cups ground red or green bell peppers (about 2 large)
- 2 cups ground onions (about 2 large)
- 3 1/3 cups sugar
- 1 quart vinegar, 5% acidity
- 2 tablespoons mustard seed
- 1 tablespoon turmeric
- Ball Pickle Crisp (optional)

PREP Wash Jerusalem artichokes under cold running water; drain. Trim artichokes as needed. Combine water and 1 cup salt in a large saucepan, stirring until salt dissolves. Add artichokes. Cover; let stand overnight in refrigerator. Drain, rinse, and dry artichokes. Coarsely grind artichokes using a food processor or food grinder. Use total amount of ground artichokes. Remove stems and seeds from red or green bell peppers. Coarsely grind bell peppers; measure 2 cups ground bell peppers. Peel onions. Coarsely grind onions; measure 2 cups ground onions.

COOK Combine sugar and vinegar in a large saucepan. Bring mixture to a boil, stirring until sugar dissolves. Reduce heat to a simmer (180°F). Add ground Jerusalem artichokes, ground bell peppers, ground onions, 1/4 teaspoon salt, and spices. Simmer relish 10 minutes, stirring to prevent sticking. Bring mixture to a boil.

FILL Pack hot relish into a hot jar, leaving 1/2-inch headspace. Add 1/16 teaspoon Pickle Crisp to half-pint jar, if desired. Remove air bubbles. Clean jar rim. Center lid on jar and adjust band to fingertip-tight. Place jar on the rack elevated over simmering water (180°F) in boiling-water canner. Repeat until all jars are filled.

PROCESS Lower the rack into simmering water. Water must cover jars by 1 inch. Adjust heat to medium-high, cover canner and bring water to a rolling boil. Process half-pint jars 10 minutes. Turn off heat and remove cover. Let jars cool 5 minutes. Remove jars from canner; do not retighten bands if loose. Cool 12 hours. Check seals. Label and store jars.

Beet or Red Relish

Yield: about 10 half-pint jars

1 quart chopped cooked beets (about 12 medium)	1 tablespoon prepared horseradish
1 quart chopped cabbage (about 1 small head)	1 tablespoon Ball Salt for Pickling & Preserving
1½ cups sugar	3 cups vinegar, 5% acidity
1 cup chopped onion (about 1 large)	Ball Pickle Crisp (optional)
1 cup chopped red bell pepper (about 1 large)	

PREP Wash beets, cabbage, and red bell pepper under cold running water; drain. Trim stem and tap root on beets to about 2 inches in length. Boil trimmed, unpeeled beets in water to cover until they give slightly when pierced with a fork. Allow beets to cool. Remove stems and tap roots from beets; peel beets. Chop beets; measure 1 quart chopped beets. Cut cabbage in half and remove core. Slice cabbage into 1-inch wedges. Coarsely chop cabbage wedges. Measure 1 quart chopped cabbage. Peel onion and chop. Measure 1 cup chopped onion. Remove stem and seeds from red bell pepper. Chop pepper; measure 1 cup chopped bell pepper.

COOK Combine all ingredients, except Pickle Crisp, in a large saucepan. Bring mixture to a simmer (180°F); simmer 10 minutes, stirring to prevent sticking. Bring mixture to a boil.

FILL Pack hot relish into a hot jar, leaving ½-inch headspace. Add ¹/₁₆ teaspoon Pickle Crisp to half-pint jar, if desired. Remove air bubbles. Clean jar rim. Center lid on jar and adjust band to fingertip-tight. Place jar on the rack elevated over simmering water (180°F) in boiling-water canner. Repeat until all jars are filled.

PROCESS Lower the rack into simmering water. Water must cover jars by 1 inch. Adjust heat to medium-high, cover canner and bring water to a rolling boil. Process half-pint jars 15 minutes. Turn off heat and remove cover. Let jars cool 5 minutes. Remove jars from canner; do not retighten bands if loose. Cool 12 hours. Check seals. Label and store jars.

Chow-Chow Relish

Yield: about 4 pint jars

1 quart chopped cabbage (about 1 small head)	3 tablespoons Ball Salt for Pickling & Preserving
3 cups cauliflowerets (about 1 medium head)	1½ cups sugar
2 cups chopped green tomatoes (about 4 medium)	2 teaspoons celery seed
	2 teaspoons dry mustard
2 cups chopped onions (about 2 medium)	1 teaspoon mustard seed
	1 teaspoon turmeric
2 cups chopped green bell peppers (about 2 large)	½ teaspoon ginger
	2½ cups vinegar, 5% acidity
1 cup chopped red bell pepper (about 1 large)	Ball Pickle Crisp (optional)

PREP Wash cabbage, cauliflower, green tomatoes, green bell peppers, and red bell pepper under cold running water; drain. Cut cabbage in half and remove core. Slice cabbage into 1-inch wedges. Coarsely chop cabbage wedges; measure 1 quart chopped cabbage. Cut cauliflower into individual flowerets; measure 3 cups cauliflowerets. Core and chop green tomatoes; measure 2 cups chopped green tomatoes. Peel onion and chop; measure 2 cups chopped onion. Remove stems and seeds from green and red bell peppers. Chop green bell peppers; measure 2 cups chopped green bell peppers. Chop red bell pepper; measure 1 cup chopped red bell pepper. Combine chopped vegetables in a large bowl. Sprinkle salt evenly over vegetables. Cover; let stand 4 to 6 hours in refrigerator. Drain vegetables. Rinse under cold running water; drain.

COOK Combine sugar, spices, and vinegar in a large saucepan. Bring mixture to a simmer (180°F); simmer 10 minutes, stirring until sugar dissolves. Add vegetables and simmer 10 minutes, stirring to prevent sticking. Bring mixture to a boil.

FILL Pack hot relish into a hot jar, leaving ½-inch headspace. Add ¹/₈ teaspoon Pickle Crisp to pint jar, if desired. Remove air bubbles. Clean jar rim. Center lid on jar and adjust band to fingertip-tight. Place jar on the rack elevated over simmering water (180°F) in boiling-water canner. Repeat until all jars are filled.

PROCESS Lower the rack into simmering water. Water must cover jars by 1 inch. Adjust heat to medium-high, cover canner and bring water to a rolling boil. Process pint jars 10 minutes. Turn off heat and remove cover. Let jars cool 5 minutes. Remove jars from canner; do not retighten bands if loose. Cool 12 hours. Check seals. Label and store jars.

Corn Relish

Yield: about 6 pint jars

2 quarts cut cooked corn (about 18 ears)	1 to 2 cups sugar
	2 tablespoons dry mustard
1 quart chopped cabbage (about 1 small head)	1 tablespoon celery seed
	1 tablespoon mustard seed
1 cup chopped onion (about 1 medium)	1 tablespoon Ball Salt for Pickling & Preserving
1 cup chopped green bell pepper (about 1 large)	1 tablespoon turmeric
	1 quart vinegar, 5% acidity
1 cup chopped red bell pepper (about 1 large)	1 cup water
	Ball Pickle Crisp (optional)

PREP Wash corn, cabbage, and green and red bell peppers under cold running water; drain. Boil ears of corn in water until fork-tender; drain. Allow corn to cool until easy to handle. Holding corn cob vertically with the stem end on a cutting board or in a bowl, cut corn kernels off the cob, starting at the small end and moving downward to the stem end. Measure 2 quarts cooked corn kernels. Cut cabbage in half and remove core. Slice cabbage into 1-inch wedges. Coarsely chop cabbage wedges. Measure 1 quart chopped cabbage. Peel onion and chop; measure 1 cup chopped onion. Remove stems and seeds from green and red bell peppers. Chop green bell pepper; measure 1 cup chopped green bell pepper. Chop red bell pepper; measure 1 cup chopped red bell pepper.

COOK Combine all ingredients, except Pickle Crisp, in a large saucepan. Bring mixture to a simmer (180°F), stirring until sugar dissolves. Simmer 20 minutes, stirring to prevent sticking.

FILL Pack hot relish into a hot jar, leaving ½-inch headspace. Add ¹/₈ teaspoon Pickle Crisp to pint jar, if desired. Remove air bubbles. Clean jar rim. Center lid on jar and adjust band to fingertip-tight. Place jar on the rack elevated over simmering water (180°F) in boiling-water canner. Repeat until all jars are filled.

PROCESS Lower the rack into simmering water. Water must cover jars by 1 inch. Adjust heat to medium-high, cover canner and bring water to a rolling boil. Process pint jars 15 minutes. Turn off heat and remove cover. Let jars cool 5 minutes. Remove jars from canner; do not retighten bands if loose. Cool 12 hours. Check seals. Label and store jars.

 To make corn relish without cabbage, substitute 1 cup chopped celery and 1 clove minced garlic for 1 quart chopped cabbage. Follow directions in recipe for cooking and processing.

Cucumber Relish

Yield: about 6 pint jars

2 quarts chopped cucumbers (about 8 medium)	1/2 cup Ball Salt for Pickling & Preserving
2 cups chopped green bell peppers (about 2 large)	4 quarts water, divided
	1 1/2 cups brown sugar
2 cups chopped red bell peppers (about 2 large)	1 quart vinegar, 5% acidity
	2 sticks cinnamon
1 cup chopped onion (about 1 medium)	1 tablespoon mustard seed
	2 teaspoons whole allspice
1 tablespoon turmeric	2 teaspoons whole cloves
	Ball Pickle Crisp (optional)

PREP Wash cucumbers and green and red bell peppers under cold running water; drain. Remove stem and blossom ends from cucumbers. Coarsely chop cucumbers; measure 2 quarts chopped cucumbers. Remove stems and seeds from green and red bell peppers. Chop green bell peppers; measure 2 cups chopped green bell peppers. Chop red bell peppers; measure 2 cups chopped red bell peppers. Peel onion and chop; measure 1 cup chopped onion. Combine cucumbers, peppers, and onions in a large bowl. Sprinkle turmeric over vegetables. Combine 2 quarts of cold water and salt, stirring until salt dissolves. Pour salted water over vegetables. Cover; let stand 3 to 4 hours in refrigerator; drain. Pour 2 quarts water over vegetables. Cover; let stand 1 hour in refrigerator; drain. Tie whole spices in a spice bag.

COOK Combine spice bag, sugar, and vinegar in a large saucepan. Bring to a boil, stirring until sugar dissolves. Ladle hot pickling liquid over vegetables. Cover and let stand in refrigerator 12 to 18 hours. Bring mixture to a boil. Reduce heat to a simmer (180°F); simmer mixture until hot throughout, stirring to prevent sticking.

FILL Pack hot relish into a hot jar, leaving 1/2-inch headspace. Add 1/8 teaspoon Pickle Crisp to pint jar, if desired. Remove air bubbles. Clean jar rim. Center lid on jar and adjust band to fingertip-tight. Place jar on the rack elevated over simmering water (180°F) in boiling-water canner. Repeat until all jars are filled.

PROCESS Lower the rack into simmering water. Water must cover jars by 1 inch. Adjust heat to medium-high, cover canner and bring water to a rolling boil. Process pint jars 10 minutes. Turn off heat and remove cover. Let jars cool 5 minutes. Remove jars from canner; do not retighten bands if loose. Cool 12 hours. Check seals. Label and store jars.

 Blend Cucumber Relish with sour cream and serve with warm pita bread and lamb. Or, thin mixture with relish juice for a creamy cucumber salad dressing.

Dill Relish

Yield: about 7 pint jars

8 pounds pickling cucumbers	1/3 cup sugar
1/2 cup Ball Salt for Pickling & Preserving	2 tablespoons dill seed
	1 quart white wine vinegar
2 teaspoons turmeric	Ball Pickle Crisp (optional)
1 quart water	
1 pound yellow onions (about 3 medium)	

PREP Wash cucumbers under cold running water; drain. Remove stem and 1/16 inch from blossom ends of cucumbers. Finely chop cucumbers using a food processor or food grinder. Put chopped cucumbers in a bowl and sprinkle with salt and turmeric. Pour cold water over cucumbers just to cover. Cover; let stand 2 hours. Peel onion and finely chop. Drain cucumbers. Rinse chopped cucumbers under cold running water; drain.

COOK Combine cucumbers, onions, sugar, dill seed, and white wine vinegar in a large saucepan. Bring mixture to a boil, stirring until sugar dissolves. Reduce heat to a simmer (180°F); simmer 10 minutes.

FILL Ladle hot relish into a hot jar, leaving 1/2-inch headspace. Add 1/8 teaspoon Pickle Crisp to pint jar, if desired. Remove air bubbles. Clean jar rim. Center lid on jar and adjust band to fingertip-tight. Place jar on the rack elevated over simmering water (180°F) in boiling-water canner. Repeat until all jars are filled.

PROCESS Lower the rack into simmering water. Water must cover jars by 1 inch. Adjust heat to medium-high, cover canner and bring water to a rolling boil. Process pint jars 15 minutes. Turn off heat and remove cover. Let jars cool 5 minutes. Remove jars from canner; do not retighten bands if loose. Cool 12 hours. Check seals. Label and store jars.

Dixie Relish

Yield: about 7 pint jars

1 quart chopped cabbage (about 1 small head)	1/2 cup Ball Salt for Pickling & Preserving
2 cups chopped green bell peppers (about 2 large)	2 quarts cold water
	3/4 cup sugar
2 cups chopped red bell peppers (about 2 large)	3 tablespoons mustard seed
	2 tablespoons celery seed
2 cups chopped onions (about 2 medium)	1 quart vinegar, 5% acidity
	Ball Pickle Crisp (optional)

PREP Wash cabbage and green and red bell peppers under cold running water; drain. Cut cabbage in half and remove core. Slice cabbage into 1-inch wedges. Coarsely chop cabbage wedges. Measure 1 quart chopped cabbage. Remove stems and seeds from green and red bell peppers. Chop green and red bell peppers; measure 2 cups chopped green bell peppers and 2 cups chopped red bell peppers. Peel onion and chop; measure 2 cups chopped onion. Mix vegetables together in a large bowl. Combine salt and water, stirring until salt dissolves. Pour salted water over vegetables. Cover; let stand 1 hour; drain. If vegetables are too salty, rinse under cold running water; drain.

COOK Combine vegetables, sugar, spices, and vinegar in a large saucepan. Bring mixture to a simmer (180°F); simmer 20 minutes. Bring mixture to a boil.

FILL Ladle hot relish into a hot jar, leaving 1/2-inch headspace. Add 1/8 teaspoon Pickle Crisp to pint jar, if desired. Remove air bubbles. Clean jar rim. Center lid on jar and adjust band to fingertip-tight. Place jar on the rack elevated over simmering water (180°F) in boiling-water canner. Repeat until all jars are filled.

PROCESS Lower the rack into simmering water. Water must cover jars by 1 inch. Adjust heat to medium-high, cover canner and bring water to a rolling boil. Process pint jars 15 minutes. Turn off heat and remove cover. Let jars cool 5 minutes. Remove jars from canner; do not retighten bands if loose. Cool 12 hours. Check seals. Label and store jars.

Mango Relish Reduced Salt, Reduced Sugar

Yield: about 4 pint jars

- 4 cups 1/2-inch cubed, underripe mango (about 4 medium)
- 3 cups 1/2-inch cubed, underripe papaya (about 1 large)
- 2 cups green seedless grapes
- 1/4 cup sliced green onions
- 3 tablespoons minced crystallized ginger
- 2 teaspoons coriander seed, toasted
- 1 teaspoon mixed peppercorns
- 1 cup white grape juice
- 1 cup white wine vinegar
- Ball Pickle Crisp (optional)

PREP Wash mango, papaya, green grapes, and green onions under cold running water; drain. Peel mango. Cut mango in half and remove seeds. Cut mango into 1/2-inch cubes; measure 4 cups cubed mango. Peel papaya. Cut papaya in half and remove seeds. Cut papaya into 1/2-inch cubes; measure 3 cups cubed papaya. Measure 2 cups green grapes. Cut off dark green leaves and root ends from onions. Peel onions. Slice onions; measure 1/4 cup sliced onions.

COOK Combine all ingredients, except Pickle Crisp, in a large saucepan. Bring mixture to a boil. Reduce heat to a simmer (180°F); simmer 10 minutes.

FILL Ladle hot relish into a hot jar, leaving 1/2-inch headspace. Add 1/8 teaspoon Pickle Crisp to pint jar, if desired. Remove air bubbles. Clean jar rim. Center lid on jar and adjust band to fingertip-tight. Place jar on the rack elevated over simmering water (180°F) in boiling-water canner. Repeat until all jars are filled.

PROCESS Lower the rack into simmering water. Water must cover jars by 1 inch. Adjust heat to medium-high, cover canner and bring water to a rolling boil. Process pint jars 15 minutes. Turn off heat and remove cover. Let jars cool 5 minutes. Remove jars from canner; do not retighten bands if loose. Cool 12 hours. Check seals. Label and store jars.

Pepper-Onion Relish

Yield: about 6 pint jars

- 2 quarts chopped green bell peppers (about 8 large)
- 2 quarts chopped red bell peppers (about 8 large)
- 1 1/2 cups chopped onions (about 1 1/2 medium)
- 2 hot red peppers
- 4 teaspoons Ball Mixed Pickling Spice
- 1 1/2 cups sugar
- 4 teaspoons Ball Salt for Pickling & Preserving
- 3 1/2 cups vinegar, 5% acidity
- Ball Pickle Crisp (optional)

PREP Wash green bell peppers, red bell peppers, and hot red peppers under cold running water; drain. Remove stems and seeds from green bell peppers and red bell peppers. Chop green and red bell peppers; measure 2 quarts chopped green bell peppers and 2 quarts chopped red bell peppers. Peel onion and chop; measure 1 1/2 cups chopped onions. Remove stems and seeds from hot red peppers. Finely chop hot red peppers. Combine vegetables in a large bowl. Pour boiling water over vegetables just to cover. Let stand 5 minutes; drain. Repeat step, letting mixture stand 10 minutes. Drain vegetables. Tie spices in a spice bag.

COOK Combine spice bag, sugar, salt, and vinegar in a large saucepan. Bring mixture to a simmer (180°F); simmer 15 minutes. Add drained vegetables; simmer 10 minutes. Remove spice bag and discard. Bring mixture to a boil.

FILL Ladle hot relish into a hot pint jar, leaving 1/2-inch headspace. Add 1/8 teaspoon Pickle Crisp to pint jar, if desired. Remove air bubbles. Clean jar rim. Center lid on jar and adjust band to fingertip-tight. Place jar on the rack elevated over simmering water (180°F) in boiling-water canner. Repeat until all jars are filled.

PROCESS Lower the rack into simmering water. Water must cover jars by 1 inch. Adjust heat to medium-high, cover canner and bring water to a rolling boil. Process pint jars 15 minutes. Turn off heat and remove cover. Let jars cool 5 minutes. Remove jars from canner; do not retighten bands if loose. Cool 12 hours. Check seals. Label and store jars.

Note: When cutting or seeding hot peppers, wear rubber gloves to prevent hands from being burned.

Piccalilli or Green Tomato Relish

Yield: about 7 pint jars

- 4 quarts chopped green tomatoes (about 32 medium)
- 2 quarts chopped cabbage (about 1 large head)
- 2 cups chopped green bell peppers (about 2 large)
- 1 cup chopped onion (about 1 medium)
- 1/2 cup Ball Salt for Pickling & Preserving
- 1 1/2 cups brown sugar
- 2 tablespoons mustard seed
- 1 tablespoon celery seed
- 1 tablespoon prepared horseradish
- 1 quart plus 1/2 cup vinegar, 5% acidity
- Ball Pickle Crisp (optional)

PREP Wash green tomatoes, cabbage, and green bell peppers under cold running water; drain. Core and chop green tomatoes. Measure 4 quarts chopped green tomatoes. Cut cabbage in half and remove core. Slice cabbage into 1-inch wedges. Coarsely chop cabbage wedges; measure 2 quarts chopped cabbage. Remove stems and seeds from green bell peppers. Chop green bell peppers; measure 2 cups chopped green bell peppers. Peel onion and chop; measure 1 cup chopped onion. Combine vegetables in a large bowl. Sprinkle salt over vegetables and mix thoroughly. Cover; let stand 3 to 4 hours in refrigerator. Drain vegetables. Rinse vegetables under cold running water; drain.

COOK Combine sugar, spices, horseradish, and vinegar in a large saucepan. Bring mixture to a simmer (180°F); simmer 15 minutes. Add drained vegetables; simmer 10 minutes. Bring mixture to a boil.

FILL Ladle hot relish into a hot jar, leaving 1/2-inch headspace. Add 1/8 teaspoon Pickle Crisp to pint jar, if desired. Remove air bubbles. Clean jar rim. Center lid on jar and adjust band to fingertip-tight.

Place jar on the rack elevated over simmering water (180°F) in boiling-water canner. Repeat until all jars are filled.

PROCESS Lower the rack into simmering water. Water must cover jars by 1 inch. Adjust heat to medium-high, cover canner and bring water to a rolling boil. Process pint jars 10 minutes. Turn off heat and remove cover. Let jars cool 5 minutes. Remove jars from canner; do not retighten bands if loose. Cool 12 hours. Check seals. Label and store jars.

Sweet Pickle Relish

Yield: about 8 half-pint jars

- 1 quart chopped cucumbers (about 4 medium)
- 2 cups chopped onions (about 2 medium)
- 1 cup chopped green bell pepper (about 1 large)
- 1 cup chopped red bell pepper (about 1 large)
- 1/4 cup Ball Salt for Pickling & Preserving
- 3 1/2 cups sugar
- 1 tablespoon celery seed
- 1 tablespoon mustard seed
- 2 cups cider vinegar, 5% acidity
- Ball Pickle Crisp (optional)

PREP Wash cucumbers and green and red bell peppers under cold running water; drain. Remove stems and 1/16 inch of blossom ends from cucumbers. Peel onions and chop; measure 2 cups chopped onions. Remove stems and seeds from green and red bell peppers. Chop green bell pepper; measure 1 cup chopped green bell pepper. Chop red bell pepper; measure 1 cup chopped red bell pepper. Combine cucumbers, onions, and green and red peppers in a large bowl. Sprinkle salt over vegetables. Pour cold water over vegetables just to cover. Let stand 2 hours. Drain vegetables. Rinse vegetables under cold running water; drain.

COOK Combine sugar, spices, and vinegar in a large saucepan. Bring mixture to a simmer (180°F); add vegetables and simmer 10 minutes.

FILL Pack hot relish into a hot jar, leaving 1/2-inch headspace. Add 1/16 teaspoon Pickle Crisp to half-pint jar, if desired. Remove air bubbles. Clean jar rim. Center lid on jar and adjust band to fingertip-tight. Place jar on the rack elevated over simmering water (180°F) in boiling-water canner. Repeat until all jars are filled.

PROCESS Lower the rack into simmering water. Water must cover jars by 1 inch. Adjust heat to medium-high, cover canner and bring water to a rolling boil. Process half-pint jars 10 minutes. Turn off heat and remove cover. Let jars cool 5 minutes. Remove jars from canner; do not retighten bands if loose. Cool 12 hours. Check seals. Label and store jars.

Zucchini Relish

Yield: about 4 half-pint jars

- 2 cups chopped zucchini (about 3 medium)
- 1 cup chopped onion (about 1 medium)
- 1/2 cup chopped green bell pepper (about 1 small)
- 1/2 cup chopped red bell pepper (about 1 small)
- 2 tablespoons Ball Salt for Pickling & Preserving
- 1 3/4 cups sugar
- 2 teaspoons celery seed
- 1 teaspoon mustard seed
- 1 cup cider vinegar, 5% acidity
- Ball Pickle Crisp (optional)

PREP Wash zucchini and green and red bell peppers under cold running water; drain. Remove stems and blossom ends from zucchini. Chop zucchini; measure 2 cups chopped zucchini. Peel onion and chop; measure 1 cup chopped onion. Remove stems and seeds from green and red bell peppers. Chop green bell pepper; measure 1/2 cup chopped green bell pepper. Chop red bell pepper; measure 1/2 cup chopped red bell pepper. Combine zucchini, onion, green pepper, and red bell pepper in a large bowl. Sprinkle salt over vegetables. Pour cold water over vegetables just to cover. Let stand 2 hours. Drain vegetables. Rinse vegetables under cold running water; drain.

COOK Combine sugar, spices, and vinegar in a large saucepan. Bring mixture to a simmer (180°F). Add vegetables; simmer 10 minutes.

FILL Pack hot relish into a hot jar, leaving 1/2-inch headspace. Add 1/16 teaspoon Pickle Crisp to half-pint jar, if desired. Remove air bubbles. Clean jar rim. Center lid on jar and adjust band to fingertip-tight. Place jar on the rack elevated over simmering water (180°F) in boiling-water canner. Repeat until all jars are filled.

PROCESS Lower the rack into simmering water. Water must cover jars by 1 inch. Adjust heat to medium-high, cover canner and bring water to a rolling boil. Process half-pint jars 10 minutes. Turn off heat and remove cover. Let jars cool 5 minutes. Remove jars from canner; do not retighten bands if loose. Cool 12 hours. Check seals. Label and store jars.

Sauces

Many of the same ingredients found in chutney recipes are found in sauce recipes. Main ingredients are typically cooked until soft, then puréed. The purée is combined with vinegar, sugar, and spices for a long, slow cook. Sauces are cooked slowly to evaporate moisture and reduce volume to achieve a thick, smooth consistency. Sauces can be used to glaze meats, as an ingredient in soups and stews, or simply for dipping.

Barbecue Sauce

Yield: about 8 half-pint or 4 pint jars

- 4 quarts chopped tomatoes (about 24 large)
- 2 cups chopped celery (about 3 stalks)
- 2 cups chopped onions (about 2 medium)
- 1 1/2 cups chopped green bell or red bell peppers (about 2 medium)
- 2 hot red peppers
- 1 teaspoon peppercorns
- 1 cup brown sugar
- 2 cloves garlic
- 1 tablespoon dry mustard
- 1 tablespoon paprika
- 1 tablespoon Ball Salt for Pickling & Preserving
- 1 teaspoon hot pepper sauce
- 1/8 teaspoon cayenne pepper
- 1 cup vinegar, 5% acidity

PREP Wash tomatoes, bell peppers, and hot red peppers under cold running water; drain. To peel tomatoes, blanch 30 to 60 seconds in boiling water. Immediately transfer to cold water. Cut off peel. Remove core and chop tomatoes; measure 4 quarts chopped tomatoes. Remove leafy tops and root ends from celery. Chop celery; measure 2 cups chopped celery. Peel and chop onion; measure 2 cups chopped onion. Remove stems and seeds from bell peppers. Chop bell peppers; measure 2 cups chopped bell peppers. Remove stem ends from hot red peppers. Finely chop hot red peppers. Peel garlic and mince. Tie peppercorns in a spice bag.

COOK Combine tomatoes, celery, onions, and peppers in a large saucepan. Bring mixture to a simmer (180°F); simmer 10 minutes. Purée vegetables using an electric food strainer or food mill. Simmer purée until reduced by one-half. Add spice bag and remaining ingredients to purée. Simmer until the purée is the consistency of ketchup, stirring to prevent sticking. Remove spice bag.

FILL Ladle hot sauce into a hot jar, leaving 1/2-inch headspace. Remove air bubbles. Clean jar rim. Center lid on jar and adjust band to fingertip-tight. Place jar on the rack elevated over simmering water (180°F) in boiling-water canner. Repeat until all jars are filled.

PROCESS Lower the rack into simmering water. Water must cover jars by 1 inch. Adjust heat to medium-high, cover canner and bring water to a rolling boil. Process half-pint or pint jars 20 minutes. Turn off heat and remove cover. Let jars cool 5 minutes. Remove jars from canner; do not retighten bands if loose. Cool 12 hours. Check seals. Label and store jars.

Note: When cutting or seeding hot peppers, wear rubber gloves to prevent hands from being burned.

Chili Sauce

Yield: about 6 pint jars

4 quarts chopped tomatoes (about 24 large)	3 tablespoons Ball Salt for Pickling & Preserving
2 cups chopped onions (about 2 medium)	3 tablespoons Ball Mixed Pickling Spice
2 cups chopped red bell peppers (about 2 large)	1 tablespoon celery seed
1 hot red pepper	1 tablespoon mustard seed
1 cup sugar	2 1/2 cups vinegar, 5% acidity

PREP Wash tomatoes, red bell peppers, and hot red pepper under cold running water; drain. To peel tomatoes, blanch 30 to 60 seconds in boiling water. Immediately transfer to cold water. Cut off peel. Remove core and chop tomatoes; measure 4 quarts chopped tomatoes. Peel and chop onion; measure 2 cups chopped onion. Remove stems and seeds from red bell peppers. Chop bell peppers; measure 1 1/2 cups chopped red bell peppers. Remove stem ends from hot red pepper. Finely chop hot red pepper. Tie spices in a spice bag.

COOK Combine tomatoes, onions, peppers, sugar, and salt in a large saucepan. Bring mixture to a simmer (180°F); simmer 45 minutes. Add spice bag. Simmer until sauce is reduced by one-half, stirring to prevent sticking. Add vinegar and simmer to desired thickness, stirring to prevent sticking. Remove spice bag.

FILL Ladle hot sauce into a hot jar, leaving 1/2-inch headspace. Remove air bubbles. Clean jar rim. Center lid on jar and adjust band to fingertip-tight. Place jar on the rack elevated over simmering water (180°F) in boiling-water canner. Repeat until all jars are filled.

PROCESS Lower the rack into simmering water. Water must cover jars by 1 inch. Adjust heat to medium-high, cover canner and bring water to a rolling boil. Process pint jars 15 minutes. Turn off heat and remove cover. Let jars cool 5 minutes. Remove jars from canner; do not retighten bands if loose. Cool 12 hours. Check seals. Label and store jars.

Note: When cutting or seeding hot peppers, wear rubber gloves to prevent hands from being burned.

Red Hot Sauce

Yield: about 4 half-pint jars

2 quarts chopped tomatoes (about 12 large)	1 cup sugar, divided
1 1/2 cups chopped hot red peppers (about 24)	2 tablespoons Ball Mixed Pickling Spice
1 quart vinegar, 5% acidity, divided	1 tablespoon Ball Salt for Pickling & Preserving

PREP Wash tomatoes and hot red peppers under cold running water; drain. To peel tomatoes, blanch 30 to 60 seconds in boiling water. Immediately transfer to cold water. Cut off peel. Remove core and chop tomatoes; measure 2 quarts chopped tomatoes. Remove stems from hot red peppers. Chop hot peppers; measure 1 1/2 cups chopped hot red peppers. Tie mixed pickling spice in a spice bag.

COOK Combine tomatoes, hot red peppers, and 2 cups vinegar in a large saucepan. Bring mixture to a simmer (180°F); simmer until tomatoes are soft. Purée mixture using an electric food strainer or food mill. Pour purée into a large saucepan. Add spice bag, sugar, and salt. Simmer until sauce is reduced by one-half, stirring to prevent sticking. Add 2 cups vinegar and simmer to desired thickness, stirring to prevent sticking. Remove spice bag and discard.

FILL Ladle hot sauce into a hot jar, leaving 1/2-inch headspace. Remove air bubbles. Clean jar rim. Center lid on jar and adjust band to fingertip-tight. Place jar on the rack elevated over simmering water (180°F) in boiling-water canner. Repeat until all jars are filled.

PROCESS Lower the rack into simmering water. Water must cover jars by 1 inch. Adjust heat to medium-high, cover canner and bring water to a rolling boil. Process half-pint jars 15 minutes. Turn off heat and remove cover. Let jars cool 5 minutes. Remove jars from canner; do not retighten bands if loose. Cool 12 hours. Check seals. Label and store jars.

Note: When cutting or seeding hot peppers, wear rubber gloves to prevent hands from being burned.

Taco Sauce

Yield: about 6 half-pint jars

3 cups tomato paste	1/2 teaspoon hot pepper sauce
2 tablespoons chili powder	1 quart plus 1 cup water
1 tablespoon Ball Salt for Pickling & Preserving	1 cup cider vinegar, 5% acidity
1 teaspoon cayenne pepper	1/2 cup corn syrup

PREP Assemble and measure ingredients.

COOK Combine tomato paste, spices, and hot pepper sauce in a large saucepan. Gradually add water, stirring until mixture is evenly blended. Stir in vinegar and corn syrup. Bring mixture to a boil. Reduce heat to a simmer (180°F); simmer until mixture thickens, stirring to prevent sticking.

FILL Ladle hot sauce into a hot jar, leaving 1/2-inch headspace. Remove air bubbles. Clean jar rim. Center lid on jar and adjust band to fingertip-tight. Place jar on the rack elevated over simmering water (180°F) in boiling-water canner. Repeat until all jars are filled.

PROCESS Lower the rack into simmering water. Water must cover jars by 1 inch. Adjust heat to medium-high, cover canner and bring water to a rolling boil. Process half-pint jars 30 minutes. Turn off heat and remove cover. Let jars cool 5 minutes. Remove jars from canner; do not retighten bands if loose. Cool 12 hours. Check seals. Label and store jars.

Tomato Ketchup

Yield: about 3 pint jars

4 quarts chopped peeled tomatoes (about 24 large)	1 teaspoon whole allspice
1 cup chopped onion (about 1 medium)	1 teaspoon mustard seed
½ cup chopped red bell pepper (about ½ medium)	1 stick cinnamon
	1 cup sugar
	1 tablespoon Ball Salt for Pickling & Preserving
1½ teaspoon celery seed	1 tablespoon paprika
	1½ cups vinegar, 5% acidity

PREP Wash tomatoes and red bell pepper under cold running water; drain. To peel tomatoes, blanch 30 to 60 seconds in boiling water. Immediately transfer to cold water. Cut off peel. Remove core and chop tomatoes; measure 4 quarts chopped tomatoes. Peel and chop onion; measure 1 cup chopped onion. Remove stem and seeds from red bell peppers. Chop red bell pepper; measure ½ cup chopped red bell pepper. Tie whole spices in a spice bag.

COOK Combine tomatoes, onion, and pepper in a large saucepan. Bring mixture to a boil. Reduce heat to a simmer (180°F); simmer until tomatoes are soft, stirring to prevent sticking. Purée mixture using an electric food strainer or food mill. Cook purée over medium-high heat until reduced by one-half. Add spice bag, sugar, salt, paprika, and vinegar to tomato purée. Cook, uncovered, until mixture thickens, stirring to prevent sticking. Remove spice bag.

FILL Ladle hot ketchup into a hot jar, leaving ½-inch headspace. Remove air bubbles. Clean jar rim. Center lid on jar and adjust band to fingertip-tight. Place jar on the rack elevated over simmering water (180°F) in boiling-water canner. Repeat until all jars are filled.

PROCESS Lower the rack into simmering water. Water must cover jars by 1 inch. Adjust heat to medium-high, cover canner and bring water to a rolling boil. Process pint jars 10 minutes. Turn off heat and remove cover. Let jars cool 5 minutes. Remove jars from canner; do not retighten bands if loose. Cool 12 hours. Check seals. Label and store jars.

Victoria or Rhubarb Sauce

Yield: about 4 pint jars

2 quarts chopped rhubarb (about 12 stalks)	½ cup vinegar, 5% acidity
1½ cups chopped raisins	1 teaspoon allspice
½ cup chopped onion (about ½ medium)	1 teaspoon cinnamon
	1 teaspoon ginger
3½ cups brown sugar	1 teaspoon Ball Salt for Pickling & Preserving

PREP Wash rhubarb under cold running water; drain. Remove leafy tops and root ends from rhubarb. Chop rhubarb into ¼-inch pieces; measure 2 quarts chopped rhubarb. Coarsely chop raisins in food processor or use a knife. Peel and chop onion; measure ½ cup onion.

COOK Combine rhubarb, raisins, onion, sugar, and vinegar in a large saucepan. Bring mixture to a boil. Reduce heat to a simmer (180°F); simmer until mixture is thick, stirring to prevent sticking. Add spices. Cook sauce 5 minutes, stirring to prevent sticking.

FILL Ladle hot sauce into a hot jar, leaving ½-inch headspace. Remove air bubbles. Clean jar rim. Center lid on jar and adjust band to fingertip-tight. Place jar on the rack elevated over simmering water (180°F) in boiling-water canner. Repeat until all jars are filled.

PROCESS Lower the rack into simmering water. Water must cover jars by 1 inch. Adjust heat to medium-high, cover canner and bring water to a rolling boil. Process pint jars 15 minutes. Turn off heat and remove cover. Let jars cool 5 minutes. Remove jars from canner; do not retighten bands if loose. Cool 12 hours. Check seals. Label and store jars.

Other Pickled VEGETABLES

Beet Pickles

Yield: about 6 pint or 3 quart jars

3 quarts beets (about 24 small)	1½ teaspoon Ball Salt for Pickling & Preserving
2 cups sugar	3½ cups vinegar, 5% acidity
2 sticks cinnamon	1½ cups water
1 tablespoon whole allspice	Ball Pickle Crisp (optional)

PREP Wash beets under cold running water; drain. Trim stem and tap root to 2 inches in length. Boil trimmed, unpeeled beets in water to cover until they give slightly when pierced with a fork. Drain beets and cool until easy to handle. Peel and chop beets. Measure 3 quarts chopped beets. Tie spices in a spice bag.

COOK Combine sugar, spice bag, salt, vinegar, and water in a large saucepan. Bring mixture to a boil. Reduce heat to a simmer (180°F); simmer 15 minutes. Remove spice bag.

FILL Pack beets into a hot jar, leaving ½-inch headspace. Add ⅛ teaspoon Pickle Crisp to pint jar or ¼ teaspoon Pickle Crisp to quart jar, if desired. Ladle hot pickling liquid over beets, leaving ½-inch headspace. Remove air bubbles. Clean jar rim. Center lid on jar and adjust band to fingertip-tight. Place jar on the rack elevated over simmering water (180°F) in boiling-water canner. Repeat until all jars are filled.

PROCESS Lower the rack into simmering water. Water must cover jars by 1 inch. Adjust heat to medium-high, cover canner and bring water to a rolling boil. Process pint or quart jars 30 minutes. Turn off heat and remove cover. Let jars cool 5 minutes. Remove jars from canner; do not retighten bands if loose. Cool 12 hours. Check seals. Label and store jars.

 If you prefer a savory approach, substitute 3 tablespoons mixed pickling spice for cinnamon sticks and whole allspice, or 2 tablespoons caraway seeds and 2 teaspoons whole black peppercorns in place of cinnamon sticks and whole allspice.

Dilled Green Tomatoes

Yield: about 6 pint jars

5 pounds small firm green tomatoes (about 25 to 30)	6 cloves garlic
	6 heads fresh dill or 1/4 cup dill seed
1/4 cup Ball Salt for Pickling & Preserving	6 bay leaves
3 1/2 cups vinegar, 5% acidity	Ball Pickle Crisp (optional)
3 1/2 cups water	

PREP Wash green tomatoes under cold running water; drain. Core green tomatoes; cut green tomatoes into halves or quarters.

COOK Combine salt, vinegar, and water in a large saucepan. Bring mixture to a boil. Reduce heat to a simmer (180°F); simmer 5 minutes.

FILL Pack green tomatoes into a hot jar, leaving 1/2-inch headspace. Add 1 clove garlic, 1 head of dill or 2 teaspoons dill seed, and 1 bay leaf to jar. Add 1/8 teaspoon Pickle Crisp to pint jar, if desired. Ladle hot pickling liquid over green tomatoes, leaving 1/2-inch headspace. Remove air bubbles. Clean jar rim. Center lid on jar and adjust band to fingertip-tight. Place jar on the rack elevated over simmering water (180°F) in boiling-water canner. Repeat until all jars are filled.

PROCESS Lower the rack into simmering water. Water must cover jars by 1 inch. Adjust heat to medium-high, cover canner and bring water to a rolling boil. Process pint jars 15 minutes. Turn off heat and remove cover. Let jars cool 5 minutes. Remove jars from canner; do not retighten bands if loose. Cool 12 hours. Check seals. Label and store jars.

Dilly Beans

Yield: about 4 pint or 2 quart jars

2 pounds green beans	4 cloves garlic
1/4 cup Ball Salt for Pickling & Preserving	4 heads fresh dill or 1/4 cup dill seed
2 1/2 cups vinegar, 5% acidity	Ball Pickle Crisp (optional)
2 1/2 cups water	
1 teaspoon cayenne pepper, divided	

PREP Wash green beans under cold running water; drain. Trim ends off green beans. Peel garlic.

COOK Combine salt, vinegar, and water in a large saucepan. Bring mixture to a boil. Reduce heat to a simmer (180°F); simmer 10 minutes.

FILL Pack green beans lengthwise into a hot jar, leaving 1/2-inch headspace. Add 1/4 teaspoon cayenne pepper, 1 clove garlic, and 1 head of dill or 2 teaspoons dill seed. Add 1/8 teaspoon Pickle Crisp to pint jar or 1/4 teaspoon Pickle Crisp to quart jar, if desired. Ladle hot pickling liquid over green beans, leaving 1/2-inch headspace. Remove air bubbles. Clean jar rim. Center lid on jar and adjust band to fingertip-tight. Place jar on the rack elevated over simmering water (180°F) in boiling-water canner. Repeat until all jars are filled.

PROCESS Lower the rack into simmering water. Water must cover jars by 1 inch. Adjust heat to medium-high, cover canner and bring water to a rolling boil. Process pint or quart jars 10 minutes. Turn off heat and remove cover. Let jars cool 5 minutes. Remove jars from canner; do not retighten bands if loose. Cool 12 hours. Check seals. Label and store jars.

Hot Peppers

Yield: about 5 pint jars

1 1/2 pounds banana peppers	2 cups water
1 pound jalapeño peppers	3 cloves garlic, crushed
1/4 pound Serrano peppers	Ball Pickle Crisp (optional)
1 quart plus 2 cups vinegar, 5% acidity	

PREP Wash banana, jalapeño, and Serrano peppers under cold running water; drain. Trim stems and blossom ends off peppers. Cut peppers into 1-inch pieces. Put peppers in a large bowl; mix to blend evenly.

COOK Combine vinegar, water, and garlic in a large saucepan. Bring mixture to a boil. Reduce heat to a simmer (180°F); simmer 5 minutes. Remove garlic and discard.

FILL Pack hot peppers into a hot jar, leaving 1/2-inch headspace. Add 1/8 teaspoon Pickle Crisp to pint jar, if desired. Ladle hot pickling liquid over peppers, leaving 1/2-inch headspace. Remove air bubbles. Clean jar rim. Center lid on jar and adjust band to fingertip-tight. Place jar on the rack elevated over simmering water (180°F) in boiling-water canner. Repeat until all jars are filled.

PROCESS Lower the rack into simmering water. Water must cover jars by 1 inch. Adjust heat to medium-high, cover canner and bring water to a rolling boil. Process pint jars 10 minutes. Turn off heat and remove cover. Let jars cool 5 minutes. Remove jars from canner; do not retighten bands if loose. Cool 12 hours. Check seals. Label and store jars.

Note: When cutting or seeding hot peppers, wear rubber gloves to prevent hands from being burned.

Okra Pickles

Yield: about 4 pint jars

3 1/2 pounds small okra pods	3 cups vinegar, 5% acidity
1/3 cup Ball Salt for Pickling & Preserving	4 cloves garlic
2 teaspoons dill seed	2 small hot red peppers
3 cups water	Ball Pickle Crisp (optional)

PREP Wash okra pods and hot red peppers under cold running water; drain. Trim stem ends off okra pods, being careful not to cut pods open. Cut hot red peppers in half. Peel garlic.

COOK Combine salt, dill seed, water, and vinegar in a large saucepan. Bring mixture to a boil. Reduce heat to a simmer (180°F); simmer 5 minutes.

FILL Pack okra pods into a hot jar, leaving 1/2-inch headspace. Put 1 clove garlic and 1 piece hot pepper in jar. Add 1/8 teaspoon Pickle Crisp to pint jar, if desired. Ladle hot pickling liquid over okra, leaving 1/2-inch headspace. Remove air bubbles. Clean jar rim. Center lid on jar and adjust band to fingertip-tight. Place jar on the rack elevated over simmering water (180°F) in boiling-water canner. Repeat until all jars are filled.

PROCESS Lower the rack into simmering water. Water must cover jars by 1 inch. Adjust heat to medium-high, cover canner and bring water to a rolling boil. Process pint jars 15 minutes. Turn off heat and remove cover. Let jars cool 5 minutes. Remove jars from canner; do not retighten bands if loose. Cool 12 hours. Check seals. Label and store jars.

Note: When cutting or seeding hot peppers, wear rubber gloves to prevent hands from being burned.

Onion Pickles

Yield: about 14 half-pint or 7 pint jars

4 quarts pearl onions (about 5 pounds)

1 cup Ball Salt for Pickling & Preserving

2 cups sugar

1/4 cup mustard seed

2 1/2 tablespoons prepared horseradish

2 quarts vinegar, 5% acidity

7 small hot red peppers

7 bay leaves

Ball Pickle Crisp (optional)

PREP Wash hot red peppers under cold running water; drain. Peel onions; measure 4 quarts peeled onions. Put onions in a large bowl and sprinkle with salt. Pour cold water over onions just to cover. Cover; let stand 12 to 18 hours in refrigerator. Drain onions. Rinse onions under cold running water; drain. Cut a small slit in each hot pepper on two opposite sides.

COOK Combine sugar, mustard seed, horseradish, and vinegar in a large saucepan. Bring mixture to a boil. Reduce heat to a simmer (180°F); simmer 15 minutes.

FILL Pack onions into a hot jar, leaving 1/2-inch headspace. Put 1/2 hot red pepper and 1/2 bay leaf into half-pint jar or 1 hot red pepper and 1 bay leaf into pint jar. Add 1/16 teaspoon Pickle Crisp to half-pint jar or 1/8 teaspoon Pickle Crisp to pint jar, if desired. Ladle hot pickling liquid over onions, leaving 1/2-inch headspace. Remove air bubbles. Clean jar rim. Center lid on jar and adjust band to fingertip-tight. Place jar on the rack elevated over simmering water (180°F) in boiling-water canner. Repeat until all jars are filled.

PROCESS Lower the rack into simmering water. Water must cover jars by 1 inch. Adjust heat to medium-high, cover canner and bring water to a rolling boil. Process half-pint or pint jars 10 minutes. Turn off heat and remove cover. Let jars cool 5 minutes. Remove jars from canner; do not retighten bands if loose. Cool 12 hours. Check seals. Label and store jars.

Note: When cutting or seeding hot peppers, wear rubber gloves to prevent hands from being burned.

 For Sour Onion Pickles, omit bay leaves and all or part of sugar.

Pickled Butternut Squash

Yield: about 4 pint jars

2 medium butternut squash (about 4 pounds)

1 1/2 tablespoons Ball Salt for Pickling & Preserving

1 cup sugar

2 cloves garlic

2 teaspoons fennel seeds

1/4 teaspoon black peppercorns

2 1/2 cups white wine vinegar

1/2 cup water

4 sprigs fresh thyme

PREP Wash butternut squash under cold running water. Remove stems and blossom ends from butternut squash. Peel squash. Cut squash in half lengthwise and remove seeds. Cut squash into 1-inch cubes. Combine squash and salt in a large bowl, tossing to coat squash evenly with salt. Let stand 2 hours. Rinse squash under cold running water; drain.

COOK Combine sugar, garlic, fennel seeds, black peppercorns, white wine vinegar, and water in a large saucepan. Bring mixture to a boil, stirring until sugar dissolves. Reduce heat to a simmer (180°F); cover, and simmer 10 minutes. Remove garlic and discard.

FILL Pack squash into a hot jar, leaving 1/2-inch headspace. Add 1 sprig of thyme to pint jar. Ladle hot pickling liquid over squash, leaving 1/2 inch headspace. Remove air bubbles. Clean jar rim. Center lid on jar and adjust band to fingertip-tight. Place jar on the rack elevated over simmering water (180°F) in boiling-water canner. Repeat until all jars are filled.

PROCESS Lower the rack into simmering water. Water must cover jars by 1 inch. Adjust heat to medium-high, cover canner and bring water to a rolling boil. Process pint jars 10 minutes. Turn off heat and remove cover. Let jars cool 5 minutes. Remove jars from canner; do not retighten bands if loose. Cool 12 hours. Check seals. Label and store jars.

Pickled Cauliflower

Yield: about 5 pint jars

3 quarts cauliflowerets (about 2 large heads)

1 1/2 cups pearl onions

1/4 cup Ball Salt for Pickling & Preserving

2 cups sugar

2 tablespoons mustard seed

1 tablespoon celery seed

1 teaspoon turmeric

1 quart vinegar, 5% acidity

1 hot red pepper (optional)

Ball Pickle Crisp (optional)

PREP Wash cauliflower and hot red pepper, if using, under cold running water; drain. Cut cauliflower into individual cauliflowerets; measure 3 quarts cauliflowerets. Peel onions; measure 1 1/2 cups peeled onions. Combine cauliflowerets, onions, and salt. Cover onions with ice. Cover; let stand 2 to 3 hours in refrigerator. Drain onions. Rinse onions under cold running water; drain. Cut a small slit in hot pepper on two opposite sides.

COOK Combine sugar, mustard seed, celery seed, turmeric, and vinegar in a large saucepan. Add hot pepper, if desired. Bring mixture to a boil. Add cauliflowerets and onions. Bring mixture to a boil. Reduce heat to a simmer (180°F); simmer 5 minutes. Remove hot pepper and discard.

FILL Pack hot vegetables and pickling liquid into a hot jar, leaving 1/2-inch headspace. Add 1/8 teaspoon Pickle Crisp to pint jar, if desired. Remove air bubbles. Clean jar rim. Center lid on jar and adjust band to fingertip-tight. Place jar on the rack elevated over simmering water (180°F) in boiling-water canner. Repeat until all jars are filled.

PROCESS Lower the rack into simmering water. Water must cover jars by 1 inch. Adjust heat to medium-high, cover canner and bring water to a rolling boil. Process pint jars 10 minutes. Turn off heat and remove cover. Let jars cool 5 minutes. Remove jars from canner; do not retighten bands if loose. Cool 12 hours. Check seals. Label and store jars.

Note: When cutting or seeding hot peppers, wear rubber gloves to prevent hands from being burned.

 Want to dial up the heat? Substitute 1 cup sliced banana peppers and 1/2 cup sliced jalapeño peppers for pearl onions.

 Pickled cauliflower is more than just an appetizer. Use it as an ingredient in green salads and pasta salads, add it to vegetarian burritos and quesadillas, or make batter-fried cauliflower to dip in cheese sauce.

Pickled Garlic Onions

Yield: about 6 half-pint jars

2 quarts pearl onions	1 cup sugar
6 cloves garlic	1 1/2 teaspoons Ball Salt for Pickling & Preserving
4 cups vinegar, 5% acidity	
1 cup water	Ball Pickle Crisp (optional)

PREP To peel pearl onions blanch in boiling water for 30 seconds. Immediately immerse onions in cold water. When onions are cool enough to touch, cut off 1/16-inch from root end and peel. Trim 1/16-inch from blossom end, if desired. Peel garlic and finely mince.

COOK Combine vinegar, water, sugar, salt, and minced garlic in a medium saucepan. Bring mixture to a boil. Reduce heat to a simmer (180° F); simmer 5 minutes.

FILL Pack onions into hot jars, leaving 1/2-inch headspace. Add 1/16 teaspoon Pickle Crisp to half-pint jar, if desired. Ladle hot pickling liquid over onions, leaving 1/2-inch headspace. Remove air bubbles. Clean jar rim. Center lid on jar and adjust band to fingertip-tight. Place jar on the rack elevated over simmering water (180° F) in boiling-water canner. Repeat until all jars are filled.

PROCESS Lower rack into simmering water. Water must cover jars by 1 inch. Adjust heat to medium-high, cover canner and bring water to a rolling boil. Process half-pint jars 10 minutes. Turn off heat and remove cover. Let jars cool 5 minutes. Remove jars from canner; do not retighten bands if loose. Cool 12 hours. Check seals. Label and store jars.

Pickled Grape Tomatoes

Yield: about 4 pint jars

2 quarts grape tomatoes	1 quart water
1 teaspoon Ball Salt for Pickling & Preserving	4 cloves garlic
1 cup white wine vinegar	4 sprigs fresh rosemary
1 cup white vinegar, 5% acidity	Ball Pickle Crisp (optional)

PREP Wash grape tomatoes under cold running water; drain. Peel garlic. Prick each grape tomato with a thin metal skewer to help prevent the peels from bursting open when processed. Pricking tomatoes will not prevent the peels from cracking.

COOK Combine salt, white wine vinegar, white vinegar, and water in a large saucepan. Bring mixture to a boil. Reduce heat to a simmer (180°F); simmer 10 minutes.

FILL Pack grape tomatoes into a hot jar, leaving 1/2-inch headspace. Add 1 clove garlic and 1 rosemary sprig to pint jar. Add 1/8 teaspoon Pickle Crisp to pint jar, if desired. Ladle hot pickling liquid over grape tomatoes, leaving 1/2-inch headspace. Remove air bubbles. Clean jar rim. Center lid on jar and adjust band to fingertip-tight. Place jar on the rack elevated over simmering water (180°F) in boiling-water canner. Repeat until all jars are filled.

PROCESS Lower the rack into simmering water. Water must cover jars by 1 inch. Adjust heat to medium-high, cover canner and bring water to a rolling boil. Process pint jars 10 minutes. Turn off heat and remove cover. Let jars cool 5 minutes. Remove jars from canner; do not retighten bands if loose. Cool 12 hours. Check seals. Label and store jars.

Pickled Pepper Mix

Yield: about 12 half-pint or 6 pint jars

3 quarts mixed long red, green, and yellow peppers (Hungarian, banana, etc.)	3 tablespoons sugar
	1 1/2 teaspoons prepared horseradish
1 cup Ball Salt for Pickling & Preserving	2 cloves garlic
3 1/2 quarts water, divided	1 1/2 quarts vinegar, 5% acidity
	Ball Pickle Crisp (optional)

PREP Wash peppers under cold running water; drain. Cut a small slit in each pepper on two opposite sides. Combine salt and water in a large bowl, stirring until salt dissolves. Add peppers. Let peppers stand 12 to 18 hours in refrigerator. Drain peppers. Rinse peppers under cold running water; drain.

COOK Combine 2 cups water, sugar, horseradish, garlic, and vinegar in a large saucepan. Bring mixture to a boil. Reduce heat to a simmer (180°F); simmer 15 minutes. Remove garlic and discard.

FILL Pack peppers into a hot jar, leaving 1/2-inch headspace. Add 1/16 teaspoon Pickle Crisp to half-pint jar or 1/8 teaspoon Pickle Crisp to pint jar, if desired. Ladle hot pickling liquid over peppers, leaving 1/2-inch headspace. Remove air bubbles. Clean jar rim. Center lid on jar and adjust band to fingertip-tight. Place jar on the rack elevated over simmering water (180°F) in boiling-water canner. Repeat until all jars are filled.

PROCESS Lower the rack into simmering water. Water must cover jars by 1 inch. Adjust heat to medium-high, cover canner and bring water to a rolling boil. Process half-pint or pint jars 10 minutes. Turn off heat and remove cover. Let jars cool 5 minutes. Remove jars from canner; do not retighten bands if loose. Cool 12 hours. Check seals. Label and store jars.

Note: When cutting or seeding hot peppers, wear rubber gloves to prevent hands from being burned.

Spiced Red Cabbage

Yield: about 5 quart jars

12 pounds red cabbage (about 3 large heads)	1/4 cup whole cloves
1/2 cup Ball Salt for Pickling & Preserving	1/4 cup whole allspice
	1/4 cup peppercorns
1 cup brown sugar	1/4 cup celery seed
1/2 cup mustard seed	2 sticks cinnamon
1/4 cup mace	Ball Pickle Crisp (optional)
2 quarts red wine vinegar	

PREP Wash cabbage under cold running water; drain. Remove large outer leaves. Cut cabbage in half and remove core. Shred cabbage. Layer cabbage in a large bowl; sprinkle each layer with salt. Cover; let cabbage stand 24 hours in refrigerator. Drain cabbage. Rinse cabbage under cold running water; drain. Put shredded cabbage on paper towel-lined trays; let stand about 6 hours. Tie whole cloves, allspice, peppercorns, celery seed, and cinnamon sticks in a spice bag.

COOK Combine spice bag, sugar, mustard seed, mace, and vinegar in a large saucepan. Bring mixture to a boil. Reduce heat to a simmer (180°F); simmer 5 minutes. Remove spice bag.

FILL Pack cabbage into a hot jar, leaving 1/2-inch headspace. Add 1/4 teaspoon Pickle Crisp to quart jar, if desired. Ladle hot pickling liquid over cabbage, leaving 1/2-inch headspace. Remove air bubbles. Clean jar rim. Center lid on jar and adjust band to fingertip-tight. Place jar on the rack elevated over simmering water (180°F) in boiling-water canner. Repeat until all jars are filled.

PROCESS Lower the rack into simmering water. Water must cover jars by 1 inch. Adjust heat to medium-high, cover canner and bring water to a rolling boil. Process quart jars 20 minutes. Turn off heat and remove cover. Let jars cool 5 minutes. Remove jars from canner; do not retighten bands if loose. Cool 12 hours. Check seals. Label and store jars.

Vinegared Red Onions

Yield: about 6 half-pint jars

- 3 pounds red onions (about 6 medium)
- 4 cups red wine vinegar
- 1 clove garlic
- Ball Pickle Crisp (optional)

PREP Peel onions. Cut onions crosswise into 1/4-inch slices. Separate onion slices into rings.

COOK Combine vinegar and garlic in a large saucepan. Bring mixture to a boil. Reduce heat to a simmer (180°F); simmer 5 minutes. Add onion rings. Simmer, covered, 5 minutes. Remove garlic and discard.

FILL Pack hot onion rings into a hot jar, leaving 1/2-inch headspace. Add 1/16 teaspoon Pickle Crisp to half-pint jar, if desired. Ladle hot pickling liquid over onion rings, leaving 1/2-inch headspace. Remove air bubbles. Clean jar rim. Center lid on jar and adjust band to fingertip-tight. Place jar on the rack elevated over simmering water (180°F) in boiling-water canner. Repeat until all jars are filled.

PROCESS Lower the rack into simmering water. Water must cover jars by 1 inch. Adjust heat to medium-high, cover canner and bring water to a rolling boil. Process half-pint jars 10 minutes. Turn off heat and remove cover. Let jars cool 5 minutes. Remove jars from canner; do not retighten bands if loose. Cool 12 hours. Check seals. Label and store jars.

Our Tip Vinegared Red Onions is a versatile recipe. Use a portion of the pickling liquid to marinade a cut of beef for grilling, then combine the remaining pickling liquid with brown sugar, honey, soy sauce, horseradish sauce, and cracked black pepper to use as a mopping sauce. Baste beef with mopping sauce the last 10 minutes of grilling. Sauté red onions with mushrooms in a scant amount of olive oil. Serve with beef.

Zucchini Pickles

Yield: about 4 half-pint jars

- 2 pounds zucchini (about 6 medium)
- 1/3 pound onion (about 1 medium)
- 1/4 cup Ball Salt for Pickling & Preserving
- 2 cups sugar
- 2 teaspoons mustard seed
- 1 teaspoon celery salt
- 1 teaspoon turmeric
- 3 cups vinegar, 5% acidity
- Ball Pickle Crisp (optional)

PREP Wash zucchini under cold running water; drain. Remove stems and blossom ends from zucchini. Cut zucchini crosswise into 1/4-inch slices. Peel onions. Cut onions into quarters, then cut into 1/4-inch slices. Combine zucchini and onion in a large bowl; sprinkle with salt. Pour cold water over vegetables just to cover.

Let stand 2 hours. Drain vegetables. Rinse vegetables under cold running water; drain.

COOK Combine sugar, mustard seed, celery salt, turmeric, and vinegar in a large saucepan. Bring mixture to a boil. Turn off heat. Add zucchini and onions. Let stand 2 hours. Bring mixture to a boil. Reduce heat to a simmer (180°F); simmer 5 minutes.

FILL Pack hot vegetables and liquid into a hot jar, leaving 1/2-inch headspace. Add 1/16 teaspoon Pickle Crisp to half-pint jar, if desired. Remove air bubbles. Clean jar rim. Center lid on jar and adjust band to fingertip-tight. Place jar on the rack elevated over simmering water (180°F) in boiling-water canner. Repeat until all jars are filled.

PROCESS Lower the rack into simmering water. Water must cover jars by 1 inch. Adjust heat to medium-high, cover canner and bring water to a rolling boil. Process half-pint jars 15 minutes. Turn off heat and remove cover. Let jars cool 5 minutes. Remove jars from canner; do not retighten bands if loose. Cool 12 hours. Check seals. Label and store jars.

Zucchini-Hot Pepper Pickles

Yield: about 6 pint jars

- 3 pounds zucchini (about 10 to 12 medium)
- 1 pound hot peppers (Serrano, jalapeño, chili, etc.)
- 1/3 pound onion (about 1 medium)
- 1/4 cup Ball Salt for Pickling & Preserving
- 1 1/2 cups sugar
- 2 teaspoons mustard seed
- 1 teaspoon black peppercorns
- 1 teaspoon crushed red pepper
- 4 cups vinegar, 5% acidity
- 1 2/3 cups water
- Ball Pickle Crisp (optional)

PREP Wash zucchini under cold running water; drain. Remove stems and blossom ends from zucchini. Cut zucchini crosswise into 1/2-inch slices. Remove stem ends from hot peppers. Cut peppers crosswise into 1/2-inch slices. Peel onions. Cut onions into quarters, then cut into 1/2-inch slices. Combine zucchini, peppers, and onion in a large bowl; sprinkle with salt. Pour cold water over vegetables just to cover. Let stand 2 hours. Drain vegetables. Rinse vegetables under cold running water; drain.

COOK Combine sugar, mustard seed, peppercorns, crushed red pepper, vinegar, and water in a large saucepan. Bring mixture to a boil. Turn off heat. Add zucchini, peppers, and onion. Let stand 2 hours. Bring mixture to a boil. Reduce heat to a simmer (180°F); simmer 5 minutes.

FILL Pack hot vegetables and liquid into a hot jar, leaving 1/2-inch headspace. Add 1/8 teaspoon Pickle Crisp to pint jar, if desired. Remove air bubbles. Clean jar rim. Center lid on jar and adjust band to fingertip-tight. Place jar on the rack elevated over simmering water (180°F) in boiling-water canner. Repeat until all jars are filled.

PROCESS Lower the rack into simmering water. Water must cover jars by 1 inch. Adjust heat to medium-high, cover canner and bring water to a rolling boil. Process pint jars 15 minutes. Turn off heat and remove cover. Let jars cool 5 minutes. Remove jars from canner; do not retighten bands if loose. Cool 12 hours.

Meats, Seafoods & Vegetables

Few things can make an evening run more smoothly than a well-stocked pantry. In this chapter, you'll find recipes that will guide you through canning the proteins, vegetables, and soups that can make putting dinner on the table such a breeze. Preserving meats, seafoods, and vegetables by canning them gives you the flexibility of having pantry goods prepared just to your liking. With staples like these, you'll be able to create healthy, delicious meals that are flavorful from the start.

Getting Started

Vegetables, meats, poultry, seafoods, and combination recipes like the soups and stews you'll find in this chapter are classified as low-acid foods, meaning they register a pH level higher than 4.6 on the acidity-alkalinity scale (see page 6). Possessing little of the natural acid needed to guard against bacterial spores and their toxins makes it necessary to process all low-acid foods at 240°F. This is achieved using a pressure canner. All the guidance you need to successfully and safely preserve these pantry staples can be found in this chapter.

Success is in the preparation

Canning meats with or without broth, brining seafoods, and blanching or cooking vegetables are some of the techniques used in the preparation of these recipes. You can adjust spices and dried herbs to create flavor combinations that you enjoy. Salt may be omitted, except when it is used to brine seafoods or cure meats.

Food safety checklist

Conduct annual maintenance on your pressure canner. If you have a dial gauge canner, have the gauge tested for accuracy at least once each year. Pressure canning is the only safe method for preserving low-acid foods for shelf storage. Other methods are either outdated or incorrect—do not use them.

Altitude makes a difference

All processing times for low-acid foods in this book are based on canning at 10 pounds pressure (240°F), using a weighted gauge canner, at or below 1,000 feet above sea level. If you're at an elevation over 1,000 feet above sea level or using a dial gauge canner, refer to the Altitude Chart (see page 9).

Featured Recipe | **Creole-Style Shrimp Po' Boy** page 176

Pictured Above | **Spicy Creole Sauce** page 117 | **Asparagus** page 110 | **Green Beans** page 111

Good Things to Know

Meats

The flavor and texture of canned meats depends largely upon the breed of animal and the manner of handling the meat at the time of slaughter. If you slaughter your own meat, contact your County Cooperative Extension service for complete information on slaughtering, chilling, and aging the meat.

To prepare meat for processing, trim away gristle, bruised spots, and fat. Too much fat is likely to cause the meat to develop a strong flavor and could also contribute to seal failure.

Cut meat into pieces suitable for cooking or canning. Slice across the grain about 1 inch thick. Then cut with the grain into jar-sized pieces. Cut stew meat into uniform cubes. Meat for soups or other entrees may be cut into smaller uniform pieces, ground, or shredded according to recipe instructions.

Strong-flavored game should be soaked in salt water before canning. Soak game 1 hour in salt brine made of 1 tablespoon salt for each quart of water. Prepare, pack, and process according to the tested recipes in this book. Do not allow meat to soak in water longer than the recommended time stated in the recipe.

Poultry

Poultry that is one or two years old is best for canning. Wash poultry under cold running water; drain. Begin separating poultry into parts by cutting the skin between legs and body. Bend legs until hip joints snap; cut through connecting tissue as needed. Separate thighs from legs by cutting through the joint. Slip knife under the ends of shoulder blades and cut up to the wings. Cut back and breast apart. Wash under cold running water. Drain and dry. Do not salt. Chill poultry pieces in refrigerator 6 to 12 hours before canning.

Seafoods

Prepare freshly caught fish as for cooking. Leave backbone in small fish. Debone large fish. Soak fish in salt water before canning (refer to recipe for instructions). Process seafoods in half-pint or pint jars only to ensure there is sufficient heat penetration throughout the jar. This is particularly important since seafoods have little natural acid to inhibit the growth of bacteria and bacterial spores that produce toxins.

Combination Recipes

Recipes that combine some low-acid and some high-acid ingredients with a pH higher than 4.6 must be processed as low-acid foods using a pressure canner. Refer to the Pressure Method (see page 8). The length of processing time for combination recipes must safely preserve the ingredient requiring the longest processing time. Follow individual recipe for ingredient preparation, jar size, and processing time.

Vegetables

Vegetables are low in natural acid and thus require the high temperature achieved by a pressure canner to destroy molds, yeasts, enzymes, and bacterial spores that produce toxins. Some vegetables may be canned using either the RAW PACK or HOT PACK method, while other vegetables must only be packed into the jars while hot. Not all vegetables withstand the high temperature or processing time required to safely preserve them in a jar; therefore, for best results, freezing is the recommended preservation method.

Meats

Broth for Canning Meat

Remove meat from cooking pan. Drain juice from pan; reserving liquid. Allow fat to separate to the top of juice. Remove fat and measure. Measure the juice. Combine 1 to 2 tablespoons fat to 1 cup juice in a large saucepan. Water or broth may be added as needed for the amount of meat to be canned. Boil broth for canning 2 to 3 minutes.

Note: Do not add a thickening agent such as flour or cornstarch before processing.

Chopped Meat

Beef, Lamb, Mutton, Pork, Veal, Venison

Preserve in pint or quart jars

Meat	Salt (optional)
Water, Broth for Canning Meat (see this page), or tomato juice	

PREP Grind fresh meat using an electric or manual food grinder. Measure ground meat.

COOK Sear meat in a hot skillet. Add 1 to 1½ cups water, broth, or tomato juice for each quart of chopped meat. Bring mixture to a boil. Reduce heat to a simmer (180°F); simmer 5 minutes.

FILL Pack hot meat and liquid into a hot jar, leaving 1-inch headspace. Add ½ teaspoon salt to each pint jar; 1 teaspoon salt to each quart jar, if desired. Remove air bubbles. Clean jar rim. Center lid on jar and adjust band to fingertip-tight. Place jar on the rack in pressure canner containing 2 inches of simmering water (180°F). Repeat until all jars are filled.

PROCESS Place lid on canner and turn to locked position. Adjust heat to medium-high. Vent steam for 10 minutes. Put weighted gauge on vent; bring pressure to 10 pounds (psi). Process pint jars 1 hour and 15 minutes or quart jars 1 hour and 30 minutes. Turn off heat; cool canner to zero pressure. After 5 minutes, remove lid. Let jars cool 10 minutes. Remove jars from canner; do not retighten bands if loose. Cool 12 hours. Check seals. Label and store jars.

 You can create 101 meals at a moment's notice when you have a variety of canned meats at your fingertips. Here are a few suggestions: tamales, stuffed peppers or stuffed cabbage, Sloppy Joes, shepherd's pie, taco salad, moussaka, and pasta with meat sauce, just to name a few.

Pork Sausage

Preserve in pint or quart jars

Pork

Broth for Canning Meat
    (see page 98)

Salt and pepper, or other
    spices or herbs
    (optional)

PREP Grind fresh pork using an electric or manual food grinder. Measure ground pork. Season pork with spices in any combination or amount, if desired. Shape ground pork into patties or 3- to 4-inch links.

COOK Lightly brown patties or links; drain. Bring broth to a boil. Reduce heat to a simmer (180°F). Keep broth hot.

FILL Pack hot sausage into a hot jar, leaving 1-inch headspace. Ladle hot broth over sausage, leaving 1-inch headspace. Remove air bubbles. Clean jar rim. Center lid on jar and adjust band to fingertip-tight. Place jar on the rack in pressure canner containing 2 inches of simmering water (180°F). Repeat until all jars are filled.

PROCESS Place lid on canner and turn to locked position. Adjust heat to medium-high. Vent steam for 10 minutes. Put weighted gauge on vent; bring pressure to 10 pounds (psi). Process pint jars 1 hour and 15 minutes or quart jars 1 hour and 30 minutes. Turn off heat; cool canner to zero pressure. After 5 minutes, remove lid. Let jars cool 10 minutes. Remove jars from canner; do not retighten bands if loose. Cool 12 hours. Check seals. Label and store jars.

Note: Do not use sage to season sausage, as it may become bitter.

Spice it up three ways! For mild seasoning, add salt, pepper, parsley, garlic powder, onion powder, and basil. Give it the Italian touch with basil, marjoram, oregano, rosemary, and thyme. Add some heat for zesty sausage, using garlic powder, paprika, anise seed, fennel seed, dried red pepper flakes, salt, and pepper.

Pork Tenderloin

Preserve in pint or quart jars

Pork tenderloin

Water or Broth for Canning
    Meat (see page 98)

Salt (optional)

PREP
RAW PACK—Slice pork tenderloin crosswise into 1/2- to 1-inch slices.

HOT PACK—Prepare pork tenderloin for roasting.

COOK
RAW PACK—Bring water or broth to a boil. Reduce heat to a simmer (180°F). Keep water or broth hot.

HOT PACK—Roast whole pork tenderloin until one-third to one-half done. Slice pork tenderloin crosswise into 1/2- to 1-inch slices. Bring water or broth to a boil. Reduce heat to a simmer (180°F). Keep water or broth hot.

FILL
RAW PACK—Pack raw pork slices into a hot jar, leaving 1-inch headspace. Ladle hot water or broth over pork slices, leaving 1-inch headspace. Add 1/2 teaspoon salt to pint jar; 1 teaspoon salt to quart jar, if desired.

HOT PACK—Pack hot pork slices into a hot jar, leaving 1-inch headspace. Ladle hot water or broth over pork slices, leaving 1-inch headspace. Add 1/2 teaspoon salt to pint jar; 1 teaspoon salt to quart jar, if desired.

Remove air bubbles. Clean jar rim. Center lid on jar and adjust band to fingertip-tight. Place jar on the rack in pressure canner containing 2 inches of simmering water (180°F). Repeat until all jars are filled.

PROCESS Place lid on canner and turn to locked position. Adjust heat to medium-high. Vent steam for 10 minutes. Put weighted gauge on vent; bring pressure to 10 pounds (psi). Process RAW PACK or HOT PACK pint jars 1 hour and 15 minutes or quart jars 1 hour and 30 minutes. Turn off heat; cool canner to zero pressure. After 5 minutes, remove lid. Let jars cool 10 minutes. Remove jars from canner; do not retighten bands if loose. Cool 12 hours. Check seals. Label and store jars.

Roast

Beef, Lamb, Mutton, Pork, Veal, Venison

Preserve in pint or quart jars

Meat

Broth for Canning Meat
    (see page 98)

Salt (optional)

PREP Cut meat into jar-length strips 1/2- to 1-inch thick.

COOK Bake or roast meat until well browned but not done. Meat may also be browned in a small amount of fat. Bring broth to a boil. Reduce heat to a simmer (180°F). Keep broth hot.

FILL Pack hot meat into a hot jar, leaving 1-inch headspace. Add 1/2 teaspoon salt to pint jar; 1 teaspoon salt to quart jar, if desired. Ladle hot broth over meat, leaving 1-inch headspace. Remove air bubbles. Clean jar rim. Center lid on jar and adjust band to fingertip-tight. Place jar on the rack in pressure canner containing 2 inches of simmering water (180°F). Repeat until all jars are filled.

PROCESS Place lid on canner and turn to locked position. Adjust heat to medium-high. Vent steam for 10 minutes. Put weighted gauge on vent; bring pressure to 10 pounds (psi). Process pint jars 1 hour and 15 minutes or quart jars 1 hour and 30 minutes. Turn off heat; cool canner to zero pressure. After 5 minutes, remove lid. Let jars cool 10 minutes. Remove jars from canner; do not retighten bands if loose. Cool 12 hours. Check seals. Label and store jars.

Spareribs

Beef, Pork

Preserve in pint or quart jars

Meat

Barbecue sauce
    (see page 89) or
    Broth for Canning Meat
    (see page 98)

Salt (optional)

PREP Crack ribs evenly. Trim off excess fat.

COOK Bake or roast meat until half done. Remove bones. Cut meat into squares. Bring barbecue sauce to a boil. Reduce heat to a simmer (180°F). Keep barbecue sauce hot.

FILL Pack hot meat into a hot jar, leaving 1-inch headspace. Add 1/2 teaspoon salt to pint jar; 1 teaspoon salt to quart jar, if desired. Ladle hot barbecue sauce or hot broth over meat, leaving 1-inch headspace. Remove air bubbles. Clean jar rim. Center lid on jar and adjust band to fingertip-tight. Place jar on the rack in pressure canner containing 2 inches of simmering water (180°F). Repeat until all jars are filled.

PROCESS Place lid on canner and turn to locked position. Adjust heat to medium-high. Vent steam for 10 minutes. Put weighted gauge on vent; bring pressure to 10 pounds (psi). Process pint jars 1 hour and 15 minutes or quart jars 1 hour and 30 minutes. Turn off heat; cool canner to zero pressure. After 5 minutes, remove lid. Let jars cool 10 minutes. Remove jars from canner; do not retighten bands if loose. Cool 12 hours. Check seals. Label and store jars.

 Prepare a few jars of spareribs using broth. When you're ready to re-heat for serving, put spareribs and broth in a shallow baking dish. Pour Plum Sauce, Hot Rhubarb Grilling Sauce, or Apricot-Chipotle Sauce over spareribs and bake at 350°F until hot throughout. Enjoy!

Steaks or Chops

Beef, Lamb, Mutton, Pork, Veal, Venison

Preserve in pint or quart jars

Meat   Salt (optional)

Water or Broth for Canning
    Meat (see page 98)

PREP Cut meat into 1-inch slices. Remove large bones.

COOK

RAW PACK—Bring water or broth to a boil. Reduce heat to a simmer (180°F). Keep water or broth hot.

HOT PACK—Brown meat in a small amount of fat in a shallow saucepan. Bring water or broth to a boil. Reduce heat to a simmer (180°F). Keep water or broth hot.

FILL

RAW PACK—Pack raw meat slices into a hot jar, leaving 1-inch headspace. Add ½ teaspoon salt to pint jar; 1 teaspoon salt to quart jar, if desired. Ladle hot water or hot broth over meat slices, leaving 1-inch headspace.

HOT PACK—Pack hot meat slices into a hot jar, leaving 1-inch headspace. Add ½ teaspoon salt to pint jar; 1 teaspoon salt to quart jar, if desired. Ladle hot water or hot broth over meat slices, leaving 1-inch headspace.

Remove air bubbles. Clean jar rim. Center lid on jar and adjust band to fingertip-tight. Place jar on the rack in pressure canner containing 2 inches of simmering water (180°F). Repeat until all jars are filled.

PROCESS Place lid on canner and turn to locked position. Adjust heat to medium-high. Vent steam for 10 minutes. Put weighted gauge on vent; bring pressure to 10 pounds (psi). Process RAW PACK or HOT PACK pint jars 1 hour and 15 minutes or quart jars 1 hour and 30 minutes. Turn off heat; cool canner to zero pressure. After 5 minutes, remove lid. Let jars cool 10 minutes. Remove jars from canner; do not retighten bands if loose. Cool 12 hours. Check seals. Label and store jars.

 Beef or pork strips are the beginning of a hearty sandwich. Drain meat, reserving broth. Sauté sliced onions, sweet or hot peppers, and mushrooms in a small amount of olive oil until tender. Add meat and cook until hot throughout. Warm reserved broth. Layer meat and vegetables on a crusty roll and serve with broth for dipping.

Stew Meat

Beef, Lamb, Mutton, Pork, Veal, Venison

Preserve in pint or quart jars

Meat   Salt (optional)
Water

PREP Remove fat and gristle. Cut meat into 1½- to 2-inch cubes.

COOK Simmer (180°F) meat in water to cover until hot throughout.

FILL Pack hot meat into a hot jar, leaving 1-inch headspace. Add ½ teaspoon salt to pint jar; 1 teaspoon salt to quart jar, if desired. Ladle hot cooking liquid over meat, leaving 1-inch headspace. Remove air bubbles. Clean jar rim. Center lid on jar and adjust band to fingertip-tight. Place jar on the rack in pressure canner containing 2 inches of simmering water (180°F). Repeat until all jars are filled.

PROCESS Place lid on canner and turn to locked position. Adjust heat to medium-high. Vent steam for 10 minutes. Put weighted gauge on vent; bring pressure to 10 pounds (psi). Process pint jars 1 hour and 15 minutes or quart jars 1 hour and 30 minutes. Turn off heat; cool canner to zero pressure. After 5 minutes, remove lid. Let jars cool 10 minutes. Remove jars from canner; do not retighten bands if loose. Cool 12 hours. Check seals. Label and store jars.

Rabbit or Squirrel

Preserve in pint or quart jars

Rabbit or squirrel   Salt (optional)

Water or Broth for Canning
    Meat (see page 98)

PREP Soak fresh game meat for 1 hour in salt brine made of 1 tablespoon salt for each quart water. Rinse fresh game under cold running water. For Raw Pack, separate game at joints. Game may be canned with or without bones.

COOK

RAW PACK—Bring water or broth to a boil. Reduce heat to a simmer (180°F). Keep water or broth hot.

HOT PACK—Boil, steam, or bake rabbit or squirrel until ²/₃ done. Separate game at joints. Game may be canned with or without bones. Bring water or broth to a boil. Reduce heat to a simmer (180°F). Keep water or broth hot.

FILL

RAW PACK—Pack raw meat into a hot jar, leaving 1-inch headspace. Add ½ teaspoon salt to pint jar; 1 teaspoon salt to quart jar, if desired. Ladle hot water or hot broth over meat, leaving 1-inch headspace.

HOT PACK—Pack hot meat into a hot jar, leaving 1-inch headspace. Add ½ teaspoon salt to pint jar; 1 teaspoon salt to quart jar, if desired. Ladle hot water or hot broth over meat, leaving 1-inch headspace.

Remove air bubbles. Clean jar rim. Center lid on jar and adjust band to fingertip-tight. Place jar on the rack in pressure canner containing 2 inches of simmering water (180°F). Repeat until all jars are filled.

PROCESS Place lid on canner and turn to locked position. Adjust heat to medium-high. Vent steam for 10 minutes. Put weighted gauge on vent; bring pressure to 10 pounds (psi). Process RAW PACK or HOT PACK pint jars 1 hour and 15 minutes or quart jars 1 hour and 30 minutes. Turn off heat; cool canner to zero pressure. After 5 minutes, remove lid. Let jars cool 10 minutes. Remove jars from canner; do not retighten bands if loose. Cool 12 hours. Check seals. Label and store jars.

Chicken, Duck, Goose, Turkey, or Game Birds

Preserve in pint or quart jars

Chicken, duck, goose, turkey, game birds	Salt (optional)
Water or Broth for Canning Meat (see page 98)	

PREP For Raw Pack, separate poultry or game birds at joints. Poultry or game birds may be canned with or without bones.

COOK

RAW PACK—Bring water or broth to a boil. Reduce heat to a simmer (180°F). Keep water or broth hot.

HOT PACK—Boil, steam, or bake poultry or game birds until 2/3 done. Separate poultry or game birds at joints. Poultry or game birds may be canned with or without bones. Bring water or broth to a boil. Reduce heat to a simmer (180°F). Keep water or broth hot.

FILL

RAW PACK—Pack raw meat into a hot jar, leaving 1-inch headspace. Add 1/2 teaspoon salt to pint jar; 1 teaspoon salt to quart jar, if desired. Ladle hot water or hot broth over meat, leaving 1-inch headspace.

HOT PACK—Pack hot meat into a hot jar, leaving 1-inch headspace. Add 1/2 teaspoon salt to pint jar; 1 teaspoon salt to quart jar, if desired. Ladle hot water or hot broth over meat, leaving 1-inch headspace.

Remove air bubbles. Clean jar rim. Center lid on jar and adjust band to fingertip-tight. Place jar on the rack in pressure canner containing 2 inches of simmering water (180°F). Repeat until all jars are filled.

PROCESS Place lid on canner and turn to locked position. Adjust heat to medium-high. Vent steam for 10 minutes. Put weighted gauge on vent; bring pressure to 10 pounds (psi). Process boned RAW PACK or HOT PACK pint jars 1 hour and 15 minutes or quart jars 1 hour and 30 minutes. Process bone-in meat RAW PACK or HOT PACK pint jars 1 hour and 5 minutes or quart jars 1 hour and 15 minutes. Turn off heat; cool canner to zero pressure. After 5 minutes, remove lid. Let jars cool 10 minutes. Remove jars from canner; do not retighten bands if loose. Cool 12 hours. Check seals. Label and store jars.

Seafoods

Clams

Preserve in half-pint or pint jars

Clams	Salt
Water	Bottled lemon juice

PREP Keep clams alive, moist, and chilled until ready to process. Scrub clams under cold running water to remove sand; drain. Steam clams 5 to 10 minutes. When cool enough to handle, open shells and remove meat, reserving juice. If shell does not open, discard clam. Drop clam meat into salt water brine made by dissolving 1/2 cup salt in 4 quarts water. Drain. Wash under cold running water; drain.

COOK Combine 4 quarts water and 2 tablespoons bottled lemon juice in a large saucepan. Bring mixture to a boil. Boil clam meat in acidified water 2 minutes. Drain. Heat reserved clam juice to a boil. Reduce heat to a simmer (180°F). Keep clam juice hot.

FILL Pack hot clam meat into a hot jar, leaving 1-inch headspace. Ladle hot clam juice over meat, leaving 1-inch headspace. If there is not enough juice to cover clams, add boiling water. Remove air bubbles. Clean jar rim. Center lid on jar and adjust band to fingertip-tight. Place jar on the rack in pressure canner containing 2 inches of simmering water (180°F). Repeat until all jars are filled.

PROCESS Place lid on canner and turn to locked position. Adjust heat to medium-high. Vent steam for 10 minutes. Put weighted gauge on vent; bring pressure to 10 pounds (psi). Process half-pint jars 1 hour or pint jars 1 hour and 10 minutes. Turn off heat; cool canner to zero pressure. After 5 minutes, remove lid. Let jars cool 10 minutes. Remove jars from canner; do not retighten bands if loose. Cool 12 hours. Check seals. Label and store jars.

 Our Tip Do you need a quick-to-make appetizer or entrée? Here are some suggestions to get you started: clams in garlic butter, clam fritters, New England or Manhattan clam chowder, or linguini with white clam sauce.

Crab Meat
King, Dungeness

Preserve in half-pint or pint jars

Crabs	Bottled lemon juice or vinegar, 5% acidity
Water	
Salt	

PREP Keep crabs alive, moist, and chilled until ready to process. Wash crabs through several changes of cold water. Complete a final washing under cold running water.

COOK Combine 4 quarts water, 1/4 cup bottled lemon juice, and 2 tablespoons salt in a large saucepan. Bring mixture to a boil. Boil crabs in acidified water 20 minutes. Drain. Cover crabs with cold water to cool. Drain. Remove back shell. Remove meat from body and claws. Put crab meat in brine of 2 tablespoons salt, 2 cups bottled lemon juice or 4 cups vinegar, and 4 quarts water. Soak crab meat 2 minutes. Drain. Squeeze excess liquid from meat.

Bring additional water to a boil in a separate large saucepan. Reduce heat to a simmer (180°F). Keep water hot.

FILL Pack 6 ounces cooked crab meat into hot half-pint jar or 12 ounces cooked crab meat into hot pint jar, leaving 1-inch headspace. Add 2 tablespoons lemon juice to half-pint jar; 4 tablespoons lemon juice to pint jar. Ladle hot water over crab meat, leaving 1-inch headspace. Remove air bubbles. Clean jar rim. Center lid on jar and adjust band to fingertip-tight. Place jar on the rack in pressure canner containing 2 inches of simmering water (180°F). Repeat until all jars are filled.

PROCESS Place lid on canner and turn to locked position. Adjust heat to medium-high. Vent steam for 10 minutes. Put weighted gauge on vent; bring pressure to 10 pounds (psi). Process half-pint or pint jars 1 hour and 20 minutes. Turn off heat; cool canner to zero pressure. After 5 minutes, remove lid. Let jars cool 10 minutes. Remove jars from canner; do not retighten bands if loose. Cool 12 hours. Check seals. Label and store jars.

Fish

All varieties, including Salmon and Shad
For Tuna, see below right

Preserve in half-pint or pint jars

Fish	Salt
Water	

PREP Clean fish within 2 hours after it is caught. Keep cleaned fish chilled until ready to process. Combine 1 cup salt and 4 quarts water to make brine. Cut fish into jar-length pieces. Soak fish in brine for 1 hour. Drain fish for 10 minutes.

FILL Pack fish, skin side next to glass, into a hot jar, leaving 1-inch headspace. Clean jar rim. Center lid on jar and adjust band to fingertip-tight. Place jar on the rack in pressure canner containing 2 inches of simmering water (180°F). Repeat until all jars are filled.

PROCESS Place lid on canner and turn to locked position. Adjust heat to medium-high. Vent steam for 10 minutes. Put weighted gauge on vent; bring pressure to 10 pounds (psi). Process half-pint or pint jars 1 hour and 40 minutes. Turn off heat; cool canner to zero pressure. After 5 minutes, remove lid. Let jars cool 10 minutes. Remove jars from canner; do not retighten bands if loose. Cool 12 hours. Check seals. Label and store jars.

Oysters

Preserve in half-pint or pint jars

Oysters	Salt
Water	

PREP Keep oysters alive and chilled until ready to process. Wash shells under cold running water; drain.

COOK Bake oysters at 400°F for 5 to 7 minutes. Quickly cool hot oysters in ice water; drain. Remove oyster meat from shells. Wash meat in brine made of 1/2 cup salt and 4 quarts water. Drain. Bring water to a boil. Reduce heat to a simmer (180°F). Keep water hot.

FILL Pack oyster meat into a hot jar, leaving 1-inch headspace. Ladle hot water over oyster meat, leaving 1-inch headspace. Remove air bubbles. Clean jar rim. Center lid on jar and adjust band to fingertip-tight. Place jar on the rack in pressure canner containing 2 inches of simmering water (180°F). Repeat until all jars are filled.

PROCESS Place lid on canner and turn to locked position. Adjust heat to medium-high. Vent steam for 10 minutes. Put weighted gauge on vent; bring pressure to 10 pounds (psi). Process half-pint or pint jars 1 hour and 15 minutes. Turn off heat; cool canner to zero pressure. After 5 minutes, remove lid. Let jars cool 10 minutes. Remove jars from canner; do not retighten bands if loose. Cool 12 hours. Check seals. Label and store jars.

Shrimp

Preserve in half-pint or pint jars

Shrimp	Vinegar, 5% acidity
Water	Salt

PREP Remove heads immediately after shrimp is caught. Wash shrimp under cold running water; drain. Keep shrimp chilled until ready to process.

COOK Combine 4 quarts water, 1 cup vinegar, and 1 cup salt in a large saucepan. Bring mixture to a boil. Boil shrimp in brine for 10 minutes. Quickly cool shrimp in cold water; drain. Peel shrimp and remove sand vein. Rinse shrimp under cold running water. Combine 4 quarts water and 1 to 3 tablespoons salt in a large saucepan. Bring brine to a boil. Reduce heat to a simmer (180°F). Keep brine hot.

FILL Pack shrimp meat into a hot jar, leaving 1-inch headspace. Ladle hot brine over meat, leaving 1-inch headspace. Remove air bubbles. Clean jar rim. Center lid on jar and adjust band to fingertip-tight. Place jar on the rack in pressure canner containing 2 inches of simmering water (180°F). Repeat until all jars are filled.

PROCESS Place lid on canner and turn to locked position. Adjust heat to medium-high. Vent steam for 10 minutes. Put weighted gauge on vent; bring pressure to 10 pounds (psi). Process half-pint or pint jars 45 minutes. Turn off heat; cool canner to zero pressure. After 5 minutes, remove lid. Let jars cool 10 minutes. Remove jars from canner; do not retighten bands if loose. Cool 12 hours. Check seals. Label and store jars.

Tuna

Preserve in half-pint or pint jars

Tuna	Salt
Water	

PREP Wash tuna under cold running water; drain.

For raw pack, fillet raw tuna. Remove skin and lightly scrape surface to remove blood vessels. Cut tuna into quarters. Remove all bones and dark flesh; discard. Cut quarters crosswise into jar-length pieces.

COOK

RAW PACK—Bring water to a boil. Reduce heat to a simmer (180°F). Keep water hot.

HOT PACK—Place tuna on a rack in a large baking pan. Bake tuna at 350°F for 1 hour or until done. The internal temperature of tuna must be 165° to 175°F. Refrigerate tuna overnight. Remove skin and lightly scrape surface to remove blood vessels. Cut tuna into quarters. Remove all bones and dark flesh; discard. Cut quarters crosswise into jar-length pieces. Bring water to a boil. Reduce heat to a simmer (180°F). Keep water hot.

FILL

RAW PACK—Pack tuna into a hot jar, leaving 1-inch headspace. Add 1/2 teaspoon salt to half-pint jar; 1 teaspoon salt to pint jar, if desired. Ladle hot water over tuna, leaving 1-inch headspace.

HOT PACK—Pack cooked tuna into a hot jar, leaving 1-inch headspace. Add 1/2 teaspoon salt to half-pint jar; 1 teaspoon salt to pint jar, if desired. Ladle hot water over tuna, leaving 1-inch headspace.

Remove air bubbles. Clean jar rim. Center lid on jar and adjust band to fingertip-tight. Place jar on the rack in pressure canner containing 2 inches of simmering water (180°F). Repeat until all jars are filled.

PROCESS Place lid on canner and turn to locked position. Adjust heat to medium-high. Vent steam for 10 minutes. Put weighted gauge on vent; bring pressure to 10 pounds (psi). Process RAW PACK or HOT PACK half-pint or pint jars 1 hour and 40 minutes. Turn off heat; cool canner to zero pressure. After 5 minutes, remove lid. Let jars cool 10 minutes. Remove jars from canner; do not retighten bands if loose. Cool 12 hours. Check seals. Label and store jars.

Note: Crystals of magnesium ammonium phosphate may form in canned tuna. There is no way to prevent these crystals from forming in home canned tuna. They usually dissolve when the tuna is heated. If the crystals do not dissolve, they are safe to eat.

 Tuna is the healthy start for a wide range of dishes. Fresh tuna you preserved is sure to liven up these all-time favorites: tuna tacos, antipasto, tuna and noodle casserole, tuna salad, deviled eggs, tuna melt, stuffed mushrooms or stuffed cherry tomatoes, and tuna burgers, just to name a few.

Entrees
SOUPS, & STOCKS

Bean Soup

Yield: about 5 pint or 2 quart jars

- 2 cups dried navy beans (about 1 pound)
- 1 ham hock or 1/4 pound salt pork
- 1/2 cup chopped onion (about 1 medium)
- 1/2 hot red pepper
- Salt and pepper to taste, if desired

PREP Wash navy beans under cold running water; drain. Peel onion. Chop onion; measure 1/2 cup chopped onion. Remove stem and blossom ends from hot red pepper. Finely chop hot red pepper.

COOK Put navy beans in a large saucepan. Add water to cover beans by 2 inches. Bring mixture to a boil over medium-high heat; boil 2 minutes. Remove from heat. Let navy beans soak 1 hour; drain. Return navy beans to a large saucepan and cover with water by 2 inches. Add ham or salt pork, onion, and hot red pepper. Bring mixture to a boil over medium-high. Reduce heat to a simmer (180°F); simmer, covered, 2 hours. Remove ham or salt pork; dice meat, discarding bone. Return meat to soup. Season soup with salt and pepper to taste, if desired.

FILL Ladle hot soup into a hot jar, leaving 1-inch headspace. Remove air bubbles. Clean jar rim. Center lid on jar and adjust band to fingertip-tight. Place jar on the rack in pressure canner containing 2 inches of simmering water (180°F). Repeat until all jars are filled.

PROCESS Place lid on canner and turn to locked position. Adjust heat to medium-high. Vent steam for 10 minutes. Put weighted gauge on vent; bring pressure to 10 pounds (psi). Process pint jars 1 hour and 15 minutes or quart jars 1 hour and 30 minutes. Turn off heat; cool canner to zero pressure. After 5 minutes, remove lid. Let jars cool 10 minutes. Remove jars from canner; do not retighten bands if loose. Cool 12 hours. Check seals. Label and store jars.

Note: When cutting or seeding hot peppers, wear rubber gloves to prevent hands from being burned.

Beef in Wine Sauce

Yield: about 3 pint jars

- 2 pounds round steak, cut into 1-inch cubes
- 1 tablespoon vegetable oil
- 1 cup shredded apple (about 1 large)
- 1 cup shredded carrot (about 2 medium)
- 3/4 cup sliced onions (about 2 medium)
- 1/2 cup water
- 1/2 cup red cooking wine
- 1 teaspoon salt
- 2 cloves garlic, minced
- 2 beef bouillon cubes
- 2 bay leaves
- 1/2 teaspoon browning and seasoning sauce

PREP Wash apple and carrots under cold running water; drain. Peel and core apple. Shred apples; measure 1 cup shredded apple. Remove stems from carrots and peel. Shred carrots; measure 1 cup shredded carrots. Peel onions. Cut onions crosswise into 1/4-inch slices; measure 3/4 cup sliced onions. Peel garlic. Finely mince garlic. Cut round steak into 1-inch cubes.

COOK Brown cubed meat in oil in a large saucepan. Add all ingredients, except browning and seasoning sauce. Simmer 1 hour, stirring to prevent sticking. Remove bay leaves. Stir in browning and seasoning sauce.

FILL Pack hot beef and sauce into a hot jar, leaving 1-inch headspace. Remove air bubbles. Clean jar rim. Center lid on jar and adjust band to fingertip-tight. Place jar on the rack in pressure canner containing 2 inches of simmering water (180°F). Repeat until all jars are filled.

PROCESS Place lid on canner and turn to locked position. Adjust heat to medium-high. Vent steam for 10 minutes. Put weighted gauge on vent; bring pressure to 10 pounds (psi). Process pint jars 1 hour and 15 minutes or quart jars 1 hour and 30 minutes. Turn off heat; cool canner to zero pressure. After 5 minutes, remove lid. Let jars cool 10 minutes. Remove jars from canner; do not retighten bands if loose. Cool 12 hours. Check seals. Label and store jars.

Note: A thickener is added to the wine sauce when reheating for serving (see recipe below). Do not add thickener before processing, as it slows heat penetration and may result in under-processed food.

To Serve—Add 2 teaspoons cornstarch to each pint jar; 1 tablespoon plus 1 teaspoon cornstarch to each quart jar of Beef and Wine Sauce and cook until sauce thickens.

Beef Stew with Vegetables

Yield: about 14 pint or 7 quart jars

4 to 5 pounds beef stew meat	3 cups chopped celery (about 6 stalks)
1 tablespoon vegetable oil	3 cups chopped onions (about 4 to 5 medium)
3 quarts cubed potatoes (about 18 medium)	1½ teaspoons salt
2 quarts sliced carrots (about 15 small)	1 teaspoon thyme
	½ teaspoon pepper

PREP Wash potatoes, carrots, and celery under cold running water; drain. Peel potatoes. Cut potatoes into 1-inch cubes; measure 3 quarts cubed potatoes. Remove stems from carrots and peel. Slice carrots ½-inch thick; measure 2 quarts sliced carrots. Remove leafy tops and root ends from celery. Slice celery ½-inch thick; measure 3 cups sliced celery. Peel onions. Chop onions; measure 3 cups chopped onions. Cut stew meat into 1½-inch cubes.

COOK Brown cubed meat in oil in a large saucepan. Stir in remaining ingredients. Add just enough boiling water to cover. Bring mixture to a boil.

FILL Pack hot stew into a hot jar, leaving 1-inch headspace. Remove air bubbles. Clean jar rim. Center lid on jar and adjust band to fingertip-tight. Place jar on the rack in pressure canner containing 2 inches of simmering water (180°F). Repeat until all jars are filled.

PROCESS Place lid on canner and turn to locked position. Adjust heat to medium-high. Vent steam for 10 minutes. Put weighted gauge on vent; bring pressure to 10 pounds (psi). Process pint jars 1 hour and 15 minutes or quart jars 1 hour and 30 minutes. Turn off heat; cool canner to zero pressure. After 5 minutes, remove lid. Let jars cool 10 minutes. Remove jars from canner; do not retighten bands if loose. Cool 12 hours. Check seals. Label and store jars.

 Customize our recipe to make it your very own. Here's how you do it: combine potatoes and turnips to equal 3 quarts cubed root vegetables, reduce the measure of onion to 2 cups, then add 1 cup peas, green beans, or corn. Sprinkle in additional dried herbs and spices to your liking. To finish it off, add a splash of hot sauce, or maybe wine. Perfect!

Beef Stock

Yield: about 4 pint or 2 quart jars

4 pounds meaty beef bones	1 medium onion
2 quarts water	1 bay leaf
1 carrot	Salt and pepper to taste
1 stalk celery	Beef bouillon cubes or granules (optional)

PREP Wash carrot and celery under cold running water; drain. Remove stem end from carrot. Cut carrot into medium chunks. Remove leafy tops and root ends from celery. Cut celery into medium chunks. Coarsely chop onion.

COOK Combine beef bones and water in a large saucepan. Bring mixture to a boil over medium-high heat. Reduce heat; skim off foam if needed. Add carrot, celery, onion, and bay leaf. Cover saucepan and simmer 2 to 3 hours. If a more concentrated flavor is desired, simmer longer or add beef bouillon cubes or granules to the stock. Remove beef bones from stock. Strain stock through a fine sieve or several layers of cheesecloth, reserving liquid. Let stock cool until fat solidifies on top; skim off fat. Put stock in a large saucepan. Season stock with salt and pepper to taste. Bring stock to a boil.

FILL Ladle hot stock into a hot jar, leaving 1-inch headspace. Clean jar rim. Center lid on jar and adjust band to fingertip-tight. Place jar on the rack in pressure canner containing 2 inches of simmering water (180°F). Repeat until all jars are filled.

PROCESS Place lid on canner and turn to locked position. Adjust heat to medium-high. Vent steam for 10 minutes. Put weighted gauge on vent; bring pressure to 10 pounds (psi). Process pint jars 20 minutes or quart jars 25 minutes. Turn off heat; cool canner to zero pressure. After 5 minutes, remove lid. Let jars cool 10 minutes. Remove jars from canner; do not retighten bands if loose. Cool 12 hours. Check seals. Label and store jars.

Chicken Soup

Yield: about 8 pint or 4 quart jars

4 quarts chicken stock (see page 105)	1½ cups sliced carrots (about 3 medium)
3 cups diced, cooked chicken (about one 3-pound chicken)	1 cup chopped onion (about 1 large)
1½ cups chopped celery (about 3 stalks)	Salt and pepper to taste
	3 chicken bouillon cubes or granules (optional)

PREP Wash celery and carrots under cold running water; drain. Remove leafy tops and root ends from celery. Coarsely chop celery; measure 1½ cups chopped celery. Remove stem ends from carrots and peel. Slice carrots ¼-inch thick; measure 1½ cups sliced carrots. Peel onion. Coarsely chop onion; measure 1 cup chopped onion.

COOK Combine chicken stock, chicken, celery, carrots, and onion in a large saucepan. Bring mixture to a boil. Reduce heat to a simmer (180°F); simmer soup 30 minutes. Season soup with salt and pepper to taste. Add bouillon cubes or granules, cooking until dissolved, if desired.

FILL Ladle hot soup into a hot jar, leaving 1-inch headspace. Clean jar rim. Center lid on jar and adjust band to fingertip-tight. Place jar on the rack in pressure canner containing 2 inches of simmering water (180°F). Repeat until all jars are filled.

PROCESS Place lid on canner and turn to locked position. Adjust heat to medium-high. Vent steam for 10 minutes. Put weighted gauge on vent; bring pressure to 10 pounds (psi). Process pint jars 1 hour and 15 minutes or quart jars 1 hour and 30 minutes. Turn off heat; cool canner to zero pressure. After 5 minutes, remove lid. Let jars cool 10 minutes. Remove jars from canner; do not retighten bands if loose. Cool 12 hours. Check seals. Label and store jars.

Chicken Stock

Yield: about 8 pint or 4 quart jars

1 whole chicken (3 to 4 pounds)	2 medium onions
4 quarts water	10 peppercorns
2 medium carrots	2 bay leaves
2 stalks celery	1 tablespoon salt

PREP Wash chicken under cold running water; drain. Leave chicken whole or cut into pieces; set aside. Wash carrots and celery under cold running water; drain. Remove stems from carrots. Cut carrots into quarters. Remove leafy tops and root ends from celery. Cut celery in half. Peel onions. Cut onions into quarters.

COOK Combine chicken and water in a large saucepan. Bring mixture to a boil. Reduce heat; skim foam if needed. Add remaining ingredients. Cover saucepan and simmer 2 hours or until chicken is tender. Remove from heat; skim foam. Remove chicken from stock, reserving it for another use. Strain stock through a fine sieve or several layers of cheesecloth. Allow stock to cool until fat solidifies on top; skim off fat. Put stock in a large saucepan. Bring stock to a boil.

FILL Ladle hot stock into a hot jar, leaving 1-inch headspace. Clean jar rim. Center lid on jar and adjust band to fingertip-tight. Place jar on the rack in pressure canner containing 2 inches of simmering water (180°F). Repeat until all jars are filled.

PROCESS Place lid on canner and turn to locked position. Adjust heat to medium-high. Vent steam for 10 minutes. Put weighted gauge on vent; bring pressure to 10 pounds (psi). Process pint jars 20 minutes or quart jars 25 minutes. Turn off heat; cool canner to zero pressure. After 5 minutes, remove lid. Let jars cool 10 minutes. Remove jars from canner; do not retighten bands if loose. Cool 12 hours. Check seals. Label and store jars.

Chili

Yield: about 6 pint or 3 quart jars

5 pounds ground beef	1/2 cup chili powder
2 cups chopped onions (about 3 to 4 medium)	1 1/2 tablespoons salt
1 clove garlic, minced	1 hot red pepper, finely chopped
6 cups diced canned tomatoes with juice	1 teaspoon cumin seed

PREP Peel onions. Chop onions; measure 2 cups chopped onions. Peel garlic. Finely mince garlic. Wash pepper under cold running water; drain. Finely chop pepper, discarding stem.

COOK Brown meat in a large saucepan. Drain off excess fat. Add onions and garlic. Cook slowly until onions are tender. Add remaining ingredients. Simmer chili 20 minutes. Remove from heat. Skim off excess fat if needed.

FILL Ladle hot chili into a hot jar, leaving 1-inch headspace. Remove air bubbles. Clean jar rim. Center lid on jar and adjust band to fingertip-tight. Place jar on the rack in pressure canner containing 2 inches of simmering water (180°F). Repeat until all jars are filled.

PROCESS Place lid on canner and turn to locked position. Adjust heat to medium-high. Vent steam for 10 minutes. Put weighted gauge on vent; bring pressure to 10 pounds (psi). Process pint jars 1 hour and 15 minutes or quart jars 1 hour and 30 minutes. Turn off heat; cool canner to zero pressure. After 5 minutes, remove lid. Let jars cool 10 minutes. Remove jars from canner; do not retighten bands if loose. Cool 12 hours. Check seals. Label and store jars.

Note: When cutting or seeding hot peppers, wear rubber gloves to prevent hands from being burned.

Add cooked or canned beans when reheating chili for serving, if desired. Do not add beans before processing, as doing so may slow heat penetration, resulting in underprocessed food.

Clam Chowder Base

Yield: about 20 half-pint or 10 pint jars

1/2 pound salt pork	2 quarts diced potatoes (about 12 medium)
1 cup chopped onion (about 1 large)	2 quarts boiling water
3 to 4 quarts cleaned, chopped clams with juice	Salt and pepper to taste

PREP Cut salt pork into small, uniform pieces. Peel onion. Chop onion; measure 1 cup chopped onion. Peel potatoes. Dice potatoes into medium, uniform cubes; measure 2 quarts diced potatoes.

COOK Brown salt pork in a large saucepan. Drain off excess fat. Add onion and cook slowly until onion is tender but not browned. Add clams with juice, potatoes, and boiling water. Boil 10 minutes. Season clam chowder base with salt and pepper to taste.

FILL Ladle hot chowder base into a hot jar, leaving 1-inch headspace. Remove air bubbles. Clean jar rim. Center lid on jar and adjust band to fingertip-tight. Place jar on the rack in pressure canner containing 2 inches of simmering water (180°F). Repeat until all jars are filled.

PROCESS Place lid on canner and turn to locked position. Adjust heat to medium-high. Vent steam for 10 minutes. Put weighted gauge on vent; bring pressure to 10 pounds (psi). Process half-pint or pint jars 1 hour and 40 minutes. Turn off heat; cool canner to zero pressure. After 5 minutes, remove lid. Let jars cool 10 minutes. Remove jars from canner; do not retighten bands if loose. Cool 12 hours. Check seals. Label and store jars.

Note: This is the base recipe for making clam chowder. Butter and milk are added to the base when reheating for serving (see recipe below). Do not add butter or milk before processing, as it may have an adverse effect on heat penetration, resulting in underprocessed food.

To Serve—For New England Chowder, add 1 tablespoon butter and 1 cup milk to a half-pint jar of clam chowder base (double this amount for a pint jar); cook the chowder until hot throughout.

For Manhattan Clam Chowder, add the following ingredients, removing bay leaf before processing.

- 2 cups chopped tomatoes with juice
- 1/2 cup chopped celery (about 1 stalk)
- 1/2 bay leaf
- 1/2 teaspoon thyme

Goulash

Yield: about 4 pint or 2 quart jars

4 pounds boneless beef chuck roast	1/3 cup vegetable oil
6 stalks celery	20 peppercorns
4 large carrots	3 bay leaves
3 medium onions	2 teaspoons caraway seeds
1 tablespoon salt	1 cup water
3 tablespoons paprika	1/3 cup vinegar, 5% acidity
2 teaspoons dry mustard	

PREP Cut beef roast into 1-inch cubes. Wash celery and carrots under cold running water; drain. Remove leafy tops and root ends from celery; cut celery in half. Remove stems from carrots; cut carrots in half. Peel onions; cut onions in half. Combine salt, paprika, and dry mustard, stirring to blend evenly. Roll cubed meat in spice blend. Tie peppercorns, bay leaves, and caraway seeds in a spice bag.

COOK Brown meat slowly in hot vegetable oil in a large saucepan. Sprinkle excess spice mixture over meat. Add spice bag and remaining ingredients to beef mixture. Cover; simmer until beef is almost tender. Remove spice bag and vegetables; discard.

FILL Ladle hot meat and sauce into a hot jar, leaving 1-inch headspace. Remove air bubbles. Clean jar rim. Center lid on jar and adjust band to fingertip-tight. Place jar on the rack in pressure canner containing 2 inches of simmering water (180°F). Repeat until all jars are filled.

PROCESS Place lid on canner and turn to locked position. Adjust heat to medium-high. Vent steam for 10 minutes. Put weighted gauge on vent; bring pressure to 10 pounds (psi). Process pint jars 1 hour and 15 minutes or quart jars 1 hour and 30 minutes. Turn off heat; cool canner to zero pressure. After 5 minutes, remove lid. Let jars cool 10 minutes. Remove jars from canner; do not retighten bands if loose. Cool 12 hours. Check seals. Label and store jars.

Meat Sauce

Yield: about 6 pint or 3 quart jars

5 pounds ground beef	2 tablespoons brown sugar
2 cups chopped onions (about 2 to 3 medium)	2 tablespoons minced parsley
1 cup chopped green bell pepper (about 1 large)	1 1/2 tablespoons salt
	1 tablespoon oregano
2 quarts plus 1 cup cooked or canned diced tomatoes with juice	1/2 teaspoon pepper
	1/2 teaspoon ginger
	1/2 teaspoon allspice
2 2/3 cups tomato paste (about 24 ounces)	2 tablespoons vinegar, 5% acidity

PREP Wash pepper and parsley under cold running water; drain. Peel onions. Chop onions; measure 2 cups chopped onions. Remove stem and seeds from pepper. Chop pepper; measure 1 cup chopped pepper. Mince parsley; measure 2 tablespoons minced parsley.

COOK Brown beef in a large saucepan. Drain off excess fat. Add onions and pepper. Cook slowly until onions and pepper are tender. Add remaining ingredients. Bring mixture to a boil. Reduce heat to a simmer (180°F); simmer until thick, stirring to prevent sticking. Skim off excess fat, if necessary.

FILL Ladle hot meat sauce into a hot jar, leaving 1-inch headspace. Remove air bubbles. Clean jar rim. Center lid on jar and adjust band to fingertip-tight. Place jar on the rack in pressure canner containing 2 inches of simmering water (180°F). Repeat until all jars are filled.

PROCESS Place lid on canner and turn to locked position. Adjust heat to medium-high. Vent steam for 10 minutes. Put weighted gauge on vent; bring pressure to 10 pounds (psi). Process pint jars 1 hour or quart jars 1 hour and 15 minutes. Turn off heat; cool canner to zero pressure. After 5 minutes, remove lid. Let jars cool 10 minutes. Remove jars from canner; do not retighten bands if loose. Cool 12 hours. Check seals. Label and store jars.

Seasoned Ground Beef

Yield: about 5 pint or 2 quart jars

4 pounds lean ground beef	1 1/2 cups beef broth
1 1/2 cups chopped onions (about 2 medium)	1 teaspoon seasoned salt
	1/2 teaspoon pepper
2 cloves garlic, minced	
2 cups tomato juice	

PREP Peel onions. Chop onions; measure 1 1/2 cups chopped onions. Peel garlic. Finely mince garlic.

COOK Brown ground beef in a large saucepan. Drain off excess fat. Add onions and garlic. Cook mixture slowly until onions are tender. Add remaining ingredients; simmer 15 minutes or until hot throughout, stirring to prevent sticking. Skim off excess fat, if necessary.

FILL Ladle hot meat sauce into a hot jar, leaving 1-inch headspace. Remove air bubbles. Clean jar rim. Center lid on jar and adjust band to fingertip-tight. Place jar on the rack in pressure canner containing 2 inches of simmering water (180°F). Repeat until all jars are filled.

PROCESS Place lid on canner and turn to locked position. Adjust heat to medium-high. Vent steam for 10 minutes. Put weighted gauge on vent; bring pressure to 10 pounds (psi). Process pint jars 1 hour and 15 minutes or quart jars 1 hour and 30 minutes. Turn off heat; cool canner to zero pressure. After 5 minutes, remove lid. Let jars cool 10 minutes. Remove jars from canner; do not retighten bands if loose. Cool 12 hours. Check seals. Label and store jars.

Spiced Tomato Soup

Yield: about 8 pint jars

4 quarts chopped tomatoes (about 20 to 24 medium)	1 cup sliced carrots (about 2 medium)
3 1/2 cups chopped onions (about 5 to 6 medium)	7 bay leaves
	1 teaspoon whole cloves
2 1/2 cups chopped celery (about 5 stalks)	1 clove garlic
2 cups chopped red bell peppers (about 2 large)	1 cup brown sugar
	2 teaspoons salt

PREP Wash tomatoes, celery, peppers, and carrots under cold running water; drain. To peel tomatoes, blanch 30 to 60 seconds in boiling water. Immediately transfer to cold water. Cut off peel and core tomatoes. Chop tomatoes; measure 4 quarts chopped tomatoes. Peel onions. Chop onions; measure 3 1/2 cups chopped onions. Remove leafy tops and root ends from celery. Chop celery; measure 2½ cups chopped celery. Remove stem and seeds from peppers. Chop peppers; measure 2 cups chopped peppers. Remove stem end from carrots and peel. Slice carrots ¼-inch thick; measure 1 cup sliced carrots. Tie bay leaves and whole cloves in a spice bag. Peel garlic. Finely mince garlic.

COOK Combine tomatoes, onions, celery, peppers, carrots, spice bag, and garlic in a large saucepan. Simmer until vegetables are tender. Remove spice bag. Purée mixture using an electric food strainer or food mill. Return purée to saucepan. Add sugar and salt. Bring mixture to a boil. Reduce heat to a simmer (180°F); simmer 15 minutes.

FILL Ladle hot soup into a hot jar, leaving 1-inch headspace. Remove air bubbles. Clean jar rim. Center lid on jar and adjust band to fingertip-tight. Place jar on the rack in pressure canner containing 2 inches of simmering water (180°F). Repeat until all jars are filled.

PROCESS Place lid on canner and turn to locked position. Adjust heat to medium-high. Vent steam for 10 minutes. Put weighted gauge on vent; bring pressure to 10 pounds (psi). Process pint jars 20 minutes. Turn off heat; cool canner to zero pressure. After 5 minutes, remove lid. Let jars cool 10 minutes. Remove jars from canner; do not retighten bands if loose. Cool 12 hours. Check seals. Label and store jars.

Southwestern Vegetable Soup

Yield: about 9 pint or 4 quart jars

- 1½ quarts whole kernel corn, uncooked (about 12 medium ears)
- 1 quart chopped tomatoes (about 5 to 6 medium)
- 2 cups chopped tomatillos (about 16 medium)
- 1 cup sliced carrots (about 2 medium)
- 1 cup chopped onions (about 2 medium)
- 1 cup chopped red bell pepper (about 1 large)
- 1 cup chopped green bell pepper (about 1 large)
- ¾ cup chopped banana peppers (about 3 to 4)
- ¼ cup chopped jalapeño peppers (about 2 to 3)
- 3 tablespoons minced cilantro
- 2 teaspoons chili powder
- 1 teaspoon cayenne pepper
- 1 teaspoon black pepper
- 1 teaspoon salt
- 1½ quarts tomato juice
- 1 cup water
- 4 teaspoons hot pepper sauce

PREP Wash corn, tomatoes, tomatillos, carrots, bell, banana and jalapeño peppers, and cilantro under cold running water; drain. Cut corn off the cob. Start at the small end of the cob and cut downward to the stem end. Measure 1½ quarts corn. To peel tomatoes, blanch 30 to 60 seconds in boiling water. Immediately transfer to cold water. Cut off peel and core. Chop tomatoes; measure 1 quart chopped tomatoes. Remove husk from tomatillos. Chop tomatillos; measure 2 cups chopped tomatillos. Remove stem ends from carrots and peel. Slice carrots ¼-inch thick; measure 1 cup sliced carrots. Peel onions. Chop onions; measure 1 cup chopped onions. Remove stems and seeds from red and green bell peppers. Chop red and green bell peppers; measure 1 cup each chopped red and green bell peppers. Remove stems and seeds from banana peppers. Chop banana peppers; measure ¾ cup chopped banana peppers. Remove stems and seeds from jalapeño peppers. Chop jalapeño peppers; measure ¼ cup chopped jalapeño peppers. Mince cilantro; measure 3 tablespoons minced cilantro.

COOK Combine all ingredients in a large saucepan. Bring mixture to a boil. Reduce heat to a simmer (180°F); simmer 15 minutes.

FILL Ladle hot soup into a hot jar, leaving 1-inch headspace. Remove air bubbles. Clean jar rim. Center lid on jar and adjust band to fingertip-tight. Place jar on the rack in pressure canner containing 2 inches of simmering water (180°F). Repeat until all jars are filled.

PROCESS Place lid on canner and turn to locked position. Adjust heat to medium-high. Vent steam for 10 minutes. Put weighted gauge on vent; bring pressure to 10 pounds (psi). Process pint jars 55 minutes or quart jars 1 hour and 25 minutes. Turn off heat; cool canner to zero pressure. After 5 minutes, remove lid. Let jars cool 10 minutes. Remove jars from canner; do not retighten bands if loose. Cool 12 hours. Check seals. Label and store jars.

Note: When cutting or seeding hot peppers, wear rubber gloves to prevent hands from being burned.

Split Pea Soup

Yield: about 5 pint or 2 quart jars

- 1 (16-ounce) package dried split peas
- 2 quarts water
- 1½ cups sliced carrots (about 3 medium)
- 1 cup chopped onion (about 1 medium)
- 1 cup diced, cooked ham
- 1 bay leaf
- ¼ teaspoon allspice
- Salt and pepper to taste

PREP Wash dried split peas and carrots under cold running water; drain. Remove stem ends from carrots and peel. Slice carrots ¼-inch thick; measure 1½ cups sliced carrots. Peel onion. Chop onion; measure 1 cup chopped onion.

COOK Combine dried split peas and water in a large saucepan. Bring mixture to a boil. Reduce heat to a simmer (180°F); simmer, covered, 1 hour or until split peas are soft. For a smooth consistency, purée mixture using a food processor or food mill. Return purée to saucepan. Add remaining ingredients and simmer 30 minutes. Add boiling water if soup is too thick.

FILL Ladle hot soup into a hot jar, leaving 1-inch headspace. Remove air bubbles. Clean jar rim. Center lid on jar and adjust band to fingertip-tight. Place jar on the rack in pressure canner containing 2 inches of simmering water (180°F). Repeat until all jars are filled.

PROCESS Place lid on canner and turn to locked position. Adjust heat to medium-high. Vent steam for 10 minutes. Put weighted gauge on vent; bring pressure to 10 pounds (psi). Process pint jars 1 hour and 15 minutes or quart jars 1 hour and 30 minutes. Turn off heat; cool canner to zero pressure. After 5 minutes, remove lid. Let jars cool 10 minutes. Remove jars from canner; do not retighten bands if loose. Cool 12 hours. Check seals. Label and store jars.

Ten Bean Soup

Yield: about 6 quart jars

½ cup dried black beans	1½ cups diced ham (optional)
½ cup dried kidney beans	½ cup cut fresh green beans
½ cup navy beans	2 bay leaves
½ cup dried pinto beans	1 tablespoon tarragon
½ cup dried Great Northern beans	1 tablespoon summer savory
¼ cup dried blackeye peas	Salt and pepper to taste, if desired
¼ cup dried split peas	
¼ cup dried chick peas	
¼ cup dried lentils	

PREP Wash dried beans, peas, lentils, and green beans under cold running water; drain. Remove ends from green beans. Cut green beans into ½-inch pieces; measure ½ cup cut green beans.

COOK Combine dried beans, peas, and lentils in a large saucepan. Add water to cover by 2 inches. Bring mixture to a boil; boil 2 minutes. Remove from heat and let beans soak 1 hour. Drain. Return beans to a large saucepan. Add water to cover by 2 inches. Add ham, if desired. Stir in remaining ingredients. Bring soup to a boil. Reduce heat to a gentle boil; boil 30 minutes. Season soup with salt and pepper to taste, if desired. Remove bay leaves.

FILL Ladle hot soup into a hot jar, leaving 1-inch headspace. Remove air bubbles. Clean jar rim. Center lid on jar and adjust band to fingertip-tight. Place jar on the rack in pressure canner containing 2 inches of simmering water (180°F). Repeat until all jars are filled.

PROCESS Place lid on canner and turn to locked position. Adjust heat to medium-high. Vent steam for 10 minutes. Put weighted gauge on vent; bring pressure to 10 pounds (psi). Process quart jars 1 hour and 30 minutes. Turn off heat; cool canner to zero pressure. After 5 minutes, remove lid. Let jars cool 10 minutes. Remove jars from canner; do not retighten bands if loose. Cool 12 hours. Check seals. Label and store jars.

Vegetable Soup

Yield: about 14 pint or 7 quart jars

2 quarts chopped tomatoes (about 12 medium)	2 cups sliced celery (about 4 stalks)
1½ quarts cubed potatoes (about 9 medium)	2 cups chopped onions (about 2 to 3 medium)
1½ quarts sliced carrots (about 12 medium)	1½ quarts water
1 quart lima beans	Salt and pepper to taste, if desired
1 quart whole kernel corn, uncooked (about 8 medium ears)	

PREP Wash tomatoes, potatoes, carrots, lima beans, corn, and celery under cold running water; drain. To peel tomatoes, blanch 30 to 60 seconds in boiling water. Immediately transfer to cold water. Cut off peel and core tomatoes. Chop tomatoes; measure 2 quarts chopped tomatoes. Peel potatoes. Cut potatoes into ½-inch cubes; measure 1½ quarts cubed potatoes. Remove stem end from carrots and peel. Slice carrots ¼-inch thick; measure 1½ quarts sliced carrots. Cut corn off the cob, starting at the small end and moving downward to the stem end; measure 1 quart whole kernel corn. Remove leafy tops and root ends from celery. Cut celery into 1-inch slices; measure 2 cups sliced celery. Peel onions. Chop onions; measure 2 cups chopped onions.

COOK Combine all ingredients, except salt and pepper, in a large saucepan. Bring mixture to a boil. Reduce heat to a simmer (180°F); simmer 15 minutes. Season soup with salt and pepper to taste, if desired.

FILL Ladle hot soup into a hot jar, leaving 1-inch headspace. Remove air bubbles. Clean jar rim. Center lid on jar and adjust band to fingertip-tight. Place jar on the rack in pressure canner containing 2 inches of simmering water (180°F). Repeat until all jars are filled.

PROCESS Place lid on canner and turn to locked position. Adjust heat to medium-high. Vent steam for 10 minutes. Put weighted gauge on vent; bring pressure to 10 pounds (psi). Process pint jars 55 minutes or quart jars 1 hour and 25 minutes. Turn off heat; cool canner to zero pressure. After 5 minutes, remove lid. Let jars cool 10 minutes. Remove jars from canner; do not retighten bands if loose. Cool 12 hours. Check seals. Label and store jars.

Vegetable Stock

Yield: about 8 pint or 4 quart jars

5 to 6 medium carrots (about 1 pound)	2 medium turnips, diced
6 stalks celery	3 cloves garlic, crushed
3 medium onions (about 1 pound)	3 bay leaves
2 medium red bell peppers	1 teaspoon crushed thyme
2 medium tomatoes, diced	8 peppercorns
	7 quarts water

PREP Wash carrots, celery, peppers, tomatoes, and turnips under cold running water; drain. Remove stem ends from carrots. Cut carrots into 1-inch pieces. Remove leafy tops and root ends from celery. Cut celery into 1-inch pieces. Cut onions into quarters. Remove stems and seeds from peppers. Cut peppers into 1-inch strips. Remove cores and seeds from tomatoes. Coarsely chop tomatoes. Remove stem ends from turnips. Coarsely chop turnips. Crush garlic.

COOK Combine all ingredients in a large saucepan. Bring mixture to a boil. Reduce heat to a simmer (180°F); simmer, covered, 2 hours. Uncover saucepan; continue simmering 2 hours. Strain stock through a fine sieve or several layers of cheesecloth. Discard vegetables and herbs.

FILL Ladle hot stock into a hot jar, leaving 1-inch headspace. Clean jar rim. Center lid on jar and adjust band to fingertip-tight. Place jar on the rack in pressure canner containing 2 inches of simmering water (180°F). Repeat until all jars are filled.

PROCESS Place lid on canner and turn to locked position. Adjust heat to medium-high. Vent steam for 10 minutes. Put weighted gauge on vent; bring pressure to 10 pounds (psi). Process pint jars 30 minutes or quart jars 35 minutes. Turn off heat; cool canner to zero pressure. After 5 minutes, remove lid. Let jars cool 10 minutes. Remove jars from canner; do not retighten bands if loose. Cool 12 hours. Check seals. Label and store jars.

Savory Fillings

Green Tomato Mincemeat

Yield: about 10 pint or 5 quart jars

- 2 quarts chopped green tomatoes (about 20 small)
- 1 tablespoon salt
- 2½ quarts chopped apples (about 10 medium)
- 3½ cups brown sugar
- 1½ cups chopped suet (about 6 ounces)
- 1 pound golden raisins
- 3 tablespoons grated orange peel (about 1 medium)
- ⅔ cup chopped orange pulp (about 2 medium)
- 2 teaspoons cinnamon
- 1 teaspoon nutmeg
- 1 teaspoon cloves
- ½ teaspoon ginger
- ½ cup vinegar, 5% acidity

PREP Wash green tomatoes, apples, and orange under cold running water; drain. Remove cores from green tomatoes. Coarsely chop tomatoes; measure 2 quarts chopped tomatoes. Put chopped green tomatoes in a large bowl. Sprinkle salt over green tomatoes; let stand 1 hour. Core and peel apples. Coarsely chop apples; measure 2½ quarts chopped apples. Grate orange peel; measure 3 tablespoons grated orange peel. Cut orange in half crosswise. Remove orange pulp from individual sections. Chop orange pulp; measure ⅔ cup chopped orange pulp. Rinse tomatoes under cold running water; drain. Cover tomatoes with boiling water; let stand 5 minutes. Drain.

COOK Combine all ingredients in a large saucepan. Bring mixture to a boil. Reduce heat and simmer 15 minutes.

FILL Ladle hot mincemeat into a hot jar, leaving 1-inch headspace. Remove air bubbles. Clean jar rim. Center lid on jar and adjust band to fingertip-tight. Place jar on the rack in pressure canner containing 2 inches of simmering water (180°F). Repeat until all jars are filled.

PROCESS Place lid on canner and turn to locked position. Adjust heat to medium-high. Vent steam for 10 minutes. Put weighted gauge on vent; bring pressure to 10 pounds (psi). Process pint or quart jars 1 hour and 30 minutes. Turn off heat; cool canner to zero pressure. After 5 minutes, remove lid. Let jars cool 10 minutes. Remove jars from canner; do not retighten bands if loose. Cool 12 hours. Check seals. Label and store jars.

Madeira Pear Mincemeat

Yield: about 8 pint or 4 quart jars

- 2 quarts coarsely chopped pears (about 12 medium)
- 1 cup golden raisins
- 1 cup dried cherries
- 1 cup sugar
- 1 cup water
- 1 cup Madeira wine
- 1 quart sliced zucchini (about 4 medium)
- 1 quart sliced yellow squash (about 4 medium)
- 2 cups chopped yellow bell peppers (about 2 large)
- 2 cups diced mushrooms (about 8 ounces)
- 1 cup chopped onion (about 1 medium)
- ¼ cup minced crystallized ginger
- 1 tablespoon grated fresh ginger
- 2 teaspoons allspice
- 1 teaspoon salt

PREP Wash pears, zucchini, squash, and peppers under cold running water; drain. Gently clean dirt from mushrooms using a soft vegetable brush. Rinse mushrooms under cold running water; drain. Cut pears in half lengthwise. Remove stem and core from pears. Coarsely chop pears; measure 2 quarts chopped pears. Remove stem and blossom ends fom zucchini and squash. Cut zucchini and squash crosswise into ¼-inch slices. Measure 1 quart each sliced zucchini and sliced squash. Remove stems and seeds from peppers. Chop peppers; measure 2 cups chopped peppers. Coarsely chop mushrooms; measure 2 cups chopped mushrooms. Peel onion. Chop onion; measure 1 cup chopped onion. Peel a small piece of fresh ginger. Grate fresh ginger; measure 1 tablespoon grated fresh ginger.

COOK Combine pears, raisins, dried cherries, sugar, water, and Madeira wine in a large saucepan. Let mixture stand 1 hour. Add remaining ingredients. Bring mixture to a boil. Reduce heat to a simmer (180°F); simmer 15 minutes.

FILL Ladle hot mincemeat into a hot jar, leaving 1-inch headspace. Remove air bubbles. Clean jar rim. Center lid on jar and adjust band to fingertip-tight. Place jar on the rack in pressure canner containing 2 inches of simmering water (180°F). Repeat until all jars are filled.

PROCESS Place lid on canner and turn to locked position. Adjust heat to medium-high. Vent steam for 10 minutes. Put weighted gauge on vent; bring pressure to 10 pounds (psi). Process pint or quart jars 25 minutes. Turn off heat; cool canner to zero pressure. After 5 minutes, remove lid. Let jars cool 10 minutes. Remove jars from canner; do not retighten bands if loose. Cool 12 hours. Check seals. Label and store jars.

Mincemeat – Traditional

Yield: about 12 pint or 6 quart jars

5 cups cooked ground beef (about 2 pounds)	1 (8-ounce) package candied citron, minced
1 quart ground suet (about 1 pound)	4½ cups brown sugar
1½ pounds golden raisins	1 tablespoon salt
1½ pounds dark raisins	1 tablespoon cinnamon
2 pounds dried currants	1 tablespoon allspice
3 quarts chopped tart apples (about 12 medium)	2 teaspoons nutmeg
	1 teaspoon cloves
1½ cups chopped orange pulp (about 3 medium)	¼ teaspoon ginger
	1 quart sweet apple cider or white grape juice
⅓ cup finely chopped orange peel (about 1 medium)	¼ cup lemon juice, fresh or bottled

PREP Wash apples and oranges under cold running water; drain. Core and peel apples. Chop apples; measure 3 quarts chopped apples. Cut oranges in half crosswise and remove seeds. Remove orange pulp from individual sections; measure 1½ cups orange pulp. Remove membrane and white pith from 2 halves of orange peel. Chop orange peel; measure ⅓ cup chopped orange peel.

COOK Brown ground beef in a large saucepan. Drain off excess fat. Measure 5 cups cooked beef. Return cooked beef to saucepan. Add remaining ingredients; simmer 30 minutes, stirring to prevent sticking.

FILL Ladle hot mincemeat into a hot jar, leaving 1-inch headspace. Remove air bubbles. Clean jar rim. Center lid on jar and adjust band to fingertip-tight. Place jar on the rack in pressure canner containing 2 inches of simmering water (180°F). Repeat until all jars are filled.

PROCESS Place lid on canner and turn to locked position. Adjust heat to medium-high. Vent steam for 10 minutes. Put weighted gauge on vent; bring pressure to 10 pounds (psi). Process pint or quart jars 1 hour and 30 minutes. Turn off heat; cool canner to zero pressure. After 5 minutes, remove lid. Let jars cool 10 minutes. Remove jars from canner; do not retighten bands if loose. Cool 12 hours. Check seals. Label and store jars.

Vegetables

Asparagus

Yield: about 6 pint or 3 quart jars

10½ pounds asparagus	Water
Salt (optional)	

PREP Wash asparagus under cold running water; drain. Remove tough root ends and scales. For HOT PACK, cut asparagus into 1-inch pieces.

COOK

RAW PACK—Bring water to a boil; reduce heat to a simmer (180°F). Keep water hot.

HOT PACK—Put asparagus in a large saucepan. Add water to cover asparagus. Boil asparagus 3 minutes.

FILL

RAW PACK—Pack raw asparagus, as tightly as possible without crushing, into a hot jar, leaving 1-inch headspace. Add ½ teaspoon salt to pint jar; 1 teaspoon salt to quart jar, if desired. Ladle hot water over asparagus, leaving 1-inch headspace.

HOT PACK—Pack cooked asparagus into a hot jar, leaving 1-inch headspace. Add ½ teaspoon salt to pint jar; 1 teaspoon salt to quart jar, if desired. Ladle hot cooking liquid or boiling water over asparagus, leaving 1-inch headspace.

Remove air bubbles. Clean jar rim. Center lid on jar and adjust band to fingertip-tight. Place jar on the rack in pressure canner containing 2 inches of simmering water (180°F). Repeat until all jars are filled.

PROCESS Place lid on canner and turn to locked position. Adjust heat to medium-high. Vent steam for 10 minutes. Put weighted gauge on vent; bring pressure to 10 pounds (psi). Process pint jars 30 minutes or quart jars 40 minutes. Turn off heat; cool canner to zero pressure. After 5 minutes, remove lid. Let jars cool 10 minutes. Remove jars from canner; do not retighten bands if loose. Cool 12 hours. Check seals. Label and store jars.

Beans – Boston Baked

Yield: about 6 pint or 3 quart jars

1 quart dried navy beans (about 1 pound)	⅔ cup brown sugar
½ pound salt pork, cut into ½-inch pieces	2 teaspoons salt
	2 teaspoons dry mustard
3 large onions	⅔ cup molasses

PREP Wash dried beans under cold running water; drain. Peel onions. Cut onions into ¼-inch slices.

COOK Put dried beans in a large saucepan. Add water to cover by 2 inches. Bring mixture to a boil; boil 2 minutes. Remove from heat and let beans soak 1 hour. Drain. Return beans to a large saucepan. Add water to cover by 2 inches. Bring beans to a boil. Reduce heat to a simmer (180°F); simmer, covered, until skins begin to split. Drain beans, reserving cooking liquid. Put beans, salt pork, and onions in a baking dish. Combine remaining ingredients in a large bowl. Stir in 4 cups reserved cooking liquid, adding water to equal 4 cups, if needed. Pour sauce over beans; cover dish. Bake at 350°F for 3½ hours. Add water, if needed, to keep beans soupy while baking.

FILL Ladle hot beans and sauce into a hot jar, leaving 1-inch headspace. Remove air bubbles. Clean jar rim. Center lid on jar and adjust band to fingertip-tight. Place jar on the rack in pressure canner containing 2 inches of simmering water (180°F). Repeat until all jars are filled.

PROCESS Place lid on canner and turn to locked position. Adjust heat to medium-high. Vent steam for 10 minutes. Put weighted gauge on vent; bring pressure to 10 pounds (psi). Process pint jars 1 hour and 20 minutes or quart jars 1 hour and 35 minutes. Turn off heat; cool canner to zero pressure. After 5 minutes, remove lid. Let jars cool 10 minutes. Remove jars from canner; do not retighten bands if loose. Cool 12 hours. Check seals. Label and store jars.

Beans or Peas – Dried

Cranberry, Chickpea, Great Northern, Kidney, Pinto

Yield: about 6 pint or 3 quart jars

2¼ pounds dried beans or peas   Water

Salt (optional)

PREP Wash beans or peas under cold running water; drain.

COOK Put beans or peas in a large saucepan. Add water to cover by 2 inches. Bring mixture to a boil; boil 2 minutes. Remove from heat and let beans or peas soak 1 hour. Drain. Return beans or peas to a large saucepan. Add water to cover by 2 inches. Bring beans or peas to a boil. Reduce heat to a gentle boil; boil, covered, for 30 minutes.

FILL Pack hot beans or peas into a hot jar, leaving 1-inch headspace. Add ½ teaspoon salt to pint jar; 1 teaspoon salt to quart jar, if desired. Ladle hot cooking liquid or boiling water over beans or peas, leaving 1-inch headspace.

Remove air bubbles. Clean jar rim. Center lid on jar and adjust band to fingertip-tight. Place jar on the rack in pressure canner containing 2 inches of simmering water (180°F). Repeat until all jars are filled.

PROCESS Place lid on canner and turn to locked position. Adjust heat to medium-high. Vent steam for 10 minutes. Put weighted gauge on vent; bring pressure to 10 pounds (psi). Process pint jars 1 hour and 15 minutes or quart jars 1 hour and 30 minutes. Turn off heat; cool canner to zero pressure. After 5 minutes, remove lid. Let jars cool 10 minutes. Remove jars from canner; do not retighten bands if loose. Cool 12 hours. Check seals. Label and store jars.

Beans – Green, Snap, or Wax

Green, Hull, Italian, Pole, Purple, Snap, Wax

Yield: about 6 pint or 3 quart jars

4½ to 7½ pounds beans   Water

Salt (optional)

PREP Wash beans under cold running water; drain. Remove string and trim ends from beans. Cut or break beans into 2-inch pieces.

COOK

RAW PACK—Bring water to a boil; reduce heat to a simmer (180°F). Keep water hot.

HOT PACK—Bring water to a boil in a large saucepan. Blanch beans in boiling water 5 minutes; remove beans. Reduce heat to a simmer (180°F). Keep water hot.

FILL

RAW PACK—Pack raw beans, as tightly as possible without crushing, into a hot jar, leaving 1-inch headspace. Add ½ teaspoon salt to pint jar; 1 teaspoon salt to quart jar, if desired. Ladle hot water over beans, leaving 1-inch headspace.

HOT PACK—Pack hot beans into a hot jar, leaving 1-inch headspace. Add ½ teaspoon salt to pint jar; 1 teaspoon salt to quart jar, if desired. Ladle the hot cooking water over beans, leaving 1-inch headspace.

Remove air bubbles. Clean jar rim. Center lid on jar and adjust band to fingertip-tight. Place jar on the rack in pressure canner containing 2 inches of simmering water (180°F). Repeat until all jars are filled.

PROCESS Place lid on canner and turn to locked position. Adjust heat to medium-high. Vent steam for 10 minutes. Put weighted gauge on vent; bring pressure to 10 pounds (psi). Process RAW PACK and HOT PACK pint jars 20 minutes or quart jars 25 minutes. Turn off heat; cool canner to zero pressure. After 5 minutes, remove lid. Let jars cool 10 minutes. Remove jars from canner; do not retighten bands if loose. Cool 12 hours. Check seals. Label and store jars.

 Add 1 or 2 pieces of fresh lemon peel to each jar for a touch of citrus flavor. Use only the yellow portion of the peel. Process jars as for Beans—Green, Snap, or Wax.

Beans – Lima or Butter

Yield: about 6 pint or 3 quart jars

9 to 15 pounds beans   Water

Salt (optional)

PREP Wash beans under cold running water; drain. Shell the beans. Rinse and drain.

COOK

RAW PACK—Bring water to a boil; reduce heat to a simmer (180°F). Keep water hot.

HOT PACK—Bring water to a boil in a large saucepan. Blanch beans in boiling water 3 minutes; remove beans. Reduce heat to a simmer (180°F). Keep water hot.

FILL

RAW PACK—Pack raw beans loosely into a hot jar, leaving 1-inch headspace. Add ½ teaspoon salt to pint jar; 1 teaspoon salt to quart jar, if desired. Ladle hot water over beans, leaving 1-inch headspace.

HOT PACK—Pack hot beans into a hot jar, leaving 1-inch headspace. Add ½ teaspoon salt to pint jar; 1 teaspoon salt to quart jar, if desired. Ladle the hot cooking water over beans, leaving 1-inch headspace.

Remove air bubbles. Clean jar rim. Center lid on jar and adjust band to fingertip-tight. Place jar on the rack in pressure canner containing 2 inches of simmering water (180°F). Repeat until all jars are filled.

PROCESS Place lid on canner and turn to locked position. Adjust heat to medium-high. Vent steam for 10 minutes. Put weighted gauge on vent; bring pressure to 10 pounds (psi). Process RAW PACK and HOT PACK pint jars 40 minutes or quart jars 50 minutes. Turn off heat; cool canner to zero pressure. After 5 minutes, remove lid. Let jars cool 10 minutes. Remove jars from canner; do not retighten bands if loose. Cool 12 hours. Check seals. Label and store jars.

Beans with Pork and Tomato Sauce

Yield: about 6 pint or 3 quart jars

1 quart dried navy beans (about 2 pounds)	2 teaspoons salt
1/4 pound salt pork	1/4 teaspoon cloves
1 cup chopped onion (about 1 medium)	1/4 teaspoon allspice
3 tablespoons sugar	1 quart tomato juice

PREP Wash beans under cold running water; drain. Cut salt pork into 1/2-inch pieces. Peel onion. Chop onion; measure 1 cup chopped onion.

COOK Put beans in a large saucepan. Add water to cover beans by 2 inches. Bring mixture to a boil; boil 2 minutes. Remove from heat and let beans soak 1 hour. Drain. Return beans to a large saucepan. Cover beans with boiling water by 2 inches. Boil beans 3 minutes. Remove from heat and let stand 10 minutes. Combine onion, sugar, salt, spices, and tomato juice in a medium saucepan. Bring sauce to a boil.

FILL Pack hot beans into a hot jar to 3/4 full. Add 1 piece of salt pork. Ladle hot sauce over beans, leaving 1-inch headspace. Remove air bubbles. Clean jar rim. Center lid on jar and adjust band to fingertip-tight. Place jar on the rack in pressure canner containing 2 inches of simmering water (180°F). Repeat until all jars are filled.

PROCESS Place lid on canner and turn to locked position. Adjust heat to medium-high. Vent steam for 10 minutes. Put weighted gauge on vent; bring pressure to 10 pounds (psi). Process pint jars 1 hour and 5 minutes or quart jars 1 hour and 15 minutes. Turn off heat; cool canner to zero pressure. After 5 minutes, remove lid. Let jars cool 10 minutes. Remove jars from canner; do not retighten bands if loose. Cool 12 hours. Check seals. Label and store jars.

Beets

Yield: about 6 pint or 3 quart jars

6 to 10 1/2 pounds beets, about 1- to 2-inch diameter	Salt (optional)
	Water

PREP Wash beets under cold running water; drain. Trim stems and tap roots to 2 inches in length.

COOK Boil beets in a large saucepan until skins slip off. Remove skins. Cut off stems and tap roots. Slice, dice, or leave beets whole.

FILL Pack hot beets into a hot jar, leaving 1-inch headspace. Add 1/2 teaspoon salt to pint jar; 1 teaspoon salt to quart jar, if desired. Ladle hot cooking liquid or boiling water over beets, leaving 1-inch headspace. Remove air bubbles. Clean jar rim. Center lid on jar and adjust band to fingertip-tight. Place jar on the rack in pressure canner containing 2 inches of simmering water (180°F). Repeat until all jars are filled.

PROCESS Place lid on canner and turn to locked position. Adjust heat to medium-high. Vent steam for 10 minutes. Put weighted gauge on vent; bring pressure to 10 pounds (psi). Process pint jars 30 minutes or quart jars 35 minutes. Turn off heat; cool canner to zero pressure. After 5 minutes, remove lid. Let jars cool 10 minutes. Remove jars from canner; do not retighten bands if loose. Cool 12 hours. Check seals. Label and store jars.

Carrots

Yield: about 6 pint or 3 quart jars

6 to 9 pounds carrots, about 1- to 1 1/2-inch diameter	Salt (optional)
	Water

PREP Wash carrots under cold running water; drain. Remove stem ends and peel carrots. Slice, dice, or leave carrots whole.

COOK

RAW PACK—Bring water to a boil; reduce heat to a simmer (180°F). Keep water hot.

HOT PACK—Put carrots in a large saucepan. Add water just to cover. Bring mixture to a boil. Reduce heat to a simmer (180°F); simmer 5 minutes; remove carrots. Keep water hot.

FILL

RAW PACK—Pack raw carrots tightly into a hot jar, leaving 1-inch headspace. Add 1/2 teaspoon salt to pint jar; 1 teaspoon salt to quart jar, if desired. Ladle hot water over carrots, leaving, 1-inch headspace.

HOT PACK—Pack hot carrots into a hot jar, leaving 1-inch headspace. Add 1/2 teaspoon salt to pint jar; 1 teaspoon salt to quart jar, if desired. Ladle the hot cooking liquid or boiling water over carrots, leaving 1-inch headspace.

Remove air bubbles. Clean jar rim. Center lid on jar and adjust band to fingertip-tight. Place jar on the rack in pressure canner containing 2 inches of simmering water (180°F). Repeat until all jars are filled.

PROCESS Place lid on canner and turn to locked position. Adjust heat to medium-high. Vent steam for 10 minutes. Put weighted gauge on vent; bring pressure to 10 pounds (psi). Process pint jars 25 minutes or quart jars 30 minutes. Turn off heat; cool canner to zero pressure. After 5 minutes, remove lid. Let jars cool 10 minutes. Remove jars from canner; do not retighten bands if loose. Cool 12 hours. Check seals. Label and store jars.

You Choose To make glazed carrots, bring 2 cups brown sugar, 2 cups water, and 1 cup orange juice to a boil, stirring until sugar dissolves. Reduce heat to a simmer (180°F). Use hot syrup as the canning liquid in place of water. Process jars as for RAW PACK Carrots.

Corn – Cream Style

Yield: about 6 pint jars

3 to 4 1/2 pounds ears of corn	Salt (optional)
	Water

PREP Remove husk and silk from ears of corn. Wash corn under cold running water; drain. Cut corn off the cob, leaving tip ends of kernels in place. Start at the small end of the cob and cut downward to the stem end. Scrape cob to extract pulp and milk. Measure kernels, pulp, and milk together.

COOK Put corn, pulp, and milk in a large saucepan. Add 1/2 teaspoon salt, if desired, and 1 1/4 cups boiling water for each 2 cups of corn mixture. Boil mixture 3 minutes.

FILL Ladle hot corn and liquid into a hot jar, leaving 1-inch headspace. Remove air bubbles. Clean jar rim. Center lid on jar and adjust band to fingertip-tight. Place jar on the rack in pressure canner containing 2 inches of simmering water (180°F). Repeat until all jars are filled.

PROCESS Place lid on canner and turn to locked position. Adjust heat to medium-high. Vent steam for 10 minutes. Put weighted gauge on vent; bring pressure to 10 pounds (psi). Process pint jars 1 hour and 25 minutes. Turn off heat; cool canner to zero pressure. After 5 minutes, remove lid. Let jars cool 10 minutes. Remove jars from canner; do not retighten bands if loose. Cool 12 hours. Check seals. Label and store jars.

Note: Process cream style corn only in pint jars.

Corn – Whole Kernel

Yield: about 6 pint or 3 quart jars

9 to 18 pounds ears of corn	Salt (optional)
	Water

PREP Remove husk and silk from ears of corn. Wash corn under cold running water; drain. Cut corn off the cob. Start at the small end of the cob and cut downward to the stem end. Do not scrape cob.

COOK

RAW PACK—Bring water to a boil; reduce heat to a simmer (180°F). Keep water hot.

HOT PACK—Measure cut corn. Put cut corn in a large saucepan. Add 1/2 teaspoon salt, if desired, and 1 cup boiling water for each 2 cups cut corn. Bring mixture to a boil. Reduce heat to a simmer (180°F); simmer 5 minutes.

FILL

RAW PACK—Pack raw corn loosely into a hot jar, leaving 1-inch headspace. Add 1/2 teaspoon salt to pint jar; 1 teaspoon salt to quart jar, if desired. Ladle hot water over corn, leaving 1-inch headspace.

HOT PACK—Pack hot corn and liquid into a hot jar, leaving 1-inch headspace.

Remove air bubbles. Clean jar rim. Center lid on jar and adjust band to fingertip-tight. Place jar on the rack in pressure canner containing 2 inches of simmering water (180°F). Repeat until all jars are filled.

PROCESS Place lid on canner and turn to locked position. Adjust heat to medium-high. Vent steam for 10 minutes. Put weighted gauge on vent; bring pressure to 10 pounds (psi). Process pint jars 55 minutes or quart jars 1 hour and 25 minutes. Turn off heat; cool canner to zero pressure. After 5 minutes, remove lid. Let jars cool 10 minutes. Remove jars from canner; do not retighten bands if loose. Cool 12 hours. Check seals. Label and store jars.

Note: The sugar content in young ears of corn or sweet varieties of corn may caramelize during processing, causing some browning.

 For a flavor variation, add 1 or 2 strips of red bell pepper and 1/4 teaspoon basil to each pint jar; 3 or 4 strips red bell pepper and 1/2 teaspoon basil to each quart jar. Process jars as for Corn–Whole Kernel.

Greens

Beet, Chard, Kale, Mustard, Poke, Spinach, Turnip

Yield: about 6 pint or 3 quart jars

6 to 18 pounds greens	Water
Salt (optional)	

PREP Wash greens thoroughly under cold running water; drain. Cut off large, tough stems.

COOK Put greens in a large saucepan. Add just enough water to prevent sticking. Cook greens until wilted, stirring to cook evenly and to prevent sticking. Cut through greens several times using a sharp knife. Bring additional water for canning to a boil in a separate saucepan; reduce heat to a simmer (180°F). Keep water hot.

FILL Pack hot greens into a hot jar, leaving 1-inch headspace. Add 1/2 teaspoon salt to pint jar; 1 teaspoon salt to quart jar, if desired. Ladle hot cooking liquid or boiling water over greens, leaving 1-inch headspace.

Remove air bubbles. Clean jar rim. Center lid on jar and adjust band to fingertip-tight. Place jar on the rack in pressure canner containing 2 inches of simmering water (180°F). Repeat until all jars are filled.

PROCESS Place lid on canner and turn to locked position. Adjust heat to medium-high. Vent steam for 10 minutes. Put weighted gauge on vent; bring pressure to 10 pounds (psi). Process pint jars 1 hour and 10 minutes or quart jars 1 hour and 30 minutes. Turn off heat; cool canner to zero pressure. After 5 minutes, remove lid. Let jars cool 10 minutes. Remove jars from canner; do not retighten bands if loose. Cool 12 hours. Check seals. Label and store jars.

Mixed Vegetables

Yield: about 6 pint or 3 quart jars

3 1/2 cups sliced carrots (about 7 medium)	3 cups cubed zucchini (about 3 medium)
3 1/2 cups whole kernel corn (about 7 medium)	1 cup chopped red bell pepper (about 1 large)
3 1/2 cups lima beans (about 6 pounds)	Salt (optional)
	Water

PREP Wash carrots, corn, lima beans, zucchini, and red bell pepper under cold running water; drain. Remove stem end from carrots and peel. Slice carrots 1/4-inch thick; measure 3 1/2 cups sliced carrots. Cut corn off the cob. Start at the small end of the cob and cut downward to the stem end. Do not scrape cob. Measure 3 1/2 cups of whole kernel corn. Shell lima beans; measure 3 1/2 cups lima beans. Remove stem and blossom ends from zucchini and peel. Cut zucchini into 1/2-inch cubes; measure 3 cups cubed zucchini. Remove stem and seeds from pepper. Cut pepper into 1/2-inch pieces; measure 1 cup chopped pepper.

COOK Combine all vegetables in a large saucepan. Add water to cover vegetables. Bring mixture to a boil. Reduce heat to a gentle boil; boil 5 minutes.

FILL Pack hot vegetables and liquid into a hot jar, leaving 1-inch headspace. Remove air bubbles. Clean jar rim. Center lid on jar and adjust band to fingertip-tight. Place jar on the rack in pressure canner containing 2 inches of simmering water (180°F). Repeat until all jars are filled.

PROCESS Place lid on canner and turn to locked position. Adjust heat to medium-high. Vent steam for 10 minutes. Put weighted gauge on vent; bring pressure to 10 pounds (psi). Process pint jars 1 hour and 15 minutes or quart jars 1 hour and 30 minutes. Turn off heat; cool canner to zero pressure. After 5 minutes, remove lid. Let jars cool 10 minutes. Remove jars from canner; do not retighten bands if loose. Cool 12 hours. Check seals. Label and store jars.

Mushrooms
Cultivated Mushrooms

Yield: about 12 half-pint or 6 pint jars

6 pounds cultivated mushrooms	Salt (optional)
	Water

PREP Gently clean dirt from mushrooms using a soft vegetable brush. Rinse mushrooms under cold running water; drain. Trim ends. Leave small mushrooms whole; cut large mushrooms in half.

COOK Put mushrooms in a large saucepan. Add just enough water to cover mushrooms. Bring mixture to a boil. Reduce heat to a gentle boil; boil 5 minutes.

FILL Pack hot mushrooms and liquid into a hot jar, leaving 1-inch headspace. Add 1/4 teaspoon salt to half-pint jar; 1/2 teaspoon salt to pint jar, if desired. Remove air bubbles. Clean jar rim. Center lid on jar and adjust band to fingertip-tight. Place jar on the rack in pressure canner containing 2 inches of simmering water (180°F). Repeat until all jars are filled.

PROCESS Place lid on canner and turn to locked position. Adjust heat to medium-high. Vent steam for 10 minutes. Put weighted gauge on vent; bring pressure to 10 pounds (psi). Process half-pint or pint jars 45 minutes. Turn off heat; cool canner to zero pressure. After 5 minutes, remove lid. Let jars cool 10 minutes. Remove jars from canner; do not retighten bands if loose. Cool 12 hours. Check seals. Label and store jars.

Note: Do not can wild mushrooms.

Okra

Yield: about 6 pint or 3 quart jars

4 1/2 to 6 pounds okra	Water
Salt (optional)	

PREP Wash okra under cold running water; drain. Remove stems and blossom ends without cutting pods open. Leave pods whole or slice 1/4-inch thick.

COOK Put okra in a large saucepan. Add just enough water to cover okra. Bring mixture to a boil. Reduce heat to a gentle boil; boil 2 minutes.

FILL Pack hot okra into a hot jar, leaving 1-inch headspace. Add 1/2 teaspoon salt to pint jar; 1 teaspoon salt to quart jar, if desired. Ladle hot cooking liquid or boiling water over okra. Remove air bubbles. Clean jar rim. Center lid on jar and adjust band to fingertip-tight. Place jar on the rack in pressure canner containing 2 inches of simmering water (180°F). Repeat until all jars are filled.

PROCESS Place lid on canner and turn to locked position. Adjust heat to medium-high. Vent steam for 10 minutes. Put weighted gauge on vent; bring pressure to 10 pounds (psi). Process pint jars 25 minutes; quart jars 40 minutes. Turn off heat; cool canner to zero pressure. After 5 minutes, remove lid. Let jars cool 10 minutes. Remove jars from canner; do not retighten bands if loose. Cool 12 hours. Check seals. Label and store jars.

Parsnips, Rutabagas, or Turnips

Yield: about 6 pint or 3 quart jars

4 1/2 to 6 pounds vegetables	Water
Salt (optional)	

PREP Wash parsnips, rutabagas, or turnips under cold running water; drain. Remove stem ends and peel vegetables. Cut vegetables into 1/4-inch slices; quarter lengthwise, or chop into 1/2-inch cubes.

COOK Put vegetables in a large saucepan. Add water to cover vegetables. Bring mixture to a boil. Reduce heat to a gentle boil; boil 3 minutes.

FILL Pack hot vegetables into a hot jar, leaving 1-inch headspace. Add 1/2 teaspoon salt to pint jar; 1 teaspoon salt to quart jar, if desired. Ladle hot cooking liquid or boiling water over vegetables. Remove air bubbles. Clean jar rim. Center lid on jar and adjust band to fingertip-tight. Place jar on the rack in pressure canner containing 2 inches of simmering water (180°F). Repeat until all jars are filled.

PROCESS Place lid on canner and turn to locked position. Adjust heat to medium-high. Vent steam for 10 minutes. Put weighted gauge on vent; bring pressure to 10 pounds (psi). Process pint jars 30 minutes; quart jars 35 minutes. Turn off heat; cool canner to zero pressure. After 5 minutes, remove lid. Let jars cool 10 minutes. Remove jars from canner; do not retighten bands if loose. Cool 12 hours. Check seals. Label and store jars.

Note: Rutabaga usually discolors when canned and may develop a strong flavor.

Peas – Blackeye, Crowder, or Field

Yield: about 6 pint or 3 quart jars

6 to 6 3/4 pounds pea pods	Water
Salt (optional)	

PREP Wash pea pods under cold running water; drain. Shell peas. Rinse under cold running water; drain.

COOK
RAW PACK—Bring water to a boil; reduce heat to a simmer (180°F). Keep water hot.

HOT PACK—Put peas in a large saucepan. Add water to cover peas. Bring mixture to a boil. Reduce heat to a gentle boil; boil 3 minutes.

FILL
RAW PACK—Pack raw peas loosely into a hot jar, leaving 1-inch headspace. Add 1/2 teaspoon salt to pint jar; 1 teaspoon salt to quart jar, if desired. Ladle hot water over peas, leaving 1-inch headspace.

HOT PACK—Ladle hot peas and liquid into a hot jar, leaving 1-inch headspace. Add 1/2 teaspoon salt to pint jar; 1 teaspoon salt to quart jar, if desired.

Remove air bubbles. Clean jar rim. Center lid on jar and adjust band to fingertip-tight. Place jar on the rack in pressure canner containing 2 inches of simmering water (180°F). Repeat until all jars are filled.

PROCESS Place lid on canner and turn to locked position. Adjust heat to medium-high. Vent steam for 10 minutes. Put weighted gauge on vent; bring pressure to 10 pounds (psi). Process RAW PACK and HOT PACK pint jars 40 minutes or quart jars 50 minutes. Turn off heat; cool canner to zero pressure. After

5 minutes, remove lid. Let jars cool 10 minutes. Remove jars from canner; do not retighten bands if loose. Cool 12 hours. Check seals. Label and store jars.

Peas – Green or "English"

Yield: about 6 pint or 3 quart jars

    9 to 18 pounds pea pods   Water
Salt (optional)

PREP Wash pea pods under cold running water; drain. Shell peas. Rinse shelled peas under cold running water; drain.

COOK
RAW PACK—Bring water to a boil; reduce heat to a simmer (180°F). Keep water hot.

HOT PACK—Bring water to a boil; reduce heat to a simmer (180°F). Keep water hot. Put peas in a separate large saucepan. Add water to cover peas. Bring mixture to a boil. Reduce heat to a gentle boil; boil small peas (less than 1/4-inch) 3 minutes; medium peas (1/4- to 1/3-inch) 5 minutes. Drain.

FILL
RAW PACK—Pack raw peas loosely into a hot jar, leaving 1-inch headspace. Add 1/2 teaspoon salt to pint jar; 1 teaspoon salt to quart jar, if desired. Ladle hot water over peas, leaving 1-inch headspace.

HOT PACK—Pack hot peas loosely into a hot jar, leaving 1-inch headspace. Add 1/2 teaspoon salt to pint jar; 1 teaspoon salt to quart jar, if desired. Ladle hot water over peas, leaving 1-inch headspace.

Remove air bubbles. Clean jar rim. Center lid on jar and adjust band to fingertip-tight. Place jar on the rack in pressure canner containing 2 inches of simmering water (180°F). Repeat until all jars are filled.

PROCESS Place lid on canner and turn to locked position. Adjust heat to medium-high. Vent steam for 10 minutes. Put weighted gauge on vent; bring pressure to 10 pounds (psi). Process RAW PACK and HOT PACK pint or quart jars 40 minutes. Turn off heat; cool canner to zero pressure. After 5 minutes, remove lid. Let jars cool 10 minutes. Remove jars from canner; do not retighten bands if loose. Cool 12 hours. Check seals. Label and store jars.

Turn this recipe into Herbed Peas simply by adding 1/4 teaspoon chervil and 1/4 teaspoon thyme to each pint jar; 1/2 teaspoon chervil and 1/2 teaspoon thyme to each quart jar. Now that's simple!

Peppers – Bell

Green, Red, or Yellow

Yield: about 12 half-pint or 6 pint jars

    6 pounds bell green,   Vinegar, 5% acidity
    red, or yellow peppers   Water
Salt

PREP Wash peppers under cold running water; drain. Remove stems and seeds from peppers. Cut peppers lengthwise into quarters.

COOK Put peppers in a large saucepan. Add water to cover peppers. Bring mixture to a boil. Reduce heat to a gentle boil; boil 3 minutes.

FILL Pack hot peppers into a hot jar, leaving 1-inch headspace. Add 1/4 teaspoon salt and 1 1/2 teaspoons vinegar to half-pint jar; 1/2 teaspoon salt and 1 tablespoon vinegar to pint jar. Ladle hot cooking liquid or boiling water over peppers. Remove air bubbles. Clean jar rim. Center lid on jar and adjust band to fingertip-tight. Place jar on the rack in pressure canner containing 2 inches of simmering water (180°F). Repeat until all jars are filled.

PROCESS Place lid on canner and turn to locked position. Adjust heat to medium-high. Vent steam for 10 minutes. Put weighted gauge on vent; bring pressure to 10 pounds (psi). Process half-pint and pint jars 35 minutes. Turn off heat; cool canner to zero pressure. After 5 minutes, remove lid. Let jars cool 10 minutes. Remove jars from canner; do not retighten bands if loose. Cool 12 hours. Check seals. Label and store jars.

Potatoes – Sweet

Yield: about 6 pint or 3 quart jars

    6 to 9 pounds   Salt (optional)
    sweet potatoes
Water

PREP Wash sweet potatoes under cold running water; drain.

COOK Boil or steam sweet potatoes until peel can be easily removed; drain. Peel potatoes. Cut potatoes into quarters. In a separate saucepan, bring water to a boil; reduce heat to a simmer (180°F). Keep water hot.

FILL Pack hot potatoes into a hot jar, leaving 1-inch headspace. Ladle hot water over potatoes, leaving 1-inch headspace. Remove air bubbles. Clean jar rim. Center lid on jar and adjust band to fingertip-tight. Place jar on the rack in pressure canner containing 2 inches of simmering water (180°F). Repeat until all jars are filled.

PROCESS Place lid on canner and turn to locked position. Adjust heat to medium-high. Vent steam for 10 minutes. Put weighted gauge on vent; bring pressure to 10 pounds (psi). Process pint jars 1 hour and 5 minutes; quart jars 1 hour and 30 minutes. Turn off heat; cool canner to zero pressure. After 5 minutes, remove lid. Let jars cool 10 minutes. Remove jars from canner; do not retighten bands if loose. Cool 12 hours. Check seals. Label and store jars.

Stock up on variety. Take this basic recipe for canned sweet potatoes and turn it into something very special. Instead of using water as the liquid for canning, pack sweet potatoes in light syrup (see page 16). Take "special" one step further: use brown sugar or honey to prepare the syrup.

Potatoes – White

Yield: about 6 pint or 3 quart jars

6 to 9 pounds white potatoes	Salt (optional) Water

PREP Wash white potatoes under cold running water; drain. Peel potatoes. Rinse under cold running water. Potatoes that are 2 inches in diameter or smaller may be canned whole. Cut large potatoes into quarters.

COOK Put white potatoes in a large saucepan. Add water to cover potatoes. Bring mixture to a boil; boil 10 minutes.

FILL Pack hot white potatoes into a hot jar, leaving 1-inch headspace. Add ½ teaspoon salt to pint jar; 1 teaspoon salt to quart jar, if desired. Ladle hot cooking liquid or boiling water over potatoes, leaving 1-inch headspace. Remove air bubbles. Clean jar rim. Center lid on jar and adjust band to fingertip-tight. Place jar on the rack in pressure canner containing 2 inches of simmering water (180°F). Repeat until all jars are filled.

PROCESS Place lid on canner and turn to locked position. Adjust heat to medium-high. Vent steam for 10 minutes. Put weighted gauge on vent; bring pressure to 10 pounds (psi). Process pint jars 35 minutes; quart jars 40 minutes. Turn off heat; cool canner to zero pressure. After 5 minutes, remove lid. Let jars cool 10 minutes. Remove jars from canner; do not retighten bands if loose. Cool 12 hours. Check seals. Label and store jars.

Red Onions with Honey

Yield: about 4 pint jars

2½ quarts sliced red onions (about 15 large)	1 cup honey
1 tablespoon salt	1½ cups water
	½ cup white wine

PREP Peel red onions. Cut onions into ⅓- to ½-inch slices. Separate slices into individual rings. Place onion rings in a large bowl. Sprinkle with salt,

COOK Combine remaining ingredients in a large saucepan. Bring mixture to a boil. Reduce heat to a simmer (180°F); simmer until sauce is reduced by one-half, about 30 minutes.

FILL Pack red onion rings into a hot jar, leaving 1-inch headspace. Ladle hot sauce over onions, leaving 1-inch headspace. Remove air bubbles. Clean jar rim. Center lid on jar and adjust band to fingertip-tight. Place jar on the rack in pressure canner containing 2 inches of simmering water (180°F). Repeat until all jars are filled.

PROCESS Place lid on canner and turn to locked position. Adjust heat to medium-high. Vent steam for 10 minutes. Put weighted gauge on vent; bring pressure to 10 pounds (psi). Process pint jars 15 minutes. Turn off heat; cool canner to zero pressure. After 5 minutes, remove lid. Let jars cool 10 minutes. Remove jars from canner; do not retighten bands if loose. Cool 12 hours. Check seals. Label and store jars.

Our Tip! These savory onions with a hint of honey pair nicely with grilled beef, pork, or chicken. Combine a jar of onions with your favorite barbecue sauce. Simmer over low heat until reduced to a spreadable consistency. Generously coat each side of meat with onion barbecue sauce during the last 5 to 10 minutes of grilling. Serve extra sauce on the side.

Succotash

Yield: about 6 pint or 3 quart jars

6 cups whole kernel corn (about 4 medium ears)	Salt (optional) Water
6 cups lima beans (about 3 pounds)	

PREP Wash corn and lima beans under cold running water; drain. Cut corn off the cob. Start at the small end and cut downward to the stem end; measure 3½ cups whole kernel corn. Shell lima beans; measure 3½ cups lima beans.

COOK Combine corn and lima beans in a large saucepan. Add water to cover vegetables. Bring mixture to a boil. Reduce heat to a gentle boil; boil 5 minutes.

FILL Pack hot vegetables into a hot jar, leaving 1-inch headspace. Add ½ teaspoon salt to pint jar; 1 teaspoon salt to quart jar, if desired. Ladle cooking liquid or boiling water over vegetables, leaving 1-inch headspace. Remove air bubbles. Clean jar rim. Center lid on jar and adjust band to fingertip-tight. Place jar on the rack in pressure canner containing 2 inches of simmering water (180°F). Repeat until all jars are filled.

PROCESS Place lid on canner and turn to locked position. Adjust heat to medium-high. Vent steam for 10 minutes. Put weighted gauge on vent; bring pressure to 10 pounds (psi). Process pint jars 1 hour or quart jars 1 hour and 25 minutes. Turn off heat; cool canner to zero pressure. After 5 minutes, remove lid. Let jars cool 10 minutes. Remove jars from canner; do not retighten bands if loose. Cool 12 hours. Check seals. Label and store jars.

Tomatoes

Creole Sauce

Yield: about 4 pint or 2 quart jars

3 quarts chopped tomatoes (about 12 medium)	1 hot red chili pepper, finely chopped
2 cups chopped onions (about 3 to 4 medium)	1 tablespoon minced parsley
1 cup chopped red bell pepper (about 1 large)	1 tablespoon sugar
½ cup chopped celery (about 1 stalk)	2 teaspoons salt
	½ teaspoon marjoram
1 clove garlic	¼ teaspoon chili powder

PREP Wash tomatoes, bell and chili peppers, celery, and parsley under cold running water; drain. To peel tomatoes, blanch 30 to 60 seconds in boiling water. Immediately transfer to cold water. Cut off peel and core tomatoes. Coarsely chop tomatoes; measure 3 quarts chopped tomatoes. Peel onions. Chop onions; measure 2 cups chopped onions. Remove stem and seeds from bell pepper. Chop bell pepper; measure 1 cup chopped bell pepper. Remove leafy tops and root ends from celery. Chop celery; measure ½ cup chopped celery. Peel garlic. Finely mince garlic. Remove stem from chili pepper. Finely chop chili pepper. Mince parsley, discarding stems. Measure 1 tablespoon minced parsley.

COOK Combine all ingredients in a large saucepan. Cook slowly until thick, stirring to prevent sticking.

FILL Ladle hot sauce into a hot jar, leaving 1-inch headspace. Remove air bubbles. Clean jar rim. Center lid on jar and adjust band to fingertip-tight. Place jar on the rack in pressure canner containing 2 inches of simmering water (180°F). Repeat until all jars are filled.

PROCESS Place lid on canner and turn to locked position. Adjust heat to medium-high. Vent steam for 10 minutes. Put weighted gauge on vent; bring pressure to 10 pounds (psi). Process pint jars 25 minutes or quart jars 30 minutes. Turn off heat; cool canner to zero pressure. After 5 minutes, remove lid. Let jars cool 10 minutes. Remove jars from canner; do not retighten bands if loose. Cool 12 hours. Check seals. Label and store jars.

Note: When cutting or seeding hot peppers, wear rubber gloves to prevent hands from being burned.

Spicy Creole Sauce

Yield: about 4 pint jars or 2 quart jars

3 quarts chopped tomatoes (about 12 large)	1½ tablespoons minced fresh parsley
1½ cups minced onions (about 2 medium)	¾ cup balsamic vinegar
1 cup diced red bell pepper (about 1 large)	1 tablespoon cayenne pepper
3 Anaheim peppers	1 tablespoon salt
3 cloves garlic, minced	1½ teaspoons paprika
3 tablespoons minced fresh oregano	1 teaspoon black pepper
3 tablespoons minced fresh thyme	

PREP Wash tomatoes, bell and Anaheim peppers, and fresh herbs under cold running water; drain. To peel tomatoes, blanch 30 to 60 seconds in boiling water. Immediately transfer to cold water. Cut off peel and core tomatoes. Coarsely chop tomatoes; measure 3 quarts chopped tomatoes. Peel onions. Chop onions; measure 1½ cups chopped onions. Remove stem and seeds from bell pepper. Chop bell pepper; measure 1 cup chopped bell pepper. Remove stems and seeds from Anaheim peppers. Mince Anaheim peppers. Peel garlic. Finely mince garlic. Mince fresh herbs, discarding stems. Measure 3 tablespoons each of minced oregano and thyme. Measure 1½ tablespoons of minced parsley.

COOK Combine all ingredients in a large saucepan. Bring mixture to a boil. Reduce heat to a gentle boil. Boil gently, uncovered, 1 to 2 hours or to desired thickness, stirring to prevent sticking.

FILL Ladle hot sauce into a hot jar, leaving 1 inch headspace. Remove air bubbles. Clean jar rim. Center lid on jar and adjust band to fingertip-tight. Place jar on the rack in pressure canner containing 2 inches of simmering water (180°F). Repeat until all jars are filled.

PROCESS Place lid on canner and turn to locked position. Adjust heat to medium-high. Vent steam for 10 minutes. Put weighted gauge on vent; bring pressure to 10 pounds (psi). Process pint jars 25 minutes or quart jars 30 minutes. Turn off heat; cool canner to zero pressure. After 5 minutes, remove lid. Let jars cool 10 minutes. Remove jars from canner; do not retighten bands if loose. Cool 12 hours. Check seals. Label and store jars.

Note: When cutting or seeding hot peppers, wear rubber gloves to prevent hands from being burned.

Tomatoes with Okra

Yield: about 6 pint or 3 quart jars

9 pounds tomatoes	Salt (optional)
6 pounds okra	

PREP Wash tomatoes and okra under cold running water; drain. To peel tomatoes, blanch 30 to 60 seconds in boiling water. Immediately transfer to cold water. Cut off peel and core tomatoes. Chop tomatoes into large pieces. Remove stem ends from okra. Slice okra ½-inch thick.

COOK Put tomatoes in a large saucepan. Gently boil 15 minutes, stirring to prevent sticking. Add okra; continue cooking 5 minutes, stirring to prevent sticking.

FILL Ladle hot vegetables into a hot jar, leaving 1-inch headspace. Add ½ teaspoon salt to pint jar; 1 teaspoon salt to quart jar, if desired. Remove air bubbles. Clean jar rim. Center lid on jar and adjust band to fingertip-tight. Place jar on the rack in pressure canner containing 2 inches of simmering water (180°F). Repeat until all jars are filled.

PROCESS Place lid on canner and turn to locked position. Adjust heat to medium-high. Vent steam for 10 minutes. Put weighted gauge on vent; bring pressure to 10 pounds (psi). Process pint jars 30 minutes or quart jars 35 minutes. Turn off heat; cool canner to zero pressure. After 5 minutes, remove lid. Let jars cool 10 minutes. Remove jars from canner; do not retighten bands if loose. Cool 12 hours. Check seals. Label and store jars.

Stewed Tomatoes

Yield: about 6 pint or 3 quart jars

4 quarts chopped tomatoes (about 24 large)	¼ cup chopped green bell pepper (about 1 small)
1 cup chopped celery (about 2 stalks)	1 tablespoon sugar
½ cup chopped onion (about 1 small)	2 teaspoons salt (optional)

PREP Wash tomatoes, celery, and pepper under cold running water; drain. To peel tomatoes, blanch 30 to 60 seconds in boiling water. Immediately transfer to cold water. Cut off peel and core tomatoes. Chop tomatoes into large pieces. Remove leafy tops and root ends from celery. Chop celery; measure 1 cup chopped celery. Peel onion. Chop onion; measure ½ cup chopped onion. Remove stem and seeds from pepper. Chop pepper; measure ¼ cup chopped pepper.

COOK Combine all ingredients in a large saucepan. Bring mixture to a boil. Reduce heat to a simmer (180°F); simmer, covered, 10 minutes, stirring to prevent sticking.

FILL Ladle hot vegetables into a hot jar, leaving 1-inch headspace. Remove air bubbles. Clean jar rim. Center lid on jar and adjust band to fingertip-tight. Place jar on the rack in pressure canner containing 2 inches of simmering water (180°F). Repeat until all jars are filled.

PROCESS Place lid on canner and turn to locked position. Adjust heat to medium-high. Vent steam for 10 minutes. Put weighted gauge on vent; bring pressure to 10 pounds (psi). Process pint jars 15 minutes or quart jars 20 minutes. Turn off heat; cool canner to zero pressure. After 5 minutes, remove lid. Let jars cool 10 minutes. Remove jars from canner; do not retighten bands if loose. Cool 12 hours. Check seals. Label and store jars.

Canning Low-Acid Foods Step-By-Step

Using a Pressure Canner

Some of the most flavorful and nutritious home canned foods are those categorized as low-acid foods. Vegetables, meats, poultry, game, seafoods, and some combination recipes have a pH value higher than 4.6, meaning they have little natural acid needed to prevent bacterial growth. This is an important factor to understand when processing low-acid foods, because low-acid foods must be processed at 240°F in order to destroy heat-resistant bacteria, bacterial spores, and the toxins they produce. A pressure canner creates a controlled steam environment that can achieve the high temperature needed to safely preserve low-acid foods.

Prep

With all of the ingredients and equipment assembled, you're ready to start canning! Begin by washing the size and number of jars, lids, and bands needed for your recipe in hot, soapy water. Rinse in hot water. Dry bands and lids and set them aside to use later. Submerge jars in a saucepan filled with simmering (180°F) water; simmer jars 10 minutes. Keep jars warm in simmering water until they are needed. Remember, preheating jars is just as important when using the RAW PACK method as it is for the HOT PACK method.

Recipes in this book will guide you through each step for preparing ingredients, which may include washing vegetables or poultry under cold running water, slicing, cubing, or deboning meat, poultry, or game, or brining seafoods in a salt-water solution.

Cooking

Refer to your recipe for the correct cooking technique to use. Blanching or steaming helps control enzyme activity for most vegetables until they are processed. Meat, poultry, or game may be partially or fully cooked before canning. Some recipes give you the option to use either the RAW PACK or HOT PACK method to fill jars. These recipes will use either hot water, hot broth, or hot sauce to cover the food. Meat or seafood that is packed into the jar and processed without added liquid will create its own liquid during processing. Juice extracted from the meat or seafood during processing surrounds the food in the jar.

Filling

❶ Lift one jar from the simmering water, using a jar lifter. Carefully empty excess water from the jar. Stand it upright on a dry towel or cutting board. ❷ Place a jar funnel onto the jar. Fill the jar with your prepared green beans, leaving 1-inch headspace. Ingredients like salt, herbs, or whole spices can be added at this time, following the recipe directions. Ladle hot water into the jar, leaving 1-inch headspace.

❸ Use the notched end of the bubble remover/headspace tool to accurately measure headspace. ❹ Slide the narrow end of the tool (or other non-metallic utensil) inside the jar, placing it between the jar and the food. Gently move the food away from the side of the jar to release trapped air. Repeat 2 or 3 times around the inside perimeter of the jar. ❺ Clean the jar rim and threads with a clean, damp cloth to remove food particles, seeds, or other residue that may prevent the jar from sealing. ❻ Center a lid onto the jar rim. Adjust the band onto the jar just until fingertip-tight.

Processing

❼ Set the filled jar on the rack in the canner. Repeat until the canner is filled with jars or the entire recipe is gone. Check the water level in the canner, it should be about 2 inches deep, add boiling water if needed. Place the lid on the canner and turn it to the locked position. Bring the water to a boil over medium-high heat. As steam begins to fill the canner, air and steam is forced through the vent. After the air is exhausted from the canner, steam will form a steady stream; time it for 10 minutes. This is called venting or exhausting. Place the canner's pressure weight on the vent. Bring the canner to 10 pounds pressure if your elevation is below 1,000 feet above sea level. Start counting the processing time when the gauge indicates the canner is at 10 pounds pressure. If your canner has a dial gauge or you are at an elevation higher than 1,000 feet above sea level, refer to the Altitude Chart (see page 9).

Keep pressure steady during the entire processing period, adjusting the heat slowly to maintain pressure without causing the temperature to fluctuate unnecessarily. Turn off the heat when the processing time is over and let the canner cool naturally. Remove the weighted gauge after the canner is depressurized—at zero pressure. Let the canner cool 10 minutes before removing the lid. ❽ Unlock the lid and lift it towards you so that steam escapes in the opposite direction. Allow the jars to remain in the canner for 10 minutes to adjust to the lower room temperature. ❾ Remove the jars from the canner using a jar lifter. Set the jars upright 1 to 2 inches apart on a dry towel or cutting board. Do not retighten bands if they come loose during processing. Let jars cool undisturbed for 12 hours.

After the jars are cooled, the lid will appear to be concave. Gently press the center of the lid with your fingertip. If the lid does not move, the jar is vacuum sealed. Remove the band; wipe the lid and jar using a clean, damp cloth to remove food particles or other residue. Jars can be stored with or without the bands. Label jars with the name of the recipe and the date it was processed. Store home-canned foods in a cool (50° to 70°F), dry, dark place. For the best quality and nutritional value, use home-canned foods within 1 year.

① Remove one hot jar from simmering water.

② Fill hot jar with green beans, then add hot water.

③ Measure headspace for accuracy.

④ Remove trapped air bubbles from jar.

⑤ Wipe jar rim with a clean, damp cloth.

⑥ Center lid onto the jar and adjust band until fingertip-tight.

⑦ Place filled jar onto canner rack; repeat until all jars are filled. Put lid onto canner and lock in place.

⑧ Start processing time after canner reaches 10 pounds pressure. Let canner return to zero pressure before removing lid.

⑨ Let jars cool 12 hours. Test jars for a vacuum seal.

Something Extra

The beauty of creating one's own pantry full of basic staples is that there's always room for surprising and decadent extras. For that sauce, condiment, or syrup that will awe your guests, family, or friends, there is always space on the shelf. This chapter will guide you through a number of recipes for the little extras that can elevate basic meals, desserts, snacks, or even drinks. Each is unique in flavor and uses, but as a whole, they are that bit of fun you can pull off the shelf exactly when it's needed. Enjoy the possibilities before you.

Getting Started

Most recipes in this section stand on their own merit. They also act as lively ingredients when used in prepared dishes. Don't be limited by traditional convention—find new ways to use these extraordinary recipes. We've provided a few tips to get you started.

Preserve it using the boiling water method

Recipes in this section are processed using the boiling water method. For a quick review of the boiling water process, see "Follow the 'How-To' of Processing" on page 12. To preserve your soft spreads in 4-ounce jars or 12-ounce jars, follow the same processing time as given for 8-ounce jars.

Fascinating flavors worth sharing

You'll discover that the recipes in this section have an added spark, a culinary twist that is fresh, contemporary, and delicious. We'll show you the "ins and outs" of creating these unique flavor combinations that are sure to inspire your gourmet spirit. These recipes will add flair and versatility to meal preparation, making everyday meals special occasions, and special dishes even more enticing. Celebrate your passion for fresh, homemade food by sharing them as gifts. They are sure to get rave reviews, because you handcrafted them fresh from your own kitchen.

Featured Recipe | **Red Cabbage Slaw-Topped Burger** page 175

Pictured Above | **Red Cabbage Slaw** page 136 | **Peach-Papaya Jam** page 124 | **Maple-Walnut Syrup** page 130   **121**

Good Things to Know

Fruit Syrups and Sauces

Fruit syrup made fresh at home is typically thinner than its commercial counterpart. Even if the cooking time is extended to evaporate the liquid, the resulting reduction may not achieve the desired viscosity. Fruit syrups can be thickened just before serving by dissolving up to 1 tablespoon of cornstarch into 1 pint fruit syrup and gently boiling the syrup to the desired consistency for serving. Some fruit sauces that are not puréed before they are processed may also require thickening. Unless otherwise stated in the recipe, follow the guidelines for thickening fruit syrup. Do not add cornstarch or other thickening agents before processing.

Salsas

Preserved homemade salsa is usually juicier than salsa served fresh. Fresh tomatoes and fruits contain natural juice that is extracted when they are cut or chopped. Even more juice may be extracted when the salsa recipe is cooked. Additional liquid in the form of lime juice, lemon juice, or vinegar is necessary to impart flavor and to achieve the correct pH level (acidity). The total amount of liquid in the recipe is needed to conduct heat throughout the jar during processing. If a chunkier salsa is desired, drain off some of the juice before serving. Customizing the "heat" level in salsa recipes is easily managed by the selection of mild versus hot peppers, and by removing or not removing the pepper seeds and veins.

Altitude Check

The processing times given for the sweet and savory condiments in this section apply when canning at 0 to 1,000 feet above sea level. Barometric pressure affects the boiling point of water, so if you are canning at a higher elevation, refer to the Boiling-Water Canner Altitude Adjustments (see page 9).

Sweet & Savory
SPREADS

Apple-Maple Jam

Yield: about 8 half-pint jars

3 quarts chopped apples (about 6 pounds)	1/2 teaspoon nutmeg
6 cups sugar	1/4 teaspoon cloves
1 teaspoon cinnamon	1 cup maple syrup
1/2 teaspoon allspice	

PREP Wash apples under cold running water; drain. Core and peel apples. Chop apples into 1/2-inch pieces; measure 3 quarts chopped apples.

COOK Combine all ingredients in a large saucepan. Bring mixture to a boil over medium-high heat, stirring until sugar dissolves. Bring mixture to a rolling boil that cannot be stirred down. Boil rapidly to gelling point (220°F), stirring to prevent sticking. Remove from heat. Skim off foam if necessary.

FILL Ladle hot jam into a hot jar, leaving 1/4-inch headspace. Remove air bubbles. Clean jar rim. Center lid on jar and adjust band to fingertip-tight. Place jar on the rack elevated over simmering water (180°F) in boiling-water canner. Repeat until all jars are filled.

PROCESS Lower the rack into simmering water. Water must cover jars by 1 inch. Adjust heat to medium-high, cover canner and bring water to a rolling boil. Process half-pint jars 10 minutes. Turn off heat and remove cover. Let jars cool 5 minutes. Remove jars from canner; do not retighten bands if loose. Cool 12 hours. Check seals. Label and store jars.

Our Tip Pure maple syrup adds the richness and depth of flavor this recipe deserves. There are a number of yummy fall apples to choose from for jam, like Cortland, McIntosh, Empire, and Cameo.

Chablis Jelly

Yield: about 5 half-pint jars

3 1/2 cups Chablis wine	4 1/2 cups sugar
1/2 cup lemon juice	
6 tablespoons Ball Classic Pectin	

PREP Wine should be at room temperature.

COOK Combine wine, lemon juice, and pectin in a large saucepan. Bring mixture to a boil over medium-high heat, stirring to blend in pectin. Add sugar, stirring until sugar dissolves. Bring mixture to a rolling boil that cannot be stirred down. Boil hard 1 minute, stirring constantly. Remove from heat. Skim off foam if necessary.

FILL Ladle hot jelly into a hot jar, leaving 1/4-inch headspace. Clean jar rim. Center lid on jar and adjust band to fingertip-tight. Place jar on the rack elevated over simmering water (180°F) in boiling-water canner. Repeat until all jars are filled.

PROCESS Lower the rack into simmering water. Water must cover jars by 1 inch. Adjust heat to medium-high, cover canner and bring water to a rolling boil. Process half-pint jars 10 minutes. Turn off heat and remove cover. Let jars cool 5 minutes. Remove jars from canner; do not retighten bands if loose. Cool 12 hours. Check seals. Label and store jars.

Champagne Blush Jelly

Yield: about 6 half-pint jars

3 cups raspberry or cranberry-raspberry juice, fresh or bottled (without added calcium)	6 tablespoons Ball Classic Pectin
1/4 cup lemon juice	4 cups sugar
	1 1/4 cups Champagne

PREP Champagne should be at room temperature.

COOK Combine raspberry juice, lemon juice, and pectin in a large saucepan. Bring mixture to a boil over medium-high heat, stirring to blend in pectin. Add sugar, stirring until sugar dissolves. Bring mixture to a rolling boil that cannot be stirred down. Boil hard 1 minute, stirring constantly. Remove from heat. Stir in Champagne. Skim off foam if necessary.

FILL Ladle hot jelly into a hot jar, leaving 1/4-inch headspace. Clean jar rim. Center lid on jar and adjust band to fingertip-tight. Place jar on the rack elevated over simmering water (180°F) in boiling-water canner. Repeat until all jars are filled.

PROCESS Lower the rack into simmering water. Water must cover jars by 1 inch. Adjust heat to medium-high, cover canner

and bring water to a rolling boil. Process half-pint jars 10 minutes. Turn off heat and remove cover. Let jars cool 5 minutes. Remove jars from canner; do not retighten bands if loose. Cool 12 hours. Check seals. Label and store jars.

Cherry-Almond Jam

Yield: about 6 half-pint jars

- 3 (12-ounce) bags frozen sweet cherries, thawed and drained
- 6 tablespoons Ball Classic Pectin
- 3/4 cup almond liqueur
- 3 tablespoons lemon juice
- 4 1/2 cups sugar

PREP Thaw frozen cherries and drain. Finely chop cherries.

COOK Combine cherries, pectin, almond liqueur, and lemon juice in a large saucepan. Bring mixture to a boil over medium-high heat, stirring to blend in pectin. Add sugar, stirring until sugar dissolves. Bring mixture to a rolling boil that cannot be stirred down. Boil hard 1 minute, stirring constantly. Remove from heat. Skim off foam if necessary.

FILL Ladle hot jam into a hot jar, leaving 1/4-inch headspace. Remove air bubbles. Clean jar rim. Center lid on jar and adjust band to fingertip-tight. Place jar on the rack elevated over simmering water (180°F) in boiling-water canner. Repeat until all jars are filled.

PROCESS Lower the rack into simmering water. Water must cover jars by 1 inch. Adjust heat to medium-high, cover canner and bring water to a rolling boil. Process half-pint jars 10 minutes. Turn off heat and remove cover. Let jars cool 5 minutes. Remove jars from canner; do not retighten bands if loose. Cool 12 hours. Check seals. Label and store jars.

Cinnamon Anise Jelly

Yield: about 3 half-pint jars

- 2 cups apple juice, fresh or bottled (without added calcium)
- 2 sticks cinnamon
- 1 teaspoon anise seed
- 3 1/2 cups sugar
- 1 (3-ounce) pouch Ball Liquid Pectin

PREP Fresh or bottled juice may be used to prepare this recipe. See Juice for Jelly (page 28) to make fresh apple juice. Tie spices in a spice bag.

COOK Combine apple juice and spice bag in a large saucepan. Simmer 10 minutes. Add sugar, stirring until sugar dissolves. Bring mixture to a boil over medium-high heat, stirring frequently. Stir in pectin. Bring mixture to a rolling boil that cannot be stirred down. Boil hard 1 minute, stirring constantly. Remove from heat. Remove spice bag. Skim off foam if necessary.

FILL Ladle hot jelly into a hot jar, leaving 1/4-inch headspace. Clean jar rim. Center lid on jar and adjust band to fingertip-tight. Place jar on the rack elevated over simmering water (180°F) in boiling-water canner. Repeat until all jars are filled.

PROCESS Lower the rack into simmering water. Water must cover jars by 1 inch. Adjust heat to medium-high, cover canner and bring water to a rolling boil. Process half-pint jars 10 minutes. Turn off heat and remove cover. Let jars cool 5 minutes. Remove jars from canner; do not retighten bands if loose. Cool 12 hours. Check seals. Label and store jars.

 Anise seed is sweet and aromatic with a distinct licorice-like taste. It is used in regional and ethnic confectionery around the world. You may make a substitution if anise seed is not to your liking. Here are a few suggestions to get you started: allspice, pink peppercorns, coriander, or chili pepper.

 Try Cinnamon Anise Jelly as the filling for Apple Spiced Oat Muffins (see page 173). Enjoy!.

Cranberry-Cider Jelly

Yield: about 6 half-pint jars

- 3 cups apple cider
- 1 cup cranberry juice cocktail (without added calcium)
- 1 teaspoon lemon juice
- 6 tablespoons Ball Classic Pectin
- 5 cups sugar

PREP Pasteurized apple cider should be used to prepare this recipe.

COOK Combine apple cider, cranberry juice cocktail, lemon juice, and pectin in a large saucepan. Bring mixture to a boil over medium-high heat, stirring to blend in pectin. Add sugar, stirring until sugar dissolves. Bring mixture to a rolling boil that cannot be stirred down. Boil hard 1 minute, stirring constantly. Remove from heat. Skim off foam if necessary.

FILL Ladle hot jelly into a hot jar, leaving 1/4-inch headspace. Clean jar rim. Center lid on jar and adjust band to fingertip-tight. Place jar on the rack elevated over simmering water (180°F) in boiling-water canner. Repeat until all jars are filled.

PROCESS Lower the rack into simmering water. Water must cover jars by 1 inch. Adjust heat to medium-high, cover canner and bring water to a rolling boil. Process half-pint jars 10 minutes. Turn off heat and remove cover. Let jars cool 5 minutes. Remove jars from canner; do not retighten bands if loose. Cool 12 hours. Check seals. Label and store jars.

Cranberry Wine Jelly

Yield: about 4 half-pint jars

- 2 cups cranberry juice cocktail (without added calcium)
- 3 1/2 cups sugar
- 1 (3-ounce) pouch Ball Liquid Pectin
- 1/4 cup Burgundy wine

PREP Wine should be at room temperature.

COOK Combine cranberry juice cocktail and sugar in a large saucepan, stirring until sugar dissolves. Bring mixture to a boil over medium-high heat, stirring frequently. Stir in pectin. Bring mixture to a rolling boil that cannot be stirred down. Boil hard 1 minute, stirring constantly. Remove from heat. Stir in wine. Skim off foam if necessary.

FILL Ladle hot jelly into a hot jar, leaving 1/4-inch headspace. Clean jar rim. Center lid on jar and adjust band to fingertip-tight. Place jar on the rack elevated over simmering water (180°F) in boiling-water canner. Repeat until all jars are filled.

PROCESS Lower the rack into simmering water. Water must cover jars by 1 inch. Adjust heat to medium-high, cover canner and bring water to a rolling boil. Process half-pint jars 10 minutes. Turn off heat and remove cover. Let jars cool 5 minutes. Remove jars from canner; do not retighten bands if loose. Cool 12 hours. Check seals. Label and store jars.

Garlic Jelly

Yield: about 5 half-pint jars

2 large garlic bulbs (about 4 ounces)	5 cups sugar
2 cups vinegar, 5% acidity, divided	1 (3-ounce) pouch Ball Liquid Pectin

PREP Roast garlic under a broiler at 425°F for 10 to 15 minutes; cool. Peel garlic. Purée garlic and ½ cup vinegar in a food processor or blender.

COOK Combine garlic purée, 1½ cups vinegar, and sugar in a large saucepan. Bring mixture to a boil over medium-high heat, stirring until sugar dissolves. Stir in pectin. Bring mixture to a rolling boil that cannot be stirred down. Boil hard 1 minute, stirring constantly. Remove from heat. Skim off foam if necessary.

FILL Ladle hot jelly into a hot jar, leaving ¼-inch headspace. Clean jar rim. Center lid on jar and adjust band to fingertip-tight. Place jar on the rack elevated over simmering water (180°F) in boiling-water canner. Repeat until all jars are filled.

PROCESS Lower the rack into simmering water. Water must cover jars by 1 inch. Adjust heat to medium-high, cover canner and bring water to a rolling boil. Process half-pint jars 10 minutes. Turn off heat and remove cover. Let jars cool 5 minutes. Remove jars from canner; do not retighten bands if loose. Cool 12 hours. Check seals. Label and store jars.

 Serve Garlic Jelly with smoky bacon cheddar cheese and toasted pumpernickel bread. Used as a glaze, Garlic Jelly is the perfect complement for savory roast chicken, Cornish hen, or quail.

Peach-Papaya Jam

Yield: about 6 half-pint jars

2½ cups peeled, diced peaches	¼ cup lemon juice
2 cups peeled, diced papaya	2 (3-ounce) pouches Ball Liquid Pectin
5½ cups sugar	

PREP Wash peaches and papaya under cold running water; drain. To peel peaches, blanch in boiling water for 30 to 60 seconds. Immediately transfer to cold water. Cut off peel. Treat peaches with Fruit-Fresh to prevent darkening (see page 16). Dice peaches; measure 2½ cups diced peaches. Cut papaya in half lengthwise. Remove seeds and peel papaya. Dice papaya; measure 2 cups diced papaya. Combine papaya and peaches in a large bowl. Lightly crush fruit with a potato masher.

COOK Combine crushed fruit, sugar, and lemon juice in a large saucepan. Bring mixture to a boil over medium-high heat, stirring until sugar dissolves. Stir in pectin. Bring mixture to a rolling boil that cannot be stirred down. Boil hard 1 minute, stirring constantly. Remove from heat. Skim off foam if necessary.

FILL Ladle hot jam into a hot jar, leaving ¼-inch headspace. Remove air bubbles. Clean jar rim. Center lid on jar and adjust band to fingertip-tight. Place jar on the rack elevated over simmering water (180°F) in boiling-water canner. Repeat until all jars are filled.

PROCESS Lower the rack into simmering water. Water must cover jars by 1 inch. Adjust heat to medium-high, cover canner and bring water to a rolling boil. Process half-pint jars 10 minutes. Turn off heat and remove cover. Let jars cool 5 minutes. Remove jars from canner; do not retighten bands if loose. Cool 12 hours. Check seals. Label and store jars.

Plum-Orange Jam

Yield: about 6 half-pint jars

5 cups chopped plums (about 3½ pounds)	6 tablespoons Ball Classic Pectin
1 tablespoon grated orange peel (about ½ medium)	5½ cups sugar
	¼ cup orange liqueur

PREP Wash plums and orange under cold running water; drain. Cut plums in half lengthwise; remove pits and fibrous flesh. Chop plums; measure 5 cups chopped plums. Grate orange peel; measure 1 tablespoon grated orange peel.

COOK Combine plums, grated orange peel, and pectin in a large saucepan. Bring mixture to a boil over medium-high heat, stirring to blend in pectin. Add sugar, stirring until sugar dissolves. Bring mixture to a rolling boil that cannot be stirred down. Boil hard 1 minute, stirring constantly. Remove from heat. Stir in orange liqueur. Skim off foam if necessary.

FILL Ladle hot jam into a hot jar, leaving ¼-inch headspace. Remove air bubbles. Clean jar rim. Center lid on jar and adjust band to fingertip-tight. Place jar on the rack elevated over simmering water (180°F) in boiling-water canner. Repeat until all jars are filled.

PROCESS Lower the rack into simmering water. Water must cover jars by 1 inch. Adjust heat to medium-high, cover canner and bring water to a rolling boil. Process half-pint jars 10 minutes. Turn off heat and remove cover. Let jars cool 5 minutes. Remove jars from canner; do not retighten bands if loose. Cool 12 hours. Check seals. Label and store jars.

 Substitute ¼ cup orange liqueur with ¼ cup fresh orange juice. Add orange juice to plums, grated orange peel, and pectin before cooking.

Red Chili Cherry Jam

Yield: about 6 half-pint jars

1 quart chopped, pitted tart red cherries (about 2 pounds)	6 tablespoons Ball Classic Pectin
1 cup red bell pepper (about 1 large)	2 tablespoons lime juice
1 cayenne pepper	4½ cups sugar

PREP Wash cherries, bell pepper, and cayenne pepper under cold running water; drain. Remove stems and pit cherries. Coarsely chop cherries. Measure 1 quart chopped cherries. Remove stems and seeds from bell and cayenne peppers. Finely chop peppers using a food processor or food grinder.

COOK Combine cherries, peppers, pectin, and lime juice in a large saucepan, stirring to blend in pectin. Bring mixture slowly to a boil over medium-high heat. Add sugar, stirring until sugar dissolves. Bring mixture to a rolling boil that cannot be stirred down. Boil hard for 1 minute, stirring constantly. Remove from heat. Skim off foam if necessary.

FILL Ladle hot jam into a hot jar, leaving ¼-inch headspace. Remove air bubbles. Clean jar rim. Center lid on jar and adjust band to fingertip-tight. Place jar on the rack elevated over simmering water (180°F) in boiling-water canner. Repeat until all jars are filled.

PROCESS Lower the rack into simmering water. Water must cover jars by 1 inch. Adjust heat to medium-high, cover canner and bring water to a rolling boil. Process half-pint jars 10 minutes. Turn off heat and remove cover. Remove jars from canner; do not retighten bands if loose. Cool 12 hours. Check seals. Label and store jars.

Note: When cutting or seeding hot peppers, wear rubber gloves to prevent hands from being burned.

Roasted Red Pepper Spread

Yield: about 5 half-pint jars

6 pounds red bell peppers (about 12 large)	2 tablespoons minced basil
1 pound Roma tomatoes (about 10 medium)	1 tablespoon sugar
2 large cloves garlic, chopped	1 teaspoon coarse salt
1/4 cup chopped white onion (about 1 medium)	1/2 cup red wine vinegar, 5% acidity

PREP Wash peppers, tomatoes, and basil under cold running water; drain. Roast peppers under a broiler at 425°F until skins wrinkle and char in spots, turning peppers over to roast evenly. Remove peppers from broiler and place in a paper bag; secure bag closed; cool 15 minutes. Roast tomatoes, garlic, and onion under a broiler at 425°F for 10 to 15 minutes. Remove vegetables from broiler. Place tomatoes in a paper bag; secure bag closed; cool 15 minutes. Peel garlic and onion. Chop garlic; set aside. Chop onion; measure 1/4 cup chopped onion; set aside. Cut off peel from peppers; remove stems and seeds. Cut peppers into quarters. Cut off peel from tomatoes and core. Cut tomatoes into quarters. Purée peppers, tomatoes, garlic, and onion using a food processor or food mill.

COOK Combine all ingredients in a large saucepan. Bring mixture to a boil over medium-high heat, stirring to prevent sticking. Reduce heat to a simmer (180°F); simmer until mixture thickens, stirring frequently.

FILL Ladle hot spread into a hot jar, leaving 1/4-inch headspace. Remove air bubbles. Clean jar rim. Center lid on jar and adjust band to fingertip-tight. Place jar on the rack elevated over simmering water (180°F) in boiling-water canner. Repeat until all jars are filled.

PROCESS Lower the rack into simmering water. Water must cover jars by 1 inch. Adjust heat to medium-high, cover canner and bring water to a rolling boil. Process half-pint jars 10 minutes. Turn off heat and remove cover. Let jars cool 5 minutes. Remove jars from canner; do not retighten bands if loose. Cool 12 hours. Check seals. Label and store jars.

Strawberry-Kiwi Jam

Yield: about 6 half-pint jars

3 cups crushed strawberries (about 2 pounds)	6 tablespoons Ball Classic Pectin
3 kiwi, peeled and diced	1 tablespoon lemon juice
1 tablespoon minced crystallized ginger	5 cups sugar

PREP Wash strawberries under cold running water; drain. Remove stems and caps from strawberries. Crush strawberries one layer at a time using a potato masher. Measure 3 cups crushed strawberries. Peel kiwi and dice.

COOK Combine strawberries, kiwi, ginger, pectin, and lemon juice in a large saucepan. Bring mixture to a boil over medium-

high heat, stirring to blend in pectin. Add sugar, stirring until sugar dissolves. Bring mixture to a rolling boil that cannot be stirred down. Boil hard 1 minute, stirring constantly. Remove from heat. Skim off foam if necessary.

FILL Ladle hot jam into a hot jar, leaving 1/4-inch headspace. Remove air bubbles. Clean jar rim. Center lid on jar and adjust band to fingertip-tight. Place jar on the rack elevated over simmering water (180°F) in boiling-water canner. Repeat until all jars are filled.

PROCESS Lower the rack into simmering water. Water must cover jars by 1 inch. Adjust heat to medium-high, cover canner and bring water to a rolling boil. Process half-pint jars 10 minutes. Turn off heat and remove cover. Let jars cool 5 minutes. Remove jars from canner; do not retighten bands if loose. Cool 12 hours. Check seals. Label and store jars.

Our Tip Turn Strawberry-Kiwi Jam into a light dressing to complement a simple fresh fruit salad. Begin by combining 1 cup vanilla low-fat yogurt, 1/2 cup Strawberry-Kiwi Jam, and 2 tablespoons orange juice, stirring to blend evenly. Top spring lettuce with melon balls, sliced kiwi, raspberries, and toasted sliced almonds. Serve with Strawberry-Kiwi Dressing (see page 174).

Tangerine Jelly

Yield: about 5 half-pint jars

6 cups chopped tangerine pulp (about 3 1/2 pounds)	1 cup water
1 cup chopped lemon pulp (about 2 medium)	6 tablespoons Ball Classic Pectin
1/2 cup thinly sliced tangerine peel (about 3 medium)	5 cups sugar

PREP Wash tangerines and lemons under cold running water; drain. Cut tangerines and lemons in half crosswise and remove seeds. Remove tangerine pulp and lemon pulp from each half of fruit, keeping fruit pulp separate. Chop tangerine pulp; measure 6 cups chopped tangerine pulp. Chop lemon pulp; measure 1 cup chopped lemon pulp. Thinly slice tangerine peel; measure 1/2 cup sliced tangerine peel.

COOK Combine tangerine pulp, lemon pulp, tangerine peel, and water in a large saucepan. Cover; simmer 10 minutes, stirring occasionally. Strain mixture through a damp jelly bag or several layers of cheesecloth; measure 4 cups juice. Combine juice and pectin in a large saucepan. Bring mixture to a boil over medium-high heat, stirring to blend in pectin. Add sugar, stirring until sugar dissolves. Bring mixture to a rolling boil that cannot be stirred down. Boil hard 1 minute, stirring constantly. Remove from heat. Skim off foam if necessary.

FILL Ladle hot jelly into a hot jar, leaving 1/4-inch headspace. Clean jar rim. Center lid on jar and adjust band to fingertip-tight. Place jar on the rack elevated over simmering water (180°F) in boiling-water canner. Repeat until all jars are filled.

PROCESS Lower the rack into simmering water. Water must cover jars by 1 inch. Adjust heat to medium-high, cover canner and bring water to a rolling boil. Process half-pint jars 10 minutes. Turn off heat and remove cover. Let jars cool 5 minutes. Remove jars from canner; do not retighten bands if loose. Cool 12 hours. Check seals. Label and store jars.

Salsas

Papaya-Pineapple Salsa

Yield: about 6 half-pint jars

4 cups cubed papaya (about 1 medium)

2 cups cubed pineapple (about 1 pound)

1 cup golden raisins

1/2 cup chopped Anaheim peppers (about 8 medium)

2 tablespoons minced green onions (about 2)

2 tablespoons minced cilantro

2 tablespoons brown sugar

1 cup lemon juice

1/2 cup lime juice

1/2 cup pineapple juice

PREP Wash papaya, pineapple, peppers, onions, and cilantro under cold running water; drain. Cut papaya in half lengthwise, remove seeds, and peel. Cut papayas into 1/2- to 1-inch cubes; measure 4 cups cubed papaya. Cut off top and bottom ends of pineapple; core and peel. Cut pineapple into 1/2- to 1-inch cubes; measure 2 cups cubed pineapple. Remove stems and seeds from peppers. Chop peppers; measure 1/2 cup chopped peppers. Peel onion and cut off root and dark green ends. Mince onion; measure 2 tablespoons minced onion. Trim stems from cilantro and mince; measure 2 tablespoons minced cilantro.

COOK Combine all ingredients in a large saucepan. Bring mixture to a boil over medium-high heat. Reduce heat to a simmer (180°F); simmer 10 minutes.

FILL Ladle hot salsa into a hot jar, leaving 1/2-inch headspace. Remove air bubbles. Clean jar rim. Center lid on jar and adjust band to fingertip-tight. Place jar on the rack elevated over simmering water (180°F) in boiling-water canner. Repeat until all jars are filled.

PROCESS Lower the rack into simmering water. Water must cover jars by 1 inch. Adjust heat to medium-high, cover canner and bring water to a rolling boil. Process half-pint jars 15 minutes. Turn off heat and remove cover. Let jars cool 5 minutes. Remove jars from canner; do not retighten bands if loose. Cool 12 hours. Check seals. Label and store jars.

Note: When cutting or seeding hot peppers, wear rubber gloves to prevent hands from being burned.

 Serve Papaya-Pineapple Salsa with toasted pita chips. Pita chips are easy to make. Brush pita bread with extra-virgin olive oil, cut into quarters, and toast over an open grill or under the broiler.

Peach-Chili Salsa

Yield: about 8 half-pint jars

6 cups chopped peaches (about 6 medium)

1 1/4 cups chopped red onion (about 1 medium)

4 jalapeño peppers, finely chopped

1 red bell pepper, chopped

1/2 cup loosely packed cilantro, finely chopped

1 clove garlic, finely chopped

1 1/2 teaspoon cumin

1/2 teaspoon cayenne pepper

1/2 cup vinegar, 5% acidity

2 tablespoons honey

PREP Wash peaches, peppers, and cilantro under cold running water; drain. To peel peaches, blanch in boiling water for 30 to 60 seconds. Immediately transfer to cold water. Cut off peel. Treat peaches with Fruit-Fresh to prevent darkening (see page 16). Chop peaches; measure 6 cups chopped peaches. Peel and chop red onion; measure 1 1/4 cups chopped red onion. Remove stems and seeds from jalapeño and bell peppers. Finely chop jalapeño peppers. Chop bell peppers. Finely chop cilantro.

COOK Combine all ingredients in a large saucepan. Bring mixture to a boil over medium-high heat, stirring to prevent sticking. Reduce heat to a gentle boil; cook until mixture thickens, about 5 minutes, stirring to prevent sticking.

FILL Ladle hot salsa into a hot jar, leaving 1/2-inch headspace. Remove air bubbles. Clean jar rim. Center lid on jar and adjust band to fingertip-tight. Place jar on the rack elevated over simmering water (180°F) in boiling-water canner. Repeat until all jars are filled.

PROCESS Lower the rack into simmering water. Water must cover jars by 1 inch. Adjust heat to medium-high, cover canner and bring water to a rolling boil. Process half-pint jars 15 minutes. Turn off heat and remove cover. Let jars cool 5 minutes. Remove jars from canner; do not retighten bands if loose. Cool 12 hours. Check seals. Label and store jars.

Note: When cutting or seeding hot peppers, wear rubber gloves to prevent hands from being burned.

 For added flavor, replace 1 cup of chopped peaches with 1 cup chopped, peeled apricots.

Zesty Salsa

Yield: about 6 pint jars

10 cups chopped tomatoes (about 6 pounds)

5 cups chopped banana peppers (about 2 pounds)

5 cups chopped onions (about 1 1/2 pounds)

2 1/2 cups chopped jalapeño (about 1 pound)

3 cloves garlic, minced

2 tablespoons cilantro, minced

3 teaspoons salt

1 1/4 cups cider vinegar, 5% acidity

1 teaspoon hot pepper sauce (optional)

PREP Wash tomatoes and peppers under cold running water; drain. To peel tomatoes, blanch 30 to 60 seconds in boiling water. Immediately transfer to cold water. Cut off peel. Cut tomatoes in half, core, and remove seeds. Chop tomatoes; measure 10 cups chopped tomatoes. Stem and seed banana and jalapeño peppers. Chop peppers, keeping them separate. Measure 5 cups chopped banana peppers; measure 2 1/2 cups chopped jalapeño peppers. Peel onions. Chop onions; measure 5 cups chopped onions.

COOK Combine all ingredients in a large saucepan. Bring mixture to a boil over medium-high heat. Reduce heat to a simmer (180°F); simmer 10 minutes or until thickened.

FILL Ladle hot salsa into a hot jar, leaving 1/2-inch headspace. Remove air bubbles. Clean jar rim. Center lid on jar and adjust band to fingertip-tight. Place jar on the rack elevated over simmering water (180°F) in boiling-water canner. Repeat until all jars are filled.

PROCESS Lower the rack into simmering water. Water must cover jars by 1 inch. Adjust heat to medium-high, cover canner and bring water to a rolling boil. Process pint jars 15 minutes. Turn off heat and remove cover. Let jars cool 5 minutes. Remove jars from canner; do not retighten bands if loose. Cool 12 hours. Test seals. Label and store jars.

Note: When cutting or seeding hot peppers, wear rubber gloves to prevent hands from being burned.

Sauces, Syrups, & VINEGARS

Sauces

Apricot-Chipotle Sauce

Yield: about 6 half-pint jars

5 cups chopped apricots (about 14 medium)	1 cup sugar
2 cups water, divided	1 teaspoon cumin
4 dried chipotle peppers	1/2 teaspoon salt
1/4 cup finely chopped onion (about 1 small)	1/2 teaspoon coarsely ground white peppercorns
1 clove garlic, minced	1 1/2 cups white wine vinegar, 5% acidity
1 tablespoon grated lemon peel	

PREP Wash apricots under cold running water; drain. Cut apricots in half lengthwise. Remove pits and fibrous flesh. Chop apricots; measure 5 cups chopped apricots. Remove stems from peppers. Peel and finely chop onion; measure 1/4 cup chopped onion. Peel garlic and mince.

COOK Combine chopped apricots and 1 cup water in a large saucepan. Cook over medium-high heat until apricots are tender. Purée apricot mixture using a food processor or food mill. Return purée to a large saucepan; set aside. Bring 1 cup water to a boil in a small saucepan; remove from heat. Add dried peppers and cover saucepan. Let peppers steep for 15 minutes. Purée pepper mixture using a food processor or food mill. Add puréed peppers and remaining ingredients to apricot purée. Bring mixture to a boil over medium-high heat, stirring to prevent sticking.

FILL Ladle hot sauce into a hot jar, leaving 1/2-inch headspace. Clean jar rim. Center lid on jar and adjust band to fingertip-tight. Place jar on the rack elevated over simmering water (180°F) in boiling-water canner. Repeat until all jars are filled.

PROCESS Lower the rack into simmering water. Water must cover jars by 1 inch. Adjust heat to medium-high, cover canner and bring water to a rolling boil. Process half-pint jars 10 minutes. Turn off heat and remove cover. Let jars cool 5 minutes. Remove jars from canner; do not retighten bands if loose. Cool 12 hours. Check seals. Label and store jars.

Note: When cutting or seeding hot peppers, wear rubber gloves to prevent hands from being burned.

Blackberry Liqueur Sauce

Yield: about 3 half-pint jars

4 cups blackberries (about 2 pounds)	1 tablespoon lemon zest
1/2 cup Chambord liqueur	1 tablespoon lemon juice
3/4 cup sugar	1 (3-ounce) pouch Ball Liquid Pectin

PREP Wash blackberries under cold running water; drain. Combine blackberries, Chambord, and sugar in a large saucepan. Let mixture stand 2 hours, stirring occasionally.

COOK Add lemon zest and lemon juice to blackberry mixture. Bring mixture to a boil over medium-high heat, stirring to prevent sticking. Stir in pectin. Bring mixture to a rolling boil that cannot be stirred down. Boil hard 1 minute, stirring constantly. Remove from heat. Skim off foam if necessary.

FILL Ladle hot sauce into a hot jar, leaving 1/2-inch headspace. Remove air bubbles. Clean jar rim. Center lid on jar and adjust band to fingertip-tight. Place jar on the rack elevated over simmering water (180°F) in boiling-water canner. Repeat until all jars are filled.

PROCESS Lower the rack into simmering water. Water must cover jars by 1 inch. Adjust heat to medium-high, cover canner and bring water to a rolling boil. Process half-pint jars 10 minutes. Turn off heat and remove cover. Let jars cool 5 minutes. Remove jars from canner; do not retighten bands if loose. Cool 12 hours. Check seals. Label and store jars.

Note: Any brand of black raspberry liqueur may be used.

Danish Cherry Sauce

Yield: about 3 pint jars

4 1/2 pounds dark sweet cherries	1 cup water
1 1/2 cups sugar	3/4 cup corn syrup
3 sticks cinnamon	1 1/2 tablespoons almond extract

PREP Wash cherries under cold running water; drain. Pit cherries.

COOK Combine sugar, cinnamon sticks, water, corn syrup, and almond extract in a large saucepan. Bring mixture to a boil, stirring until sugar dissolves. Reduce heat to a simmer (180°F); add cherries and simmer until cherries are hot throughout. Remove cinnamon sticks.

FILL Ladle hot sauce into a hot jar, leaving 1/2-inch headspace. Clean jar rim. Center lid on jar and adjust band to fingertip-tight. Place jar on the rack elevated over simmering water (180°F) in boiling-water canner. Repeat until all jars are filled.

PROCESS Lower the rack into simmering water. Water must cover jars by 1 inch. Adjust heat to medium-high, cover canner and bring water to a rolling boil. Process pint jars 10 minutes. Turn off heat and remove cover. Let jars cool 5 minutes. Remove jars from canner; do not retighten bands if loose. Cool 12 hours. Check seals. Label and store jars.

Note: To thicken sauce for serving, dissolve 1 tablespoon cornstarch in 2 tablespoons water in a small saucepan. Add 1 pint Danish Cherry Sauce. Bring mixture to a boil, cooking until sauce thickens. Do not add cornstarch before processing.

Garlic Mustard Sauce

Yield: about 8 half-pint jars

2 pounds garlic bulbs (about 16 to 18)	8 Serrano peppers
1/3 cup extra virgin olive oil	1/4 cup mustard powder
1 pound Granny Smith apples (about 3)	2 tablespoons mustard seeds
2 cups apple juice, divided	1 tablespoon coriander seeds
1 pound Anaheim peppers (about 18 to 20)	1 1/2 cups white wine vinegar, 5% acidity

PREP Wash apples and peppers under cold running water; drain. Core and peel apples. Chop apples into 1/2-inch pieces. Cut tops off garlic bulbs to expose individual cloves.

COOK Combine apples and 1 cup apple juice in a large saucepan. Simmer apples and juice 5 minutes; set aside. Place garlic bulbs in a baking dish. Pour olive oil over cut surface of garlic. Bake garlic at 350°F until tender. Cool garlic. Separate cloves of garlic and peel. Roast peppers under a broiler until skins wrinkle and char in spots, turning to roast evenly. Put roasted peppers in a paper bag and secure closed. Cool 15 minutes. Remove stems and skins from peppers. Purée apple mixture, garlic, and peppers using food processor or food mill. Combine purée, 1 cup apple juice, and remaining ingredients in a large saucepan. Bring mixture to a boil over medium-high heat; boil 10 minutes, stirring to prevent sticking.

FILL Ladle hot sauce into a hot jar, leaving 1/2-inch headspace. Clean jar rim. Center lid on jar and adjust band to fingertip-tight. Place jar on the rack elevated over simmering water (180°F) in boiling-water canner. Repeat until all jars are filled.

PROCESS Lower the rack into simmering water. Water must cover jars by 1 inch. Adjust heat to medium-high, cover canner and bring water to a rolling boil. Process half-pint jars 10 minutes. Turn off heat and remove cover. Let jars cool 5 minutes. Remove jars from canner; do not retighten bands if loose. Cool 12 hours. Check seals. Label and store jars.

Note: When cutting or seeding hot peppers, wear rubber gloves to prevent hands from being burned.

Hot Rhubarb Grilling Sauce

Yield: about 5 half-pints

4 cups chopped rhubarb (about 6 stalks)	1 1/3 cups brown sugar
2 cups finely chopped tart cherries (about 1 to 1 1/2 pounds)	1 cup red wine vinegar, 5% acidity
2/3 cup finely minced Serrano peppers (about 8 to 10)	4 teaspoons grated fresh ginger
1/2 cup finely chopped onion (about 1/2 medium)	1 1/2 teaspoons grated lemon peel

PREP Wash rhubarb, cherries, and Serrano peppers under cold running water; drain. Remove leafy tops and root ends from rhubarb. Chop rhubarb into 1/2-inch pieces; measure 4 cups chopped rhubarb. Remove stems and pits from cherries. Finely chop cherries; measure 2 cups chopped cherries. Remove stems and seeds from peppers. Finely mince peppers; measure 2/3 cup minced peppers. Peel onion and chop; measure 1/2 cup chopped onion. Peel fresh ginger and grate; measure 4 teaspoons grated fresh ginger.

COOK Combine rhubarb, cherries, peppers, onion, sugar, and vinegar in a medium saucepan. Cook over medium-high heat until rhubarb is tender. Add grated ginger and lemon peel. Cook 5 minutes, stirring to prevent sticking.

FILL Ladle hot sauce into a hot jar, leaving 1/2-inch headspace. Clean jar rim. Center lid on jar and adjust band to fingertip-tight. Place jar on the rack elevated over simmering water (180°F) in boiling-water canner. Repeat until all jars are filled.

PROCESS Lower the rack into simmering water. Water must cover jars by 1-inch. Adjust heat to medium-high, cover canner and bring water to a rolling boil. Process half-pint jars 10 minutes. Turn off heat and remove cover. Let jars cool 5 minutes. Remove jars from canner; do not retighten bands if loose. Cool 12 hours. Check seals. Label and store jars.

Pineapple Sauce

Yield: about 5 half-pint jars

5 cups crushed pineapple (about 4 pounds)	4 cups sugar

PREP Wash fresh pineapple under cold running water; drain. Cut off top and bottom ends of pineapple; core and peel. Crush pineapple using a food processor or food grinder.

COOK Combine crushed pineapple and sugar in a large saucepan. Bring mixture slowly to a boil, stirring until sugar dissolves. Cook rapidly almost to the gelling point (about 220°F), stirring to prevent sticking. Remove from heat. Skim off foam if necessary.

FILL Ladle hot sauce into a hot jar, leaving 1/2-inch headspace. Remove air bubbles. Clean jar rim. Center lid on jar and adjust band to fingertip-tight. Place jar on the rack elevated over simmering water (180°F) in boiling-water canner. Repeat until all jars are filled.

PROCESS Lower the rack into simmering water. Water must cover jars by 1 inch. Adjust heat to medium-high, cover canner and bring water to a rolling boil. Process half-pint jars 15 minutes. Turn off heat and remove cover. Let jars cool 5 minutes. Remove jars from canner; do not retighten bands if loose. Cool 12 hours. Check seals. Label and store jars.

Plum Sauce

Yield: about 4 pint jars

4 pounds plums (about 12 large)	1 (1/4 x 1 inch) piece fresh ginger, minced
2 cups brown sugar	1 tablespoon salt
1 cup granulated sugar	1 clove garlic, minced
3/4 cup chopped onion (about 1 medium)	1 cup cider vinegar, 5% acidity
2 tablespoons mustard seed	
2 tablespoons finely chopped green chili peppers	

PREP Wash plums and chili peppers under cold running water; drain. Cut plums in half lengthwise and remove pits and fibrous flesh. Chop plums. Peel and chop onion. Measure 3/4 cup chopped onion. Remove stems and seeds from chili peppers. Finely chop chili peppers; measure 2 tablespoons chopped chili peppers.

COOK Combine all ingredients, except plums, in a large saucepan. Bring mixture to a boil over medium-high heat, stirring until sugar dissolves. Reduce heat to a gentle boil. Add chopped plums. Cook until sauce is thick and syrupy.

FILL Ladle hot sauce into a hot jar, leaving 1/2-inch headspace. Clean jar rim. Center lid on jar and adjust band to fingertip-tight. Place jar on the rack elevated over simmering water (180°F) in boiling-water canner. Repeat until all jars are filled.

PROCESS Lower the rack into simmering water. Water must cover jars by 1 inch. Adjust heat to medium-high, cover canner and bring water to a rolling boil. Process pint jars 20 minutes. Turn off heat and remove cover. Let jars cool 5 minutes. Remove jars from canner; do not retighten bands if loose. Cool 12 hours. Check seals. Label and store jars.

Note: When cutting or seeding hot peppers, wear rubber gloves to prevent hands from being burned.

Pomegranate Sauce

Yield: about 4 half-pint jars

5 cups pomegranate juice (about 10 large)	1/2 cup lemon juice
	1 cup sugar

PREP Wash pomegranates under cold running water; drain. Cut pomegranates in half crosswise. Extract juice from seeds with a juice reamer. Strain juice through a damp jelly bag or several layers of cheesecloth; measure 5 cups pomegranate juice.

COOK Combine all ingredients in a large saucepan. Bring mixture to a boil, stirring until sugar dissolves. Reduce heat to a simmer (180°F); simmer until sauce is reduced by half.

FILL Ladle hot sauce into a hot jar, leaving 1/2-inch headspace. Clean jar rim. Center lid on jar and adjust band to fingertip-tight. Place jar on the rack elevated over simmering water (180°F) in boiling-water canner. Repeat until all jars are filled.

PROCESS Lower the rack into simmering water. Water must cover jars by 1 inch. Adjust heat to medium-high, cover canner and bring water to a rolling boil. Process half-pint jars 10 minutes. Turn off heat and remove cover. Let jars cool 5 minutes. Remove jars from canner; do not retighten bands if loose. Cool 12 hours. Check seals. Label and store jars.

Soy Plum Sauce

Yield: about 4 half-pint jars

4 cups chopped plums (about 7 medium)	1 clove garlic, finely minced
1/2 cup brown sugar	2 tablespoons coarsely grated fresh ginger
1 cup pineapple juice	
1/4 cup finely minced Serrano peppers	1 1/4 cups red wine vinegar, 5% acidity
1/4 cup thinly sliced green onions (about 5 to 6)	1/4 cup soy sauce
	1 teaspoon Hoisin sauce

PREP Wash plums, peppers, and onions under cold running water; drain. Cut plums in half lengthwise and remove pits and fibrous flesh. Chop plums into 1/2-inch pieces; measure 4 cups chopped plums. Remove stems from peppers. Finely mince peppers; measure 1/4 cup minced peppers. Peel and thinly slice onions; measure 1/4 cup sliced onions. Peel garlic and finely mince. Peel fresh ginger and grate; measure 2 tablespoons grated fresh ginger.

COOK Combine chopped plums, sugar, and pineapple juice in a large saucepan. Cook over medium-high heat until plums

are tender. Purée mixture using a food processor or food mill. Return purée to a large saucepan. Add remaining ingredients. Cook mixture over medium-high heat for 10 minutes, stirring to prevent sticking.

FILL Ladle hot sauce into a hot jar, leaving 1/2-inch headspace. Clean jar rim. Center lid on jar and adjust band to fingertip-tight. Place jar on the rack elevated over simmering water (180°F) in boiling-water canner. Repeat until all jars are filled.

PROCESS Lower the rack into simmering water. Water must cover jars by 1 inch. Adjust heat to medium-high, cover canner and bring water to a rolling boil. Process half-pint jars 10 minutes. Turn off heat and remove cover. Let jars cool 5 minutes. Remove jars from canner; do not retighten bands if loose. Cool 12 hours. Check seals. Label and store jars.

Note: When cutting or seeding hot peppers, wear rubber gloves to prevent hands from being burned.

Syrups

Fruit syrup is typically thin. If a thick syrup is desired for serving, dissolve up to 1 tablespoon cornstarch in double the measure of water in a small saucepan. Stir in 1 cup of syrup. Bring mixture to a boil, cooking until syrup thickens. Do not add cornstarch before processing.

Apple-Cinnamon Syrup

Yield: about 6 pint jars

6 cups apple juice, fresh or bottled (without added calcium)	4 cups water
	3 cups corn syrup
3 sticks cinnamon, broken	1/4 cup lemon juice
5 cups sugar	

PREP Refer to Apple Juice (see page 28) to prepare juice from fresh apples.

COOK Combine apple juice and cinnamon sticks in a medium saucepan. Simmer 5 minutes; set aside. Combine sugar and water in a medium saucepan; boil to 230°F. Add apple juice, cinnamon sticks, and corn syrup to sugar syrup; boil 5 minutes. Remove from heat. Stir in lemon juice. Remove cinnamon sticks.

FILL Ladle hot syrup into a hot jar, leaving 1/4-inch headspace. Clean jar rim. Center lid on jar and adjust band to fingertip-tight. Place jar on the rack elevated over simmering water (180°F) in boiling-water canner. Repeat until all jars are filled.

PROCESS Lower the rack into simmering water. Water must cover jars by 1 inch. Adjust heat to medium-high, cover canner and bring water to a rolling boil. Process pint jars 10 minutes. Turn off heat and remove cover. Let jars cool 5 minutes. Remove jars from canner; do not retighten bands if loose. Cool 12 hours. Check seals. Label and store jars.

Blueberry Syrup

Yield: about 3 pint jars

2 quarts blueberries	3 cups sugar
6 cups water, divided	2 tablespoons lemon juice
1 tablespoon grated lemon peel	

PREP Wash blueberries under cold running water; drain. Crush blueberries.

COOK Combine blueberries, 2 cups water, and lemon juice in a medium saucepan. Simmer 5 minutes. Strain mixture through a damp jelly bag or several layers of cheesecloth. Combine sugar and 4 cups water in a medium saucepan; boil to 230°F. Add blueberry juice to sugar syrup; boil 5 minutes. Stir in lemon juice.

FILL Ladle hot syrup into a hot jar, leaving 1/4-inch headspace. Clean jar rim. Center lid on jar and adjust band to fingertip-tight. Place jar on the rack elevated over simmering water (180°F) in boiling-water canner. Repeat until all jars are filled.

PROCESS Lower the rack into simmering water. Water must cover jars by 1 inch. Adjust heat to medium-high, cover canner and bring water to a rolling boil. Process pint jars 10 minutes. Turn off heat and remove cover. Let jars cool 5 minutes. Remove jars from canner; do not retighten bands if loose. Cool 12 hours. Check seals. Label and store jars.

Maple-Walnut Syrup

Yield: about 4 half-pint jars

1 1/2 cups corn syrup	1/2 cup sugar
1 cup maple syrup	2 cups walnut pieces
1/2 cup water	

PREP Put walnut pieces into a sieve and shake vigorously to remove small particles that will cloud syrup.

COOK Combine corn syrup, maple syrup, and water in a large saucepan. Add sugar, stirring until sugar dissolves. Bring mixture to a boil, stirring occasionally. Reduce heat to a simmer (180°F); simmer until syrup begins to thicken, about 15 minutes. Stir in walnuts; cook 5 minutes.

FILL Ladle hot syrup into a hot jar, leaving 1/4-inch headspace. Remove air bubbles. Clean jar rim. Center lid on jar and adjust band to fingertip-tight. Place jar on the rack elevated over simmering water (180°F) in boiling-water canner. Repeat until all jars are filled.

PROCESS Lower the rack into simmering water. Water must cover jars by 1 inch. Adjust heat to medium-high, cover canner and bring water to a rolling boil. Process half-pint jars 10 minutes. Turn off heat and remove cover. Let jars cool 5 minutes. Remove jars from canner; do not retighten bands if loose. Cool 12 hours. Check seals. Label and store jars.

Praline Syrup

Yield: about 4 half-pint jars

2 cups dark corn syrup	1 cup pecan pieces
1/2 cup water	1/2 teaspoon vanilla
1/3 cup dark brown sugar	

PREP Put pecan pieces into a sieve and shake vigorously to remove small particles that will cloud syrup.

COOK Combine dark corn syrup and water in a large saucepan. Add sugar, stirring until sugar dissolves. Bring mixture to a boil over medium-high heat; boil hard 1 minute. Reduce heat to a simmer (180°F); stir in pecan pieces and vanilla; simmer 5 minutes.

FILL Ladle hot syrup into a hot jar, leaving 1/4-inch headspace. Clean jar rim. Center lid on jar and adjust band to fingertip-tight. Place jar on the rack elevated over simmering water (180°F) in boiling-water canner. Repeat until all jars are filled.

PROCESS Lower the rack into simmering water. Water must cover jars by 1 inch. Adjust heat to medium-high, cover canner and bring water to a rolling boil. Process half-pint jars 10 minutes. Turn off heat and remove cover. Let jars cool 5 minutes. Remove jars from canner; do not retighten bands if loose. Cool 12 hours. Check seals. Label and store jars.

Strawberry Syrup

Yield: about 3 pint jars

2 1/2 quarts strawberries (about 5 to 6 pounds)	2 1/2 cups sugar
3 cups water, divided	3 1/2 cups corn syrup
1 2-inch strip of lemon peel	2 tablespoons lemon juice (about 1 medium)

PREP Wash strawberries and lemon under cold running water; drain. Remove stems and caps from strawberries. Crush strawberries using a potato masher. Cut yellow portion of lemon peel into a 2- inch strip. Cut lemon in half crosswise and extract juice. Measure 2 tablespoons lemon juice.

COOK Combine strawberries, 1 1/2 cups water, and lemon peel in a medium saucepan. Bring mixture to a simmer (180°F); simmer 5 minutes. Strain mixture through a damp jelly bag or several layers of cheesecloth; set aside. Combine sugar and 1 1/2 cups water in a large saucepan. Boil mixture to 230°F. Stir in strawberry juice and corn syrup. Boil 5 minutes. Stir in lemon juice.

FILL Ladle hot syrup into a hot jar, leaving 1/4-inch headspace. Clean jar rim. Center lid on jar and adjust band to fingertip-tight. Place jar on the rack elevated over simmering water (180°F) in boiling-water canner. Repeat until all jars are filled.

PROCESS Lower the rack into simmering water. Water must cover jars by 1 inch. Adjust heat to medium-high, cover canner and bring water to a rolling boil. Process pint jars 10 minutes. Turn off heat and remove cover. Let jars cool 5 minutes. Remove jars from canner; do not retighten bands if loose. Cool 12 hours. Check seals. Label and store jars.

 Vinegars

Blueberry-Basil Vinegar

Yield: about 2 pint jars

4 cups blueberries	1 cup basil, loosely packed
4 cups white wine vinegar, 5% acidity, divided	Zest of 1 lemon

PREP Wash blueberries and lemon under cold running water; drain. Combine blueberries and 1 cup white wine vinegar in a large glass bowl. Lightly crush blueberries. Add remaining white wine vinegar. Crush basil and add to blueberry mixture. Grate lemon peel; add lemon peel to blueberry mixture. Cover bowl with waxed paper or plastic wrap and secure. Let vinegar steep in a cool, dark place for 4 weeks, stirring every 2 to 3 days. Taste vinegar each week for desired flavor. Strain mixture through a damp jelly bag or several layers of cheesecloth.

COOK Pour blueberry vinegar into a medium saucepan. Bring vinegar to a simmer (180°F) over medium heat.

FILL Ladle hot vinegar into a hot jar, leaving ¼-inch headspace. Clean jar rim. Center lid on jar and adjust band to fingertip-tight. Place jar on the rack elevated over simmering water (180°F) in boiling-water canner. Repeat until all jars are filled.

PROCESS Lower the rack into simmering water. Water must cover jars by 1 inch. Adjust heat to medium-high, cover canner and bring water to a rolling boil. Process pint jars 10 minutes. Turn off heat and remove cover. Let jars cool 5 minutes. Remove jars from canner; do not retighten bands if loose. Cool 12 hours. Check seals. Label and store jars.

Cranberry-Orange Vinegar

Yield: about 2 pint jars

1 pound fresh cranberries, divided	1 cup sugar
4 whole cloves	3 cups white wine vinegar, 5% acidity
2 sticks cinnamon	2 orange slices

PREP Wash cranberries under cold running water; drain. Measure ½ cup cranberries; set aside. Prepare cranberry juice with remaining cranberries (see page 28); measure 1 cup cranberry juice. Tie spices in a spice bag.

COOK Combine cranberry juice, spice bag, and sugar in a large saucepan. Cook over medium heat, stirring until sugar dissolves. Add reserved cranberries and white wine vinegar. Bring vinegar to a simmer (180°F) over medium heat; simmer 10 minutes. Remove spice bag.

FILL Put one orange slice into a hot jar. Ladle hot vinegar into jar, leaving ¼-inch headspace. Clean jar rim. Center lid on jar and adjust band to fingertip-tight. Place jar on the rack elevated over simmering water (180°F) in boiling-water canner. Repeat until all jars are filled.

PROCESS Lower the rack into simmering water. Water must cover jars by 1 inch. Adjust heat to medium-high, cover canner and bring water to a rolling boil. Process pint jars 10 minutes. Turn off heat and remove cover. Let jars cool 5 minutes. Remove jars from canner; do not retighten bands if loose. Cool 12 hours. Check seals. Label and store jars.

Lemon-Mint Vinegar

Yield: about 2 pint jars

4 cups white wine vinegar, 5% acidity	2 cups mint leaves, loosely packed
¼ cup sugar	Peel of 2 lemons

PREP Wash lemons under cold running water; drain. Cut yellow peel off lemon and cut into 1-inch strips. Set aside 2 strips of lemon peel and 2 sprigs of mint. Lightly crush remaining mint leaves.

COOK Combine white wine vinegar and sugar in a medium saucepan. Heat mixture to a simmer (180°F), stirring until sugar dissolves. Pour mixture into a large glass bowl. Add crushed mint leaves and lemon peel. Cover bowl with waxed paper or plastic wrap and secure. Let vinegar steep in a cool, dark place for 1 to 4 weeks, stirring every 2 to 3 days. Taste vinegar each week to determine desired flavor. Strain vinegar through a damp jelly bag or several layers of cheesecloth. Pour vinegar into a medium saucepan. Bring vinegar to a simmer (180°F) over medium heat.

FILL Put one strip of lemon peel and 1 sprig of mint into a hot jar. Ladle hot vinegar into jar, leaving ¼-inch headspace. Clean jar rim. Center lid on jar and adjust band to fingertip-tight. Place jar on the rack elevated over simmering water (180°F) in boiling-water canner. Repeat until all jars are filled.

PROCESS Lower the rack into simmering water. Water must cover jars by 1 inch. Adjust heat to medium-high, cover canner and bring water to a rolling boil. Process pint jars 10 minutes. Turn off heat and remove cover. Let jars cool 5 minutes. Remove jars from canner; do not retighten bands if loose. Cool 12 hours. Check seals. Label and store jars.

Loganberry Vinegar

Yield: about 2 pint jars

4 cups loganberries	4 cups red wine vinegar, 5% acidity

PREP Wash loganberries under cold running water; drain. Combine loganberries and red wine vinegar in a large glass bowl. Cover bowl with waxed paper or plastic wrap and secure. Let vinegar steep in a cool, dark place for 1 to 4 weeks, stirring every 2 to 3 days. Taste vinegar each week for desired flavor. Strain vinegar through a damp jelly bag or several layers of cheesecloth.

COOK Pour loganberry vinegar into a medium saucepan. Bring vinegar to a simmer (180°F) over medium heat.

FILL Ladle hot vinegar into a hot jar, leaving ¼-inch headspace. Clean jar rim. Center lid on jar and adjust band to fingertip-tight. Place jar on the rack elevated over simmering water (180°F) in boiling-water canner. Repeat until all jars are filled.

PROCESS Lower the rack into simmering water. Water must cover jars by 1 inch. Adjust heat to medium-high, cover canner and bring water to a rolling boil. Process pint jars 10 minutes. Turn off heat and remove cover. Let jars cool 5 minutes. Remove jars from canner; do not retighten bands if loose. Cool 12 hours. Check seals. Label and store jars.

Mulled Blackberry Vinegar

Yield: about 3 pint jars

4 cups blackberries	2 sticks cinnamon
4 cups cider vinegar, 5% acidity, divided	1 tablespoon whole cloves
	1 tablespoon whole allspice

PREP Wash blackberries under cold running water; drain. Combine blackberries and 1 cup cider vinegar in a large glass bowl. Lightly crush blackberries. Add remaining cider vinegar and spices. Cover bowl with waxed paper or plastic wrap and secure. Let vinegar steep in a cool, dark place for 4 weeks, stirring every 2 to 3 days. Taste vinegar each week for desired flavor. Strain vinegar through a damp jelly bag or several layers of cheesecloth.

COOK Pour mulled blackberry vinegar into a medium saucepan. Bring vinegar to a simmer (180°F) over medium heat.

FILL Ladle hot vinegar into a hot jar, leaving 1/4-inch headspace. Clean jar rim. Center lid on jar and adjust band to fingertip-tight. Place jar on the rack elevated over simmering water (180°F) in boiling-water canner. Repeat until all jars are filled.

PROCESS Lower the rack into simmering water. Water must cover jars by 1 inch. Adjust heat to medium-high, cover canner and bring water to a rolling boil. Process pint jars 10 minutes. Turn off heat and remove cover. Let jars cool 5 minutes. Remove jars from canner; do not retighten bands if loose. Cool 12 hours. Check seals. Label and store jars.

Sweet Cherry Vinegar

Yield: about 2 pint jars

4 cups pitted sweet cherries (about 2 pounds)	4 cups white wine vinegar, 5% acidity, divided
	Zest of 1 lemon

PREP Wash sweet cherries under cold running water; drain. Remove stems and pit cherries. Measure 4 cups pitted cherries. Combine cherries and 1 cup white wine vinegar in a large glass bowl. Lightly crush cherries. Add remaining white wine vinegar and lemon zest. Cover bowl with waxed paper or plastic wrap and secure. Let vinegar steep in a cool, dark place for 4 weeks, stirring every 2 to 3 days. Taste vinegar each week for desired flavor. Strain vinegar through a damp jelly bag or several layers of cheesecloth.

COOK Pour sweet cherry vinegar into a medium saucepan. Bring vinegar to a simmer (180°F) over medium heat.

FILL Ladle hot vinegar into a hot jar, leaving 1/4-inch headspace. Clean jar rim. Center lid on jar and adjust band to fingertip-tight. Place jar on the rack elevated over simmering water (180°F) in boiling-water canner. Repeat until all jars are filled.

PROCESS Lower the rack into simmering water. Water must cover jars by 1 inch. Adjust heat to medium-high, cover canner and bring water to a rolling boil. Process pint jars 10 minutes. Turn off heat and remove cover. Let jars cool 5 minutes. Remove jars from canner; do not retighten bands if loose. Cool 12 hours. Check seals. Label and store jars.

Flavorful Sampler

Almond Pears

Yield: about 5 pint jars

7 pounds pears (about 21 medium)	4 cups water
Ball Fruit-Fresh Produce Protector	1/3 cup blanched almonds
2 cups sugar	1/2 cup almond liqueur

PREP Wash pears under cold running water; drain. Cut pears in half lengthwise, core, and peel. Treat with Fruit-Fresh to prevent darkening (see page 16).

COOK Cook pears in a small amount of water, one layer at a time, until hot throughout; keep pears hot. Combine sugar and 4 cups water in a medium saucepan. Bring mixture to a boil over medium-high heat, stirring until sugar dissolves. Reduce heat to a simmer (180°F); simmer 5 minutes. Remove syrup from heat. Stir in almond liqueur.

FILL Pack hot pears, cavity side down and layers overlapping, into a hot jar, leaving 1/2-inch headspace. Add 1 tablespoon almonds. Ladle hot syrup over pears, leaving 1/2-inch headspace. Remove air bubbles. Clean jar rim. Center lid on jar and adjust band to fingertip-tight. Place jar on the rack elevated over simmering water (180°F) in boiling-water canner. Repeat until all jars are filled.

PROCESS Lower the rack into simmering water. Water must cover jars by 1 inch. Adjust heat to medium-high, cover canner and bring water to a rolling boil. Process pint jars 20 minutes. Turn off heat and remove cover. Let jars cool 5 minutes. Remove jars from canner; do not retighten bands if loose. Cool 12 hours. Check seals. Label and store jars.

Blackberries in Framboise

Yield: about 4 half-pint jars

6 cups blackberries, divided (about 2 1/2 pounds)	1/2 teaspoon freshly grated nutmeg
2 cups sugar	2 cups water
1 stick cinnamon, broken	1/2 cup Framboise brandy
1 tablespoon grated lemon peel	

PREP Wash blackberries under cold running water; drain. Extract the juice from 2 cups of blackberries (see page 28). Measure 1/2 cup blackberry juice; set aside.

COOK Combine sugar, cinnamon stick, lemon peel, nutmeg, and water in a large saucepan. Bring mixture to a boil over medium-high heat, stirring until sugar dissolves. Reduce heat to a simmer (180°F); simmer 5 minutes. Strain syrup through a sieve. Combine syrup, blackberry juice, remaining blackberries, and brandy in a large saucepan. Bring mixture to a boil.

FILL Pack hot blackberries into a hot jar, leaving 1/2-inch headspace. Ladle hot syrup over blackberries, leaving 1/2-inch headspace. Remove air bubbles. Clean jar rim. Center lid on jar and adjust band to fingertip-tight. Place jar on the rack elevated over simmering water (180°F) in boiling-water canner. Repeat until all jars are filled.

PROCESS Lower the rack into simmering water. Water must cover jars by 1 inch. Adjust heat to medium-high, cover canner

and bring water to a rolling boil. Process half-pint jars 10 minutes. Turn off heat and remove cover. Let jars cool 5 minutes. Remove jars from canner; do not retighten bands if loose. Cool 12 hours. Check seals. Label and store jars.

Brandied Apple Rings

Yield: about 3 pint jars

4½ pounds apples (12 to 14 medium)	3 cups water
Ball Fruit-Fresh Produce Protector	Red food coloring (optional)
	1 cup brandy
4 cups sugar	

PREP Wash apples under cold running water; drain. Core apples, but do not peel. Cut apples crosswise into ¼-inch rings. Treat with Fruit-Fresh to prevent darkening (see page 16).

COOK Combine sugar and water in a medium saucepan. Bring mixture to a boil over medium-high heat, stirring until sugar dissolves. Stir in a few drops of red food coloring, if desired. Drain apple rings. Add apple rings to syrup. Bring mixture to a boil over medium-high heat. Reduce heat to a simmer (180°F); simmer 30 minutes, or until apple rings are desired color. Remove from heat; cool to room temperature. Remove apple rings; set aside. Bring syrup to a boil. Remove from heat. Stir in brandy.

FILL Pack apple rings loosely into a hot jar, leaving ½-inch headspace. Ladle hot syrup over apple rings, leaving ½-inch headspace. Remove air bubbles. Clean jar rim. Center lid on jar and adjust band to fingertip-tight. Place jar on the rack elevated over simmering water (180°F) in boiling-water canner. Repeat until all jars are filled.

PROCESS Lower the rack into simmering water. Water must cover jars by 1 inch. Adjust heat to medium-high, cover canner and bring water to a rolling boil. Process pint jars 15 minutes. Turn off heat and remove cover. Let jars cool 5 minutes. Remove jars from canner; do not retighten bands if loose. Cool 12 hours. Check seals. Label and store jars.

CONDIMENTS

Apricot and Date Chutney

Yield: about 6 half-pint jars

1 pound dried apricots	1 teaspoon ginger
1¼ cups dried dates	½ teaspoon coriander
1½ cups brown sugar	1 cup white wine vinegar, 5% acidity
1¼ cups raisins	
1½ teaspoons mustard seed	1 cup water
1½ teaspoons salt	

PREP Soak apricots in enough water to cover for 30 minutes. Drain apricots. Chop dates into ¼- to ⅓-inch pieces.

COOK Combine all ingredients in a large saucepan. Cook mixture over medium-low heat until thickened, stirring to prevent sticking. Bring mixture to a boil.

FILL Pack hot chutney into a hot jar, leaving ½-inch headspace. Remove air bubbles. Clean jar rim. Center lid on jar and adjust band to fingertip-tight. Place jar on the rack elevated over simmering water (180°F) in boiling-water canner. Repeat until all jars are filled.

PROCESS Lower the rack into simmering water. Water must cover jars by 1 inch. Adjust heat to medium-high, cover canner and bring water to a rolling boil. Process half-pint jars 10 minutes. Turn off heat and remove cover. Let jars cool 5 minutes. Remove jars from canner; do not retighten bands if loose. Cool 12 hours. Check seals. Label and store jars.

Brandied Mincemeat

Yield: about 4 quart jars

2 quarts diced tart apples (about 8 large)	½ cup minced candied orange peel
4 cups cranberries (about 1 pound)	½ cup minced candied lemon peel
1 (14-ounce) package golden raisins	2 cups brown sugar
1 (14-ounce) package dark raisins	1 tablespoon cinnamon
1 (11-ounce) package dried currants	2 teaspoons allspice
1 (12-ounce) package dried figs, chopped	2 teaspoons nutmeg
1⅓ cups ground oranges (about 2 medium)	1 teaspoon cloves
1 cup ground lemons (about 2 large)	1 teaspoon ginger
	1 quart apple cider
	¾ cup brandy
	½ cup dry sherry

PREP Wash apples, cranberries, oranges, and lemons under cold running water; drain. Core, peel, and dice apples; measure 2 quarts diced apples. Chop dried figs into ½-inch pieces. Cut oranges and lemons in half crosswise and remove seeds. Do not peel oranges or lemons. Grind oranges and lemons separately using a food processor or food grinder. Measure 1⅓ cups ground orange and 1 cup ground lemon.

COOK Combine all ingredients, except brandy and sherry, in a large saucepan. Simmer mixture over medium-low heat 1 hour, stirring to prevent sticking. Remove from heat. Stir in brandy and sherry. Return mixture to medium-low heat and simmer 30 minutes.

FILL Pack hot mincemeat into a hot jar, leaving ½-inch headspace. Remove air bubbles. Clean jar rim. Center lid on jar and adjust band to fingertip-tight. Place jar on the rack elevated over simmering water (180°F) in boiling-water canner. Repeat until all jars are filled.

PROCESS Lower the rack into simmering water. Water must cover jars by 1 inch. Adjust heat to medium-high, cover canner and bring water to a rolling boil. Process quart jars 30 minutes. Turn off heat and remove cover. Let jars cool 5 minutes. Remove jars from canner; do not retighten bands if loose. Cool 12 hours. Check seals. Label and store jars.

If you want to make a non-alcoholic version of this recipe, replace brandy and sherry with 1¼ cups white grape juice or apple juice.

Crabapple Pickles

Yield: about 6 pint jars

2 quarts crabapples with stems (about 2½ pounds)	2 sticks cinnamon
6 cups sugar	1½ tablespoons whole allspice
3 cups vinegar, 5% acidity	1½ tablespoons whole cloves
3 cups water	

PREP Wash crabapples under cold running water; drain. Prick crabapples with a thin metal skewer to help prevent peel from bursting; set aside. Tie spices in a spice bag.

COOK Combine sugar, vinegar, and water in a large saucepan. Bring mixture to a boil, stirring until sugar dissolves. Reduce heat to a simmer (180°F); add spice bag and simmer 5 minutes. Add crabapples, one layer at a time, and simmer until tender. Remove crabapples, to a large bowl. Bring pickling liquid to a boil. Pour pickling liquid over crabapples. Cover bowl; let stand 12 to 18 hours in the refrigerator. Remove spice bag. Return mixture to a large saucepan. Bring mixture to a boil.

FILL Pack crabapples into a hot jar, leaving ½-inch headspace. Ladle hot pickling liquid over fruit, leaving ½-inch headspace. Remove air bubbles. Clean jar rim. Center lid on jar and adjust band to fingertip-tight. Place jar on the rack elevated over simmering water (180°F) in boiling-water canner. Repeat until all jars are filled.

PROCESS Lower the rack into simmering water. Water must cover jars by 1 inch. Adjust heat to medium-high, cover canner and bring water to a rolling boil. Process pint jars 15 minutes. Turn off heat and remove cover. Let jars cool 5 minutes. Remove jars from canner; do not retighten bands if loose. Cool 12 hours. Check seals. Label and store jars.

Curried Fruit Compote

Yield: about 4 quart jars

3 pounds peaches (about 12)	3 cups sugar
2 pounds apricots (about 16)	3 tablespoons curry powder
Ball Fruit-Fresh Produce Protector	4 cups water
1 fresh pineapple (about 5 pounds)	¼ cup lemon juice
1 cantaloupe (about 4 pounds)	½ cup thinly sliced lime (about 1 small)

PREP Wash peaches, apricots, pineapple, and lime under cold running water; drain. To peel peaches and apricots, blanch in boiling water for 30 to 60 seconds. Immediately transfer to cold water. Cut off peels. Cut peaches and apricots in half lengthwise; remove pits and fibrous flesh. Slice peaches; leave apricots cut in half. Treat with Fruit-Fresh to prevent darkening (see page 16). Cut off top and bottom ends of pineapple; core and peel. Cut pineapple into 1-inch pieces. Peel and seed cantaloupe; cut cantaloupe into 1-inch pieces or shape into balls. Thinly slice lime, discarding ends.

COOK Combine sugar, curry powder, water, and lemon juice in a large saucepan. Bring mixture to a boil; reduce heat to a simmer (180°F). Drain peaches and apricots. Add peaches, apricots, pineapple, and cantaloupe to syrup. Simmer until fruit is hot throughout.

FILL Pack hot fruit into a hot jar, leaving ½-inch headspace. Put one lime slice into jar. Ladle hot syrup over fruit, leaving ½-inch headspace. Remove air bubbles. Clean jar rim. Center lid on jar and adjust band to fingertip-tight. Place jar on the rack elevated over simmering water (180°F) in boiling-water canner. Repeat until all jars are filled.

PROCESS Lower the rack into simmering water. Water must cover jars by 1 inch. Adjust heat to medium-high, cover canner and bring water to a rolling boil. Process quart jars 30 minutes. Turn off heat and remove cover. Let jars cool 5 minutes. Remove jars from canner; do not retighten bands if loose. Cool 12 hours. Check seals. Label and store jars.

Jardinière

Yield: about 6 pint jars

1 pound green bell peppers (about 3 medium)	½ pound mushrooms
1¼ pounds onions (about 3 medium)	1 cup sugar
¾ pound zucchini (about 4 medium)	2 tablespoons Ball Mixed Pickling Spice
1 pound Anaheim peppers (about 4 small)	2 teaspoons basil
½ pound carrots (about 5 medium)	1 teaspoon oregano
3⅔ cups sliced celery (about 6 stalks)	1 teaspoon peppercorns
¼ pound banana peppers (about 4 medium)	1 clove garlic
	1 teaspoon Ball Salt for Pickling & Preserving
	1 quart cider vinegar, 5% acidity
	1½ cups water
	Ball Pickle Crisp (optional)

PREP Wash bell peppers, zucchini, carrots, celery, and mushrooms under cold running water; drain. Remove stems and seeds from peppers. Cut peppers into ½-inch strips. Peel and slice onions. Remove stem and blossom ends from zucchini. Cut zucchini crosswise into ¼-inch slices. Remove stem end from carrots. Peel carrots. Cut carrots crosswise in half, then cut lengthwise into quarters. Remove leafy tops and root ends from celery. Chop celery into ½-inch pieces; measure 3½ cups chopped celery. Cut mushrooms in half. Peel garlic and mince.

COOK Combine sugar, spices, vinegar, and water in a large saucepan. Bring mixture to a boil, stirring until sugar dissolves. Reduce heat to a simmer (180°F); add vegetables and simmer until vegetables are just tender. Remove spice bag.

FILL Pack hot vegetables into a hot jar, leaving ½-inch headspace. Ladle hot pickling liquid over vegetables, leaving ½-inch headspace. Add Pickle Crisp, if desired. Remove air bubbles. Clean jar rim. Center lid on jar and adjust band to fingertip-tight. Place jar on the rack elevated over simmering water (180°F) in boiling-water canner. Repeat until all jars are filled.

PROCESS Lower the rack into simmering water. Water must cover jars by 1 inch. Adjust heat to medium-high, cover canner and bring water to a rolling boil. Process pint jars 20 minutes. Turn off heat and remove cover. Let jars cool 5 minutes. Remove jars from canner; do not retighten bands if loose. Cool 12 hours. Check seals. Label and store jars.

Note: When cutting or seeding hot peppers, wear rubber gloves to prevent hands from being burned.

Mango-Pineapple Relish

Yield: about 6 pint jars

4 cups chopped mangoes (about 8 small)	1/4 cup diced red onion (about 1/2 small)
3 cups chopped pineapple (about 4 pounds)	1/4 cup cider vinegar, 5% acidity
1/2 cup diced green bell pepper (about 1/2 large)	1/4 cup lemon juice
	1/4 cup pineapple juice
1/2 cup diced red bell pepper (about 1/2 large)	1 tablespoon sugar
	2 teaspoons cinnamon
	1/4 teaspoon ginger

PREP Wash mangoes, pineapple, and green and red bell peppers under cold running water; drain. Cut each mango lengthwise into two large pieces, starting at the top and cutting down to the bottom. Make cuts about 1/3 inch from the center of the fruit to avoid the pit and fibrous flesh. Peel mango pieces and chop; measure 4 cups chopped mango. Cut off top and bottom ends of pineapple; core and peel. Coarsely chop pineapple; measure 3 cups chopped pineapple. Remove stems and seeds from green and red bell peppers. Dice peppers separately. Measure 1/4 cup diced green bell pepper and 1/4 cup diced red bell pepper. Peel onion and dice; measure 1/2 cup diced onion.

COOK Combine all ingredients in a large saucepan. Bring mixture to a boil. Reduce heat to a simmer (180°F); simmer 20 minutes, stirring to prevent sticking.

FILL Pack hot relish into a hot jar, leaving 1/2-inch headspace. Remove air bubbles. Clean jar rim. Center lid on jar and adjust band to fingertip-tight. Place jar on the rack elevated over simmering water (180°F) in boiling-water canner. Repeat until all jars are filled.

PROCESS Lower the rack into simmering water. Water must cover jars by 1 inch. Adjust heat to medium-high, cover canner and bring water to a rolling boil. Process pint jars 15 minutes. Turn off heat and remove cover. Let jars cool 5 minutes. Remove jars from canner; do not retighten bands if loose. Cool 12 hours. Check seals. Label and store jars.

Pickled Green Tomato-Hot Pepper Mix

Yield: about 5 quart jars

7 pounds green tomatoes (about 21 medium)	5 cloves garlic
	1 tablespoon Ball Salt for Pickling & Preserving
2 pounds Hungarian peppers (about 40)	1 cup sugar
	2 quarts vinegar, 5% acidity
1 pound banana peppers (about 16 to 18)	1 quart water
	1/4 cup Ball Mixed Pickling Spice
1 pound Anaheim peppers (about 18 to 20)	2 tablespoons mustard seed
1/2 pound pearl onions	Ball Pickle Crisp (optional)

PREP Wash tomatoes and Hungarian, banana, and Anaheim peppers under cold running water; drain. Core tomatoes and cut lengthwise into eighths. Remove stems from peppers. Cut peppers crosswise into 1/2-inch rings. To peel pearl onions, cover with boiling water and let stand 2 minutes; drain. Quickly rinse under cold running water. Cut off peel. Peel garlic. Tie spices in a spice bag.

COOK Combine tomatoes, peppers, onions, garlic, and salt in a large bowl; set aside. Combine sugar, vinegar, and water in a large saucepan. Bring mixture to a boil, stirring until sugar dissolves. Add spice bag. Reduce heat to a simmer (180°F); simmer 10 minutes. Add vegetables and simmer 10 minutes. Remove spice bag.

FILL Pack hot vegetables into a hot jar, leaving 1/2-inch headspace. Ladle hot pickling liquid over vegetables, leaving 1/2-inch headspace. Add Pickle Crisp, if desired. Remove air bubbles. Clean jar rim. Center lid on jar and adjust band to fingertip-tight. Place jar on the rack elevated over simmering water (180°F) in boiling-water canner. Repeat until all jars are filled.

PROCESS Lower the rack into simmering water. Water must cover jars by 1 inch. Adjust heat to medium-high, cover canner and bring water to a rolling boil. Process quart jars 15 minutes. Turn off heat and remove cover. Let jars cool 5 minutes. Remove jars from canner; do not retighten bands if loose. Cool 12 hours. Check seals. Label and store jars.

Pickled Pineapple

Yield: about 4 pint jars

2 cups brown sugar	3 sticks cinnamon, broken
1 cup red wine vinegar, 5% acidity	1/2 teaspoon whole allspice
	1/4 teaspoon whole cloves
1 cup unsweetened pineapple juice, fresh or canned	2 fresh pineapples (about 5 pounds each)

PREP Wash pineapples under cold running water; drain. Cut off top and bottom ends of pineapples; core and peel. Cut pineapples lengthwise into 1-inch-wide spears. Tie spices in a spice bag.

COOK Combine brown sugar, red wine vinegar, pineapple juice, and spice bag in a large saucepan. Bring mixture to a boil. Reduce heat to a simmer (180°F); simmer, covered, 20 minutes, stirring occasionally. Add pineapple spears and simmer until hot throughout. Remove pineapple spears from syrup; keep hot. Bring syrup to a boil; remove spice bag.

FILL Pack hot spears vertically into a hot jar, leaving 1/2-inch headspace. Ladle hot pickling liquid over spears, leaving 1/2-inch headspace. Remove air bubbles. Clean jar rim. Center lid on jar and adjust band to fingertip-tight. Place jar on the rack elevated over simmering water (180°F) in boiling-water canner. Repeat until all jars are filled.

PROCESS Lower the rack into simmering water. Water must cover jars by 1 inch. Adjust heat to medium-high, cover canner and bring water to a rolling boil. Process pint jars 10 minutes. Turn off heat and remove cover. Let jars cool 5 minutes. Remove jars from canner; do not retighten bands if loose. Cool 12 hours. Check seals. Label and store jars.

Pickled Three Bean Salad

Yield: about 5 pint jars

1½ pounds green beans	2½ cups sugar
1½ pounds wax beans	1 tablespoon mustard seed
1 pound fresh lima beans, shelled	1 teaspoon celery seed
2 cups sliced celery (about 3 stalks)	4 teaspoons Ball Salt for Pickling & Preserving
½ pound onion (about 1 large)	3 cups vinegar, 5% acidity
1 cup diced red bell pepper (about 1 medium)	1¼ cups water
	Ball Pickle Crisp (optional)

PREP Wash beans, celery, and pepper under cold running water; drain. Cut green and wax beans into 1½-inch pieces, discarding ends. Shell lima beans. Rinse lima beans under cold running water; drain. Remove leafy tops and root ends from celery. Cut celery into ½-inch pieces. Peel onion and slice. Remove stem and seeds from pepper. Dice pepper; measure 1 cup diced pepper. .

COOK Combine beans, celery, onion and pepper in a large saucepan. Cover with boiling water and cook 8 to 10 minutes over medium heat. Drain vegetables; keep hot. Combine sugar, mustard seed, celery seed, salt, vinegar, and water in a large saucepan. Bring mixture to a boil. Reduce heat to a simmer (180°F); simmer 15 minutes, stirring occasionally.

FILL Pack hot vegetables into a hot jar, leaving ½-inch headspace. Ladle hot pickling liquid over vegetables, leaving ½-inch headspace. Add Pickle Crisp, if desired. Remove air bubbles. Clean jar rim. Center lid on jar and adjust band to fingertip-tight. Place jar on the rack elevated over simmering water (180°F) in boiling-water canner. Repeat until all jars are filled.

PROCESS Lower the rack into simmering water. Water must cover jars by 1 inch. Adjust heat to medium-high, cover canner and bring water to a rolling boil. Process pint jars 15 minutes. Turn off heat and remove cover. Let jars cool 5 minutes. Remove jars from canner; do not retighten bands if loose. Cool 12 hours. Check seals. Label and store jars.

Red Cabbage Slaw

Yield: about 5 pint jars

6 pounds red cabbage (about 2 to 3 small heads)	2 tablespoons caraway seeds
¼ cup Ball Salt for Pickling & Preserving	2 tablespoons whole allspice
½ cup sugar	2 tablespoons peppercorns
2 sticks cinnamon, broken	1 quart red wine vinegar, 5% acidity
2 tablespoons mustard seeds	Ball Pickle Crisp (optional)

PREP Wash cabbage under cold running water; drain. Remove large outer leaves. Cut cabbage into quarters and core. Shred cabbage using a grater or knife. Layer the cabbage and salt in a large bowl. Cover; let stand 24 hours in refrigerator. Rinse cabbage under cold running water; drain. Drain thoroughly on paper towel-lined baking sheets, about 6 hours. Tie spices in a spice bag.

COOK Combine sugar, vinegar, and spice bag in a large saucepan. Bring mixture to a boil; boil 5 minutes. Remove spice bag.

FILL Pack cabbage into a hot jar, leaving ½-inch headspace. Ladle hot pickling liquid over cabbage, leaving ½-inch headspace. Add Pickle Crisp, if desired. Remove air bubbles. Clean jar rim. Center lid on jar and adjust band to fingertip-tight. Place jar on the rack elevated over simmering water (180°F) in boiling-water canner. Repeat until all jars are filled.

PROCESS Lower the rack into simmering water. Water must cover jars by 1 inch. Adjust heat to medium-high, cover canner and bring water to a rolling boil. Process pint jars 20 minutes. Turn off heat and remove cover. Let jars cool 5 minutes. Remove jars from canner; do not retighten bands if loose. Cool 12 hours. Check seals. Label and store jars.

 Our Tip Red Cabbage Slaw adds spicy crunch to burgers and brats. Toss it with yogurt or mayonnaise for a creamy side to accompany grilled fish or fried chicken.

Spicy Pickled Beets

Yield: about 4 pint jars

4 pounds beets, 1- to 1½-inch diameter (about 20 to 24 medium)	1 teaspoon whole allspice
	1 teaspoon whole cloves
3 cups thinly sliced onions (about 3 medium)	1 teaspoon Ball Salt for Pickling & Preserving
2 cups sugar	2½ cups cider vinegar, 5% acidity
3 sticks cinnamon, broken	1½ cups water
1 tablespoon mustard seed	Ball Pickle Crisp (optional)

PREP Wash beets under cold running water; drain. Trim beet stems and tap roots to 2 inches in length.

COOK Put beets in a large saucepan and cover with water by 1 inch. Bring water to a boil. Cook beets until just tender. Drain. When beets are cool enough to handle, peel and cut off ends. Combine remaining ingredients in a large saucepan. Bring mixture to a boil. Reduce heat to a simmer (180°F); simmer 5 minutes. Add beets and cook until hot throughout. Remove cinnamon sticks.

FILL Pack hot beets into a hot jar, leaving ½-inch headspace. Ladle hot pickling liquid over beets, leaving ½-inch headspace. Add Pickle Crisp, if desired. Remove air bubbles. Clean jar rim. Center lid on jar and adjust band to fingertip-tight. Place jar on the rack elevated over simmering water (180°F) in boiling-water canner. Repeat until all jars are filled.

PROCESS Lower the rack into simmering water. Water must cover jars by 1 inch. Adjust heat to medium-high, cover canner and bring water to a rolling boil. Process pint jars 30 minutes. Turn off heat and remove cover. Let jars cool 5 minutes. Remove jars from canner; do not retighten bands if loose. Cool 12 hours. Check seals. Label and store jars.

Sweet and Sour Pepper Relish

Yield: about 7 half-pint jars

4 cups finely chopped green bell peppers (about 4 medium)

3 cups chopped Granny Smith apples (about 3 large)

2 cups chopped cabbage (about ½ small head)

1 cup finely chopped banana peppers (about 6 large)

2 tablespoons Ball Salt for Pickling & Preserving

3 cups sugar

1 teaspoon mustard seed

3 cups cider vinegar, 5% acidity

Ball Pickle Crisp (optional)

PREP Wash peppers, apples, and cabbage under cold running water; drain. Remove stems and seeds from peppers. Finely chop peppers separately. Measure 4 cups chopped green bell peppers and 1 cup chopped banana peppers. Core apples and chop. Measure 3 cups chopped apples. Remove outer leaves from cabbage and core. Chop cabbage; measure 2 cups chopped cabbage. Combine peppers, apples, cabbage, and salt in a large bowl. Toss gently to blend evenly. Let stand 2 hours; drain.

COOK Combine sugar, mustard seed, and vinegar in a large saucepan. Bring mixture to a boil. Reduce heat to a simmer (180°F); add vegetables and simmer 10 minutes.

FILL Pack hot relish into a hot jar, leaving ½-inch headspace. Add Pickle Crisp, if desired. Remove air bubbles. Clean jar rim. Center lid on jar and adjust band to fingertip-tight. Place jar on the rack elevated over simmering water (180°F) in boiling-water canner. Repeat until all jars are filled.

PROCESS Lower the rack into simmering water. Water must cover jars by 1 inch. Adjust heat to medium-high, cover canner and bring water to a rolling boil. Process half-pint jars 10 minutes. Turn off heat and remove cover. Let jars cool 5 minutes. Remove jars from canner; do not retighten bands if loose. Cool 12 hours. Check seals. Label and store jars.

Zucchini Bread and Butter Pickles

Yield: about 5 pint jars

14 to 16 small zucchini, sliced

8 small onions, sliced

2 medium green bell peppers, diced

⅓ cup Ball Salt for Pickling & Preserving

2 cups sugar

2 tablespoons mustard seed

1 teaspoon turmeric

1 teaspoon celery seed

1 teaspoon peppercorns

3 cups vinegar, 5% acidity

Ball Pickle Crisp (optional)

PREP Wash zucchini and peppers under cold running water; drain. Remove stem and blossom ends from zucchini. Cut zucchini crosswise into ¼-inch slices. Remove stems and seeds from peppers. Dice peppers. Peel onions; cut into ¼-inch slices. Combine zucchini, peppers, onions, and salt in a large bowl. Toss gently to blend evenly. Let stand 2 hours; drain. Rinse vegetables under cold running water; drain.

COOK Combine remaining ingredients in a large saucepan. Bring mixture to a boil. Reduce heat to a simmer (180°F); add vegetables and simmer 10 minutes.

FILL Pack vegetables into a hot jar, leaving ½-inch headspace. Ladle hot pickling liquid over vegetables, leaving ½-inch headspace. Add Pickle Crisp, if desired. Remove air bubbles. Clean jar rim. Center lid on jar and adjust band to fingertip-tight. Place jar on the rack elevated over simmering water (180°F) in boiling-water canner. Repeat until all jars are filled.

PROCESS Lower the rack into simmering water. Water must cover jars by 1 inch. Adjust heat to medium-high, cover canner and bring water to a rolling boil. Process pint jars 10 minutes. Turn off heat and remove cover. Let jars cool 5 minutes. Remove jars from canner; do not retighten bands if loose. Cool 12 hours. Check seals. Label and store jars.

Freezing

While much of this book guides you through canning, having an arsenal of techniques to preserve fresh foods gives home cooks the means to prepare a vast array of foods in the best ways possible. In this chapter, we'll go through the basics of freezing, one of the simplest and most convenient ways to preserve food—from storing prepared foods, fresh produce, and meats to creating plan-ahead meals, we'll show you the best ways to keep your food tasting its best. You may discover a few new delicious favorites that are simple to make like pesto, freezer jam, or lemon curd. Once you learn the secrets to successful freezing, you can create a freezer that is as much a go-to as the well-stocked pantry for cooking fast, easy, nutritious meals.

Getting Started

Freezing preserves the natural color, fresh flavor, and much sought-after nutritive quality of most foods better than a process where high heat is required. Spoilers, such as mold, yeast, and bacteria are kept in check at below-freezing temperatures.

Freezing is simple, safe, and easy

Freezing is one of the simplest ways to preserve foods. There is no need to know the food's acidity levels (pH). Following the simple steps outlined in this section will keep your fresh frozen food looking and tasting its best. But not every food freezes well; see page 141 for a checklist of those items that are unsatisfactory when frozen.

Start with quality ingredients

The original quality of foods selected for freezing is the most important factor in the quality of the preserved foods when served—so be sure to use the best, freshest foods you can when freezing. Over time, the quality of frozen foods deteriorates, even when prepared and packaged correctly. The chart found on page 141 gives the recommended length of storage for many frozen foods.

Freeze it fast

Rapid freezing of fruits, vegetables, meats, and prepared foods prevents quality loss due to organic and environmental spoilers. In this chapter we share techniques to maximize frozen food quality. The most important factor is to maintain the freezer temperature at 0°F or lower at all times. If your freezer does not display the actual internal temperature, a freestanding freezer thermometer placed inside the freezer will allow you to monitor the temperature, so that you will know if the temperature control requires adjustment.

Featured Recipe | **Pesto Pizza with Artichoke Hearts and Italian Tomatoes** page 177

Pictured Above | **Pesto** page 152 | **Chicken Vegetable Soup** page 151 | **Lemon Curd** page 152

Good Things to Know

Freezing as a method of food preservation is based on the principle that extreme cold delays growth of microorganisms, and also slows down enzyme activity and the effects of oxidation. Unlike canning, freezing does not sterilize food. Freezing is an effective, safe method for preserving fruits, vegetables, meats, seafoods, game, and precooked foods. Directions in this chapter have been established to minimize changes in frozen food that result in the loss of quality. There are two types of spoilers that must be controlled when freezing foods: organic spoilers and environmental spoilers:

Organic Spoilers

Bacteria, yeasts, and molds present in fresh foods will multiply rapidly and cause spoilage if they are not stopped. The following steps will stop or slow down the effects of these spoilers:

a) select only quality foods

b) prepare foods under the most sanitary conditions

c) prepare foods according to recipe directions

d) use containers and flexible wraps designed for freezing foods

e) store frozen foods at or below 0°F

Enzymes are organic spoilers that cause chemical changes in food. Some changes are desirable and even necessary. For example, beef is aged in a chill room to give enzymes time to tenderize the meat. However, if enzymes are not inactivated before vegetables are frozen, the enzymes can cause an "off" color and destroy flavor. A short heat treatment known as blanching slows the growth of enzymes in vegetables long enough for them to freeze. Controlling enzyme activity in fruits is accomplished by the addition of sugar or an antioxidant like Ball Fruit-Fresh Produce Protector.

Environmental Spoilers

Environmental spoilers are easily controlled by using the correct method of preparing foods for freezing, selecting the right type and size of packaging, and freezing the packaged food quickly.

Freezer Burn

Freezer burn is a condition that can occur if frozen food is improperly wrapped. Dry air circulates throughout the freezer. Food exposed to this dry air may undergo a loss of moisture, causing a dry, pithy, tough surface to develop. Exposure to dry air can also cause chemical changes that include loss of color, loss of vitamins, absorption of odors, and development of "off" flavors.

Ice Crystals

Slow freezing causes moisture from within food fibers to form ice crystals between groups of fibers. This may result in physical changes like loss of liquid, diminished weight, and a dark appearance. Freezing food quickly at 0°F or lower helps the cells in the food fibers to retain their natural structure.

Oxidation

Oxidative changes are commonly encountered chemical changes in frozen foods. Food will suffer a loss in quality if exposed to oxygen due to incorrect storage or packaging.

Packaging

Packaging designed specifically for freezing foods minimizes the adverse effect spoilers have during freezer storage. It is not necessary for frozen foods to be hermetically sealed; however, the container or wrap should be secured to prevent oxidation and freezer burn. Select packaging that is moisture- and vapor-proof, odorless, tasteless, grease-proof, and capable of being tightly closed. There are two types of packaging recommended for home freezing use: rigid and flexible.

Rigid Containers—These include plastic, glass, and coated paper. Rigid containers should be used for most frozen foods, and are recommended for all foods that are soft or liquid at room temperature. Products suitable for storage in rigid containers are fruits packed in syrup or sugar, soft berries, butter, eggs, stews and soups, creamed foods, and meats with gravy or sauce. Ball® Plastic Freezer Containers are available in 8-ounce and 16-ounce sizes. Ball tapered glass jars may also be used for freezing all types of foods. Ball tapered glass jars come in 4-ounce, 8-ounce, 12-ounce, 16-ounce, and 24-ounce sizes. Coated paper boxes are available in pint and quart sizes.

Flexible Bags—These are convenient to use and particularly suited for foods having irregular shapes, such as whole turkeys or hens, fish, and all cuts of meat. Bags can be used for vegetables and fruits without syrup or added sugar. Bags are also best for precooked foods that are not liquid at room temperature. Plastic freezer bags come in the following sizes: pint, quart, two-quart, and one-gallon. Bags are closed by pressing out the air, twisting the top, doubling the top over, and securing it with a handy tie, or by closing the self-seal channel.

Flexible Wraps—These are similar to flexible bags, but they come on rolls of varying widths and can be cut to the desired length. Flexible wrap is available in plastic, foil, and coated paper. Wraps are best for irregular sizes of meat, fish, game, and poultry. They are also perfect for baked goods like pies, cakes, and breads. To use: mold the flexible wrap tightly around the food so there are no air pockets. Secure the wrap closed using freezer tape.

Freezer Tape and Freezer Labels—Freezer tape and freezer labels are designed to withstand the moist, cold environment of a freezer for long periods of time. Freezer tape may be used to secure flexible wraps of all types. Label containers and packages using freezer tape or freezer labels. Identify each with the name of the product, date it was stored in the freezer, number of servings or weight, and how the product was prepared.

It's a good idea to keep a record of the frozen foods stored in the freezer. Post the list near the freezer so it can be easily updated as needed. This list will let you know exactly what foods you have on hand and how long they have been stored in the freezer, thus helping you use all frozen foods within the recommended storage period (see figure 11).

Freezers

Regardless of the style of freezer you have, it should be located in a cool, dry, well-ventilated location. Use a freezer thermometer to register the freezer temperature. Keep the freezer temperature at 0°F or lower at all times. Maintaining the temperature at -10°F will help keep the temperature below 0°F when unfrozen food is added to the freezer. Make adjustments to the temperature setting as needed to maintain 0°F or lower at all times.

Store like foods together, placing the most recently frozen foods at the bottom or back of the freezer. At the same time, move foods that have been stored in the freezer longer toward the top or front of the freezer. For economical use of your freezer, all foods should be used within one year. Most foods should be held for much less time. By continuously using foods from the freezer and replacing them as other types of foods become readily available, the freezer space is effectively utilized during the entire year. This efficient use of freezer space lowers the cost per pound to store frozen foods.

The quantity of food that can be successfully frozen at one time depends on the type of food, type of package and its size, and style of freezer. Add no more unfrozen food than will freeze within 24 hours, about 2 to 3 pounds of food per cubic foot of capacity. Overloading the freezer with unfrozen food slows down the rate of freezing and can raise the temperature in the freezer. This will have a detrimental effect on the quality of unfrozen food, as well as the existing inventory of frozen food.

Follow the freezer's user manual instructions for defrosting, deodorizing, and cleaning.

Freezer Storage Expectancy

Gradual loss of quality occurs over time in all frozen foods. Deterioration of frozen foods accelerates rapidly with a rise in storage temperature. This is why it's important to maintain the storage temperature at 0°F or lower at all times. Properly wrapping foods for freezing helps to lengthen the time foods can be stored in the freezer without diminishing

their quality. Individual recipes in this chapter give options for correctly preparing and packaging foods for freezing.

Figure 11 | **Recommended Length of Storage at 0°F**

Bakery	Months		Months
Breads, Quick (Baked)	2	Cookies (Baked)	6
Breads, Yeast (Baked)	4-8	Cookies (Unbaked)	4
Breads, Yeast (Unbaked)	½	Pastry (Unbaked)	2
Cakes	6	Pies (Baked)	1
Cakes, Fruit	12	Pies (Unbaked)	3

Dairy	Months		Months
Butter	5-6	Cheese, Soft	4
Cheese, Cottage	1	Eggs	12
Cheese, Hard or Semi-Hard	6-12	Ice Cream, Sherbet	1-3
		Milk	1

Fruits	Months		Months
Fruits, Citrus	3-4	Fruits (Except Citrus)	12

Meat, Poultry, Seafood & Game	Months		Months
Seafood & Game		Crab, Fish Roe, Lobster, Oysters	3-4
Beef, Lamb, Mutton, Veal, Venison	8-12	Pork (Cured)	1-2
Fish	2-3	Pork (Fresh)	6-8
Ground Meat	3-4	Sausage	4-6
Liver	3	Shrimp	6
Rabbit, Squirrel	6-8	Turkey, Chicken	12

Prepared Foods	Months		Months
Candies	12	Salads	2
Gravy	2	Sandwiches	1
Pizza	1	Soups, Stews	6
Prepared Main Dishes	3-6		

Soft Spreads	Months		Months
Freezer Jams & Jellies	12		

Vegetables	Months		Months
Onions	3-6	Vegetables (Except Onions)	12
Vegetables (Cooked)	1		

Foods That Do Not Freeze Well

- Cake icings made with egg whites can become frothy or can "weep" when thawed.
- Cream fillings and soft frostings are unsatisfactory when frozen.
- Custards and cream-pie fillings become watery and lumpy.
- Egg whites become cracked, tough, and rubbery when frozen.
- Use less fat when making gravy to be frozen. If too much fat is used in proportion to the amount of starch, the fat can separate. Stir well when reheating.
- Fried foods lose their crispness and become soggy. (Exceptions are French-fried potatoes and onion rings.)
- Fruit jelly in sandwiches may soak into the bread.

- Macaroni, spaghetti, and some types of rice (frozen separately) have a warmed-over flavor and often are mushy.
- Mayonnaise separates during freezing and thawing, except when used in some salads.
- Meringue toughens and sticks to paper after a few days of freezing.
- Peppers, onions, cloves, and synthetic vanilla become strong and bitter when frozen as an ingredient in a prepared food.
- Potatoes (white) cooked in stews and soups become mushy and can darken.
- Salt loses flavor when frozen.
- Sauces tend to separate unless beaten or stirred when reheated.
- Vegetables (raw) lose their crispness.

Thawing and Preparing

Methods for Thawing

Frozen foods spoil more rapidly than fresh foods. Thaw only the amount of food that will be actually used on the same day. Thaw each product to the desired point by placing the sealed container or package:

1. in the refrigerator,
2. at room temperature for two hours; complete thawing in refrigerator as needed,
3. in the microwave oven on the defrost cycle, following manufacturer's directions, or
4. submerged in cold water.

Methods for Cooking

Frozen foods must be cooked immediately after thawing and should be served as soon as the correct internal temperature is reached. Prepared or cooked foods may be thawed and made ready for serving by one of the following ways:

1. Serve food while it is still frozen: cookies, candies, ice cream, salads, and similar foods,
2. Serve food immediately after thawing: cakes, sandwiches, and similar foods,
3. Heat food to serving temperature: soups, meat dishes, stews, and similar dishes,
4. Cook frozen food before serving: uncooked pies, rolls, and casseroles.

Refreezing

Thawing of frozen foods can occur unexpectedly during a power outage, or due to a similar unforeseen cause. Partially-thawed foods may be safely refrozen. Foods considered partially-thawed are those having a large percentage of ice crystals remaining in the product. However, partial thawing has an adverse affect on food quality. These foods will likely undergo additional deterioration and yield a very poor-quality product. Refrozen foods should be used as soon as possible.

Foods that are completely thawed should not be refrozen. These foods may be refrigerated for immediate use if they became thawed within the past two-hour period and remained chilled below 40°F during that time.

Foods that have been subjected to gradual thawing and warming to a temperature of 40°F, occurring over a two-hour period, should not be refrozen. Under these conditions, the food may be unsafe to eat. Eating foods of unknown quality may result in food loss or illness. Dispose of food so that no other human or animal will come in contact with it. Carefully clean and sanitize containers and surfaces that were exposed to the questionable food.

Handling Frozen Foods in Emergencies

When you know or suspect the power will be off in your home, immediately set the freezer control at its coldest setting. The lower temperature of the freezer and that of the frozen food will delay thawing if the power does go off. If normal operation of the freezer will not resume before the food thaws, use dry ice to keep it cold, or transfer the food in insulated boxes to a meat processing plant for freezer storage until the problem is resolved.

A fully-loaded freezer at 0°F usually will stay cold enough to keep frozen foods frozen for a couple of days. A freezer that is filled to half its capacity may not keep frozen food frozen for more than one day.

Fifty pounds of dry ice placed in a 20-cubic-foot freezer filled to capacity shortly after a power outage should keep the temperature of frozen food below freezing for 3 to 4 days. If the freezer is filled to half its capacity or less, the frozen food will likely remain frozen for 2 to 3 days. Place dry ice on thick cardboard or boards on top of frozen food. Do not put dry ice directly on food packaging. Protect hands from exposure to dry ice and ensure the room has adequate air circulation.

Do not open the freezer door while the freezer is inoperative, except as part of food-saving procedures.

Dairy Products

Butter

Freeze only high-quality butter made from pasteurized cream. Mold into desired shapes or freeze as a log. Wrap butter tightly in freezer film and pack into plastic freezer bags or plastic freezer containers. Seal, label, and freeze.

Basil-Garlic Butter

Yield: about 1 cup

1 cup unsalted butter	3 tablespoons chopped fresh basil
3 cloves garlic	1/4 teaspoon freshly ground black peppercorns
1 teaspoon extra-virgin olive oil	

Bring butter to room temperature. Put garlic cloves in a small baking dish and drizzle with olive oil. Roast garlic in an oven at 375°F for 15 minutes. Peel garlic. Press garlic cloves with the back of a spoon to form a smooth paste. Combine butter, roasted garlic paste, basil, and pepper in a medium bowl, stirring until well-blended and smooth. Pack butter into a plastic freezer jar, or shape into a log and wrap in freezer wrap. Seal, label, and freeze.

Dill Butter

Yield: about 1/2 cup

1/2 cup unsalted butter	1/2 teaspoon grated lemon peel
1 tablespoon minced fresh dill	1/8 teaspoon salt

Bring butter to room temperature. Combine butter, dill, lemon peel, and salt in a medium bowl, stirring until well-blended and smooth. Pack into a plastic freezer jar, or shape into a log and wrap in freezer wrap. Seal, label, and freeze.

Fresh Herb Butter

Yield: about 1/2 cup

1/2 cup unsalted butter	1 teaspoon minced fresh oregano
1 1/2 teaspoons minced fresh flat leaf parsley	1/4 teaspoon freshly ground black peppercorns
1 teaspoon minced fresh tarragon	
1 teaspoon minced fresh thyme	

Bring butter to room temperature. Combine butter, herbs, and pepper in a medium bowl, stirring until well-blended and smooth. Pack into plastic freezer jar, or shape into a log and wrap in freezer wrap. Seal, label, and freeze.

Lemon Balm Butter

Yield: about 1/2 cup

1/2 cup unsalted butter	1 tablespoon minced fresh chives
1 tablespoon minced fresh lemon balm	1/8 teaspoon salt
1 tablespoon minced fresh parsley	

Bring butter to room temperature. Combine butter, herbs, and salt in a medium bowl, stirring until well-blended and smooth. Pack into plastic freezer jar, or shape into a log and wrap in freezer wrap. Seal, label, and freeze.

Cheese

Hard Or Semi-Hard Cheese: Cut in 1/2- to 1-pound pieces. Wrap tightly in freezer wrap and pack cheese into plastic freezer bags or plastic freezer containers. Seal, label, and freeze.

Soft Cheese: Wrap tightly in freezer wrap and pack cheese into plastic freezer bags or plastic freezer containers. Seal, label, and freeze.

Cottage Cheese: Pack cottage cheese into plastic freezer jars or plastic freezer containers. Seal, label, and freeze.

Cream

Freeze only heavy cream containing 40 percent or more butterfat. Heat between 170° to 180°F for 15 minutes. Add 3 tablespoons sugar per pint of cream. Cool quickly and ladle cream into plastic freezer jars or plastic freezer containers, leaving 1/2-inch headspace. Seal, label, and freeze.

Eggs

Select eggs as fresh as possible. Wash eggs in clear water; break each egg separately into a small bowl; examine eggs by smell and appearance for spoilage before mixing with other eggs.

Whole: Gently mix the whites and yolks without forming air bubbles by putting them through a sieve or colander. Pack eggs into plastic freezer jars or plastic freezer containers, leaving 1/2-inch headspace. Seal, label, and freeze.

Yolks: Gently mix the yolks without forming air bubbles. To each 6 yolks add 1 teaspoon sugar or 1/2 teaspoon salt to reduce coagulation. Pack same as Eggs, Whole.

Whites: Gently mix whites without forming air bubbles. Pack same as Eggs, Whole.

Measuring for cooking:
• 3 tablespoons whole egg = 1 egg
• 2 tablespoons egg white = 1 egg white
• 1 tablespoon egg yolk = 1 egg yolk

Ice Cream and Sherbet

Homemade: Prepare your favorite recipe and freeze in a hand-turned or electrically-turned ice cream freezer. Pack ice cream or sherbet into plastic freezer jars or plastic freezer containers. Seal, label, and freeze.

Commercially Made: Place original carton in plastic freezer bag or repack ice cream into plastic freezer jars or plastic freezer containers. Seal, label, and freeze.

Milk

Freeze only pasteurized milk. Ladle milk into plastic freezer jars or plastic freezer containers, leaving 1/2-inch headspace. Seal, label, and freeze.

Thawing And Preparing Dairy Products

Place the frozen product in the refrigerator to thaw. After thawing, use as fresh.

Fruits & FRUIT FILLINGS

There are three methods used to pack whole or sliced fruits for freezing, including dry pack, sugar pack, and syrup pack. Some fruits freeze exceptionally well using the dry pack method, like blueberries, cranberries, and rhubarb. Other types of fruit benefit from the addition of sugar or sugar syrup. Using one of these methods to pack fruit for freezing helps to retain texture, color, and flavor. Peaches, strawberries, and cherries are enhanced when packed using one of these methods. Select the type of pack from the options given in the recipe. Fruits that brown quickly after cutting and peeling may require pretreatment with an antioxidant to aid in color retention during preparation for freezing. To prepare the pretreatment, dissolve 4 tablespoons Fruit-Fresh in 2 quarts cold water.

Figure 12 | Syrup Pack and Sugar Pack for Freezing

Syrup Pack	Fruit-Fresh	Sugar	Water	Yield
Extra-Light	6 Rounded Teaspoons	1¼ Cups	5½ Cups	6 Cups
Light	6½ Rounded Teaspoons	2¼ Cups	5¼ Cups	6½ Cups
Medium	7 Rounded Teaspoons	3¼ Cups	5 Cups	7 Cups
Heavy	7 Rounded Teaspoons	4¼ Cups	4¼ Cups	7 Cups

Sugar Pack	Fruit-Fresh	Sugar	Fruit	Yield
	4 Rounded Tablespoons	1 Cup	4 Cups	2 Pint or 1 Quart Containers

Apples

Select apples that are crisp and firm. Wash, peel, and core. Cut into ¼-inch slices. Treat with Fruit-Fresh to prevent darkening.

Syrup Pack: Use heavy syrup; add 1 teaspoon Fruit-Fresh (see figure 12) to each cup of syrup. Ladle ½ cup cold syrup into plastic freezer jars or plastic freezer containers. Press apple slices down in container and add enough syrup to cover, leaving ½-inch headspace. Seal, label, and freeze.

Pie Apples: Place apple slices in boiling water 2 minutes and cool in ice water. Drain. Pack apples slices into plastic freezer bags, plastic freezer jars, or plastic freezer containers. Seal, label, and freeze.

Applesauce: Wash apples; peel, if desired; core and slice. To each quart of apples, add ⅓ cup water and 1 tablespoon Fruit-Fresh (see figure 12). Cook apples until tender; purée. To each quart of hot purée, add ¼ cup sugar, stirring until dissolved. Cool. Ladle applesauce into plastic freezer jars or plastic freezer containers, leaving ½-inch headspace. Seal, label, and freeze.

Apple Pie Filling

Yield: about 6 pint containers

6 pounds apples	¼ cup flour
Ball Fruit-Fresh Produce Protector	1½ teaspoons cinnamon
	¼ teaspoon nutmeg
2 cups sugar	2 tablespoons lemon juice

Wash, peel, core, and slice apples. Treat with Fruit-Fresh to prevent darkening. Combine sugar, flour, and spices. Rinse and drain apples; stir into sugar mixture. Let stand until juices begin to flow, about 30 minutes. Stir in lemon juice. Cook over medium heat until mixture begins to thicken. Ladle pie filling into plastic freezer jars or plastic freezer containers, leaving ½-inch headspace. Cool at room temperature, not to exceed 2 hours. Seal, label, and freeze.

Berries

Blackberries, Mulberries, Red Raspberries, Black Raspberries

Select fully-ripe, firm berries. Wash berries in cold water. Drain and dry berries. Discard soft, underripe, or imperfect berries. Remove stems. Pack using one of the following methods:

Sugar Pack: Mix 1 part sugar with 4 parts berries. Pack into plastic freezer jars or plastic freezer containers. Seal, label, and freeze.

Syrup Pack: Prepare a heavy syrup (see figure 12). Pack drained berries into plastic freezer jars or plastic freezer containers. Shake the container gently to pack berries. Cover berries with syrup, leaving ½-inch headspace. Seal, label, and freeze.

Purée: Select fully-ripe berries. Purée using a food processor or food mill. Ladle berry purée into plastic freezer jars or plastic freezer containers, leaving ½-inch headspace. Seal, label, and freeze.

Blueberries, Huckleberries, Elderberries, or Gooseberries

Wash berries; drain. Dry berries. Remove stems and underripe or imperfect berries. Pack using one of the following methods:

Dry Pack: Pack berries into plastic freezer bags, plastic freezer jars, or plastic freezer containers. Seal, label, and freeze.

Sugar Pack: Mix 1 quart berries with ⅔ cup sugar. Pack into plastic freezer jars or plastic freezer containers. Seal, label, and freeze.

Syrup Pack: Pack same as Berries, Syrup Pack.

Blueberry Pie Filling

Yield: about 5 pint containers

12 cups blueberries	1 tablespoon grated lemon peel
3 cups sugar	
¾ cup cornstarch	¼ cup lemon juice

Wash and drain blueberries. Combine sugar and cornstarch. Stir in blueberries; let stand until juice begins to flow, about 30 minutes. Add lemon peel and lemon juice. Cook over medium heat until mixture begins to thicken. Ladle pie filling into plastic freezer jars or plastic freezer containers, leaving ½-inch headspace. Cool at room temperature, not to exceed 2 hours. Seal, label, and freeze.

Cherries – Sour

Select tender-skinned, bright red cherries with a characteristic tart flavor. Wash cherries; drain. Stem and pit. Pack using one of the following methods:

Sugar Pack: Mix 1 part sugar with 4 parts cherries. Pack cherries into plastic freezer jars or plastic freezer containers. Seal, label, and freeze.

Syrup Pack: Prepare heavy syrup (see figure 12). Pack drained cherries into plastic freezer jars or plastic freezer containers. Shake the container gently to pack cherries. Cover cherries with syrup, leaving ½-inch headspace. Seal, label, and freeze.

Cherries – Sweet

Select bright, fully-ripe sweet cherries of a dark color variety. Wash cherries; drain. Stem and pit.

Syrup Pack: Prepare heavy syrup (see page 144). Pack cherries into plastic freezer jars or plastic freezer containers. Shake container gently to pack cherries. Cover cherries with syrup, leaving 1/2-inch headspace. Seal, label, and freeze.

Cherry Pie Filling

Yield: about 4 pint containers

8 cups tart cherries	5 tablespoons cornstarch
2 1/2 cups sugar	

Wash cherries; drain. Pit cherries. Combine sugar and cornstarch. Stir in cherries; let stand until juice begins to flow, about 30 minutes. Cook over medium heat until mixture begins to thicken. Ladle pie filling into plastic freezer jars or plastic freezer containers, leaving 1/2-inch headspace. Cool at room temperature, not to exceed 2 hours. Seal, label, and freeze.

Coconut

Grate coconut by hand or use a food processor. Pack using one of the following methods:

Dry Pack: Pack grated coconut into plastic freezer bags, plastic freezer jars, or plastic freezer containers. Seal, label, and freeze.

Sugar Pack: Mix 1 part sugar with 8 parts shredded coconut. Pack coconut into plastic freezer jars or plastic freezer containers. Seal, label, and freeze.

Milk Pack: Mix grated coconut with its own milk. Pack coconut into plastic freezer jars or plastic freezer containers, leaving 1/2-inch headspace. Seal, label, and freeze.

Cranberries

Select firm cranberries of uniform color with glossy skins. Wash cranberries in cold water; drain. Dry and stem. Pack cranberries into plastic freezer bags, plastic freezer jars, or plastic freezer containers. Seal, label, and freeze.

Sauce: Prepare selected recipe as for serving. Pack into plastic freezer jars or plastic freezer containers, leaving 1/2-inch headspace. Cool at room temperature, not to exceed 2 hours. Seal, label, and freeze.

Currants

Select ripe currants. Wash currants in cold water; drain. Stem. Pack using one of the following methods:

Dry Pack: Pack currants into plastic freezer bags, plastic freezer jars, or plastic freezer containers. Seal, label, and freeze.

Sugar Pack: Lightly crush currants. Mix 3 parts currants with 1 part sugar. Allow to stand until sugar dissolves, about 10 minutes. Pack currants and syrup into plastic freezer jars or plastic freezer containers, leaving 1/2-inch headspace. Seal, label, and freeze.

Figs

Select fully-ripe figs. Wash figs; drain. Peel figs. Prepare using one of the following methods:

Dry Pack: Pack figs into plastic freezer bags, plastic freezer jars, or plastic freezer containers. Seal, label, and freeze.

Sugar Pack: Leave figs whole or cut in half. Mix 1 part sugar with 4 parts figs. Pack into plastic freezer jars or plastic freezer containers. Seal, label, and freeze.

Syrup Pack: Prepare a heavy syrup (see page 144). Pack whole or halved figs into plastic freezer jars or plastic freezer containers. Ladle heavy syrup over figs, leaving 1/2-inch headspace. Seal, label, and freeze.

Fruit Juices

Most fruits make excellent frozen juice, retaining their natural fruit flavor when thawed. Prepare juice using your favorite recipe. Cool. Ladle into plastic freezer jars or plastic freezer containers, leaving 1/2-inch headspace. Seal, label, and freeze.

Fruit Sorbet

Yield: about 7 half-pint containers

4 cups sliced fruit (any soft variety)	1 cup orange juice
2 cups sugar	2 tablespoons lemon juice

Purée fruit using a food processor or blender. Combine sugar, orange juice, and lemon juice in a saucepan. Cook over medium heat, stirring until sugar dissolves. Remove from heat. Stir in purée. Pour sorbet into a 13- x 9-inch pan. Freeze until fully frozen. Working in small batches, process frozen purée using a food processor or blender until light and fluffy. Ladle sorbet into plastic freezer jars or plastic freezer containers, leaving 1/2-inch headspace. Seal, label, and freeze.

Note: Any soft fruit such as peaches, strawberries, raspberries, or melon can be used for sorbet. Prepare fruit as for eating fresh.

Grapefruit or Oranges

Select firm, tree-ripened fruit. Heaviness of fruit indicates maturity. Wash fruit; drain. Chill. Peel and section fruit, removing membrane and seeds.

Syrup Pack: Prepare a medium syrup (see page 144). Pack fruit into plastic freezer jars or plastic freezer containers. Ladle syrup over fruit, leaving 1/2-inch headspace. Seal, label, and freeze.

Grapes
Green, Red, Purple

Select ripe, firm, sweet grapes. Wash grapes; drain. Stem. Prepare using one of the following methods:

Syrup Pack: Prepare medium syrup (see page 144). Pack grapes into plastic freezer jars or plastic freezer containers. Ladle medium syrup over grapes, leaving 1/2-inch headspace. Seal, label, and freeze.

Purée: Lightly crush grapes. Heat grapes to a boil, adding just enough water to prevent sticking. Press through a sieve or food mill to remove seeds and peels. Mix 1 part sugar with 5 parts purée. Cool at room temperature, not to exceed 2 hours. Pack purée into plastic freezer jars or plastic freezer containers, leaving 1/2-inch headspace. Seal, label, and freeze.

Juice: Prepare and heat grapes same as for Purée. Strain juice through a damp jelly bag or several layers of cheesecloth. Sweeten to taste with sugar. Cool. Ladle juice into plastic freezer jars or plastic freezer containers, leaving 1/2-inch headspace. Seal, label, and freeze.

Kiwi

Select firm, ripe kiwi. Peel. Cut kiwi into 1/4-inch slices. Pack kiwi into plastic freezer jars or plastic freezer containers. Seal, label, and freeze.

Melons

Cantaloupe, Cranshaw, Honeydew, Persian, Watermelon

Select fully-ripe, firm melons. Remove seeds and peel. Cut melon into 1/4-inch cubes, slices, or balls. Pack melon into plastic freezer jars or plastic freezer containers. Seal, label, and freeze.

Note: Serve melon before completely thawed.

Peaches, Nectarines, or Apricots

Select fully-ripe fruit and handle carefully to avoid bruising. Wash fruit; drain. Peel, pit, and slice fruit. Treat with Fruit-Fresh to prevent darkening. Prepare using one of the following methods:

Sugar Pack: Combine 2/3 cup sugar and 2 teaspoons Fruit-Fresh (see page 16); set aside. Measure 1 quart sliced fruit; sprinkle fruit with sugar mixture. Gently toss to coat fruit evenly with sugar mixture. Allow fruit to stand until sugar dissolves, about 10 minutes. Pack sliced fruit and syrup into plastic freezer jars or plastic freezer containers, leaving 1/2-inch headspace. Seal, label, and freeze.

Syrup Pack: Prepare a heavy syrup (see page 144). Ladle 1/2 cup syrup into plastic freezer jars or plastic freezer containers. Fill container with sliced fruit, gently shaking to pack fruit, leaving 1/2-inch headspace. Add more syrup if needed, leaving 1/2-inch headspace. Seal, label, and freeze.

Purée: Combine 2 cups sliced fruit, 2 tablespoons sugar, and 1 1/2 teaspoons Fruit-Fresh (see page 16). Put mixture in a food processor and purée. Pack purée into plastic freezer jars or plastic freezer containers, leaving 1/2-inch headspace. Place a piece of freezer wrap over the top of purée to prevent discoloration. Seal, label, and freeze.

Peach Pie Filling

Yield: about 4 pint containers

6 pounds peaches	1 teaspoon cinnamon
Ball Fruit-Fresh Produce Protector	1/2 teaspoon nutmeg
2 1/4 cups sugar	2 teaspoons lemon peel
1/2 cup flour	1/4 cup lemon juice

Wash peaches; drain. Peel, pit, and slice peaches. Treat with Fruit-Fresh to prevent darkening. Combine sugar, flour, and spices. Rinse peaches; drain. Add peaches to sugar mixture and

gently toss to coat fruit evenly with sugar mixture. Let stand until juices begin to flow, about 30 minutes. Stir in lemon peel and lemon juice. Cook over medium heat until mixture begins to thicken. Ladle pie filling into plastic freezer jars or plastic freezer containers, leaving 1/2-inch headspace. Cool at room temperature, not to exceed 2 hours. Seal, label, and freeze.

Pears

Select full-flavored pears that are crisp and firm. Wash pears; drain. Peel and core pears. Leave in halves or cut into quarters or slices. Treat with Fruit-Fresh to prevent darkening. Prepare a medium syrup (see page 144). Bring syrup to a boil. Drain pears. Blanch pears in syrup for 2 minutes. Cool pears and syrup at room temperature, not to exceed 2 hours. Pack pears into plastic freezer jars or plastic freezer containers. Ladle syrup over pears, leaving 1/2-inch headspace. Seal, label, and freeze.

Pineapple

Select fruit of bright appearance, dark yellow-orange color, and fragrant aroma. Green leaves pull out easily when pineapple is ripe. Wash pineapple; drain. Peel and core. Cut pineapple into wedges, slices, or cubes. Prepare using one of the following methods:

Dry Pack: Pack slices into plastic freezer jars or plastic freezer containers, layering two pieces of freezer paper between slices. Seal, label, and freeze.

Sugar Pack: Mix 1 part sugar with 8 parts pineapple. Allow pineapple to set until sugar is dissolved. Pack pineapple into plastic freezer jars or plastic freezer containers. Seal, label, and freeze.

Syrup Pack: Prepare a light syrup (see page 144). Pack pineapple into plastic freezer jars or plastic freezer containers. Ladle syrup over pineapple, leaving 1/2-inch headspace. Seal, label, and freeze.

Plums

Select firm, ripe plums soft enough to yield to slight pressure. Wash plums; drain. Leave plums whole or cut into halves, slices, or cubes. Prepare using one of the following methods:

Dry Pack: Wash and drain plums. Pack whole plums into plastic freezer bags, plastic freezer jars, or plastic freezer containers. Seal, label, and freeze.

Sugar Pack: Mix 1 part sugar with 5 parts plums. Allow to stand until sugar is dissolved. Pack plums into plastic freezer jars or plastic freezer containers. Seal, label, and freeze.

Syrup Pack: Prepare heavy syrup (see page 144). Pack halved, sliced, or cubed plums into plastic freezer jars or plastic freezer containers. Ladle syrup over plums, leaving 1/2-inch headspace. Seal, label, and freeze.

Prepared Fruits

Cooked fruits such as baked apples, baked pears, and applesauce may be prepared as for serving. Cool at room temperature, not to exceed 2 hours. Pack into plastic freezer jars or plastic freezer containers. Seal, label, and freeze.

Rhubarb

Select rhubarb with crisp, tender, red stalks. Early spring cuttings are best for freezing. Remove leaves and woody ends; discard blemished and tough stalks. Wash rhubarb under cold running water; drain. Cut rhubarb into 1-inch lengths. Prepare using one of the following methods:

Dry Pack: Pack rhubarb into plastic freezer bags, plastic freezer jars, or plastic freezer containers. Seal, label, and freeze.

Sugar Pack: Mix 1 part sugar to 4 parts rhubarb. Allow to stand until sugar is dissolved. Pack rhubarb into plastic freezer jars or plastic freezer containers. Seal, label, and freeze.

Syrup Pack: Prepare a heavy syrup (see page 144). Pack rhubarb into plastic freezer jars or plastic freezer containers. Ladle syrup over rhubarb, leaving 1/2-inch headspace. Seal, label, and freeze.

Stewed: Stew or steam rhubarb according to your favorite recipe; sweeten to taste. Cool at room temperature, not to exceed 2 hours. Pack same as Rhubarb, Syrup Pack.

Strawberries

Select fully-ripe, firm strawberries with a deep red color. Discard immature and imperfect fruit. Wash strawberries; drain. Remove caps. Prepare using one of the following methods:

Dry Pack: Pack berries into plastic freezer bags, plastic freezer jars, or plastic freezer containers. Seal, label, and freeze.

Sugar Pack: Slice berries lengthwise in half. Mix 1 part sugar with 6 parts strawberries. Allow to stand until sugar is dissolved, about 10 minutes. Gently stir. Pack strawberries and syrup into plastic freezer jars or plastic freezer containers, leaving 1/2-inch headspace. Seal, label, and freeze.

Syrup Pack: Prepare a heavy syrup (see page 144). Leave strawberries whole or slice. Pack strawberries into plastic freezer jars or plastic freezer containers. Ladle syrup over berries, leaving 1/2-inch headspace. Seal, label, and freeze.

Purée: Combine 1 pint strawberries, 4 tablespoons sugar, and 1 teaspoon lemon juice in food processor and purée. Pack purée into plastic freezer jars or plastic freezer containers, leaving 1/2-inch headspace. Seal, label, and freeze.

Thawing and Preparing Fruits

Frozen fruits may be used the same as fresh fruit in most recipes. When using frozen fruit in cooking, an allowance should be made for any sugar added at the time of freezing. For fresh fruit dessert or fruit salad, serve fruit just before it is completely thawed. A few ice crystals remaining in the fruit will help to retain a plump structure.

Freezer Spreads

Although a wide variety of frozen fruit may be used for making soft spreads, fresh fruit is superior in flavor, color, and texture. Soft spreads made using frozen fruit may yield a softer set. Recipes in this section are made using one of the four Ball pectin varieties. Ball® Instant Pectin makes a delicious freezer jam, or the jam may be refrigerated for immediate use. Use only the pectin variety listed in the recipe to be prepared. Pectin is not interchangeable; making a substitution will prevent the recipe from gelling. For more information about Ball brand pectin varieties, see page 42.

Apricot Freezer Jam No cooking required

Yield: about 6 half-pint containers

5 cups crushed apricots (about 24 medium)	6 tablespoons Ball RealFruit Instant Pectin
2 cups granulated sugar	

Wash apricots; drain. Peel and pit apricots (see page 18). Cut apricots into quarters. Lightly crush apricots in a medium bowl using a potato masher; measure 5 cups crushed apricots; set aside. Stir sugar and pectin together in a large bowl until well-blended. Add apricots to sugar mixture and stir 3 minutes. Ladle jam into plastic freezer jars, leaving 1/2-inch headspace. Adjust caps. Let jam stand 30 minutes to thicken. Label and freeze, or refrigerate up to 3 weeks.

Blackberry Freezer Jam No cooking required

Yield: about 6 half-pint containers

5 cups crushed blackberries (about 3 pounds)	2 cups granulated sugar
	6 tablespoons Ball RealFruit Instant Pectin

Wash blackberries; drain. Lightly crush blackberries in a medium bowl using a potato masher; measure 5 cups crushed blackberries; set aside. Stir sugar and pectin together in a large bowl until well-blended. Add blackberries to sugar mixture and stir 3 minutes. Ladle jam into plastic freezer jars, leaving 1/2-inch headspace. Adjust caps. Let jam stand 30 minutes to thicken. Label and freeze, or refrigerate up to 3 weeks.

Blueberry Freezer Jam No cooking required

Yield: about 4 half-pint containers

5 cups crushed blueberries (about 3 pounds)	6 tablespoons Ball RealFruit Instant Pectin
2 cups granulated sugar	

Wash blueberries; drain. Lightly crush blueberries in a medium bowl using a potato masher; measure 5 cups crushed blueberries; set aside. Stir sugar and pectin together in a large bowl until well-blended. Add blueberries to sugar mixture and stir 3 minutes. Ladle jam into plastic freezer jars, leaving 1/2-inch headspace. Adjust caps. Let jam stand 30 minutes to thicken. Label and freeze, or refrigerate up to 3 weeks.

Blueberry Freezer Jam No cooking required

Yield: about 7 half-pint containers

4 1/2 cups crushed blueberries (about 3 pounds)	2 3-ounce pouches Ball RealFruit Liquid Pectin
6 cups sugar	2 tablespoons lemon juice

Wash blueberries; drain. Lightly crush blueberries; measure 4 1/2 cups crushed blueberries. Combine blueberries with sugar in a large bowl, stirring until sugar dissolves. Let stand 10 minutes. Add pectin and lemon juice to mixture and stir 3 minutes. Ladle jam into plastic freezer jars, leaving 1/2-inch headspace. Adjust caps. Let jam stand 30 minutes to thicken. Label and freeze, or refrigerate up to 3 weeks.

Lemony Blueberry-Nectarine Freezer Jam No cooking required

Yield: about 5 half-pint containers

3 cups chopped, pitted, peeled nectarines (about 4 medium)

1 cup crushed blueberries (about 1 pint)

1 tablespoon grated lemon peel

1 teaspoon lemon juice

1½ cups sugar

5 tablespoons Ball RealFruit Instant Pectin

Combine nectarines, blueberries, lemon peel, and lemon juice in a medium bowl; set aside. Stir sugar and pectin together in a large bowl until well-blended. Add fruit mixture to sugar mixture and stir 3 minutes. Ladle jam into plastic freezer jars, leaving ½-inch headspace. Adjust caps. Let jam stand 30 minutes to thicken. Label and freeze, or refrigerate up to 3 weeks.

Peach Freezer Jam

Yield: about 5 half-pint containers

2¼ cups chopped peaches (about 5 medium)

2 tablespoons bottled lemon juice

4½ cups sugar

3 tablespoons Ball RealFruit Classic Pectin

¾ cup water

Wash peaches; drain. Peel and pit peaches (see page 24). Chop peaches; measure 2¼ cups chopped peaches. Combine peaches with lemon juice in a large bowl. Add sugar, stirring until sugar dissolves. Let stand 10 minutes. Combine pectin and water in a small saucepan. Bring mixture to a rolling boil that cannot be stirred down, stirring constantly. Boil hard for 1 minute, stirring constantly. Add pectin mixture to fruit mixture and stir 3 minutes. Ladle jam into plastic freezer jars, leaving ½-inch headspace. Adjust caps. Let jam stand 30 minutes to thicken. Label and freeze, or refrigerate up to 3 weeks.

Peach Freezer Jam No cooking required

Yield: about 6 half-pint containers

3 cups crushed peaches (about 8 medium)

6½ cups sugar

2 3-ounce pouches Ball RealFruit Liquid Pectin

⅓ cup lemon juice

Wash peaches; drain. Peel and pit peaches (see page 24). Lightly crush peaches using a potato masher; measure 3 cups crushed peaches. Combine peaches with sugar in a large bowl, stirring until sugar dissolves. Let stand 10 minutes. Add pectin and lemon juice to mixture and stir 3 minutes. Ladle jam into plastic freezer jars, leaving ½-inch headspace. Adjust caps. Let jam stand 30 minutes to thicken. Label and freeze, or refrigerate up to 3 weeks.

Plum Freezer Jam No cooking required

Yield: about 4 half-pint containers

3⅓ cups finely chopped plums (about 10 to 12 medium)

1⅓ cups sugar

4 tablespoons Ball RealFruit Instant Pectin

Wash plums; drain. Pit plums. Finely chop plums; measure 3⅓ cups finely chopped plums. Combine sugar and pectin in a large bowl, stirring until well-blended. Add plums to sugar mixture and stir 3 minutes. Ladle jam into plastic freezer jars, leaving ½-inch headspace. Adjust caps. Let jam stand 30 minutes to thicken. Label and freeze, or refrigerate up to 3 weeks.

Raspberry Freezer Jam

Yield: about 6 half-pint containers

3 cups crushed raspberries (about 2¼ pounds)

5¼ cups sugar

¾ cup water

6 tablespoons Ball RealFruit Classic Pectin

Wash raspberries; drain. Lightly crush raspberries in a medium bowl; measure 3 cups crushed raspberries. Add sugar, stirring until sugar dissolves. Let stand 10 minutes. Combine water and pectin in a small saucepan. Bring mixture to a rolling boil that cannot be stirred down, stirring constantly. Boil hard for 1 minute, stirring constantly. Add pectin mixture to fruit mixture and stir 3 minutes. Ladle jam into plastic freezer jars, leaving ½-inch headspace. Adjust caps. Let jam stand 30 minutes to thicken. Label and freeze, or refrigerate up to 3 weeks.

Raspberry Freezer Jam No cooking required

Yield: about 4 half-pint containers

3⅓ cups crushed raspberries (about 2 to 2½ pounds)

1⅓ cups sugar

4 tablespoons Ball RealFruit Instant Pectin

Wash raspberries; drain. Lightly crush raspberries in a medium bowl using a potato masher; measure 3 cups crushed raspberries. Stir sugar and pectin together in a large bowl until well-blended. Add raspberries to sugar mixture and stir 3 minutes. Ladle jam into plastic freezer jars, leaving ½-inch headspace. Adjust caps. Let jam stand 30 minutes to thicken. Label and freeze, or refrigerate up to 3 weeks.

Raspberry-Peach Freezer Jam

Low or no-sugar added

Yield: about 4 half-pint containers

2 cups finely chopped peaches (about 1½ pounds)

1 cup crushed raspberries (about 1 pound)

1¾ cups unsweetened white grape juice or apple juice

3 tablespoons Ball RealFruit Low or No-Sugar Needed Pectin

Sugar, if desired

Wash peaches and raspberries; drain. Peel and pit peaches (see page 24). Finely chop peaches; measure 2 cups finely chopped peaches. Lightly crush raspberries; measure 1 cup crushed raspberries. Put juice in a medium saucepan. Gradually add pectin to fruit juice, stirring until dissolved. Bring mixture to a rolling boil that cannot be stirred down, stirring constantly. Boil hard for 1 minute. Remove from heat. Add peaches and raspberries and stir vigorously 1 minute. Add up to 3 cups of sugar, if desired, stirring until sugar is dissolved. Ladle jam into plastic freezer jars, leaving ½-inch headspace. Adjust caps. Let jam stand in refrigerator until set, not to exceed 24 hours. Label and freeze, or refrigerate up to 3 weeks.

Strawberry Freezer Jam

Yield: about 5 half-pint containers

- 2 cups crushed strawberries (about 2 pounds)
- 2 tablespoons lemon juice
- 4½ cups sugar
- ¾ cup water
- 6 tablespoons Ball RealFruit Classic Pectin

Wash strawberries; drain. Remove stems and caps. Crush strawberries using a potato masher; measure 2 cups crushed strawberries. Combine strawberries and lemon juice in a large bowl. Add sugar, stirring until sugar dissolves. Let stand 10 minutes. Combine pectin and water in a small saucepan. Bring mixture to a rolling boil that cannot be stirred down, stirring constantly. Boil hard for 1 minute, stirring constantly. Add pectin mixture to fruit mixture and stir 3 minutes. Ladle jam into plastic freezer jars, leaving ½-inch headspace. Adjust caps. Let jam stand 30 minutes to thicken. Label and freeze, or refrigerate up to 3 weeks.

Strawberry Freezer Jam No cooking required

Yield: about 6 half-pint containers

- 5 cups crushed strawberries
- 6 tablespoons Ball RealFruit Instant Pectin
- 2 cups sugar

Wash strawberries; drain. Remove stems and caps. Crush strawberries using a potato masher; measure 5 cups crushed strawberries. Combine sugar with pectin in a large bowl, stirring until well-blended. Add strawberries to sugar mixture and stir 3 minutes. Ladle jam into plastic freezer jars, leaving ½-inch headspace. Adjust caps. Let jam stand 30 minutes to thicken. Label and freeze, or refrigerate up to 3 weeks.

Strawberry Freezer Jam

Low or no-sugar added

Yield: about 4 half-pint containers

- 3 cups crushed strawberries (about 3 pounds)
- 1¾ cups unsweetened cranberry-raspberry juice or apple juice
- 3 tablespoons Ball RealFruit Low or No-Sugar Needed Pectin
- Sugar, if desired

Wash strawberries; drain. Remove stems and caps. Crush strawberries using a potato masher; measure 3 cups crushed strawberries. Put juice into a medium saucepan. Gradually add pectin to fruit juice, stirring until dissolved. Bring mixture to a rolling boil that cannot be stirred down, stirring constantly. Boil hard for 1 minute. Remove from heat. Add strawberries and stir vigorously for 1 minute. Add up to 3 cups of sugar, if desired, stirring until sugar is dissolved. Ladle jam into plastic freezer jars, leaving ½-inch headspace. Adjust caps. Let jam stand in refrigerator until set, not to exceed 24 hours. Label and freeze, or refrigerate up to 3 weeks.

Strawberry-Banana Freezer Jam

Yield: about 5 half-pint containers

- 3 large bananas
- 3 cups crushed strawberries (about 1 pint)
- 1½ cups sugar
- 5 tablespoons Ball RealFruit Instant Pectin

Place unpeeled bananas on a foil-lined baking sheet. Bake bananas 15 minutes at 400°F. Cool bananas until they can be easily handled; peel. Crush bananas; measure 1 cup crushed bananas. Wash strawberries; drain. Remove stems and caps. Lightly crush strawberries in a medium bowl using a potato masher; combine bananas and strawberries in a medium bowl; set aside. Stir sugar and pectin together in a large bowl until well-blended. Add fruit mixture to sugar mixture and stir 3 minutes. Ladle jam into plastic freezer jars, leaving ½-inch headspace. Adjust caps. Let jam stand 30 minutes to thicken. Label and freeze, or refrigerate up to 3 weeks.

Triple Berry Freezer Jam No cooking required

Yield: about 5 half-pint containers

- 2 cups crushed strawberries (about 1 quart)
- 1 cup crushed red raspberries (about 1 pint)
- 1 cup crushed blackberries (about 1 pint)
- 1½ cups sugar
- 5 tablespoons Ball RealFruit Instant Pectin

Combine strawberries, raspberries, and blackberries in a medium bowl; set aside. Stir sugar and pectin together in a large bowl until well-blended. Add fruit mixture to sugar mixture and stir 3 minutes. Ladle jam into plastic freezer jars, leaving ½-inch headspace. Adjust caps. Let jam stand 30 minutes to thicken. Label and freeze, or refrigerate up to 3 weeks.

Meats

Freezing preserves the natural, fresh qualities of meat better than any other method of preservation.

While beef, lamb, pork, chicken, and turkey may be produced on the farm and frozen in the home, it is advisable that slaughtering, chilling, and preparation of beef, lamb, and pork be done in commercial establishments. All meats and poultry must be chilled quickly after slaughter. Beef must be aged about one week at 33° to 38°F to become tender and flavorful. The advantages of commercial meat packing are that animals may be slaughtered at any time of the year and the meat can be handled under sanitary conditions, controlled temperatures, and also be inspected by local authorities.

Equipment for handling meat products should be as free of seams and cracks as possible; equipment should be scrubbed in hot water with a good detergent and sanitizer after each use.

Many families prefer to select cuts of meat from the market and freeze these at home. Replace store packaging with moisture- and vapor-proof wrap before freezing to protect meat from freezer burn, the formation of ice crystals, and oxidation.

Beef, Lamb, Mutton, Veal, or Venison

Use only high-quality meat from carcasses that have been aged at 35°F for about one week in a relatively dry room. Cut meats as for cooking, removing as much bone and fat as possible, and package in family-size servings. Keep meat cold while being cut and wrapped. Pack using one of the following methods:

Large Cuts: Wrap individually in plastic freezer bags, freezer foil, film, paper, or vacuum package. Seal, label, and freeze.

Steaks Or Chops: Wrap individually in plastic freezer bags, freezer foil, film, paper, or vacuum package with a double layer of moisture- and vapor-proof material placed between each piece of meat to make separation for cooking easier. Seal, label, and freeze.

Ground Meat: Pack in family-size servings and wrap same as Large Cuts.

Pork, Rabbit, or Squirrel

Select cuts suitable for roasting, broiling, frying, stewing, and ground meat. Pork products should be frozen or prepared for curing as soon as they are chilled. Hold no longer than 1 day after slaughter before freezing. Pack using one of the following methods:

Fresh Meat: All cuts of this type should be frozen fresh except ham, bacon, jowls, and sausage. These may be cured instead. Cut as desired, removing as much bone and fat as possible. Wrap in plastic freezer bags, freezer foil, film, paper, or vacuum package. Seal, label, and freeze.

Cured Pork: Freshly cured pork loses desirable color and flavor during freezer storage; therefore, it has a very short storage period in the freezer. Wrap in plastic freezer bags, freezer foil, film, paper, or vacuum package. Seal, label, and freeze.

Sausage: Make sausage from trimmings of lean portions of pork. Sausage to be frozen should contain approximately three times as much lean as fat. Prepare the sausage using your favorite recipe. Pack sausage tightly into plastic freezer bags, plastic freezer jars, plastic freezer containers, or vacuum package. Seal, label, and freeze.

Prepared Meat Entrees

Stews, creamed meats, meat sauces, casserole dishes, meat with vegetables, meat pies, roasted and baked meats, meatballs, and meatloaf may be frozen. Pack into plastic freezer jars, plastic freezer containers, or vacuum package. Seal, label, and freeze.

Thawing and Preparing Beef, Pork, Lamb, Mutton, Veal, and Venison

Leave package wrapped until ready to cook. The refrigerator is the best place to thaw meats. Slow thawing allows the meat to absorb the thawed ice crystals. Also, the meat is less likely to spoil and develop an "off" flavor. If you must thaw meat fast, thaw in a microwave oven on the defrost setting, or seal in plastic wrap and submerge in cold water. Thaw frozen meat just long enough for the ice to disappear in the center. Do not let meat return to room temperature. It is best to cook meat while it still contains a few ice crystals. Usually roasts and steaks over 1½ inches thick should be thawed before cooking. Thin steaks, chops, or patties may be cooked from the frozen stage, but the cooking time must be longer to allow for thawing the meat. Use a meat cooking

chart for accurate times and temperatures for completely thawed meats. Add from 12 to 21 minutes per pound for roasting meats still frozen.

Poultry

Chicken or Turkey

Select choice birds that have grown rapidly and are plump. If practical, starve birds overnight before slaughtering. Allow carcass of whole turkey to chill two days. Pack using one of the following methods:

Whole: Wrap whole chicken or turkey in freezer foil, film, paper, or vacuum package. Seal, label, and freeze.

Pieces: Cut chicken or turkey into pieces. Pack pieces in plastic freezer jars, plastic freezer containers, freezer foil, film, paper, or vacuum package. Seal, label, and freeze.

Halves: Cut chicken or turkey in half. Wrap in freezer foil, film, paper, or vacuum package. Seal, label, and freeze.

Prepared Poultry Entrees

All chicken or turkey entrees, such as creamed chicken, chicken or turkey pies, baked chicken, chicken or turkey broth, chicken or turkey chopped for salad, and barbecue chicken or turkey freeze well. Do not freeze stuffed poultry. Cover chicken or turkey with a cream sauce or gravy if possible. Cool at room temperature, not to exceed 2 hours. Pack into plastic freezer jars or plastic freezer containers. Seal, label, and freeze.

Thawing and Preparing Chicken or Turkey

Whole or Halves: Thaw wrapped whole or halved chicken or turkey in refrigerator or submerge in cold water. Never thaw poultry at room temperature. Prepare and cook as fresh.

Pieces: Thaw chicken or turkey pieces in the refrigerator until pieces can be easily separated. Prepare and cook as fresh.

Prepared Foods

Breads – Quick

Biscuits, Fruit and Nut Breads, Muffins, and Waffles: Prepare, bake, and cool. Pack into plastic freezer bags or plastic freezer containers. Seal, label, and freeze.

Breads – Yeast

Unbaked: Shape as desired. Freeze on baking sheet. Pack into plastic freezer bags or plastic freezer containers. Seal, label, and return to freezer.

Baked: Prepare, bake, and cool. Pack same as Yeast Breads, Unbaked.

Brown-and-Serve: Bake 20 minutes at 275°F. Cool. Pack same as Yeast Breads, Unbaked.

Pizza: Prepare pizza. Do not bake. Flash freeze; remove from freezer. Wrap in freezer film, foil, paper, or vacuum package. Seal, label, and return to freezer.

Cakes

Layer, Loaf, Cupcakes, Angel, Chiffon, Sponge, and Fruit: Prepare, bake, and cool. May be frozen whole or in meal-size portions or slices. Pack into plastic freezer bags or plastic freezer containers. Seal, label, and freeze.

Frosted: Prepare, bake, cool, and frost. Place in freezer to harden the frosting. Remove from freezer and pack into plastic freezer bags or plastic freezer containers. Seal, label, and return to freezer.

Candies – Homemade

Fudge, Divinity, Brittle, Taffy, Creams, or Caramels: Wrap each piece individually in freezer film and pack into plastic freezer containers to avoid crushing. Seal, label, and freeze. Allow to thaw in the package.

Chicken Vegetable Soup

Yield: about 7 pint containers

1 cup sliced carrots (about 2 large)	2½ quarts vegetable broth (see page 108)
1 cup sliced celery (about 1 stalk)	2 cups chopped cooked chicken breast
½ cup chopped onion (about 1 medium)	½ teaspoon kosher salt
¼ cup butter or margarine	½ teaspoon coarsely ground pepper

Lightly sauté carrots, celery, and onion in butter in a large saucepan. Add vegetable broth, chicken, and salt and pepper. Bring soup to a boil; reduce heat and simmer 30 minutes. Cool, not to exceed 2 hours. Ladle soup into plastic freezer jars or plastic freezer containers, leaving ½-inch headspace. Seal, label, and freeze.

Combination Dishes

Baked Beans, Stew, Ravioli, or Meat Sauce Casseroles: Prepare as usual, keeping fat to a minimum. Cool at room temperature, not to exceed 2 hours. Pack into plastic freezer jars or plastic freezer containers. Seal, label, and freeze.

Cookies

Unbaked: For bar cookies, form into a long roll; for drop cookies, place cookies close together on a baking sheet. Flash freeze cookie roll and drop cookies; remove from freezer. Wrap in plastic freezer bags, freezer film, foil, paper, or vacuum package. Seal, label, and return to freezer.

Baked: Prepare, bake, and cool. Pack into plastic freezer bags or plastic freezer containers, placing freezer paper between cookie layers. Seal, label, and freeze.

Desserts

Mousse: Mix and pour into plastic freezer jars or plastic freezer containers. Seal, label, and freeze.

Cheesecake, Baked: Prepare, bake, and cool. Wrap in freezer film and pack in plastic freezer containers. Seal, label, and freeze.

Pudding, Steamed: Prepare, cook, and cool. Pack in covered baking mold, securing lid with freezer tape. Pack mold in plastic freezer bag. Seal, label, and freeze.

Doughnuts

Deep-Fried: Fry in high-quality cooking oil. Cool. Package same as Cookies, Baked.

Freezer Slaw

Yield: about 5 pint containers

2 pounds cabbage	2 cups sugar
1 large green pepper	1 teaspoon dry mustard
3 large carrots	1 teaspoon celery seed
¾ cup chopped onion	1 cup vinegar, 5% acidity
1 teaspoon salt	½ cup water

Shred cabbage, green pepper, and carrots. Add onion. Sprinkle with salt; let stand 1 hour. Drain. Combine remaining ingredients in a saucepan. Bring to a boil; boil 3 minutes. Cool. Ladle liquid over cabbage mixture; let stand 5 minutes. Stir well. Pack slaw into plastic freezer jars or plastic freezer containers, leaving ½-inch headspace. Seal, label, and freeze.

Gazpacho

Yield: about 7 pint containers

2 pounds tomatoes (about 6 medium)	5 cups tomato juice
1 pound cucumbers (about 2 medium)	½ cup red wine vinegar
1 cup chopped onion (about 1 large)	2 tablespoons extra-virgin olive oil
1 cup chopped green pepper (about 1 large)	½ teaspoon hot pepper sauce
½ cup chopped celery (about 1 stalk)	1 clove garlic, minced
	1 teaspoon salt
	¼ teaspoon pepper

Peel, core, seed, and chop tomatoes. Peel, seed, and chop cucumbers. Combine all ingredients. Ladle gazpacho into plastic freezer jars or plastic freezer containers, leaving ½-inch headspace. Seal, label, and freeze.

Gravy

It is better to freeze broth and thicken while reheating than to freeze gravy. Prepare broth according to favorite recipe; cool. Ladle broth into plastic freezer jars or plastic freezer containers, leaving ½-inch headspace. Seal, label, and freeze.

Herb Pizza Crust

Yield: about three 10- to 14-inch pizza crusts

2 tablespoons sugar	1/2 cup bread flour
2 1/2 teaspoons active dry yeast	1 tablespoon coarse salt
1 1/2 cups warm water (105° to 115°F or according to yeast packet)	1 tablespoon basil
	1 tablespoon oregano
	1 tablespoon thyme
3 1/2 cups all-purpose flour	3 tablespoons extra-virgin olive oil

Dissolve sugar and yeast in warm water. Let stand until mixture starts to foam, about 5 minutes. Combine all-purpose flour, bread flour, salt, and herbs in a large bowl. Mound flour mixture, then make a well in the center. Pour yeast mixture into the flour well. Add olive oil. With a fork, stir in circular motion to gradually incorporate dry ingredients into liquid ingredients. Continue stirring until dough forms.

Shape dough into a ball. Grease a large bowl with olive oil. Place dough in bowl, turning to cover entire surface of dough with a thin coating of olive oil. Cover bowl with plastic wrap and let dough rise at room temperature until doubled in size, 45 minutes to 1 hour. Punch down dough. Turn dough onto a floured surface and shape into three balls. Lightly brush individual dough balls with olive oil and cover with plastic wrap. Let rise at room temperature 30 to 45 minutes.

Shape dough by hand, working from center to outer edge to form a circle. For a crispy crust, form a 1/4-inch thickness. For a soft crust, form a 1/2-inch thickness. Transfer dough to a cardboard round. Freeze pizza crust plain or with toppings. Wrap crusts individually in plastic freezer bags, freezer foil, film, paper, or vacuum package. Seal, label, and freeze.

Lemon Curd

Makes one 9-inch tart

6 large egg yolks	1 cup fresh lemon juice
3/4 cup sugar	1/2 cup cold unsalted butter, cut into 8 pieces
Grated peel of one lemon	

Press egg yolks though a sieve set over a heavy saucepan. Add sugar, lemon peel, and lemon juice. Whisk just to combine. Cook over medium heat, stirring constantly with a wooden spoon. Make sure to stir down the sides of the saucepan. Cook until mixture coats the back of the wooden spoon, about 20 minutes. Remove saucepan from heat. Add butter, one piece at a time, stirring after each addition to ensure the mixture is smooth. Ladle lemon curd into plastic freezer jars or plastic freezer containers, leaving 1/2-inch headspace. Chill until set, about 1 hour. Seal, label, and freeze.

Onion Soup

Yield: about 5 pint containers

2 pounds onions, sliced	3 tablespoons flour
6 tablespoons butter	2 quarts beef broth
1 teaspoon sugar	1 cup white cooking wine
1 teaspoon dry mustard	Salt and pepper to taste

Cook onions in butter until transparent but not browned. Add sugar and dry mustard. Blend in flour; cook 1 minute, stirring to prevent burning. Gradually stir in beef broth and wine; simmer 30 minutes. Add salt and pepper to taste. Cool. Ladle soup into plastic freezer jars or plastic freezer containers, leaving 1/2-inch headspace. Seal, label, and freeze.

Pastry Circles, Squares, or Rectangles

Roll out dough; cut circles, squares, or rectangles large enough for pie or tart pan, adding 2 inches. Place pastry onto a piece of cardboard cut to the shape of the pastry, then wrap in freezer foil, film, or paper. Separate layers with a double thickness of freezer foil, film, or paper. Flash freeze. Place in plastic freezer bags or vacuum package. Seal, label, and return to freezer.

Pesto

Yield: about 2 half-pint containers

1 cup pine nuts	1 cup grated Parmesan cheese
4 cups fresh basil leaves, firmly packed	1 cup plus 1 tablespoon extra-virgin olive oil
2 cloves garlic, crushed	

Spread pine nuts on a baking sheet and bake at 450°F until lightly browned. Purée toasted pine nuts, basil, and garlic using a food processor or blender until smooth. Add Parmesan cheese, processing just to blend. Add 1 cup olive oil through feed tube of food processor or lid of blender in a slow, steady stream while machine is running. Pour pesto into plastic freezer jars or plastic freezer containers, leaving 1/2-inch headspace. Drizzle 1 1/2 teaspoons olive oil over pesto. Seal, label, and freeze.

Pickled Horseradish

Yield: about 2 half-pint containers

3/4 pound horseradish root	1 1/2 teaspoons Ball Fruit-Fresh Produce Protector
1 cup vinegar, 5% acidity	
1/2 teaspoon salt	

Wash horseradish root; drain. Peel and finely grate horseradish root. Combine 2 cups grated horseradish, vinegar, salt, and Fruit-Fresh in a bowl. Ladle pickled horseradish into plastic freezer jars or plastic freezer containers, leaving 1/2-inch headspace. Seal, label, and freeze.

Note: The pungency of horseradish root fades quickly. Prepare only the amount of pickled horseradish that will be used within three months.

Pie Crust

Yield: about 4 eight- or nine-inch crusts

4 1/2 cups all-purpose flour	1 egg, beaten
2 teaspoons salt	1 tablespoon vinegar
4 teaspoons sugar	1/2 cup water
1 3/4 cups vegetable shortening	

Combine dry ingredients; cut in shortening until mixture is uniformly coarse. Combine egg, vinegar, and water. Gradually add to flour mixture, stirring until mixture forms a ball. Divide dough into 4 equal portions. Roll dough out on a floured surface; cut into circles the size of the pie pan plus 2 inches. Place pastry onto cardboard round covered with freezer foil, film, or paper, or place in foil baking pan. Separate layers with a double thickness of freezer foil, film, or paper. Place in plastic freezer bags. Seal, label, and freeze. Alternatively, flash freeze; remove from freezer. Vacuum package. Label and return to freezer.

Pies

Double-crust pies, raw or cooked, as well as single-crust pies (coconut, nut, potato and similar pies), may be frozen. The pie filling to be frozen should be slightly thicker than usual. Flash freeze; remove from freezer. Pack into plastic freezer bags. Seal, label, and return to freezer.

Salads

Fruit and gelatin salads that freeze well are those made with a base of cream, cottage cheese, whipped cream, or mayonnaise. Prepare as a single dish or individual servings. Most containers suitable for freezer storage can be used to freeze the salad or gelatin. Salad molds, serving bowls, custard cups, or muffin tins are just a few of the containers that can be used. So that the container can be used for another purpose after the salad or gelatin is frozen, line it with freezer foil or film before filling. Flash freeze the salad or gelatin. After salad or gelatin is frozen, remove it from the dish and over-wrap the salad or gelatin using plastic freezer bags, plastic freezer containers, freezer foil, or film. Seal, label, and return to freezer.

Sandwiches

Filled: Sandwiches suitable for freezing include those made with cheese, chicken, meat, peanut butter, nut paste, egg yolk mixtures, and fish. Use day-old bread; spread bread with butter; add filling. Wrap sandwiches individually in freezer film or foil. Flash freeze. Overwrap with plastic freezer bags. Label and return to freezer.

Open-Face Canapés: Make canapés according to recipe. Be sure to spread filling to the very edge of bread. Place canapés on a baking sheet and flash freeze. Pack frozen canapés into plastic freezer container; separate layers with a double thickness of freezer foil, film, or paper. Seal, label, and return to freezer.

Savory Pastry Crust

Yield: about 4 five-inch crusts

2 cups all-purpose flour	3 tablespoons sugar
1/2 cup shredded cheddar cheese	1/2 teaspoon salt
2 tablespoons minced flat leaf parsley	1/2 cup butter, chilled and cut into 1/2-inch cubes
	1/3 cup cold water

Combine flour, cheese, parsley, sugar, and salt in a medium bowl. Cut in butter until mixture is uniformly coarse. Gradually add water, one tablespoon at a time, stirring gently with a fork after each addition. Use just enough water for dough to form a ball. Divide dough into 4 equal portions. Roll one portion of dough out on a floured surface into a 5-inch circle; repeat for each portion. Place pastry onto a cardboard round covered with freezer foil, film, or paper. Separate layers with a double thickness of freezer foil, film, or paper. Place in plastic freezer bag or plastic freezer container. Seal, label, and freeze.

Soups

Most soups freeze well. These include dried beans, split pea, oyster, and those made from poultry, meats, and vegetables.

Stock-Based: Prepare as usual. Cool. Pack into plastic freezer jars or plastic freezer containers, leaving 1/2-inch headspace. Seal, label, and freeze.

Spaghetti Sauce

Yield: about 6 pint containers

2 cups chopped onions	3 (8-ounce) cans tomato sauce
2 cups chopped green peppers	1 (29-ounce) can whole tomatoes, chopped
1 cup chopped celery	2 bay leaves
4 cloves garlic, minced	1 teaspoon oregano
2 tablespoons extra-virgin olive oil	1 teaspoon basil
2 pounds ground beef	1 teaspoon salt
3 (6-ounce) cans tomato paste	1/4 teaspoon pepper

Sauté onions, green peppers, celery, and garlic in oil until onions are tender. Add ground beef; cook until browned. Drain off excess fat. Add remaining ingredients; simmer 1 hour. Remove bay leaves. Cool. Ladle sauce into plastic freezer jars or plastic freezer containers, leaving 1/2-inch headspace. Seal, label, and freeze.

#

It is important that only fresh seafood be used for freezing. Seafood must be cleaned and prepared for freezing shortly after being caught. Since seafood is a perishable commodity, it must be kept under refrigeration at all times.

Crab, Lobster, or Oysters

Prepare seafood as for using fresh. Pack meat into plastic freezer jars, plastic freezer containers, or vacuum package. Seal, label, and freeze.

Fish

Select any variety of fresh fish that is good for cooking.

Whole: Prepare fish for freezing in the same manner as for cooking. Wrap each fish tightly in freezer film, foil, or paper, then pack into plastic freezer bags, plastic freezer jars, or plastic freezer containers. Alternatively, vacuum package. Seal, label, and freeze.

Fish may also be frozen in plastic freezer jars or plastic freezer containers and covered with cold water. Seal, label, and freeze.

Steaks Or Fillets: Dip fish in a 5 percent salt solution (2/3 cup salt to 1 gallon water) for 30 seconds. Pack same as Fish, Whole.

Fish Roe

Thoroughly wash roe. Pack roe into plastic freezer jars or plastic freezer containers. Seal, label, and freeze.

Shrimp

Fresh Frozen: Remove head from shrimp; wash shrimp in cold water. Pack shrimp in plastic freezer bags, plastic freezer jars, plastic freezer containers, or vacuum package. Seal, label, and freeze.

Cleaned: Remove head from shrimp. Peel, de-vein, and wash shrimp in cold water. Pack same as for Shrimp, Fresh Frozen.

Cooked: Prepare shrimp as for Shrimp, Cleaned. Boil 5 minutes in 1 gallon water and 3 tablespoons salt. Pack same as for Shrimp, Fresh Frozen.

Breaded: Remove head, peel, and de-vein. Wash shrimp in cold water. Coat with breading. Pack same as for Shrimp, Fresh Frozen.

Thawing and Preparing Seafood Products

Place unopened package in the refrigerator until thawing begins and the product softens slightly. Cook as for fresh.

Special Diet &
BABY FOODS

Freezing foods is an excellent way to meet specialized meal requirements and save time. However, ready-to-serve frozen meals do not retain quality, flavor, or texture as long as foods frozen as separate ingredients. Careful management of ready-to-serve meals will help meet individual dietary needs and still provide nutritious meals.

Foods for diabetics can be prepared and frozen without sugar or sweetened with a non-sugar sweetener. Consult your physician and follow manufacturer's instructions for use of non-sugar sweeteners.

It is often convenient to freeze single portions without salt or without fat for individuals on special diets. Plastic freezer jars and plastic freezer containers make convenient freezer storage containers for foods that are soft or liquid at room temperature. They are available in sizes that are perfect for one serving.

Purées of vegetables, fruits, and meats for babies and for individuals convalescing may be made and frozen when the foods are in season. These foods require a rigid container due to the soft texture. Four-ounce tapered glass jars or eight-ounce plastic freezer jars are most suitable for freezing baby food, while eight-ounce tapered glass or plastic jars make a perfect single serving size for adults.

Vegetables

Freezing is an excellent method for preserving most vegetables, particularly when the variety selected is suitable for freezing, they are harvested at the correct time, they are adequately blanched and cooled, and they are packaged correctly. Practically all frozen vegetables may be stored for one year.

Vegetables that are harvested from your own garden or purchased at the market should be tender and at their peak of flavor and texture. Do not use vegetables that are overripe. Prepare, package, and freeze vegetables the same day of harvest or purchase.

If it is necessary to store vegetables for a short time before freezing, store them in a cool, well-ventilated area or in the refrigerator. Prompt cooling in ice water after blanching, followed by storage in the refrigerator, will help retain flavor as well as other desirable qualities.

Most fully-cooked vegetables lose flavor rapidly and should be stored for only a few days. Loss of flavor may be slowed by covering the vegetables with a cream sauce.

Blanching

Blanching is a "must" in preparing vegetables for freezing, and it must be done carefully. Blanching cleanses off surface dirt and microorganisms, brightens the color, helps retain vitamins, and reduces enzyme activity that can destroy fresh flavors in as little as four weeks. All vegetables that are stored frozen for more than four weeks require blanching. However, those vegetables used exclusively for their flavor, such as green onions, hot peppers, and herbs, do not have to be blanched.

Before blanching, wash, drain, sort, trim, and cut the vegetables as for cooking fresh. Use 1 gallon water per 1 pound vegetables—2 gallons for leafy greens. For a large quantity of vegetables, determine how many vegetables can be blanched in 15 minutes. Prepare this amount, leaving the remaining vegetables in the refrigerator. Put vegetables into blancher (wire basket, coarse mesh bag or perforated metal strainer) and lower into vigorously boiling water. Begin counting the time as soon as vegetables are placed into the boiling water. Keep the heat on high and stir water or keep container covered during blanching. Follow the blanching time given in the recipe for each vegetable. If you live 5,000 feet or more above sea level, blanch 1 minute longer than time specified in the recipe. Underblanching stimulates the activity of enzymes and is worse than no blanching at all. Prolonged blanching causes loss of vitamins, minerals, flavor, and color.

After blanching is complete, immediately cool vegetables in cold water to stop the heating process. Vegetables should be stirred several times during cooling. Cool vegetables for the same length of time as for blanching.

Vegetables are usually packed without added seasoning. Pack vegetables into meal-size, airtight, moisture- and vapor-proof packaging. Place sealed packages into freezer in single layers, leaving 1-inch space between packages. Use coldest part of freezer for freezing foods. Foods should freeze in 12 to 24 hours.

When completely frozen, packages may be compactly stacked. Keep the freezer at 0°F or lower at all times.

Artichoke – Globe

Select globe artichokes with uniform green color, compact globes, and tightly-adhering leaves. Size has little to do with quality or flavor. Remove outer bracts until light yellow or white bracts are reached. Cut off tops of bud and trim to a cone. Wash the hearts in cold water as soon as trimming is complete. Drain. Blanch 7 minutes. Cool. Drain. Pack globe artichokes in plastic freezer jars, plastic freezer bags, plastic freezer containers, or vacuum package. Seal, label, and freeze.

Artichoke – Jerusalem

Select mature, unblemished Jerusalem artichokes. Wash thoroughly; peel or scrape; wash again. Blanch 3 to 5 minutes, depending on size. Cool. Drain. Pack artichokes into plastic freezer jars, plastic freezer containers, or vacuum package. Seal, label, and freeze.

Asparagus

Select young, tender asparagus with tightly closed tips. Wash thoroughly and sort into sizes. Trim stalks by removing scales with a sharp knife. Cut into even lengths to fit freezer containers. Blanch small spears 1½ minutes, medium spears 2 minutes, and large spears 3 minutes. Cool. Drain. Pack asparagus into plastic freezer bags, plastic freezer jars, plastic freezer containers, or vacuum package. Seal, label, and freeze.

Beans – Lima

Select lima beans while the seed is in the green stage. Wash in cold water. Shell and wash again. Sort according to size. Blanch small beans 1 minute, medium beans 2 minutes, and large beans 3 minutes. Cool. Drain. Pack beans into plastic freezer bags, plastic freezer jars, plastic freezer containers, or vacuum package. Seal, label, and freeze.

Beans – Snap

Select young, tender bean pods when the seed is first formed. Wash in cold water. Trim ends; cut into 2- to 4-inch lengths or lengths to fit freezer container. The longer cuts are the best quality. Blanch 3 minutes. Cool. Drain. Pack beans into plastic freezer bags, plastic freezer jars, plastic freezer containers, or vacuum package. Seal, label, and freeze.

Beets

Select uniformly tender, deep red beets. Trim stems and tap roots to 2 inches in length; wash. Cook beets until tender; cool. Cut off stems, tap roots, and peels. Leave whole, quarter, slice, or dice. Pack beets into plastic freezer jars, plastic freezer containers, or vacuum package. Seal, label, and freeze.

Broccoli

Select tender yet firm broccoli stalks with compact heads. Wash and remove leaves and woody portions. Separate heads into conveniently sized sections and immerse in brine (1 cup salt to 1 gallon water) 30 minutes to remove insects. Rinse and drain. Blanch medium-size sections 3 minutes and large-size sections 4 minutes. Cool. Drain. Pack broccoli into plastic freezer jars, plastic freezer containers, or vacuum package. Seal, label, and freeze.

Brussels Sprouts

Select Brussels sprouts with dark green, compact heads. Remove coarse outer leaves; wash and sort into small, medium, and large sizes. Blanch small size 3 minutes, medium size 4 minutes, and large size 5 minutes. Cool. Drain. Pack Brussels sprouts into plastic freezer jars, plastic freezer containers, or vacuum package. Seal, label, and freeze.

Cabbage

Select solid cabbage heads with crisp green leaves. Wash, discard the coarse outer leaves, and cut the head into wedges or coarsely shred. Blanch wedges 3 minutes; shredded cabbage 1½ minutes. Cool. Drain. Pack cabbage into plastic freezer jars or plastic freezer containers. Seal, label, and freeze.

Carrots

Select young, tender, coreless, medium-length carrots. Wash, peel, wash again, and dice or quarter. Small carrots may be frozen whole. Blanch cut carrots 3 minutes; whole carrots 5 minutes. Cool. Drain. Pack carrots into plastic freezer jars, plastic freezer containers, or vacuum package. Seal, label, and freeze.

Cauliflower

Select cauliflower with compact heads. Trim; break into flowerets of uniform size, about 1-inch across. Wash and drain. Immerse flowerets in brine (1 cup salt to 1 gallon water) for 30 minutes to remove insects. Rinse and drain. Blanch medium-size sections 3 minutes; large-size sections 4 minutes. Cool. Drain. Pack cauliflower into plastic freezer jars, plastic freezer containers, or vacuum package. Seal, label, and freeze.

Corn

Select only tender, freshly-gathered corn in the milk stage. Husk and trim the ears; remove silks and wash.

Corn on the Cob: Blanch ears 1½ inches in diameter 6 minutes, 2 inches in diameter 8 minutes, and larger ears 10 minutes. Cool. Drain. Wrap ears individually in moisture- and vapor-proof film. Pack wrapped ears of corn into plastic freezer bags, or vacuum package. Seal, label, and freeze.

Whole Kernel: Blanch 5 to 6 minutes, depending on size of ears. Cool; drain; cut corn from cob. Pack into plastic freezer bags, plastic freezer jars, plastic freezer containers, or vacuum package. Seal, label, and freeze.

Cream-Style: Blanch ears the same as Corn, Whole Kernel. Cool. Drain. Cut kernels, leaving tip ends; scrape cob to extract milk and pulp. Pack corn into plastic freezer jars or plastic freezer containers, leaving ½-inch headspace. Seal, label, and freeze.

Precooked: Cut and scrape corn from the cob without blanching. Put small amount of water in saucepan, add cut corn and cook over low heat, stirring constantly, about 10 minutes or until it thickens. Pour corn into a bowl; set bowl in ice water to cool. Do not cook more than 3 quarts at a time. Pack same as Corn, Cream-Style.

Eggplant

Harvest uniformly dark-colored eggplant before seeds become mature.

Plain: Wash, peel, and slice ⅓-inch thick. Prepare just enough eggplant for 1 batch at a time. Blanch 4 minutes in 1 gallon boiling water containing 3 tablespoons Fruit-Fresh (see page 16) or ½ cup lemon juice. Cool. Drain. Pack eggplant into plastic freezer jars or plastic freezer containers. Seal, label, and freeze.

For Frying: Pack same as Eggplant, Plain. Separate slices with a double thickness of freezer foil, film, or paper.

Greens

Pick young, tender, green leaves. Wash thoroughly. Cut off woody stems. Blanch 2 minutes, stirring to avoid matting leaves. Cool. Drain. Pack into plastic freezer jars or plastic freezer containers, leaving 1/2-inch headspace. Seal, label, and freeze.

Herbs – Fresh

Many fresh herbs may be frozen while in season to use later in cooking and baking. Wash, drain, and dry herbs. Do not blanch. Wrap a few sprigs or leaves in freezer film and place in plastic freezer bags, plastic freezer jars, or plastic freezer containers. Seal, label, and freeze.

Mushrooms

Select cultivated mushrooms that are firm and of even color. Mushrooms deteriorate rapidly, so freeze mushrooms the same day they are purchased. Do not let mushrooms soak in water during preparation.

Plain: Wash mushrooms; pat dry. Remove the base of the stem. Sort mushrooms by size. Smaller mushrooms may be frozen whole; larger mushrooms should be sliced. Add Fruit-Fresh (see page 16) to blanching water to help prevent discoloration. Blanch small, whole mushrooms 4 minutes; sliced mushrooms 3 minutes. Cool. Drain. Pack mushrooms into plastic freezer jars or plastic freezer containers. Seal, label, and freeze.

Sautéed: Slice mushrooms. Sauté sliced mushrooms in butter for 3 minutes. Cool. Pack same as Mushrooms, Plain. Seal, label, and freeze.

Note: If mushrooms are sautéed, blanching is not required.

Okra

Select tender okra pods. Wash and separate into two sizes: under 4 inches and larger than 4 inches. Remove stems at the end of the seed cells. Blanch small pods 3 minutes; large pods 5 minutes. Cool. Drain. Leave small pods whole; cut large pods into 1-inch lengths. Pack okra into plastic freezer jars or plastic freezer containers. Seal, label, and freeze.

Onions

Mature Bulbs: Choose mature bulbs and clean as for using fresh. Blanch onions 3 to 7 minutes or until the center is heated. Cool. Drain. Pack onions into plastic freezer jars or plastic freezer containers. Seal, label, and freeze. Best if used only for cooking.

Green: Wash and chop. Freeze without blanching. Pack same as Onions, Mature Bulbs.

Parsnips or Turnips

Choose parsnips or turnips that are firm and have smooth skin. Remove leafy tops. Wash and drain. Peel parsnips or turnips. Cut in half lengthwise, slice crosswise, or dice. Blanch 3 minutes. Cool. Drain. Pack parsnips or turnips into plastic freezer jars, plastic freezer containers, or vacuum package. Seal, label, and freeze.

Peanuts

Select fully-mature peanuts.

Green In The Shell: Wash. Leave in shell. Blanch 10 minutes. Cool. Drain. Pack peanuts into plastic freezer jars or plastic freezer containers. Seal, label, and freeze.

Shelled: Shell. Pack peanuts into plastic freezer jars, plastic freezer containers, or vacuum package. Seal, label, and freeze.

Note: Peanuts may be removed from the freezer, thawed, and used as fresh-shelled peanuts in any recipe.

Peas

Field (Blackeye): Select pods when seeds are tender and barely grown. Wash peas. Shell. Wash again. Blanch smaller sizes 1 minute and larger sizes 2 minutes. Cool. Drain. Pack peas into plastic freezer jars or plastic freezer containers. Seal, label, and freeze.

Green or "English": Harvest when pods are filled with young, tender peas that have not become starchy. Wash peas. Shell. Wash again. Blanch 2 minutes. Cool. Drain. Pack peas into plastic freezer jars or plastic freezer containers. Seal, label, and freeze.

Snow or Sugar Snap: Select firm, unblemished pods. Wash and drain. Blanch 2 minutes. Cool. Drain. Pack pea pods into plastic freezer jars, plastic freezer containers, or vacuum package. Seal, label, and freeze.

Peppers

Hot: Select crisp, tender green or red pods. Wash and drain. Pack peppers into plastic freezer jars, plastic freezer containers or vacuum package. Seal, label, and freeze.

Pimientos: Select fully-ripe pods of deep red color. Wash and drain. Remove stems and seeds. Peel by roasting at 400°F until skins blister or cover with water, and boil until peppers are tender. Cool. Drain. Peel. Pack pimientos into plastic freezer jars or plastic freezer containers. Seal, label, and freeze.

Sweet: Select crisp, tender green or red pods. Wash and drain. Remove stems and seeds. Freeze peppers whole, cut into halves or strips, or dice. Do not blanch. Pack peppers into plastic freezer jars, plastic freezer containers, or vacuum package. Seal, label, and freeze.

Note: When cutting or seeding hot peppers, wear rubber gloves to prevent hands from being burned.

Potatoes – White

Select smooth new potatoes.

Plain: Wash thoroughly. Peel. Wash again. Blanch 3 to 5 minutes, depending on size. Drain. Cool. Pack potatoes into plastic freezer jars, plastic freezer containers, or vacuum package. Seal, label, and freeze.

Baked or Stuffed: Bake at 350°F until fork-tender. For stuffed potatoes, cut off a thin slice from the long side of the potato. Sprinkle potato with cheese and replace potato slice. Cool quickly in refrigerator. Wrap individually in freezer foil or film. Freeze. Pack individually wrapped frozen potatoes in plastic freezer bags, plastic freezer containers, or vacuum package. Seal, label, and return to freezer.

French Fried: Cut potatoes into thin strips. Blanch potatoes 2 minutes; cool on a paper towel. Fry in fresh vegetable oil (370°F) until very light brown. Drain. Cool. Pack into plastic freezer bags, plastic freezer containers, or vacuum package. Seal, label, and freeze.

Scalloped: Bake potatoes in dish suitable for baking and freezing until pale in color, but not quite done. Cool at room temperature, not to exceed 2 hours. Wrap cooled dish with freezer foil or film. Place wrapped dish in plastic freezer bags or vacuum package. Seal, label, and freeze.

Potatoes – Sweet

Allow sweet potatoes to cure for a minimum of one week after harvesting. Wash and dry potatoes.

Baked: Coat peel with vegetable oil; bake at 350°F until slightly soft. Cool. Wrap individually in freezer foil or film. Place in plastic freezer bags, plastic freezer containers, or vacuum package. Seal, label, and freeze.

Sliced: Cook unpeeled potatoes in water at 130°F for 30 minutes. Peel and cut lengthwise into 1/2-inch slices. Blanch 3 minutes in boiling syrup to cover (1 1/2 cups water to 1 cup sugar and 1 tablespoon lemon juice). Cool. Pack potatoes into plastic freezer jars or plastic freezer containers. Ladle syrup over potatoes, leaving 1/2-inch headspace. Seal, label, and freeze.

Purée: Bake potatoes at 350°F until soft. Cool. Peel sweet potatoes. Purée using a food processor or food mill. For each 5 pounds of puréed potatoes, add 1/2 cup sugar, 1/2 cup cold water and 1 tablespoon lemon juice. Cool. Pack purée into plastic freezer jars or plastic freezer containers, leaving 1/2-inch headspace. Seal, label, and freeze.

Pumpkin

Select mature cooking pumpkin that has uniform color and a stem that breaks easily from the vine. Wash and drain. Peel pumpkin and remove seeds. Cut pumpkin into sections; steam until soft. Purée using a food processor or food mill. Add 1 part sugar to 6 parts purée, if desired. Cool. Pack purée into plastic freezer jars or plastic freezer containers, leaving 1/2-inch headspace. Seal, label, and freeze.

Squash – Spaghetti

Cut squash in half; remove seeds. Place squash in baking dish, cut side down. Add 1/2-inch water and bake at 350°F until tender. Using a fork, rake pulp away from peel, separating pulp into strands. Cool. Pack squash into plastic freezer jars or plastic freezer containers. Seal, label, and freeze.

Squash – Summer

Choose young squash with tender skin. Wash and drain. Cut squash crosswise into slices. Blanch 3 minutes. Cool. Pack squash into plastic freezer jars, plastic freezer containers, or vacuum package. Seal, label, and freeze.

Squash – Winter

Select fully-mature squash with a hard rind. Wash and drain. Cut squash in half; scoop out seeds and membrane. Place squash cut side down in a shallow baking dish; add 1/4-inch water and bake at 375°F until tender. Scoop out pulp. Purée using a food processor or food mill. Cool. Pack purée into plastic freezer jars or plastic freezer containers. Seal, label, and freeze.

Tomatoes

Sauce: Select firm ripe tomatoes. Wash, core, quarter, and seed tomatoes. Cook tomatoes until soft, stirring to prevent sticking. Purée using food processor or food mill. Return to saucepan and simmer until reduced by half. Cool. Pack sauce into plastic freezer jars or plastic freezer containers. Seal, label, and freeze.

Juice: Select firm, ripe tomatoes. Wash, core, quarter, and seed tomatoes. Simmer tomatoes until soft, stirring to prevent sticking. Purée using a food processor or food mill. Cool. Pack juice into plastic freezer jars or plastic freezer containers. Seal, label, and freeze.

Tomatoes – Green

Select firm green tomatoes. Wash; core; slice 1/4-inch thick. Pack tomatoes into plastic freezer jars or plastic freezer containers with a double thickness of freezer wrap between slices. Seal, label, and freeze.

Thawing and Preparing Vegetables

Most vegetables can be cooked without thawing. The exception is corn on the cob, the only vegetable which should be completely thawed before cooking. All greens should be partially thawed so that they are easy to separate before cooking. Precooked vegetables should also be partially thawed.

Cook frozen vegetables as you would fresh, but for a shorter time, since they were blanched before freezing. Use the smallest amount of water possible. Cook vegetables immediately before serving. Nutrients in frozen vegetables are quickly lost if they are allowed to stand after cooking. Cook only the amount that can be consumed at one meal.

r

Freezing Step-By-Step

Using a Freezer to Preserve Food

Freezing foods as a way to preserve them for serving long after their in-season availability has ended is easy, convenient, and requires little time. The extreme cold delays the growth of microorganisms and slows down chemical changes that affect quality or cause food to spoil. Following instructions to inactivate enzymes that cause color loss and flavor changes as well as loss of nutrients is essential in sustaining the high quality of frozen foods. Techniques you will use to help preserve the quality of frozen foods include blanching some fruits and vegetables, pre-treating certain fruits and vegetables with an antioxidant, flash freezing some foods before packaging, using moisture- and vapor-proof packaging, and controlling the rate of freezing. Following the "first in, first out" method for inventory management will help you retain the quality of frozen food and improve the economy of freezing food. Proper maintenance of your freezer helps to ensure that the internal temperature of the freezer remains consistent and helps to extend the life of the freezer. Refer to the owner's manual for use and care instructions for your freezer model.

Prep

❶ Choose appropriate moisture- and vapor-proof packaging for the type of food you are preparing to freeze. Glass freezer jars, plastic freezer containers, freezer wraps, or freezer bags provide optimal protection for food during freezer storage. Freeze foods at 0°F or lower. For rapid freezing, set the temperature control at -10°F for 24 hours before packing the freezer with unfrozen food. Add only the amount of unfrozen food that will freeze within 24 hours. Return the temperature control to 0°F after the food is frozen.

Select tender young ears of corn. Remove husks and silks. Cut off the stem end even with the base of the corn. Cut off the tip end to remove underdeveloped corn kernels. Leave the ear of corn whole for whole-kernel, cream style, and individual ears of corn. If small pieces of corn on the cob are desired, cut the ear of corn into 2- to 3-inch pieces.

Cook

❷ Submerge several ears of corn into an eight-quart saucepan of boiling water. Blanch 2-inch diameter ears of corn 6 minutes for whole-kernel corn or cream style corn; blanch 8 minutes for corn on the cob. Begin blanching time when ears of corn are put into boiling water; water must remain boiling during the entire blanching period. ❸ To stop the effects of cooking, immediately submerge ears of corn into cold water for the same length of time used to blanch the corn. Drain; dry corn on the cob.

Package

❹ To cut corn kernels off the cob, hold the ear of corn upright, resting the stem end on a cutting board. Using a knife, and working from the narrow end to the wide end, cut corn kernels off the cob while moving the knife downward. Cut kernels off the cob, leaving tip ends. If cream style corn is desired, scrape the cob with the edge of the knife after the kernels are cut off in order to extract the milk. ❺ Pack whole-kernel corn in freezer jars, containers, or bags, leaving ¼-inch headspace. Pack cream style corn in freezer jars or containers, leaving ½-inch headspace. Wrap individual ears of corn or small pieces of corn on the cob tightly in freezer wrap, then package multiple ears of corn or pieces of corn in a freezer bag or container.

Freeze

❻ Label each container with the product name, method of preparation, and the date it was prepared for freezing. Place the containers near the coldest spot in the freezer, in single layers. Containers may be stacked after the corn is frozen. Adjust freezer temperature control to 0°F. Keep the freezer temperature at or below 0°F. Refer to the recipe or Figure 11 (see page 141) for optimal length of freezer storage.

1 Select the correct packaging for freezing.

2 Blanch ears of corn in boiling water.

3 Immerse blanched ears of corn in cold water.

4 Cut corn kernels off the cob.

5 Package corn for freezer storage.

6 Label container for freezer storage.

Dehydrating

Dehydrating is one of the oldest and simplest methods of preserving food—one that creates rich, concentrated flavor in food. In the process, dehydration transforms foods by removing moisture, so they take up less pantry space and are conveniently portable—perfect for on-the-go snacks. With dehydration, you can create versatile foods that can be used to deepen the flavor of great homemade classics—from dehydrated meats in soups and stews to rehydrated fruits in pies, cookies, and quick breads!

Getting Started

An electric food dehydrator is inexpensive and easy to operate. It produces consistent results and saves money over purchased dried foods. Dehydrators typically have a power base, nesting drying trays, and a cover. Some dehydrators come with "nice to have" features like temperature controls and timers. But units without these features work equally well for drying food.

The science of dehydrating

This method of food preservation works by removing the water that microorganisms need to survive. Common spoilers such as bacteria, molds, and enzymes need water to thrive. By reducing this essential nutrient required for their growth, dried foods become shelf-stable.

It takes time to dry

Dehydration requires a steady temperature over a long period of time in order to force moisture from food. Dry air is also needed to absorb moisture released from the food. Proper air circulation is essential for carrying moist air away so it is not reabsorbed by the food. To help minimize the length of time required to dry food, dehydrate food on days with low humidity.

Handy tools to make dehydrating easy

In addition to the electric food dehydrator, you may find that flexible nonstick mesh screens, fruit-roll sheets, and parchment paper are helpful tools when drying food. The mesh screens or parchment paper will help keep small pieces of dried food, such as berries, herbs, peas, and corn from falling through the trays. Fruit-roll sheets provide a smooth surface that will hold fruit purée, while allowing air to circulate so that moisture is removed.

Good Things to Know

Drying food at home is simple to do. Dried foods are easy to use and convenient to store. However, unlike the exact methods needed for canning and freezing, finding the best technique for drying may require the trial-and-error approach. Various factors, such as the drying method used, the quality of the produce, pretreatment techniques, and even the climate may affect the finished product. Follow the general guidelines given for each specific food and then make the necessary adjustments.

The Science Behind Dehydration

Successful home food dehydration is dependent on three basic principles:

- Heat: controlled temperature high enough to force out moisture, but not hot enough to cook the food.
- Dry Air: to absorb the released moisture.
- Air Circulation: to carry the moisture away.

When food is dehydrated, 80% to 95% of the moisture is removed, inactivating the growth of bacteria and other spoilage microorganisms. This makes it a useful method of preservation.

Ingredients and Preparation

Fresh, high-quality, ripe produce is best for dehydrating. Dry foods during the peak harvest season for the specific food type, especially if produce must be purchased from farm stands or supermarkets.

Dehydrated produce will weigh much less and take up less volume than fresh produce, depending on the natural moisture content of the fruit or vegetable and the discarded inedible portions (such as peelings, cores, seeds, pits, pods, and stems). As an example, apples are usually peeled and cored prior to drying, so a purchased weight of 10 pounds will be reduced to 1 to 1½ pounds when dried.

Pretreatment Techniques

Most vegetables and some fruits benefit from pretreatment techniques, such as blanching and dipping. Although the drying process slows down the action of enzymes, the chemical substances that cause fruits and vegetables to mature and ripen, it does not stop the action entirely. Simple pretreating slows this action. Blanching (heating in steam or water for a specific time, then cooling quickly) is the most common method of pretreating vegetables. Steam blanching is preferred because more water-soluble vitamins and minerals are preserved. In steam blanching, vegetables or fruits are placed in a colander that is suspended above boiling water and heated by the steam. In water blanching, the vegetables or fruits are placed directly in the boiling water. Blanching shortens the drying and rehydration time, sets color, slows enzyme action, and kills many spoilage microorganisms.

Dipping is a pretreatment used to prevent fruits such as apples, bananas, peaches, and pears from oxidizing. Oxidation is the process that causes fruits to turn brown and lose some vitamins A and C when exposed to the oxygen in air. Common antioxidants are Ball Fruit-Fresh Produce Protector, lemon or lime juice, and ascorbic acid.

Ball Fruit-Fresh Produce Protector: a blend of ascorbic and citric acids. Dissolve 2 tablespoons in 2 quarts of water. Hold produce in solution for no longer than 30 minutes; drain before drying.

Lemon or Lime Juice: the most natural pretreatment. Use 1 cup juice to 1 quart water. Soak fruit no longer than 10 minutes; drain before drying.

Ascorbic Acid: also known as vitamin C. Dissolve 1 tablespoon ascorbic acid in 1 quart of water. Hold produce in solution no longer than 30 minutes; drain before drying.

Equipment

Other than an electric dehydrator, equipment needed for drying food is found in a well-equipped kitchen. A food processor with slicing and grating blades, vegetable slicer with adjustable blade, grater, and food blender are useful tools for cutting uniform pieces or puréeing food.

Food dehydration can be done by several methods. Natural methods, such as sun and room drying, require warm days of 90°F or more, low humidity, little air pollution and control of insects for a quality finished product. Oven drying is a good choice only for small quantities of food because the energy costs of operating a gas or an electric oven are high compared to the cost of operating an electric food dehydrator. Also, a conventional oven only heats food and does not carry away moisture.

Commercial or homemade electric dehydrators provide the most reliable and consistent results, often without pretreatment, because of the controlled temperature and air flow. Food dehydrated by this method dries quickly and evenly. The quality of the finished product can be excellent. Food can be dried 24 hours a day, summer or winter, rain or shine.

Quality, cost, efficiency, and personal needs should be assessed when considering the purchase of a food dehydrator. Inexpensive dehydrators may not operate efficiently, resulting in greater energy costs than the actual savings of preserving foods by dehydration. Selecting a dehydrator that offers greater capacity than will be practical for your needs also wastes energy dollars. If a food dehydrator is used frequently and to its maximum capacity each time it is operated, dehydration can be a very cost-effective way to preserve foods.

When looking for a dehydrator to purchase, or if you plan to build a dehydrator, be certain the following features are built into the dehydrator to ensure quality results:

Heat Source: should be efficient and durable, enclosed for safety and have sufficient wattage for the entire drying area, about 70 watts per tray.

Fan: should be proportional to the dryer's capacity, and it should be quiet.

Thermostat: should be an adjustable temperature control with a range from 85° to 160°F.

Drying Trays: should be made of safe, food-grade material, such as stainless steel, nylon, or plastic. Copper, aluminum, or plated metal (such as cadmium or zinc plate) should not come in contact with drying food. Copper reduces vitamin C in many foods. Aluminum discolors some fruits. Galvanized plated metal contains cadmium and zinc, which can be dissolved by fruit acids and cause the fruit to become toxic. Trays should have adequate spaces for air circulation and be easy to load, unload, and clean.

Construction Quality: should be of plastic or metal approved for food contact, durable, and easy to clean. Electrical components must be UL approved. The dehydrator should come with a warranty and information for factory repair service. Dehydrators may be made at home. Contact your state or county Cooperative Extension Service for more information.

The Drying Process

Temperature plays a key role in the drying process. If the temperature is too high, food may case harden; that is, cook and harden on the outside while trapping moisture on the inside. Generally, vegetables are dried at 125°F, fruits at 135°F, and meats at 145°F.

There are other variables to consider when timing foods in a dehydrator: the amount of natural water in the food, the size and thickness of the food, the relative humidity of the air, and the efficiency of the dehydrator. Vegetables may take as little as 3 to 4 hours or up to 14 hours to dry, depending on the above variables. For example, sliced cultivated mushrooms may dry in an average of 4 to 6 hours, while beets may take as long as 12 to 14 hours to dry.

Determining Weight of Dehydrated Foods

Testing fruits and vegetables for dryness can be done simply by tasting and touching. The following equation will also be helpful in determining if the correct amount of moisture has been removed from foods.

1. After peeling, coring, etc., weigh prepared produce. (For example, peeled, cored, sliced apples weigh 10 pounds.)

2. See the recipe for the water content of fruits or vegetables (apples = 84%).

3. The total weight of water equals the weight of prepared fruit multiplied by the percent of water content (10 x 0.84 = 8.4 pounds of water).

4. Most fruits need 80% of their water content removed; most vegetables need 95% of their water content removed. To find the weight of the water that needs to be removed, multiply the total weight of water by the percent of water to be removed. (For apples, 8.4 x 0.80 = 6.72 pounds of the water to remove.)

5. To find how much the produce should weigh after dehydration, subtract the weight of the water to be removed from the weight of the fresh product. (For apples, 10 pounds prepared apples - 6.72 pounds of water = 3.28 pounds of dried apples.) In this technique, if one starts out with 10 pounds of prepared apples, the apples will be sufficiently dehydrated when they weigh about 3¼ pounds (see figure 13).

Figure 13 | **Fresh Weight Vs. Dried Weight**

Fruits		Vegetables	
20 Pounds Prepared Produce	Yield Dehydrated Produce	20 Pounds Prepared Produce	Yield Dehydrated Produce
Apples	6½	Beans (Green, Wax)	3
Cherries (Sweet)	7	Carrots	3 to 3½
Peaches	6½ to 7	Corn	6
Pears	6½ to 7	Onions	3
Prune Plums	7½	Peas	5 to 5½
		Squash (Summer)	2

Storage

Any food-safe container that protects from air, moisture, light, and insects will extend the shelf life of dried foods. Home canning jars have the advantage of keeping out these spoilers while providing a convenient "see-through" container. Jars should be washed in hot, soapy water, rinsed, and dried. If a dishwasher is used to clean jars, allow the jars to cool completely before filling. Adjust cap onto the jar. Label the jar with the name of the recipe or product and the date it was dehydrated.

Glass jars with twist-on caps, plastic storage containers with snap-on lids, and vacuum packaging also keep dehydrated foods protected from air, moisture, and insects.

Store dried foods in a cool, dry, dark place. The best storage temperature for dehydrated foods is between 50° and 70°F. Most fruits and vegetables can be safely stored from 6 months to 1 year, depending on storage temperature, humidity, and storage container. Check dried fruits and vegetables occasionally for moisture. If moisture is apparent, dispose of food.

Rehydrating Dried Foods

Fruits and vegetables can be rehydrated and used like fresh foods for casseroles, salads, and other prepared dishes. Directions for rehydrating fruits and vegetables are given at the beginning of the sections for drying fruits and vegetables (see page 164 and page 166). Foods may be rehydrated before use or as a part of the cooking and baking process. Follow individual recipe guidelines for using dehydrated foods in cooking and baking.

Understanding the following points will help you achieve successful results when rehydrating foods:

- Vegetables dried to 5% residual moisture take longer to rehydrate than fruit dried to 20% residual moisture content.

- Small or thin pieces of fruits and vegetables rehydrate in less time than large pieces.

- Blanched vegetables rehydrate more quickly than unblanched vegetables.

- Boiling water shortens rehydration time.
- Rehydration is quicker in soft water than in hard water.
- Sugar and salt increase time for food rehydration; add sugar or salt during the last 5 minutes of rehydration for best results.

Fruits

As a rule, most fruits can be successfully dried. However, a few fruits, such as avocados, citrus fruits, and melons, are best if eaten fresh. Sweet, ripe fruits in their natural state will be sweet and delicious when dried.

Some fruits, such as grapes, plums, and blueberries, have a waxy coating or "bloom" that must be "checked" or removed by dipping in boiling water before beginning the drying process. Other fruits, such as peaches, plums, and apricots, benefit by using a technique called "popping the backs." This means pushing the peel side inward to expose more of the pulp surface to dry. It may take up to 24 hours to properly dry stone fruit.

Uniformly cutting slices or pieces of fruit will help fruit to dry more evenly. Dried fruit should retain some moisture, about 15% to 20%. To test for dryness, cut a piece in half; no visible moisture should be present. The piece of fruit should be pliable and chewy. Bananas and strawberries should be almost crisp for best protection against mold.

Pack dehydrated fruits in home canning jars, plastic storage containers, or vacuum package. Label and date.

Dried fruit is a natural, sweet-tasting snack. However, there may be times when you will want to rehydrate the fruit for eating and serving. To rehydrate, add just enough boiling water to cover the fruit, wait 10 minutes, and serve immediately or use in a favorite recipe.

Apples

Choose any tart, firm-textured apple. Wash, peel, and core apples. Cut into ¼- to ½-inch slices or rings. Pretreat with Fruit-Fresh by dipping. Dry at 130° to 135°F until pliable. Use as a snack, for applesauce, or in baked goods, such as pies, cobblers, or crisps. Water content 84%.

Apricots

Choose any firm, ripe apricot with a deep-yellow to orange color. Wash, cut in half, and remove pits. Pretreat with Fruit-Fresh by dipping, if desired. Dry at 130° to 135°F until pliable with no moisture pockets. Use as a snack or in meat dishes, salads, or baked goods. Water content 85%.

Bananas

Choose any large, slightly brown-speckled yellow variety. Peel and cut into ¼- to ½-inch slices. Pretreat with Fruit-Fresh by dipping, if desired. Dry at 130° to 135°F until pliable to almost crisp. Use in trail mixes, cookies, cakes, breads, on cereals, or as a snack. Water content 76%.

Blueberries

Choose large, firm blueberries with deep-blue color. Wash and remove stems. Dip in boiling water 30 seconds to "check" skins. Blueberries dried without boiling first have a puffy appearance. Dry at 130° to 135°F until leathery. Use like raisins in baked goods. Water content 83%.

Cherries

Choose sweet or sour varieties. Wash, cut in half, and remove pits. Dry at 165°F 2 to 3 hours; then dry at 135°F until leathery and slightly sticky. Use sweet cherries as a snack or like raisins in baked goods. Use sour varieties in baked goods. Water content: sweet 80%, sour 84%.

Citrus Peel

Choose peels from grapefruit, lemon, lime, orange, or tangerine. Do not use fruit labeled "Color Added." Wash well to remove surface dirt and pesticides. Cut a thin layer of peel from fruit, avoiding the bitter, white pith. Dry at 135°F until crisp. Use as a flavoring in baked goods.

Coconuts

Choose fresh coconuts heavy and full of coconut milk. Pierce eyes to remove milk; crack the hard, outer shell with a hammer. Remove coconut meat, discarding dark, outer skin. Grate or thinly slice. Dry at 135°F until crisp. Use in pies, cakes, candies, and trail mixes. Water content 51%.

Grapes Home-Dried Raisins

Choose Thompson seedless or red seedless varieties. Wash, remove stems, and leave whole. Dip in boiling water 30 to 60 seconds to "check" skins. Dry at 130° to 135°F until pliable with no moisture pockets. Use raisins as a snack or in baked goods. Water content 81%.

Nectarines

Choose bright-looking, plump fruit with an orange-yellow color between red areas. Wash, cut in half, and remove pits. Cut into ¼- to ½-inch slices. Pretreat with Fruit-Fresh by dipping, if desired. Place on drying trays peel-side down. Dry at 130° to 135°F until pliable with no moisture pockets. Use as a snack or in baked goods. Water content 82%.

Peaches

Choose either clingstone or freestone varieties. Peaches must be firm and ripe with no green color. Wash peaches; dip in boiling water 30 to 60 seconds, then dip in cold water to loosen peels. Cut off peels. Remove pits; cut into ½-inch slices or circles. Pretreat with Fruit-Fresh by dipping. Dry at 130° to 135°F until pliable with no moisture pockets. Use as a snack or in baked goods, salads, or desserts. Water content 89%.

Pears

Choose any summer or winter variety. Allow pears to ripen at home before drying. Wash, peel, and core. Cut into ½-inch slices, quarters, or halves. Pretreat with Fruit-Fresh by dipping, if desired. Dry at 130° to 135°F until leathery with no moisture pockets. Use as a snack or in baked goods. Water content 83%.

Pineapples

Choose only fully-ripe pineapples with a yellowish-brown peel. Wash, peel, and core pineapple. Cut into ½-inch slices. Dry at 130° to 135°F until leathery but not sticky. Use as a snack or in baked goods and granolas. Water content 86%.

Plums

Choose any variety of ripe, sweet plums. Wash, cut in half, and remove pits. Cut into ¼- to ½-inch slices. Dry at 130° to 135°F until pliable. Use as a snack or in puddings, muffins, or breads. Water content 87%.

Prune Plums Homemade Prunes

Remember, all prunes are plums, but not all plums can be prunes. Ripe prune plums are slightly soft with a sweet flesh. Wash, cut in half, and remove pits. "Pop the back" of fruit to increase surface area (see page 164). Dry peel side down at 130° to 135°F until pliable with no moisture pockets. Use in breads, stuffings and salads, or as a snack. Water content 79%.

Strawberries

Choose ripe, juicy red berries. Gently wash. Remove caps. Cut into ½-inch slices. Dry at 130° to 135°F until pliable to almost crisp. Use in puddings, yogurt and dessert, or as a snack. Water content 90%.

Note: Strawberries do not rehydrate well.

Fruit Leathers

Fruit leather is puréed fruit which is dried and rolled into a chewy fruit taffy. It is a delicious, nutritious snack for lunch boxes and after school snacks, or to tote along anywhere.

Apples, apricots, berries (all kinds), cherries, nectarines, peaches, pears, pineapple, and plums make excellent fruit leathers. Be sure to remove excess seeds from berries. Bananas are wonderful blended with other fruits for a smooth, naturally sweet finished product. Fresh fruit in season has the best flavor; however, do not overlook canned or frozen fruits, which may be used any time of the year.

Pack dehydrated fruit leather rolls or pieces in home canning jars or vacuum package. Label and date.

Assorted Fruit Leathers

Wash fruit and cut away blemished areas. Peel, if necessary, and remove pits or seeds. Purée fruit in a blender until smooth.

Thin purée with a little water or fruit juice if it is too thick. Add 1 tablespoon honey or corn syrup if fruit is too tart, if desired. Spices or flavorings may be added at this time. Fruits that oxidize (apples, nectarines, peaches, and pears) should be heated to 190°F and allowed to cool before proceeding. Cover drying trays with a heavy, food-grade plastic wrap or use specifically designed sheets that come with most dehydrators. Spread purée evenly, about ⅛-inch thick in the center to ½-inch thick at the edges, on dehydrator trays. Dry at 135°F until fruit purée feels pliable and leather-like. Check center to be sure there are no sticky spots. Cut fruit leather in strips or circles while still warm. Leave pieces flat or roll, jelly roll-style. Let fruit leather cool. Wrap fruit leather in parchment paper or plastic wrap, placing a piece of paper or wrap between layers. Pack into home canning jar, plastic storage container, or vacuum package. Label and date.

Mango Leather

| 2 pounds mangoes | 1 tablespoon lemon juice |
| 2 tablespoons corn syrup | |

Wash mangoes; drain. Peel, pit, and dice mangoes. Purée mangoes using a food processor or food mill. Add corn syrup and lemon juice; blend. Spread purée evenly on dehydrator trays to ¼-inch thick. Dry at 135°F until pliable, about 12 to 14 hours. Cut mango leather into 6-inch circles. Place parchment paper or plastic wrap between circles. Pack into a plastic storage container or vacuum package. Label and date.

Beef Jerky

Jerky is raw meat or fish which is salted or marinated, then dried. Although almost any type of lean meat (beef, lamb, pork, or game) or fish may be used, beef jerky is the easiest to make with the most reliable results. Choose any lean cut of beef. Flank, round, or sirloin tip are excellent choices. Rump, if it is lean, is also a good choice. Use only a commercial or homemade electric food dehydrator. Do not attempt to dry meat in the sun, because doing so increases the risk of spoilage and contamination.

Freeze meat slightly to aid in slicing. Cut beef in strips, ½-inch thick, across the grain for a tender, slightly brittle finished product. Cut with the grain for a chewy end product.

The meat must be "cured," that is, treated in such a way as to prevent spoilage. Dry cures are salt and seasonings rubbed on the meat surface. Brine cures are marinades or liquid seasoning mixtures in which the meat is soaked for a period of time. Vacuum packaging sliced meat and marinade will reduce the length of time it takes for the marinade to penetrate the meat. Not only is this method quicker, but it allows the marinade to penetrate deeper, locking in the great taste.

Dry meat in an electric dehydrator at 145°F. If fat droplets appear during the drying process, blot meat with a paper towel. To test a slice of meat, allow to cool. It should bend, but not break.

Jerky must be brought to an internal temperature of 160°F just prior to drying or immediately after drying. Two methods are recommended: heat meat strips in marinade before drying by boiling 5 minutes. Alternatively, heat dehydrated meat strips in an oven at 275°F for 10 minutes after the drying process is completed. Check the internal temperature of the jerky with a prong-type meat thermometer to ensure it has reached 160°F. Heating strips of meat in a marinade before dehydrating reduces the drying time.

Jerky that has been properly dehydrated and brought to an internal temperature of 160°F can be stored on the shelf. Pack in home canning jars or plastic storage containers. If the jerky is slightly moist after dehydrating, store in the freezer. Check jerky that is stored on the shelf periodically for indications of weeping. Weeping is any moisture from water, brine, marinade, or fat that appears on the surface of jerky. If weeping is evident, dispose of jerky.

Barbecued Beef Jerky

Yield: about 12 ounces

- 3 pounds lean beef (flank, round, or sirloin tip)
- 1 cup ketchup
- 1/2 cup red wine vinegar
- 1/4 cup brown sugar
- 2 tablespoons Worcestershire sauce
- 2 teaspoons dry mustard
- 1 teaspoon onion powder
- 1 teaspoon salt
- 1/4 teaspoon cracked pepper
- Dash of hot pepper sauce

Cut beef into strips 1/2-inch thick. Combine all marinade ingredients in a large glass baking dish. Add strips of beef; cover and refrigerate overnight. Drain beef slices. Dry in an electric dehydrator at 145°F until pliable. Package in home canning jars, plastic storage containers, or vacuum package. Label and date.

Soy Jerky

Yield: about 12 ounces

- 3 pounds lean beef (flank, round, or sirloin tip)
- 3/4 cup soy sauce
- 1/4 cup Worcestershire sauce
- 1/4 cup brown sugar
- 1 teaspoon onion powder
- 1 clove garlic, crushed
- 1/2 teaspoon cracked pepper
- 1/4 teaspoon liquid smoke (optional)

Cut beef into strips 1/2-inch thick. Combine all marinade ingredients in a large glass baking dish. Add strips of beef; cover and refrigerate overnight. Drain beef slices. Dry in an electric dehydrator at 145°F until pliable. Package in home canning jars, plastic storage containers, or vacuum package. Label and date.

Vegetables

Most vegetables, from asparagus to zucchini, can be dehydrated at home. Select garden-fresh, top-quality produce for the best results. Remember, although dried vegetables retain most of their vitamin and mineral content as well as their good flavor, the original quality cannot be improved upon.

All vegetables require some preparation, such as removing stems, peels, or seeds before drying. Like fruits, uniformly-cut slices or pieces of vegetables result in even drying. Unlike fruits, vegetables are better cut slightly smaller to hasten drying time. Vegetables lose flavor and tenderness if the drying time is prolonged. Drying time varies from about 4 to 14 hours. A temperature of 125°F is recommended for most vegetables. Finished vegetables should contain about 5% moisture. When tested, vegetables should look and feel crisp or brittle.

Vegetables can be eaten dried, but they are usually reconstituted before using. An equal volume of water and dried vegetables is needed. Boiling water will shorten the rehydration time.

It takes 15 minutes to 3 hours to reconstitute vegetables. The length of time it takes to reconstitute vegetables varies depending on the texture, thickness, and size of pieces.

If a vegetable is not listed in the following pages, freezing or canning may be a more suitable method of food preservation.

Pack dehydrated vegetables in home canning jars, plastic storage containers, or vacuum package. Label and date.

Asparagus

Choose young, tender stalks. Wash; cut off tough end. Slice into 1-inch pieces. Steam blanch 3 to 4 minutes. Dry at 125°F until brittle. Rehydrate and serve in soups or with seasoned cream sauce. Water content 92%.

Beans – Green or Wax

Choose any variety with crisp, thick walls and small seeds. Wash beans; remove strings and cut off ends. Cut beans diagonally into 1-inch pieces or French cut to expose more surface area. Steam blanch 4 to 6 minutes. Freeze beans 30 minutes to tenderize; dry at 125°F until brittle. Rehydrate and use in casseroles, soups, and stews. Water content 90%.

Beets

Choose any variety with deep red color and smooth skins. Wash; remove all but two inches of stem and tap root. Steam about 30 minutes or until tender. Cool; peel; trim stem and tap root. Cut into 1/4-inch slices or dice. Dry at 125°F until leathery. Use in soups or reconstitute for other uses. Water content 87%.

Carrots

Choose any deep orange, mature variety. Wash, remove stem ends, and peel. Slice crosswise or dice. Steam blanch 3 to 4 minutes. Dry at 125°F until almost brittle. Use in soups, stews, and carrot cake. Water content 88%.

Corn

Choose any yellow variety with tender, sweet kernels. Husk corn; remove silks and wash. Steam until milk is set. Cool. Carefully cut corn from cob. Dry at 125°F until brittle. Use in soups, chowders and fritters, or to make cornmeal. Water content 73%.

Mushrooms

Choose only edible, cultivated mushrooms with small, closed caps. Wash quickly to remove dirt; cut into 1/4-inch slices. Dry at 125°F until brittle. Use in soups, sauces, and casseroles. Water content 90%.

Okra

Choose any firm pod 2 to 4 inches long. Wash; cut off ends; slice crosswise 1/4-inch thick. Dry at 125°F until leathery. Use in soups and gumbos, rehydrate and bread okra for deep-fat frying . Water content 89%.

Onions and Leeks

Choose red, white, or yellow onions; white varieties dry best. Choose leeks about 1- to 1½-inch diameter at bulb end. Trim ends off onions; peel off paper shell; cut into slices 1/4-inch thick. Trim root end off leeks; cut white and light green portion into 1/4-inch slices; discard dark leafy top. Dry at 145°F until crisp. Use in soups, stews and casseroles, or use powdered (or flaked) for seasoning. Water content 89%.

Peas

Choose medium-size peas. Shell and wash peas. Steam blanch 3 minutes. Dry at 125°F until brittle. Use in soups and stews, or reconstitute for other uses. Water content 78%.

Peppers – Hot

Choose any hot variety. Wash; cut into pieces about 1/4- to 1-inch thick. Dry at 125°F until crisp. Crush or grind and use as a seasoning in soups, stews, casseroles, and Mexican foods. Water content 93%.

Note: When cutting or seeding hot peppers, wear rubber gloves to prevent hands from being burned.

Peppers – Bell

Choose any well-shaped bell pepper. Wash; remove stem and seeds; dice. Dry at 125°F until leathery. Use to season a variety of foods. Water content 93%.

Popcorn

Choose varieties specifically grown for popping. Leave kernels on cob until dried. Dry at 130°F until shriveled. Test a few kernels to see if they pop. Popcorn should have a dehydrated moisture content of 10%. Water content 73%.

Potatoes – Sweet and Yams

Choose thick, orange potatoes. Wash, peel, and cut into 1/4-inch slices. Steam blanch 3 minutes. Dry at 125°F until brittle. Use to make candied yams or bake in pies, and breads. Water content 71%.

Potatoes – White

Choose any white variety. Wash, peel, and cut into slices 1/4-inch thick. Steam blanch 5 to 6 minutes. Rinse well in cold water to remove starch. Dry at 125°F until crisp. Use in soups, casseroles, and potato dishes. Water content 80%.

Pumpkin

Choose a cooking variety. Wash, peel, and remove fibers and seeds. Cut into small, thin strips. Steam blanch 2 to 3 minutes or until tender. Dry at 125°F until brittle. Use in pies and baked goods. Water content 90%.

Tomatoes

Choose paste-type varieties. Wash; dip in boiling water 30 to 60 seconds; transfer to cold water. Cut off peel and core. Cut into slices 1/4-inch thick. Dry at 145°F until crisp. Use in soups and sauces, or combine with other vegetables for flavor. Can be powdered and used to make tomato sauces, paste, or ketchup. Water content 94%.

Turnips or Rutabagas

Choose firm, round turnips or rutabagas. Wash, remove tops, and peel. Cut into slices 1/4- to 1/2-inch thick. Steam blanch 3 to 5 minutes. Dry at 125°F until brittle. Use in soups or with potatoes. Thinly-sliced turnip chips are an excellent snack. Water content turnips 92%, rutabagas 87%.

Zucchini

Choose young, slender zucchini. Wash zucchini. Cut into 1/4-inch slices or 1/2-inch slices for chips. Dry at 125°F until brittle. Use in soups and casseroles. Sprinkle zucchini chips with seasoned salt and serve with dips. Water content 94%.

Dehydrating Step-By-Step

Using a dehydrator to preserve food

One of the oldest methods used to extend the shelf life of food is dehydration. Most foods can be preserved by removing moisture, so that yeasts, molds, and bacteria cannot grow and spoil the food. An electric food dehydrator adds greatly to the simplicity of drying foods. Unlike sun-drying or vine-drying, the electric food dehydrator is not dependent on Mother Nature for perfect weather conditions. ❶ An electric food dehydrator has a consistent heat source to extract moisture and a fan to carry moisture away, so that food can be dehydrated at any time of year regardless of the weather conditions outside. Oven drying is another option for indoor drying, but it is more costly to operate and lacks the controls needed to achieve the desired results. Room drying is fine for such foods as herbs, garlic, and peppers; however, this method takes much longer than the length of time needed when using an electric food dehydrator.

Prep

Not all fruits, vegetables, meats, and herbs are suitable to be dehydrated. Check this section for drying instructions for the food product you select before you begin. Determine the best type of package to use for the finished dried food. Because this method of preserving removes most of the water contained in food, it will shrink in size and weight. The number of containers needed to store dried food is considerably fewer compared to other methods of preserving food.

Apples make one of the best dried foods. Begin with fresh, tart apples to help ensure the dried version is flavorful and nutritious. ❷ Wash apples under cold running water; dry. Remove stems and cores. Apples may be dehydrated with or without their peel. Cut apples crosswise into ¼- to ½-inch slices. Cutting slices uniformly will help apples to dry evenly. ❸ Oxidation causes sliced apples to brown due to exposure to oxygen in air. Browning can be slowed by treating apple slices with an antioxidant. Treat apples to prevent browning as they are sliced. Place sliced apples in a mixture of 2 rounded tablespoons of Fruit-Fresh and 2 quarts of water. Hold apple slices in the antioxidant solution no more than 30 minutes.

Dehydrate

❹ Place apple slices onto the drying trays in a single layer, being certain the apple slices do not overlap or touch each other. Apple slices are usually large enough that they will not fall through the perforations in the tray. Even though the apple slices will shrink as moisture is removed, it's not necessary to use flexible screens or parchment paper to line the trays. Drying screens or parchment paper are needed when making apple chips or apple leather. Dry apple slices at 130° to 135°F until they are pliable and show no signs of surface moisture. To test for dryness, fold an apple slice in half; the apple slice should not stick to itself. Now squeeze the folded apple slice. The surface should remain dry. If the apple slice fails the dryness test, return all apple slices to the dehydrator for additional drying time.

Package

❺ Let the apple slices cool about 30 to 60 minutes, then package. Long delays in packaging dried foods may allow moisture that is in the air to migrate into the food. Layer dried apple slices loosely into jar, container, or bag. Pack slices close to each other without pressing them together. Adjust lid onto jar or container, or secure bag closed.

Store

❻ Label each container with the name of the dried food and the date it was dehydrated. Check the containers for the next 10 days for signs of condensation inside the container and moisture on the food. If either is present, return the food to the dehydrator for additional drying time. Dehydrated fruits, vegetables, and meats are shelf stable, but they should be evaluated periodically to ensure they do not absorb moisture during storage. If moisture is evident on fruits or vegetables, or if meats appear moist with water or fat, dispose of the food.

1 Gather together recipe ingredients, electric dehydrator, and storage containers.

2 Prepare apples for dehydrating.

3 Prevent apples from browning.

4 Arrange sliced apples on drying trays.

5 Package dried apple slices in rigid containers.

6 Store dehydrated foods in a cool, dark place, having low humidity.

Meal Creations

Creating home-cooked meals, whether for everyday meals or special occasions, is where your talents as a fresh food preserver can truly "shine through." You'll be able to elevate even the most humble of dishes to new heights by using the foods you've preserved along the way. Side dishes, fruit pies—even seafood can benefit from what you've been able to create. Even better, you'll know that you're serving your family and friends the best possible meals by ensuring that quality ingredients are being used in every aspect of your meal.

Getting Started

You can (and should!) use your home preserved foods to prepare recipes in the same ways as store-bought foods, whether they are canned, frozen, or dried. The fresh, natural taste will enhance any recipe. And you'll find it extremely satisfying, knowing that the food you are serving is free from artificial additives and preservatives.

Measure before you mix

Keep in mind that one jar of home canned food may not hold the same volume or weight as one jar of commercially-processed food, so before you mix in your fresh preserved ingredients, measure them using cup measures or a food scale. Don't use the jar as a unit of measurement, since the quantity of food packed into a jar can vary.

Stir in flavor to create new dishes

Fresh preserving allows you to make food with unique flavor combinations that shine on their own, but when you mix them into some of your favorite prepared dishes, they sing! So next time, when you're cooking something in the kitchen, think about what you've already created—reach for your fresh preserved foods to add that extra level of flavor to any recipe.

Create your own taste sensations

Some of the hottest new food trends are just rediscovered favorites. This book is loaded with recipes that will provide that one-of-a-kind taste you are seeking. Be bold—use these sauces, jams, pickles, and relishes to create your own signature foods—they make extraordinarily good toppings, glazes, or stir-ins. Our Meal Creations ideas are just the beginning of all the good things you can create.

Featured Recipe | **Apricot-Honey Mustard Grilled Chicken** page 175

Breakfast

Apple Butter Pancakes

Makes about 4 servings

- 1½ cups plus 2 tablespoons all-purpose flour
- 2 tablespoons sugar
- 2 teaspoons baking powder
- ½ teaspoon cinnamon
- ½ teaspoon salt
- ¼ teaspoon ground ginger
- ¼ teaspoon nutmeg
- 1 cup milk
- ½ cup homemade apple butter (see page 44)
- 2 tablespoons canola oil, plus extra for cooking
- 1 egg
- 1 8-ounce jar Maple-Walnut Syrup (see page 130)

PREP To Make Pancake Batter—Combine all-purpose flour, sugar, baking powder, cinnamon, salt, ground ginger, and ground nutmeg in a medium bowl. Lightly whisk milk, apple butter, canola oil, and egg to combine. Fold liquid mixture into dry ingredients until evenly blended.

COOK Warm the Maple-Walnut Syrup in a small saucepan over low heat, or warm in a microwave oven. Cover syrup to keep warm until serving.

Heat a shallow saucepan over medium heat. Add a scant amount of oil in pan. After the oil begins to sizzle, but not burn, pour in ¼ cup batter for each pancake. Cook pancakes about 2 to 3 minutes or until bubbles begin to break the surface and edges start to brown. Turn pancake over and continue cooking about 2 minutes or until cooked through.

SERVE Serve warm Apple Butter Pancakes with warm Maple-Walnut Syrup.

Banana Nut Bread

Makes one 9-inch loaf

- 1 cup dried banana chips or pieces (see page 164)
- 1 cup water
- 1¼ cups all-purpose flour
- 2¼ teaspoons baking powder
- ½ teaspoon salt
- ⅔ cup sugar
- ⅓ cup vegetable shortening
- 2 eggs, slightly beaten
- ½ cup chopped pecans or walnuts

PREP Rehydrate bananas in 1 cup water for 1 hour. Lightly coat the inside of a 9- x 5- x 3-inch loaf pan with nonstick cooking spray. Sift together flour, baking powder, and salt. Cream together sugar and shortening. Add dry ingredients to sugar mixture. Stir in bananas, eggs, and nuts until well-blended. Pour batter into prepared pan.

BAKE Place pan on the center oven rack and bake at 350°F for 1 hour, or until done. Cool on wire rack.

SERVE Cut bread into ½-inch slices.

Blueberry Focaccia

Makes about two 9-inch loaves

- 5½ cups unbleached bread flour
- 2½ cups tepid water (about 55°F)
- 2⅓ tablespoons granulated sugar
- 2 teaspoons granulated salt
- ½ teaspoon dried thyme
- ½ teaspoon dried savory
- 1 (1¼-ounce) packet instant yeast
- ½ cup extra-virgin olive oil
- 1¼ cups dried blueberries (see page 164)
- Sea salt or kosher salt, if desired

PREP Combine flour, water, sugar, salt, dried thyme, dried savory, and yeast in a large mixing bowl. Slowly mix ingredients, using a paddle beater, until the mixture forms into a ball around the paddle beater, about 30 seconds. Replace the paddle beater with a dough hook. Mix the dough on medium-low for 3 minutes. Scrape dough off the hook; let the dough rest for 5 minutes. Continue to mix the dough on medium-low for 3 minutes. The dough should be smooth. Coat the inside of a bowl that is twice the size of the dough ball with 1 tablespoon of olive oil. Place dough in the oiled bowl; turn dough over to coat the other side with olive oil.

Wet one hand with water. Holding the bowl with your dry hand, stretch the dough to about twice its size. Fold stretched dough back over itself. Rotate the bowl a quarter turn. Repeat stretching and folding dough 3 times, rotating bowl a quarter turn after each stretch. Rub about 1 tablespoon olive oil over dough; turn dough over and rub other side to lightly coat it with olive oil. Tightly cover bowl with plastic wrap. Refrigerate overnight, or at least 8 hours.

Remove dough from refrigerator 4 hours before desired baking time. Cover baking sheet with parchment paper or silicone mat. Coat surface with 2 tablespoons olive oil. Gently transfer dough to the middle of the pan. Dough will lose some volume. Drizzle 2 tablespoons olive oil over dough. Spread dough outward from the center towards the edges of the pan until it begins to resist. Start dimpling the dough using your fingertips and working from the center to the outside edges, pressing fingertips straight down to create hollows in the dough. Dimple the entire surface. Let dough rest for 20 minutes. Drizzle another 2 tablespoons of olive oil over the surface of the dough; dimple again. Dough should be about ¼- to ½-inch thick and nearly fill all space on the pan.

Cover the dough loosely with oiled plastic wrap. Set the pan on a cooling rack to allow for air circulation. Let the dough rise at room temperature until it is about 1½ times its original size. This will take about 2 to 3 hours, depending on the room temperature.

BAKE Take plastic wrap off dough. Gently press dried blueberries into the surface of the dough. Sprinkle dough lightly with sea salt or kosher salt, if desired. Bake at 450°F for 15 minutes, then rotate the pan a half turn, continue baking about 7 minutes. When the focaccia is done, it will be golden brown on top. Remove from oven and allow to cool 10 minutes.

SERVE Cut focaccia into individual servings.

Jelly-Filled Oat Muffins

Makes about 12 muffins

Muffins

1 1/2 cups all-purpose flour
1 cup quick oats
1 1/2 teaspoons baking powder
1 teaspoon cinnamon
3/4 teaspoon baking soda
1/4 teaspoon salt
1/2 cup brown sugar

1/4 cup butter or margarine, softened
1 egg
1 1/4 cups buttermilk
3/4 cup raisins
1/4 cup Cinnamon Anise Jelly (see page 123)

Crunchy Topping

1/3 cup all-purpose flour
1/2 cup finely chopped walnuts
2 tablespoons brown sugar

3 tablespoons butter or margarine

PREP To Make Muffins—Lightly coat the inside of muffin cups with nonstick cooking spray. Combine flour, quick oats, baking powder, cinnamon, baking soda, and salt in a medium bowl. Combine brown sugar, butter, and egg in a large bowl; mix well. Add dry ingredients alternately with milk to sugar mixture. Stir in raisins. Fill each muffin cup 2/3 full with batter. Spoon 1 teaspoon Cinnamon Anise Jelly into the center of each muffin. Carefully add additional batter evenly over jelly to cover; set aside.

To Make Topping—In a small bowl, combine flour, walnuts, and brown sugar. Cut in butter until mixture resembles coarse crumbs. Sprinkle crunchy topping over muffins.

BAKE Put muffin pans on the center oven rack and bake at 375°F for 18 to 25 minutes or until tops are lightly brown and spring back when lightly touched. Cool 5 minutes on wire rack.

SERVE Remove muffins from pan; serve when completely cool.

Mixed Vegetable Quiche

Makes about 8 servings

1/2 cup dried mixed vegetables (see pages 166 and 167)
1/2 cup boiling water
2 cups milk or cream
3 eggs

1/4 teaspoon salt
1/8 teaspoon pepper
1/2 cup shredded Swiss cheese
1 9-inch pastry for single-crust pie

PREP Combine dried vegetables and boiling water in a medium bowl; let stand 1 to 2 hours or until vegetables are tender. Drain. Whisk together milk or cream, eggs, salt, and pepper. Stir in mixed vegetables. Pour mixture into a prepared pie shell. Sprinkle Swiss cheese evenly over the top.

COOK Place quiche on the center oven rack and bake at 375°F for 35 to 40 minutes or until golden brown and filling is set. Cool on a wire rack 5 minutes.

SERVE Cut quiche into individual servings; serve immediately.

Zucchini-Pineapple Doughnuts

Makes about 9 doughnuts

Doughnuts

1 1/4 cups (16-ounce jar) shredded Zucchini in Pineapple Juice (see page 27)
1 1/2 cups all-purpose flour
1 1/2 teaspoons baking powder
1/4 teaspoon baking soda
1/4 teaspoon salt

4 tablespoons unsalted butter, melted
1 egg
3/4 cup sugar
3/4 cup sour cream
1/2 teaspoon cinnamon
2 teaspoons clear vanilla

Glaze

4 ounces cream cheese
1/2 cup Confectioner's sugar
1 teaspoon clear vanilla

1/4 cup milk
1/2 cup lightly toasted coconut, optional

PREP To Make Doughnuts—Drain zucchini-pineapple using a sieve or colander placed over a large bowl. Press gently on zucchini to extract juice; reserve juice. Lightly coat the wells in the doughnut pans with nonstick cooking spray.

Stir together flour, baking powder, baking soda, salt, and cinnamon in a large bowl; set aside. In a medium bowl, whisk together egg and sugar until thick and creamy. Stir in 3/4 cup sour cream and vanilla. Combine flour mixture and egg mixture, stirring to slightly moisten ingredients, some dry ingredients will remain. Fold in drained, shredded zucchini-pineapple until all ingredients are evenly incorporated.

BAKE Ladle doughnut batter into wells of doughnut pans to 3/4 full. Bake doughnuts at 350°F for 18 to 20 minutes. Place pans on a wire cooling rack to cool. Allow doughnuts to cool completely before removing from pans.

To Make Glaze—Warm cream cheese in a warm oven or microwave oven just until it begins to melt. Stir in Confectioner's sugar and vanilla. Stir in milk or reserved zucchini-pineapple juice, gradually adding 1 tablespoon at a time, stirring to the desired consistency.

SERVE Dip doughnuts into glaze to coat the top. Sprinkle with toasted coconut, if desired.

Soups

Savory Carrot-Fennel Soup

Makes about 8 servings

1 bulb fennel, sliced
2 tablespoons extra-virgin olive oil
2 pounds carrots
3 cups vegetable stock (see page 108)

3 cups water
1 teaspoon coarse salt
1/4 teaspoon white pepper
8 ounces sour cream
1/2 red bell pepper, finely minced

PREP Wash fennel, carrots, and red bell pepper under cold running water. Remove fronds from fennel bulb. Thinly slice fennel crosswise. Remove stem end from carrots and peel. Cut carrots crosswise into 1/2-inch pieces.

COOK Sauté fennel in olive oil until transparent. Combine fennel, carrots, and vegetable stock in a large saucepan. Bring mixture to a boil. Reduce heat and simmer until carrots are tender. Purée mixture in a food processor or blender. Return purée to saucepan. Add water. Simmer until heated throughout. Stir in salt and pepper. Simmer 30 minutes.

SERVE Garnish individual servings with a dollop of sour cream and finely minced red bell pepper.

Vegetable Beef Soup

Makes about 8 servings

1 large soup bone with meat	1 cup crushed tomatoes
Water	1 beef bouillon cube
2 cups dried mixed vegetables (carrots, peas, corn, potatoes, green beans, onions, or other dried vegetables) (see pages 166 and 167)	1 tablespoon parsley
	1 teaspoon salt
	1/4 teaspoon pepper
	1/4 cup rice, barley, or soup pasta
2 cups boiling water	

PREP Rehydrate vegetables in 2 cups boiling water for 2 hours.

COOK Put soup bone into a large saucepan; add water to cover by 1 inch. Bring to a boil. Reduce heat and simmer, covered, 1 to 2 hours. Remove soup bone from stock; cut off meat. Combine 3 to 4 cups stock, meat, crushed tomatoes, bouillon cube, and seasonings. Bring mixture to a boil; reduce heat and simmer 30 minutes. Add reconstituted vegetables and rice, barley, or soup pasta. Add water if soup is too thick. Simmer about 1 hour, or until vegetables are tender.

SERVE Ladle hot soup into individual serving bowls.

Salads

Antipasto Platter

Makes about 6 servings

Pickled Grape Tomatoes in Herb Marinade

1 16-ounce jar Pickled Grape Tomatoes (see page 94)	1/2 teaspoon minced fresh thyme
1/2 cup extra-virgin olive oil	1/4 teaspoon kosher salt
1/2 teaspoon minced fresh rosemary	1/4 teaspoon fresh cracked pepper
1/2 teaspoon minced fresh oregano	

Platter

6 ounces small whole portabella mushrooms	6 ounces artichoke hearts
1/4 cup extra-virgin olive oil	2 tablespoons capers
1 1/2 pounds assorted Italian cured meats: prosciutto, salami, and bresaola	1/2 pound asparagus, steamed
1/2 cantaloupe, peeled and cut into thin wedges	1 8-ounce jar Onion Pickles (see page 93)
1 pound fresh mozzarella bocconcini	1 16-ounce jar Pickled Pepper Mix (see page 94)
8 ounces black or Italian olives	

PREP To Make Marinade—Drain pickled grape tomatoes, reserving pickling liquid. Combine pickling liquid, olive oil, herbs, and spices in a small bowl. Add pickled grape tomatoes, stirring to coat evenly with marinade. Refrigerate overnight.

ASSEMBLE Bring marinated pickled grape tomatoes to room temperature. Lightly sauté mushrooms in 1/4 cup olive oil. Cool. Wrap prosciutto around cantaloupe wedges and place on platter. Roll or fold salami and bresaola, then arrange on platter. Place olives, artichoke hearts, mushrooms, and asparagus on the platter. Use half of the marinade from the tomatoes to drizzle over vegetables. Add mozzarella bocconcini.

SERVE Garnish platter with capers. Serve marinated Pickled Grape tomatoes, Onion Pickles, and Pickled Pepper Mix with antipasto platter.

Arugula and Pickled Butternut Squash Salad

Makes about 4 servings

Salad

4 cups arugula	1 cup Pickled Butternut Squash, drained (see page 93)
1/2 red onion, thinly sliced	

Dressing

1/3 cup white wine vinegar	1/3 cup extra-virgin olive oil
2 teaspoons coarsely ground brown mustard	4 ounces fresh goat cheese or feta
1/2 teaspoon freshly ground pepper	1/2 cup walnut pieces

PREP To Make Salad—Combine arugula, pickled butternut squash, and red onion in a large bowl.

To Make Dressing—In a small bowl, whisk together vinegar, mustard, and pepper. Gradually whisk in the olive oil until all is incorporated and the mixture is smooth. Pour dressing over the salad and toss to coat well.

SERVE Place salad on a serving platter or divide among individual plates. Crumble cheese over the salad, then sprinkle with walnut pieces. Serve immediately.

Fruit Salad with Strawberry-Kiwi Dressing

Makes about 4 servings

Salad

4 cups mixed spring greens	2 kiwifruits, peeled and sliced
1 cup cantaloupe melon balls or cubes	1/2 cup red raspberries
1 cup honeydew melon balls or cubes	

Dressing

1 cup vanilla low-fat yogurt	2 tablespoons orange juice
1/2 cup Strawberry-Kiwi Jam (see page 125)	

Garnish

1/4 cup sliced almonds

PREP To Make Salad—Arrange a bed of mixed greens on individual salad plates. Divide melon, kiwifruit, and raspberries evenly among salad plates.

To Make Dressing—Combine yogurt, Strawberry-Kiwi Jam, and orange juice in a small bowl until well-blended.

BAKE To Make Garnish—Spread sliced almonds in a single layer on a baking sheet. Toast sliced almonds in the oven at 350°F for about 5 minutes, or until lightly browned. Cool.

SERVE Just before serving, spoon dressing over salads. Garnish with toasted sliced almonds.

Mixed Vegetable Pickles and Bowtie Pasta Salad

Makes about 8 servings

2½ cups Mixed Pickles, (see page 80)	8 ounces bowtie pasta
4 tablespoons extra-virgin olive oil, divided	1 cup cubed salami
2 tablespoons sugar	½ cup shredded Parmesan cheese
2 cloves garlic, finely minced	

PREP Drain mixed pickles, reserving pickling liquid for dressing. Whisk together ½ cup reserved pickling liquid, 3 tablespoons olive oil, sugar, and garlic in a small bowl. Cover; let stand 1 to 2 hours.

COOK Bring water to a rolling boil in a large saucepan. Add bowtie pasta and cook to desired doneness; drain. Put pasta in a large bowl. Add 1 tablespoon olive oil and toss gently.

SERVE Add 3 tablespoons olive oil, drained vegetables, and salami to pasta; toss gently. Sprinkle Parmesan cheese over pasta salad. Serve pasta salad immediately, or chill before serving.

Spinach Salad with Warm Pomegranate Dressing

Makes about 4 servings

Salad

1 pound fresh baby spinach, stemmed	½ red onion
1 orange	2 slices bacon

Dressing

½ cup Pomegranate Sauce (see page 129)	Pinch of fresh nutmeg
1 tablespoon honey or sugar	1 cup extra-virgin olive oil
1½ teaspoons minced fresh ginger	½ cup coarsely chopped walnuts

PREP To Make Salad—Wash spinach and orange under cold running water. Spread spinach over paper towel to dry. Cut off orange peel to expose fruit pulp. Remove pulp from each section. Dice orange pulp. Cut red onion crosswise into very thin slices. Separate onion slices into rings.

To Make Dressing—Combine Pomegranate Sauce, honey, ginger, and nutmeg in a food processor. Set processor on low speed. Slowly pour olive oil through the feed tube until olive oil is completely used and dressing is evenly blended.

COOK Place bacon in a small saucepan and cook until crisp. Drain bacon on a paper towel; let bacon cool. Break bacon into bite-sized pieces. Warm salad dressing over medium heat.

SERVE Place spinach in a large bowl. Pour dressing over spinach and toss to coat evenly. Top with orange, onion rings, and bacon. Garnish with walnuts.

Entrées

Apricot-Honey Mustard Glazed Chicken

Makes about 4 servings

4 boneless, skinless chicken breast halves (about 1 pound)	⅓ cup honey mustard
2 tablespoons sugar	2 teaspoons kosher salt, divided
⅓ cup white wine vinegar	⅓ cup dry white wine
¼ cup Apricot Preserves (see page 64)	Wooden or bamboo skewers, if desired

PREP Wash chicken breasts under cold running water. Pat chicken dry with paper towel. Cut chicken breasts in half on the diagonal; set aside. Combine sugar and vinegar in a small saucepan. Bring mixture to a boil over medium heat. Remove from heat. Add apricot preserves, mustard, 1 teaspoon salt, and wine, stirring to blend well.

To Use Skewers—Soak wooden or bamboo skewers in water for 30 minutes. Thread two chicken breasts pieces onto each skewer.

COOK Brush top of chicken breasts with apricot glaze. Place chicken breasts on grill or under broiler; cook 6 to 8 minutes. Turn chicken breasts over and brush with apricot glaze. Cook 6 to 8 minutes, or until done.

SERVE Remove chicken to platter. Serve with remaining apricot glaze.

Red Cabbage Slaw-Topped Burger

Makes about 4 servings

2 pounds ground beef	4 hamburger buns
1 teaspoon salt	4 large lettuce leaves, divided
¼ teaspoon freshly ground pepper	1 8-ounce jar Red Cabbage Slaw, drained and divided (see page 136)
4 ounces sliced cheddar cheese	

PREP Season ground beef with salt and pepper, mixing lightly to distribute evenly. Shape mixture into 4 hamburger patties.

COOK Place hamburgers on a hot grill or into a hot, shallow saucepan and cook 4 to 6 minutes on each side, or to desired doneness. After hamburgers have been turned over, place a slice of cheese on each hamburger; let cheese melt. Remove hamburgers to a plate.

SERVE Layer bottom half of hamburger buns with lettuce, hamburger, Red Cabbage Slaw, and top half of hamburger bun.

Chicken Cacciatore

Makes about 4 servings

1/3 cup all-purpose flour
1 teaspoon salt
1/4 teaspoon black pepper
3 to 3 1/2-pound broiler-fryer chicken, cut into pieces
2 tablespoons vegetable oil
1/2 cup chopped onions
1 cup sliced mushrooms
1 32-ounce jar Basil-Garlic Tomato Sauce (see page 33)
1/2 cup dry white wine or chicken broth
1 1/2 teaspoons sugar
2 tablespoons minced fresh parsley
Hot, cooked fettuccine or spaghetti

PREP Combine flour, salt, and pepper in a shallow dish. Coat chicken pieces with flour mixture.

COOK Heat oil in a large saucepan until hot. Cook chicken until brown on all sides. Drain oil from saucepan. Add remaining ingredients except minced parsley and pasta. Bring mixture to a boil, stirring to blend ingredients. Reduce heat, cover, and simmer 30 to 40 minutes or until chicken is tender.

SERVE Put pasta on a platter, place chicken over pasta, and ladle sauce over chicken. Garnish with minced parsley.

Crab Cakes with Dill Mustard Sauce

Makes about 8 servings

Crab Cakes

1/2 cup finely minced green onions
1 tablespoon unsalted butter
1/2 cup soft bread crumbs
1 tablespoon heavy cream
2 eggs, beaten
3 tablespoons minced parsley
1/2 teaspoon dry mustard
1/8 teaspoon red hot sauce
1/8 teaspoon cayenne pepper
1/8 teaspoon white pepper
1/2 teaspoon salt
2 cups lump crabmeat, flaked (about two 6-ounce cans)
1 cup dry bread crumbs
Extra-virgin olive oil

Dill Mustard Sauce

1 cup Dill Relish (see page 87)
1/4 cup Dijon mustard
1/4 cup mayonnaise
Salt and white pepper

PREP To Make Patties—Sauté onion in butter until tender. Combine onion, soft bread crumbs, heavy cream, and eggs in a medium bowl. Add remaining ingredients except for dry bread crumbs and olive oil. Shape crab mixture into 8 patties. Lightly dust patties with dry bread crumbs.

To Make Sauce—Combine all ingredients in a small bowl until well-blended. Season to taste with salt and white pepper. Set aside.

COOK Put a small amount of olive oil in a heavy saucepan. Cook patties until lightly brown on both sides.

SERVE Serve warm crab cakes with Dill Mustard Sauce.

Creole-Style Shrimp Po' Boy

Makes about 4 servings

1 16-ounce jar Spicy Creole Sauce, divided (see page 117)
1/2 cup mayonnaise
1 1/2 pounds large shrimp, peeled and deveined
Vegetable oil
2 10-inch baguettes
1/4 cup melted butter
1 cup shredded lettuce
1 large beefsteak tomato, sliced
1/2 cup sliced dill pickles
Hot sauce, if desired

PREP Combine 1/3 cup Spicy Creole Sauce and mayonnaise in a small bowl. Cover bowl and chill. Put shrimp in a medium bowl. Add remaining Spicy Creole Sauce, stirring to evenly coat shrimp. Let shrimp marinate for 30 minutes.

COOK Bring grill temperature to medium-high heat (350°F); brush cooking surface lightly with vegetable oil. Grill shrimp about 2 minutes on each side, or just until firm. Cut baguettes in half crosswise, then again lengthwise. Brush cut side with butter. Grill bread, cut side down, until lightly toasted.

SERVE Butter toasted baguettes with creole spread. Divide the grilled shrimp evenly between 4 sandwiches. Add lettuce, tomato, and dill pickles. Top sandwiches with remaining baguette slices. Serve with hot sauce, if desired.

Flank Steak with Honey-Glazed Red Onions

Makes about 6 servings

1 16-ounce jar Red Onions with Honey (see page 116)
2 tablespoons extra-virgin olive oil
2 tablespoons minced garlic
1 tablespoon coriander seeds
2 teaspoons paprika
1 cup tomato purée
1/2 cup Chili Sauce (see page 90)
Juice of 1 lime
2 pounds flank steak
1 tablespoon kosher salt
2 teaspoons coarsely ground black pepper

PREP Drain onions, reserving liquid. Rub both sides of flank steak with salt and pepper; set aside.

COOK Heat olive oil in a medium saucepan; cook garlic in olive oil just until translucent. Add coriander seeds and continue cooking until seeds are lightly toasted. Stir in paprika, tomato purée, chili sauce, and lime juice; simmer 10 minutes. Add red onions and continue cooking about 5 minutes. Keep honey-glazed red onions warm.

Grill steak at 400°F about 4 minutes on each side for medium-rare, or longer for desired doneness. Baste steak with honey glaze; cook 5 minutes. Turn steak over; baste with honey glaze and continue cooking 5 minutes, or until glaze begins to form a crust.

SERVE Let steak rest 10 minutes before slicing. Cut slices about 1/4-inch thick across the grain. Serve immediately with remaining honey-glazed red onions.

Herb-Crusted Beef Stew with Vegetables

Makes 2 6-inch casseroles

Stew

- 1 16-ounce jar Beef Stew with Vegetables (see page 104)
- 2 tablespoons cornstarch
- 1½ cups water

Crust

- ¾ cup all-purpose flour
- 1 tablespoon minced mixed herbs of parsley, basil, and thyme
- ½ teaspoon baking powder
- ¼ teaspoon salt
- ¼ cup butter or margarine
- 2 tablespoons heavy cream or milk

PREP To Make Stew—Combine cornstarch and water in a medium saucepan, stirring to dissolve cornstarch.

To make crust—Combine flour, herbs, baking powder, and salt in a medium bowl. With a pastry blender or two forks, cut in butter until mixture resembles coarse crumbs. Stir in cream just until blended. Form dough into a ball. On a lightly floured surface, roll dough ¼-inch thick. Cut dough into two 6-inch circles; cut vents in the center of each dough round to allow steam to escape during baking.

COOK Place saucepan containing cornstarch mixture over medium heat. Stir in beef and vegetable mixture. Cook until mixture begins to thicken.

Divide stew mixture between two individual casserole dishes. Top each with herb crust; crimp edge of dough. Place casserole dishes on a baking sheet. Bake at 350°F for 30 to 35 minutes or until crust is golden brown. Cool on a wire rack for 10 minutes.

SERVE Add a small salad or fresh fruit to complete this meal.

Linguine with Roasted Garlic Roma Tomato Sauce and Spinach

Makes about 4 servings

- 5 ounces baby spinach
- 2 cloves garlic, minced
- 3 tablespoons extra-virgin olive oil, divided
- 1 32-ounce jar Roasted Garlic Roma Tomato Sauce (see page 33)
- ¼ teaspoon salt
- ⅛ teaspoon coarsely ground pepper
- ½ cup heavy cream
- 8 ounces linguine
- ½ cup freshly shaved Parmesan cheese

PREP Wash spinach under cold running water; drain. Peel garlic and mince.

COOK Heat 2 tablespoons olive oil in a large saucepan over medium heat. Stir in garlic and cook until tender but not browned. Add tomatoes and cook over medium-high heat until heated through. Layer spinach over tomatoes, cover pan, and continue cooking about 5 minutes. Add salt and pepper. Reduce heat; stir in cream and simmer until thickened, about 3 minutes.

Cook pasta according to package directions while tomato and spinach mixture cooks. Drain pasta; toss with remaining olive oil.

SERVE Put pasta on a serving platter. Ladle tomato and spinach mixture over pasta. Sprinkle with Parmesan cheese.

Oriental Hot Dish

Makes about 4 servings

- 1 32-ounce jar raw pack ground beef with juice (see page 98)
- 1 cup cut fresh green beans
- 1 cup sliced celery
- 8 ounces sliced water chestnuts, drained
- ½ cup rice
- ½ cup chopped onion
- ¼ cup soy sauce
- 1 4-ounce jar whole mushrooms (see page 114)
- 1 clove garlic, minced
- ½ teaspoon salt
- ¼ teaspoon ground ginger
- ½ cup chopped cashews

PREP Combine all ingredients in a large bowl, except cashews, mixing well to blend evenly. Pour mixture into a 2-quart shallow baking dish.

BAKE Put baking dish on center oven rack and bake at 350°F for 50 to 60 minutes or until rice is tender. Stir once during baking.

SERVE Sprinkle cashews over top; serve immediately.

Pesto Pizza with Artichoke Hearts and Italian Tomatoes

Makes about 4 servings

- 2 4-ounce containers Pesto, thawed (see page 152)
- 1 Herb Pizza Crust, thawed (see page 152)
- 2 large garlic cloves
- 2 tablespoons extra-virgin olive oil
- 6 ounces fresh mozzarella, cut into ¼-inch slices
- 4 ounces artichoke hearts in olive oil
- 2 Italian tomatoes
- 4 to 6 leaves fresh basil

PREP Two hours before assembling pizza, remove pesto from the freezer to thaw. About 30 minutes before serving, remove pizza crust from freezer and unwrap; set aside. Peel garlic; crush cloves. Drain artichoke hearts, cut in half; set aside. Remove cores from tomatoes; slice tomatoes crosswise into thick slices. Cut basil leaves crosswise into thin strips; set aside.

COOK Sauté garlic in olive oil, in a small, heavy saucepan, over medium-low heat until garlic turns pale yellow; do not let garlic brown. Brush pizza crust with garlic oil. Spread pesto over crust, leaving a 1-inch border. Arrange cheese on top, leaving a 2- to 3-inch border. Arrange artichoke hearts and tomato slices over cheese. Bake on baking sheet or preheated pizza stone at 450°F for 10 minutes. Reduce heat to 400°F and continue baking 10 minutes or until crust is lightly browned and pizza is cooked throughout.

SERVE Remove pizza from pan. Garnish with thin strips of basil. Cut into slices.

Pork Medallions with Pepper-Onion Relish

Makes about 8 servings

1 3/4 to 2 pounds pork tenderloin	3 tablespoons honey
Salt	2 tablespoons olive oil
Pepper	1 tablespoon Dijon mustard
Canola oil	1 16-ounce jar Pepper-Onion Relish (see page 88)
1/2 cup vinegar	

PREP Cut tenderloin crosswise into 1-inch-thick medallions. Season both sides of pork medallions with salt and pepper.

BAKE Lightly coat the bottom of a shallow saucepan with canola oil and heat over medium-high heat until hot. Sear pork medallions on each side for 1 minute, or until lightly browned. Spread Pepper-Onion Relish on the bottom of a shallow baking dish. Layer pork medallions over relish. Roast at 350°F for 10 minutes or until a meat thermometer reaches 140°F. Remove from oven; loosely cover with foil until ready to serve.

SERVE Place pork medallions on a serving plate. Serve with Pepper-Onion Relish.

Praline-Glazed Salmon with Mango Salad

Makes about 4 servings

Mango Salad

1 16-ounce jar Mango Relish (see page 88)	4 cups frisée
	1/4 cup sunflower seed oil

Praline-Glazed Salmon

1 8-ounce jar Praline Syrup (see page 130)	1/4 teaspoon salt
2 tablespoons lemon juice	1/4 teaspoon lemon-pepper
4 (5 to 6 ounce) salmon fillets, skin removed	

PREP To Make Salad—Drain Mango Relish, reserving liquid. Place frisée on a serving platter; top with mango relish; set aside. Whisk together sunflower seed oil and reserved liquid; drizzle dressing over salad.

COOK To Make Salmon—Combine Praline Syrup and lemon juice in a small saucepan. Cook over medium-high heat until reduced by half. Grill salmon about 4 minutes, basting occasionally with syrup of praline glaze. Turn salmon over and sprinkle with salt and lemon-pepper. Continue grilling about 3 minutes, basting occasionally with syrup of praline glaze. Spoon pecans over salmon and continue grilling, about 2 minutes.

SERVE Place salmon on serving platter with Mango Salad. Serve immediately.

Desserts

Apple-Cranberry Pie

Makes one 9-inch pie

Crust

2 1/2 cups all-purpose flour	3/4 cup vegetable shortening
2 tablespoons sugar	2/3 cup cold water
1 teaspoon salt	

Filling

2 32-ounce jars Apples for Baking (see page 17)	3/4 cup sweetened dried cranberries
1/2 cup sugar	3/4 cup chopped dates
2 tablespoons all-purpose flour	3/4 cup chopped walnuts
1/4 teaspoon salt	1 tablespoon freshly grated orange zest
1/4 teaspoon cinnamon	2 tablespoons unsalted butter
1/8 teaspoon allspice	

PREP To Make Crust—Combine flour, sugar, and salt in a medium bowl. Cut shortening into dry ingredients using a pastry blender just until mixture is uniformly coarse. Add water one tablespoon at a time, stirring gently with a fork after each addition. Use just enough water for dough to hold together in a ball. Divide dough into two portions with one slightly larger. Cover each portion of dough with plastic wrap and refrigerate.

To Make Filling—Drain apples, reserving liquid. Combine sugar, flour, salt, cinnamon, and allspice in a medium bowl. Add drained apples and stir gently to coat evenly with sugar mixture; set aside. Combine cranberries, dates, walnuts, and orange zest in a small bowl. Stir in two tablespoons reserved liquid from apples; let stand 10 minutes.

To Assemble Pie—Remove dough from refrigerator. Roll out larger portion of dough on a lightly floured surface to 1/8-inch-thick and 2 inches larger than pie pan. Place rolled dough into pie pan and gently work the dough to fit pan. Trim edge even with pie pan. Roll out remaining dough to 1/8-inch-thick and 1 inch larger than pie pan. Cut steam vents into crust; set aside. Spread cranberry mixture evenly over bottom of pie crust. Spoon the apple mixture evenly over cranberries to cover. Cut butter into small pieces and place evenly over apples. Center top crust over pie and trim edge, allowing 1/2-inch overhang. Fold edge of top crust under bottom crust; flute the edge to seal.

BAKE Place pie pan on center oven rack and bake at 450°F for 20 minutes, reduce heat to 350°F and continue baking 40 minutes, or until crust is lightly browned and fruit is tender. Cool pie on a wire rack.

SERVE Pie may be cut and served warm, or cool completely before serving.

Fruit Cornucopia

Makes 4 cornucopias

Mango Leather
(see page 165)
4 round pretzels
1 cup dried apricots
1 cup dried apple slices
1/2 cup dried pineapple
tidbits

1/2 cup dried cherries
1/2 cup pecan halves, lightly
toasted
4 (4- x 6-inch) strips of
parchment paper

PREP Cut dried apricots and dried apple slices into bite-size pieces.

BAKE Toast pecan halves at 350°F until lightly toasted. Cool. Turn off oven. Warm mango leather rounds in oven just until pliable.

SERVE Wrap opposite sides of one mango leather round into the center, overlapping slightly, and twist to form a cone shape. Wrap bottom of cone with a small piece of parchment paper. To secure parchment paper in place, slide narrow end of cone through pretzel until it can slide no further. Repeat with remaining mango leather rounds. Combine dried fruit and pecans in a small bowl to blend well. Fill cornucopia with a mixture of dried fruit and nuts.

PB&J Cookie Bars

Makes about 16 cookie bars

2 1/4 cups unbleached
all-purpose flour
1 1/2 teaspoons baking powder
1/2 teaspoons salt
1 1/2 cups creamy
peanut butter
1 1/2 cups light brown sugar
3/4 cup unsalted butter,
room temperature

2 medium eggs
1 1/2 teaspoons vanilla extract
1 1/2 cups grape jelly
(see page 58)
1 cup coarsely chopped
salted peanuts

PREP Line an 8- x 8- x 2-inch baking pan with heavy foil, allowing edges to hang over by about 2 inches. Spray foil with nonstick cooking spray; set aside.

Whisk flour, baking powder, and 1/2 teaspoon salt in a small bowl. Using an electric mixer, beat peanut butter, sugar, and butter in a large bowl until smooth. Add egg and vanilla; continue beating on low speed until mixture is smooth. Add flour mixture and beat on low speed just to blend. Put half of the mixture into baking pan. Wrap remaining dough in plastic wrap and chill quickly in freezer for 10 minutes. Press dough evenly onto bottom of pan using fingertips. Spread jelly over cookie dough in an even layer. Remove remaining dough from freezer. Crumble chilled dough into grape-sized pieces and sprinkle evenly over jelly mixture. Sprinkle chopped nuts evenly over the top

BAKE Bake cookie bars at 350°F for 30 minutes, or until top is golden brown. Set pan on a cooling rack until completely cooled.

SERVE Holding the foil around the edge of the pan, lift the entire square of cookie bars out of the pan. Remove foil from edges. Cut cookie bar into 16 pieces. Store in an airtight container.

Trifle with Blackberries in Rosemary Syrup

Makes about 4 servings

Yellow Sponge Cake
1 cup sugar
6 large eggs
1 1/3 cups unbleached
all-purpose flour

6 tablespoons unsalted
butter, melted
1 teaspoon vanilla extract

Blackberries in Rosemary Syrup
2 cups blackberries
2 sprigs fresh rosemary
1/2 cup sugar

2 tablespoons orange
liqueur or fresh
orange juice

Whipped Cream
1 cup
heavy whipping cream
1 to 4 tablespoons
Confectioner's sugar

Lemon Curd
(see page 152)

PREP Set lemon curd in the refrigerator to thaw the day before you plan to serve Trifle with Blackberries in Rosemary Syrup.

To Make Yellow Sponge Cake—Line a jelly-roll pan (11 1/2- x 17 1/2-inches) with parchment paper. Butter and flour the paper; set aside. Set a heat-proof mixing bowl over a pan of simmering water. Whisk sugar and eggs together in bowl until warm to the touch. Using an electric mixer, beat on high speed until mixture is very thick and pale yellow, about 6 to 8 minutes. Transfer mixture to a clean bowl. Sift 1/3 of the flour into sugar mixture; fold the flour into the sugar mixture. Repeat twice. Combine butter and vanilla in a small bowl, stirring until blended well. Slowly pour butter mixture into flour mixture, folding to incorporate evenly. Pour cake batter into prepared pan and smooth top.

To Make Blackberries In Rosemary Syrup—Put blackberries and rosemary in a small bowl. Sprinkle with sugar and orange liqueur or orange juice. Let blackberries macerate about 30 minutes, tossing gently to coat blackberries with syrup.

To Make Whipped Cream—Pour heavy whipping cream into a chilled bowl. Whip cream using chilled beaters, gradually adding Confectioner's sugar 1 tablespoon at a time, beating to the desired consistency. Chill.

BAKE Place jelly-roll pan on the middle oven rack and bake at 350°F for 18 to 20 minutes, or until cake is springy to the touch. Cool.

SERVE To Assemble Trifle—Reserve a few blackberries to garnish individual trifles. Cut or break cake into 1-inch squares. Alternate layers of cake, blackberries, lemon curd, and whipped cream into individual serving dishes or Ball jars. Garnish with reserved blackberries.

Extras

Apricot Light Jam

Yield: about 6 half-pint jars

2 cups dried apricots (see page 164)	1/2 cup chopped orange pulp (about 1 large)
1 1/2 cups crushed pineapple, unsweetened (if using canned, drain)	2 tablespoons lemon juice
	3 1/2 cups sugar

PREP Put apricots in a medium bowl and cover with cold water by 1 inch; let stand in refrigerator overnight.

COOK Put apricots and soaking water into a large saucepan. Cook over low heat, uncovered, until apricots are tender. Remove from heat and crush apricots with a potato masher. Add pineapple, orange pulp, lemon juice, and sugar. Bring mixture to a simmer, stirring until sugar dissolves. Cook over medium-high heat until thick, about 20 to 30 minutes, stirring to prevent sticking.

FILL Ladle hot jam into a hot jar, leaving 1/4-inch headspace. Remove air bubbles. Clean jar rim. Center lid on jar and adjust band to fingertip-tight. Place jar on the rack elevated over simmering water (180°F) in boiling-water canner. Repeat until all jars are filled.

PROCESS Lower the rack into simmering water, Water must cover jars by 1 inch. Adjust heat to medium-high, cover canner and bring water to a rolling boil. Process half-pint jars 10 minutes. Turn off heat and remove cover. Let jars cool 5 minutes. Remove jars from canner, do not retighten bands if loose. Cool 12 hours. Check seals. Label and store jars.

Bean Dip and Toasted Tortilla Chips

Makes about 2 cups

Dip

1 cup kidney or pinto beans (see page 111)	1 jalapeño pepper, finely chopped
1 cup Chili (see page 105)	

Chips

12 6-inch corn tortillas	Fine salt
1 tablespoon vegetable oil	

PREP To Make Dip—Drain kidney or pinto beans. Purée drained beans in a food processor or blender until smooth. Combine bean purée and chili in a small bowl. Slice jalapeño pepper, discarding stem end.

To Make Chips—Lightly brush corn tortillas with vegetable oil on both sides. Sprinkle lightly with salt on both sides. Cut corn tortillas into six wedges. Place corn tortilla wedges in a single layer on an ungreased baking sheet.

BAKE Put baking sheet on the center oven rack and bake at 400°F for 12 to 15 minutes, rotating baking sheet halfway after 6 minutes.

SERVE Place corn tortilla chips in a serving basket. Garnish bean dip with sliced jalapeño pepper. Serve bean dip with corn tortilla chips.

Note: When cutting or seeding hot peppers, wear rubber gloves to prevent hands from being burned.

Brie with Maple-Walnut Syrup

Makes about 4 servings

4 ounce round of Brie	1/2 cup Maple-Walnut Syrup (see page 130)

PREP Remove top rind from Brie. Cut cheese into 4 wedges; keeping wedges in a round, place on lightly greased baking sheet. Spoon syrup over cheese.

BAKE Place baking sheet on center oven rack and bake at 450°F for 2 to 3 minutes.

SERVE Put warm Brie and syrup on a serving plate. Serve immediately with fresh fruit and crackers.

Crostini with Hickory-Smoked Ham and Red Chili Cherry Jam

Makes about 24 appetizers

8 ounces hickory-smoked ham	Extra-virgin olive oil
1 small baguette, cut into 1/2-inch slices	1 8-ounce jar Red Chili Cherry Jam (see page 124)

PREP Cut ham into thick irregular slices; set aside. Cut baguette into 1/2-inch slices.

BAKE Place baguette slices on a baking sheet. Brush baguette slices with olive oil. Bake at 350°F for 10 minutes, or until lightly browned.

SERVE Place toasted baguette slices onto a serving plate. Top each slice with ham, then top with 2 teaspoons Red Chili Cherry Jam.

Granola

Makes about 8 cups

4 cups old fashioned or quick oats	1 teaspoon cinnamon
1/2 cup wheat germ	1/2 teaspoon salt
1 cup coconut (see page 164)	3/4 cup vegetable oil
1 cup slivered almonds	1/2 cup honey
1 cup sunflower seeds	1 teaspoon vanilla
1/2 cup brown sugar	1 cup raisins (see page 164)

PREP Combine all ingredients, except raisins; mix to blend well.

BAKE Spread granola onto a baking sheet and bake at 350°F for 25 to 30 minutes, stirring every 10 minutes.

SERVE Stir in raisins. Cool completely before serving.

Horseradish Mayonnaise

Makes about 1 cup

1/2 cup sour cream

1/2 cup mayonnaise

1 tablespoon grated
horseradish

1 tablespoon Dill Relish
(see page 87)

1 tablespoon chopped
chives

PREP Whisk all ingredients together in a small bowl.

CHILL Cover bowl and refrigerate 2 hours.

SERVE Spread mayonnaise on crackers or small bread rounds
and top with cheese and roast beef.

Parmesan Crisps

Yield: about 12 crisps

1 cup finely grated
Parmigiano-Reggiano
cheese (from moist cut)

PREP Line baking sheet with silicone nonstick baking mat.
Sprinkle about 2 teaspoons of grated cheese on mat and spread
into a 2-inch circle. Repeat.

BAKE Put baking sheet on center oven rack and bake at 350°F
for 8 to 10 minutes, or until cheese is golden brown. Remove
cheese rounds to a paper towel to cool. To give cheese crisps a
curl, lay paper towel over a rolling pin; place warm cheese crisp
on paper towel to cool.

SERVE Parmesan Crisps make a wonderful accompaniment
to Vine-Fresh Tomato Soup (see page 35).

Peach and Pineapple Jam

Yield: about 6 half-pint jars

1 pound dried peaches
(see page 164)

Peel of 1/2 orange

2 1/2 cups water

3 1/2 cups sugar

1 1/2 cups crushed pineapple
with juice

1/2 cup chopped orange pulp
(about 1 large)

1/2 teaspoon ginger

1/4 teaspoon salt

PREP Rinse peaches under cold water; drain. Cut peaches into
small pieces. Cut orange peel into three pieces. Combine peaches,
orange peel, and water in a medium bowl; let stand in refrigerator
overnight.

COOK Put fruit mixture into a large saucepan. Add remaining
ingredients. Bring mixture to a boil over medium-high heat,
stirring until sugar dissolves. Boil until mixture is thick, stirring to
prevent sticking. Remove orange peel.

FILL Ladle hot jam into a hot jar, leaving 1/4-inch headspace.
Remove air bubbles. Clean jar rim. Center lid on jar and adjust
band to fingertip-tight. Place jar on the rack elevated over
simmering water (180°F) in boiling-water canner. Repeat until all
jars are filled.

PROCESS Lower the rack into simmering water, Water must
cover jars by 1 inch. Adjust heat to medium-high, cover canner
and bring water to a rolling boil. Process half-pint jars 10 minutes.
Turn off heat and remove cover. Let jars cool 5 minutes. Remove
jars from canner, do not retighten bands if loose. Cool 12 hours.
Check seals. Label and store jars.

Roasted Red Pepper Dip

Makes about 1 cup

2 4-ounce jars Roasted
Red Pepper Spread
(see page 125)

1/2 cup Greek-style
whole-milk yogurt

1 teaspoon extra-virgin
olive oil

1/2 teaspoon smoked paprika

Salt and freshly ground
pepper, to taste

1/2 lime

PREP Whisk Roasted Red Pepper Spread, yogurt, olive oil,
paprika, and salt and pepper together in a small bowl.

CHILL Cover bowl and refrigerate 1 hour.

SERVE Shred lime peel. Garnish dip with shredded lime peel.
Serve with fresh vegetables.

Home Canning Planning Guide

Seasonal availability is dependent upon growing conditions and location within a region. The actual weight or quantity of produce needed to yield one quart jar is an approximate amount and may vary based on size of produce, recipe preparation, and cooking method.

■ Northern
■ Central
■ Southern

Fresh Fruits & Vegetables

FRUITS	NORTHERN REGION SEASON AVAILABILITY	CENTRAL REGION SEASON AVAILABILITY	SOUTHERN REGION SEASON AVAILABILITY	PURCHASE WEIGHT	UNITS PER POUND	POUNDS PER QUART
APPLES	June–December	June–November	May–November	1 lb	3–4 Medium	2½–3
APRICOTS	July–September	June–August	May–August	1 lb	8–12 Medium	2–2½
BERRIES	June–October	June–October	May–October	6-oz Container	3 Containers	1½–3
BLUEBERRIES	July–August	June–July	May–July	6-oz Container	3 Containers	1½–3
CHERRIES	June–August	May–August	May–August	1 lb	3 Cups	2–2½
FIGS	Market Availability	Market Availability	June–October	1 lb	12–14 Small	2½
GRAPES	September–October	July–October	June–November	1 lb	3 Cups	2
KIWIFRUITS	Market Availability	Market Availability	Market Availability	1 lb	5–6 Medium	For Jam
MELONS	August–October	June–August	June–July	3 lb	½ Medium	1½–3
NECTARINES	Market Availability	Market Availability	April–October	1 lb	3 Medium	2–2½
PEACHES	July–September	June–October	April–September	1 lb	3–4 Medium	2–3
PEARS	August–October	August–October	April–November	1 lb	3 Medium	2–3
PLUMS	August–October	July–September	May–August	1 lb	8–10 Medium	1½–2½
RASPBERRIES	September–November	June–September	May–July	6-oz Container	3 Containers	1½–3
RHUBARB	April–July	April–July	April–July	1 lb	4–8 Stalks	1½–2
STRAWBERRIES	June–August	May–September	January–October	1 lb	4 Cups	2½–3
TOMATOES	July–October	May–October	January–December	1 lb	3–4 Medium	2½–3½

VEGETABLES	NORTHERN REGION SEASON AVAILABILITY	CENTRAL REGION SEASON AVAILABILITY	SOUTHERN REGION SEASON AVAILABILITY	PURCHASE WEIGHT	UNITS PER POUND	POUNDS PER QUART
ASPARAGUS	May–June	April–June	February–May	1 lb	16–20 Medium	3–3½
BEANS, GREEN	July–September	July–October	Year Round	1 lb	6 Cups	1½–2½
BEANS, LIMA	August–September	June–October	Year Round	1 lb	3–4 Cups	3–5
BEETS	July–November	May–November	April–November	1 lb	5–6 Medium	2–3½
CABBAGE	July–November	June–November	January–April	1 lb	⅓ Head	2½–3
CARROTS	July–November	May–November	Year Round	1 lb	5–6 Medium	2–3
CORN, SWEET	July–September	June–October	April–November	1 lb	2–3 Medium Ears	3–6
CUCUMBERS, PICKLING	July–September	July–October	March–November	1 lb	6–7 Medium	1½–2
OKRA	June–September	June–October	May–October	1 lb	50 Small	1½–3
ONIONS	Year Round	Year Round	Year Round	1 lb	3 Medium	1½–2
PEAS, GREEN	June–September	May–August	April–May	1 lb	In Shell	2–2¼
PEPPERS, BELL	July–September	July–October	May–December	1 lb	2–3 Large	1 lb Per Pint Jar
PEPPERS, CHILI	July–September	July–October	May–December	1 lb	15 Medium	1 lb Per Pint Jar
POTATOES, SWEET	August–November	September–October	July–November	1 lb	3 Medium	2–3
POTATOES, WHITE	June–December	June–December	Year Round	1 lb	3 Medium	2
SQUASH, SUMMER	June–September	June–October	February–October	1 lb	3 Medium	2
TOMATILLOS	Market Availability	Market Availability	Market Availability	1 lb	6 Medium	2

Equivalents Guide

Weight & Measure Equivalents

DRY MEASURE EQUIVALENTS		
UNITED STATES IMPERIAL	AUSTRALIA METRIC	GREAT BRITAIN METRIC
¼ teaspoon	1 ml	1 ml
½ teaspoon	2 ml	2 ml
1 teaspoon	5 ml	5 ml
3 teaspoons = 1 tablespoon	20 ml	15 ml
4 tablespoons = ¼ cup	60 ml	50 ml
5 tablespoons = ⅓ cup	80 ml	75 ml
8 tablespoons = ½ cup	125 ml	125 ml
10 tablespoons + 2 teaspoons = ¾ cup	180 ml	150 ml
12 tablespoons = 1 cup	190 ml	175 ml
1 cup = ½ pint	250 ml	250 ml
2 cups = 1 pint	500 ml	500 ml
4 cups or 2 pints = 1 quart	1 liter	1 liter
4 quarts or 2 half-gallons = 1 gallon	4 liters	4 liters

LIQUID MEASURE & DRY WEIGHT EQUIVALENTS		
UNITED STATES IMPERIAL	AUSTRALIA METRIC	GREAT BRITAIN METRIC
1 fluid ounce = ⅛ cup or 2 tablespoons	30 ml	30 ml
2 fluid ounces = ¼ cup or 4 tablespoons	60 ml	60 ml
4 fluid ounces = ½ cup or 8 tablespoons	120 ml	120 ml
6 fluid ounces = ¾ cup or 12 tablespoons	180 ml	180 ml
8 fluid ounces = 1 cup or 16 tablespoons	250 ml	250 ml
16 fluid ounces = 1 pint or 2 cups	500 ml	500 ml
32 fluid ounces = 1 quart or 2 pints	1 liter	1 liter
64 fluid ounces = 1 half-gallon or 2 quarts	2 liters	2 liters
DRY WEIGHTS		
4 ounces = ¼ pound	125 g	125 g
8 ounces = ½ pound	250 g	250 g
16 ounces = 1 pound	500 g	500 g

Canning & Jar Size Equivalents

HEADSPACE MEASUREMENT EQUIVALENTS		
UNITED STATES IMPERIAL	AUSTRALIA METRIC MILLIMETERS	GREAT BRITAIN METRIC CENTIMETERS
¼ inch	6 mm	0.5 cm
½ inch	13 mm	1 cm
1 inch	25 mm	2.5 cm

JAR SIZE EQUIVALENTS			
JAR SIZE	UNITED STATES IMPERIAL FLUID OUNCE	AUSTRALIA FLUID OUNCE	GREAT BRITAIN METRIC MILLILITER
Half-Pint Jar	8 ounces	8 ounces	250 ml
Pint Jar	16 ounces	16 ounces	500 ml
Pint and Half Jar	24 ounces	24 ounces	750 ml
Quart Jar	32 ounces	32 ounces	1 L

Temperature Conversions

TEMPERATURE EQUIVALENTS: FAHRENHEIT (°F) = CELSIUS (°C)																										
Fahrenheit	-10°	0°	8°	20°	32°	40°	50°	60°	70°	80°	90°	100°	120°	139°	140°	160°	179°	180°	190°	200°	212°	220°	240°	350°	375°	450°
Celsius	-23°	-17°	-4°	-6.6°	0°	4.4°	10°	15.5°	21°	27°	32°	38°	49°	59°	60°	71°	81°	82°	87°	93°	100°	104°	116°	176°	190°	232°

Jar Size Comparison

Regular Mouth Quilted Crystal® Jelly Jar (4 oz)*   Regular Mouth Quilted Crystal® Jelly Jar (8 oz)*   Regular Mouth Quilted Crystal® Jelly Jar (12 oz)*   Regular Mouth Half Pint (8 oz)*   Regular Mouth Pint (16 oz)   Regular Mouth Quart (32 oz)   Wide Mouth Pint (16 oz)*   Wide Mouth Pint and Half (24 oz)*   Wide Mouth Quart (32 oz)

*Jars having straight tapered sides are suitable for home canning and freezing.

The Problem Solver

The general information in Canning Basics (see pages 4–13) and the tested recipes in this book will guide you to successful home canning results. However, should you experience a problem, refer to the problem solving list below for help. This list identifies some conditions that might occur in home canned foods, the causes for them, and how best to remedy them. Review the cause and prevention for your particular problem and make the necessary adjustments in your canning procedures. If the condition of any home canned food indicates spoilage, dispose of it in a manner that humans or animals will not come in contact with the suspect food (see page 188).

Jar fails to seal

Use food immediately, refrigerate immediately, or correct cause of failure and reprocess within 24 hours.

A. **Failure to heat-process filled jars using the correct method and adequate length of time.**
Heat-process all filled jars using the method and time recommended in a tested home canning recipe for the specific food and jar size.

B. **Improper adjustment of screw bands.**
Center lid on jar rim. Screw band down until fingertip-tight. Do not use force.

C. **Improper headspace.**
Use the headspace recommended in recipe for food product being processed.

D. **Food particles on jar rim.**
Clean jar rim using a clean, damp cloth to remove residue before applying lid.

E. **Failure to adjust processing time or pressure for high altitude.**
Know the altitude of your location and adjust processing time for boiling-water canning or pressure (psi) for pressure canning as required.

Jar seals or appears to seal and then unseals

If spoilage is evident, or you do not know when the jar came unsealed, do not use.

A. **Minimum or inadequate vacuum, caused by underprocessing filled jar for the specific food and jar size.**
Heat-process all filled jars using the method and time recommended in a tested home canning recipe.

B. **Particles of food left on sealing surface.**
Clean jar rim using a clean, damp cloth to remove residue before applying lid.

C. **Crack or chip in jar rim.**
Visually examine all jars prior to use to ensure there are no nicks or cracks on the rim that can prevent a seal.

D. **Excess air left in jar.**
Leave the recommended headspace when filling the jar and remove air bubbles to release trapped air before applying lid.

Lid buckles, appearing to warp or bulge upward

If spoilage is evident, do not use food.

A. **Buckling that occurs immediately after heat processing is caused by overly-tight application of the band.**
Adjust the band using only your fingertips; screw band downward until fintertip-tight.

B. **When buckling becomes apparent during storage, the cause is food spoilage.**
Heat processing has been insufficient to destroy all spoilage microorganisms. Foods on which lids buckle during storage must be disposed of in a way that prevents consumption by both humans and animals (see page 188).

Rust appears on underside of metal lid

A. **Coating on underside of lid is scratched.**
Use care when washing lids in hot, soapy water so they do not become scratched by abrasive objects. Store unused lids carefully to prevent scratching.

Liquid is lost during processing

Do not open jar to replace liquid.

A. **Food not heated before filling jar.**
Use the hot-pack method.

B. **Food packed too tightly into jar.**
Pack food closely, leaving room for liquid to circulate around food pieces.

C. **Air bubbles not removed after filling jar.**
Slide a nonmetallic utensil between the food and the jar, pressing against the food to release trapped air. Repeat 2 or 3 times around inside perimeter of the jar.

D. **Light band torque: the band is applied too loosely.**
Adjust band using your fingertips until it is fingertip-tight. Do not use force.

E. **Pressure canner was not operated correctly.**
Regulate heat so that pressure does not fluctuate, avoiding sudden temperature changes.

F. **Starchy foods absorb liquid.**
Pack starchy foods loosely.

Liquid is lost immediately after processing

A. **Jars removed from canner before the internal temperature stabilizes to room temperature.**
For boiling-water canner, when processing time is complete, turn off heat and remove cover. Wait 5 minutes before removing jars.
For pressure canner, follow manufacturer's instructions for cooling canner and removing cover. Wait 10 minutes before removing jars.

Food floats in jar

A. **Fruit is lighter than syrup.**
Use firm, fully-ripe fruit. Heat fruit before packing. Use a light to medium syrup. Pack fruit closely without crushing.

B. **Tomatoes no longer contain the natural pectin needed to hold juice and pulp together.**
Peeling, cutting, and cooking tomatoes can break down pectin, causing the pulp and juice to separate. Work quickly when canning tomatoes or tomato juice.

C. **Pickles are lighter than the pickling liquid or pickles are packed too loosely in the jar.**
Ensure ingredients are measured accurately. Prick the peel in several places around the cucumber with a thin metal skewer so that the pickling liquid is easily absorbed.

Soft spread "weeps"

A. Syneresis or "weeping" occurs in quick-setting soft spreads and is due to the quantity of acid and quality of pectin in the fruit.
None.

B. Storage conditions are not ideal.
Store soft spreads in a dry, dark place between 50° and 70°F.

Soft spread made using added pectin is too soft

See remake instructions on page 69.

A. Proportions of sugar, juice or fruit, acid, and pectin are not in balance.
Follow instructions for Soft Spreads (see page 43).

B. Too large a batch was prepared at one time.
Use no more than 4 to 6 cups of juice or fruit in each batch. Do not double the recipe.

C. Fruit used to prepare soft spread is overripe.
Selection of fruit should include some slightly underripe fruit along with some fully-ripe fruit.

D. Soft spread is not boiled at a rolling boil for the recommended length of time.
Soft spread mixture must be brought to a hard boil that cannot be stirred down, and boiled hard for the length of time stated in the recipe.

E. The wrong type of pectin is used in the recipe.
Pectin types are not interchangeable. Use only the type of pectin listed in the recipe.

F. An incorrect amount of pectin was used.
Measure powdered pectin carefully.

Soft spread made without added pectin is too soft

See remake instructions on page 69.

A. Proportions of sugar, juice or fruit, acid, and pectin is not in balance.
Follow instructions for Soft Spreads (see page 43).

B. Too large a batch was made.
Use no more than 4 to 6 cups of juice or fruit in each batch. Do not double the recipe.

C. Fruit used was too ripe.
Fruit selected should include some fruit that is slightly underripe (but not green) along with some fully-ripe fruit.

D. Soft spread was not boiled to the correct temperature.
Use Gelling Test (see page 43).

Soft spread is cloudy

A. Fruit used is too green.
Fruit should be firm and fully-ripe.

B. Fruit may have been cooked too long before straining.
Fruit should be cooked only until it is slightly soft.

C. Some fruit pulp may have been extracted when juice was strained from fruit.
For clear juice, let fruit pulp drain through a damp jelly bag or several layers of cheesecloth. Do not squeeze jelly bag.

D. Soft spread was ladled into jars too slowly.
Work quickly to fill jars before soft spread starts to gel.

E. Soft spread set too long before filling jars.
When cooking period is complete, ladle soft spread into jars and process immediately.

Bubbles in soft spread

If bubbles denote spoilage, do not use.

A. If bubbles are moving when the jar is stationary, the soft spread is spoiled.
Process all soft spreads in a boiling-water canner for the time indicated in the tested recipe.

B. Bubbles that do not move inside the jar when it is stationary indicate air is trapped in the gel structure.
Ladle the soft spread quickly into the jar, holding the ladle near the rim of the jar or funnel.

Soft spread molds

Do not use.

A. Headspace is too great.
Leave 1/4-inch headspace.

B. Soft spread was not processed long enough to destroy molds, allowing them to grow on the surface of the soft spread.
Process soft spread in boiling-water canner for the time indicated in the tested recipe.

Soft spread is tough or stiff

A. Too much natural pectin in fruit.
Use less underripe fruit and more fully-ripe fruit.

B. Soft spread was cooked too long.
When commercial pectin is not added, use Gelling Test (see page 43) to determine doneness.

C. Too much sugar used.
If commercial pectin is not used, 3/4 to 1 cup sugar for each cup of juice or fruit should be adequate. Use standard dry measuring cups and level sugar even with the top edge of the cup.

Soft spread ferments

Do not use.

A. Soft spread was not brought to the correct temperature before filling jars.
Bring soft spread to a rolling boil that cannot be stirred down when using commercial pectin, or 220°F when making a recipe without added pectin.

B. Soft spread was either not processed or it was underprocessed.
Process all soft spreads in a boiling-water canner for the time indicated in the tested recipe.

Soft spread contains glass-like particles

A. Too much sugar was used.
Follow remake instructions for Soft Spreads (see page 69).

B. The soft spread may have been undercooked.
Too short of a cooking time results in sugar not dissolving completely and not mixing thoroughly with the juice or fruit.

C. The soft spread may have been cooked too slowly or too long.
Long, slow cooking results in too much evaporation of the water content of the fruit.

D. Undissolved sugar that was sticking to the pan washed into the soft spread as it was poured.
Carefully wipe the side of the pan with a damp cloth to remove sugar crystals before filling jars. Ladle soft spread into the jars instead of pouring soft spread directly from the pan.

E. Crystals in grape jelly may be tartaric acid, a natural substance in grapes.
Allow juice to stand in the refrigerator 12 to 24 hours. Ladle strained juice from the container, being careful not to disturb sediment that may have settled in the bottom. Strain juice through a damp jelly bag or several layers of cheesecloth.

Hollow pickles

A. Faulty growth of cucumbers.
None. Hollow cucumbers are best used for relish. Hollow cucumbers can be identified during cleaning, as they will float in water.

White sediment in the bottom of a jar of pickles

A. Harmless yeasts have grown on the surface and then settled to the bottom of the jar.
None. The presence of a small amount of white sediment is normal.

B. Additives in salt.
Use pickling or canning salt or salt without anti-caking agents.

Shriveled pickles

A. Too much salt, sugar, or vinegar was added at one time.
Gradually add salt, sugar, or vinegar until the full amount is incorporated.

B. Whole cucumbers were not pricked before canning.
Use a thin metal skewer to pierce the cucumber peel in multiple places around the entire cucumber to allow the brine to saturate and plump the flesh of the cucumber.

C. Cucumbers had a wax coating that prevented the brine from penetrating the peel.
Use only unwaxed pickling cucumbers for pickling.

Soft or slippery pickles

Do not use if spoilage is evident.

A. Blossom end was not removed from cucumbers.
Cut 1/16-inch off the blossom end of the cucumbers before pickling.

B. Brine or vinegar was too weak.
Use pure granulated salt, pickling salt, or canning salt, 5% acidity vinegar, and a tested recipe.

C. Scum was not removed daily.
Completely remove scum daily during the brining process.

D. Pickles not completely covered with brine.
Pickles must be completely covered with liquid during fermentation, or completely covered inside the filled jar.

E. Pickles were underprocessed.
Process all pickled foods in a boiling-water canner.

Darkened or discolored pickles

A. Minerals present in hard water used in making the pickles.
Use soft water or distilled water.

B. Brass, iron, copper, aluminum, or zinc utensils were used in making the pickles, or are present in the water used to make pickles.
Use enamelware, glass, stainless-steel, stoneware, or food grade plastic utensils. Use distilled water.

C. Ground spices used.
Use whole spices.

D. Whole spices left in jars of pickles.
Remove whole spices used for flavoring the pickling liquid before filling jars.

Black spots on underside of metal lid

A. Natural compounds in some foods cause a brown or black deposit on the underside of the lid. This deposit is harmless and does not mean the food is unsafe to eat.
None.

Cloudy liquid

If cloudiness denotes spoilage, do not use.

A. Food spoilage from underprocessing.
Process each food following recommended method and recommended length of time.

B. Minerals in water.
Use soft water or distilled water.

C. Starch in vegetables.
None.

D. Fillers in table salt.
Use pickling salt, canning salt, or granulated salt without additives.

White sediment in the bottom of a jar of vegetables

If sediment denotes spoilage, do not use.

A. Starch from food.
None.

B. Minerals in water used.
Use soft water or distilled water.

C. Bacterial spoilage; liquid is usually murky and food is soft. (Do not use.)
Process each food by recommended method and for recommended length of time.

Food in jar darkens on top

A. Liquid did not cover food product.
Completely cover food product with brine, syrup, juice, or water before adjusting two-piece cap.

B. Food not processed long enough to inactivate enzymes.
Process each food for recommended length of time.

C. Manner of packing and processing did not expel enough air.
Use hot pack when indicated in the recipe.

D. Air was sealed in the jar either because headspace was too large or because air bubbles were not removed.
Use headspace recommended in recipe. Slide a nonmetallic spatula between food and jar; press back gently on the food to release trapped air.

Fruit darkens after removed from jar

A. Fruit has not been processed long enough to inactivate enzymes. Enzyme activity causes fruit to darken.
Process each fruit by recommended method and for recommended length of time. Time is counted when water reaches a rolling boil in a boiling-water canner.

Corn turns brown after processing

A. Variety of corn was not suitable for canning, or corn was not harvested at the correct time.
Select only varieties of corn recommended for preserving and choose ears of corn with plump, shiny kernels filled with milk.

B. Liquid did not cover corn.
Cover corn with liquid before adjusting two-piece cap.

C. Jars were processed at too high a temperature.
Keep pressure in canner at recommended pounds; dial gauge may be faulty and must be checked for accuracy.

Pink, red, blue, or purple color in canned apples, pears, peaches, or quinces

A. A natural chemical change which occurs in cooking the fruit.
None.

Some foods become black, brown, or gray

A. Natural chemical substances (tannins, sulfur compounds, and acids) in food react with minerals in water or with metal utensils used in preparing the food.

Use soft water. Avoid using brass, copper, iron, aluminum, zinc, or chipped enamelware, and utensils from which tin plate is worn.

White crystals in canned spinach

A. Calcium and oxalic acid in spinach combine to form harmless calcium oxalate.
None.

Identifying & Disposing
OF SPOILED FOODS

Do not taste food from a jar that came unsealed or shows signs of spoilage.

Examine each jar of food carefully before using it to ensure a vacuum seal is present. Lids that are concave indicate the jar is sealed. Do not use any jar of food that is unsealed, has a bulged lid, or does not require a can opener for the lid to be removed. Food spoilage produces gases that cause the lids to swell and/or break their seals. Follow the detoxification process for disposing of food, jar, and cap.

Visually examine jars of food for other signs of spoilage that might be present. Indications that the food has spoiled include:

- Broken seal
- Mold
- Gassiness
- Cloudiness
- Spurting liquid
- Bubbles rising in jar
- Seepage
- Yeast growth
- Fermentation
- Slime
- Disagreeable odor

Jars that are suspected of containing spoiled low-acid or tomato products must be handled carefully. They may exhibit different signs of spoilage or no signs of spoilage. Thus, suspect jars should be treated as having produced botulinum toxin and handled carefully, following these guidelines:

- Place jars of sealed home canned food showing signs of spoilage in a garbage bag. Secure the bag closed and place it in the regular trash container or dispose of it at a landfill.

- Unsealed, open, or leaking jars of spoiled home canned food should be detoxified before disposal.

Home canned food that shows signs of spoilage must be discarded in a manner that no human or animal will come in contact with the product. Contact with botulinum toxin can be fatal whether it is ingested or enters the body through the skin. Avoid contact with suspect food.

Detoxification Process—Wear rubber gloves when handling suspect jars. Carefully place the suspect jars on their sides, keeping lids and bands in place, in a deep saucepan. It is not necessary to remove contents from the jars. Wash your hands with gloves thoroughly. Carefully add water to cover all items by 1 inch. Place the cover on the saucepan. Bring the water to a boil and boil 30 minutes, being careful not to splash water or food product outside the saucepan. Allow the contents of the saucepan to cool. Discard the jars, lids and bands, and food in the regular trash or landfill.

Sanitation Process—Wear rubber gloves when cleaning work surfaces and equipment. Make a solution of 1 part unscented liquid household chlorine bleach and 5 parts clean water. Spray or wet contaminated surfaces with bleach solution and let stand for 30 minutes. Wipe up treated spills with paper towels, being careful to minimize the spread of contamination. Place paper towels in a plastic bag and dispose of the bag in the regular trash. Apply bleach solution to surfaces and equipment again; let stand 30 minutes and rinse. Thoroughly wash all detoxified counters, containers, equipment, and clothing. Discard rubber gloves in the regular trash when the sanitation process is complete.

Glossary

Acetic Acid
A pungent, colorless liquid acid that mixes readily with water and is the principal acid of vinegar. Acetic acid gives vinegar its sour flavor.

Altitude
The vertical elevation (distance) of a location above sea level.

Antioxidant
An agent, such as citric acid (lemon or lime juice), ascorbic acid (vitamin C), or a blend of ascorbic and citric acids that inhibits oxidation. When used as an antioxidant, each of these acids helps to control browning of peeled or cut light-colored fruits and vegetables.

Ascorbic Acid
The chemical name for vitamin C, a natural, water-soluble vitamin commonly derived from citrus fruits. Lemon juice contains a high concentration of ascorbic acid. Ascorbic acid is also available commercially in powdered form. Ascorbic acid and lemon juice are used to increase the acid (pH level) in tomatoes and tomato recipes.

Bacteria
A group of one-celled microorganisms widespread in the soil, water, and air that is around us. Some bacteria can be harmful under certain conditions common to low-acid canned food; thus requiring low-acid food to be processed at 240°F (at sea level) for a specific length of time in a pressure canner.

Band
A threaded metal ring used in combination with a flat metal vacuum sealing lid to form a two-piece metal cap used for home canning.

Blanch
A technique used to inactivate enzymes by submerging food in boiling water or exposing food to steam for a short period of time, followed by rapid cooling in ice water. This technique is effective in loosening the skin of fruits and vegetables, making them easy to peel.

Boil
A boil is achieved when a liquid is heated to a temperature that causes bubbles to break the surface and, at the same time, continually maintains bubbling activity.

Boiling Point
The temperature at which liquid reaches a boil at sea level, 212°F (see Altitude Chart).

Boiling-Water Canner
A large, deep saucepan with lid and rack, having the capacity to hold jars immersed in water to cover by 1 inch. Additional space of 2 to 3 inches is needed to prevent the water from boiling over. Standard liquid capacity is approximately 21 quarts, which typically accommodates 7 quart jars or 9 pint jars.

Boiling-Water Method
Method recommended for heat processing high-acid foods and acidified foods by which filled jars are immersed in water, then boiled for the length of time specified by a recipe tested to be safe for home canning.

Botulism
An illness caused by ingestion of a toxin produced by spores of the bacterium Clostridium botulinum. These spores are ever-present in wind and soil. They belong to a species of bacteria that cannot grow in the presence of air, and do not normally thrive in high-acid foods. These spores can survive in a sealed jar of moist, low-acid food, having little oxygen, and stored between 40° to 120°F. Heat processing at 240°F (at sea level), for the correct length of time, destroys this bacterium in home canned food.

Brine
A salt and water solution used in pickling or preserving foods. Sugar and spices are sometimes added for flavor.

Bubble Remover
A nonmetallic utensil used in home canning to remove or free air bubbles trapped inside the jar. To ensure appropriate headspace, air bubbles should be removed before the two-piece cap is applied.

Candy or Jelly Thermometer
A kitchen thermometer that usually comes with an adjustable clip to allow it to be attached to the saucepan. During the preparation of soft spreads without added pectin, it is used to determine when the gel stage is reached (this occurs at 220°F, or 8°F above the boiling point of water). Always insert the thermometer vertically into the mixture and ensure that it does not come in contact with the surface of the saucepan.

Canning
A method of preserving food in an air-tight jar by applying sufficient temperature for a specific length of time in order to achieve sterilization and to vacuum seal the jar, enabling the sealed jar to be safely stored at optimal room temperatures (50° to 70°F).

Canning Liquid
Any one of many types of liquids, such as water, cooking liquid, pickling liquid, broth, juice, or syrup, used to cover solid food packed in a home canning jar. Canning liquid prevents oxidation that causes food to darken and aids in heat penetration during processing.

Canning Salt
See Salt.

Cap
See Two-piece closure.

Case Harden
The formation of a hard shell on the outside of produce that traps moisture inside and causes deterioration of dehydrated food.

Cheesecloth
A lightweight, woven cloth that has many uses in the kitchen. It can be used in place of a spice bag to hold herbs and whole spices. Cheesecloth can also replace a jelly bag to strain juice from fruit pulp.

Citric Acid
A form of natural acid often derived from citrus fruits. It is available as white granules and is used to increase the acidity of foods like canned tomatoes. Citric acid may be blended with ascorbic acid for use as an antioxidant to prevent discoloration of peeled or cut fresh fruits and vegetables. Citric acid is also blended with pectin to aid in gel formation of jams and jellies by increasing the acidity.

Cold Pack
See Raw pack.

Cool Place
A term used to describe the best storage temperature for home-canned foods. The ideal temperature is 50° to 70°F.

Dehydrating (or drying)
The process of removing water or moisture from food.

Dry Pack
A method of packing food for freezing in a container without added liquid or sugar.

E. coli
A species of bacteria that is normally present in the human intestines. A common strain, Escherichia coli 0157:H7, produces high levels of toxins and, when consumed, can cause symptoms such as diarrhea, chills, headaches, and high fever. In some cases, it can be fatal.

Enzymes
Proteins in food that act to accelerate changes to flavor, color, texture, and nutritional value, especially when food is peeled, cut, crushed, damaged, or exposed to air. Enzyme action can be destroyed or neutralized by following recommended food preservation methods.

Exhausting
Removal of air from within food, from within jars, or from within canners. Blanching and cooking food exhausts air from food tissue. Processing exhausts air from home canning jars before they seal. Venting a pressure canner exhausts cool air from the canner for a uniform steam environment.

Fermentation
A method of changing food by causing the intentional growth of bacteria, yeast, or mold. Bacteria present in food converts sugars to lactic acid that acts to flavor and preserve some foods like sauerkraut and fermented dill pickles. Foods that ferment due to improper processing are spoiled and must not be eaten (see page 188).

Fermented Pickles
Vegetables, usually cucumbers, that are submerged in a salt-water brine to ferment or cure for up to 6 weeks. Dill, garlic, and other herbs and spices are often added to the brine for flavoring. Fermented pickles are also called "brined pickles."

Fingertip-Tight
The degree to which bands are properly applied to home canning jars. Screw bands onto the jars using your fingertips. Adjust the bands until fingertip-tight, but not forced. Overtightening the bands can result in seal failure.

Flash Freezing
A method of freezing foods quickly in a single layer on a baking sheet. The frozen food is then packed into freezer containers or freezer bags for long-term freezing.

Freezer Burn
A condition that occurs when frozen food is exposed to air due to poor or improper packaging. Air that comes in contact with the surface of the food can cause it to dry out, lose color, or develop a pithy surface or tough texture.

Fresh-Pack Pickles
Cucumbers that are canned in a spicy vinegar solution without fermenting, although they are frequently brined for several hours or overnight. All fresh-pack pickles should stand for 3 to 6 weeks after processing to cure and develop optimal flavor.

Funnel
A plastic or metal utensil that is placed on the rim of a home canning jar to allow for easy ladling of food into the jar. A canning funnel helps prevent spillage and waste.

Gel Stage
The point at which a soft spread becomes a full gel. The gelling point is 220°F, or 8°F above the boiling point of water.

Headspace
The unfilled space inside a home canning jar measured from the surface of the food or liquid to the rim of the jar. Accurate headspace is essential for food expansion as the jar heats, and to form a vacuum as the jar seals (see Measuring Headspace).

Heat Penetration/Heat Processing
See Processing.

Heat Processing
Applying sufficient heat to jars of food that enables them to be stored at optimal room temperature (50° to 70°F).

Hermetic Seal
An airtight seal on a food container that prevents reentry of air or microorganisms and maintains commercial sterility.

High-Acid Foods
Foods having enough acid to measure a pH of 4.6 or lower. High-acid foods may be processed in a boiling-water canner. High-acid foods include all fruits (except figs) and most tomatoes. Foods acidified to a pH of 4.6 or lower, such as fermented and pickled vegetables, relishes, chutneys, sauces, and salsas can be processed in a boiling-water canner.

Hot Pack
Describes the method of filling jars with hot food. Food is boiled in water, steamed, cooked, baked, or prepared using other techniques according to recipe instructions before it is packed into hot jars.

Jar
A glass container able to be sealed with a threaded closure, sometimes called a Mason jar or home canning jar. Designed to withstand repeated use and heat processing in a boiling-water canner or pressure canner.

Jar Lifter
Large tongs usually having a heat-resistant coating on one end and easy-to-grip handle on the other end. These tongs are designed to lift home canning jars out of hot water.

Jelly Bag
A mesh or cloth bag used to strain juice from fruit pulp when making jellies. A strainer lined with several layers of cheesecloth may be substituted. Both the jelly bag and cheesecloth need to be dampened before use.

Jelly Strainer

A stainless steel tripod stand fitted with a large ring used to elevate a filled jelly bag above a bowl for the purpose of extracting juice from fruit pulp. A jelly bag is placed over the large ring, then the stand is positioned over a large bowl. Prepared fruit is spooned into the bag, allowing only the juice to be extracted.

Lactic Acid

The acid produced during fermentation. The fermentation process converts the natural sugars in food to lactic acid, which, in turn, controls the growth of undesirable microorganisms by lowering the pH (increasing the acidity) of the food product and its environment. Lactic acid also adds a distinctive tart flavor and transforms low-acid foods into high-acid foods that can be safely processed in a boiling-water canner.

Lid

A flat metal disc with sealing compound. Used in combination with a metal band for vacuum sealing home canning jars.

Long-Boil Soft Spread

A sugar and fruit mixture boiled for an extended time in order to concentrate the fruit's natural pectin and evaporate moisture until a gelled texture is achieved. Long boiling works best with fruits containing naturally high pectin levels. Long-boil soft spreads usually yield smaller quantities per pound of fruit.

Low-Acid Foods

Foods having very little acid and a pH above 4.6. To control all risks of botulism, jars of these foods must be heat-processed in a pressure canner. Low-acid foods include vegetables, some tomatoes, figs, rhubarb, poultry, and seafoods.

Microorganisms

Independent living plants or animals of microscopic size, such as molds, yeasts, or bacteria, that can cause spoilage in canned or frozen food.

Molds

Microscopic fungi that grow as silken threads and appear as fuzz on food. Molds thrive on acids and can produce mycotoxins. Because molds also grow downward, food having visible signs of mold growth should be discarded, including jams and jellies. Processing high-acid foods in a boiling-water canner will destroy molds.

Mycotoxins

Toxins produced by the growth of certain molds on foods.

Non-Sugar Sweetener

Any one of many synthetically produced non-nutritive sweet substances. Non-sugar sweeteners vary in sweetness but are usually many times sweeter than granulated sugar.

Overnight

A period of time from 8 to 12 hours.

Pasteurization

Adequately heating a specific food to destroy the most heat-resistant pathogenic or disease-causing microorganism known to be associated with the specific food.

Pectin

A naturally occurring carbohydrate found in fruits and vegetables. Pectin is available commercially in powdered and liquid form, and is typically extracted from apples or citrus fruit. Pectin assists fruit, sugar, and acid in forming the gel structure in jams, jellies, and other soft spreads.

pH (potential of hydrogen)

A measuring system to determine how acid or alkaline a substance is. Values on a pH scale range from 0 to 14, with 7 being neutral. For the purpose of home canning, foods are divided into two groups: high-acid and low-acid. A boiling-water canner is used for processing high-acid foods; a pressure canner must be used for processing low-acid foods.

Pickle Crisp®

A crisping agent that uses calcium chloride, a naturally occurring salt found in some mineral deposits, to enhance the texture of pickles. Pickle Crisp may be added to jars of quick-process or fresh-pack pickles before processing. Look for it where canning supplies are sold.

Pickling

Preserving food, especially low-acid foods, in a brine or vinegar solution to lower its pH to 4.6 or lower. Herbs or spices are often used for added flavor. Foods that are properly pickled may be safely heat-processed in a boiling-water canner.

Pressure Canner

A heavy saucepan fitted with a lid that locks onto the base to form a steam-tight fit. The lid has a safety valve, vent, and pressure gauge to control and maintain the correct pressure. Pressure canners are available with either a weighted gauge or a dial gauge. The average pressure canner designed for home canning will hold approximately 5 to 7 quart jars. Do not use pressure canners with a capacity of less than 4 quart jars.

Pressure Canning Method

The only method recommended to heat-process low-acid foods. Low-acid foods must reach an internal temperature sufficient to destroy potentially harmful bacteria, their spores, and the toxins they produce. The steam inside a pressurized canner is able to reach the high temperature of 240°F (at sea level) needed to safely process low-acid foods.

Pretreatment

Blanching or treating produce with an antioxidant to prevent color change, slow enzyme activity, or destroy bacteria.

Processing Time

The period of time in which a filled jar is heated in a boiling-water canner or a pressure canner. The processing time must be sufficient to heat food at the coldest spot in the jar to a specific temperature for a specified length of time.

Produce Protector

See Antioxidant.

Raw Pack

Describes the method of filling jars with raw (unheated) food prior to processing. Food is peeled, pitted, cored, chopped, crushed, or prepared using other techniques according to recipe instructions, then packed into hot jars. This method is sometimes referred to as "Cold Pack;" however, Raw Pack is the preferred term for describing this technique.

Rehydration (or reconstitution)
Restoring water (liquid) to dried food.

Reprocessing
Repeating the heat processing of filled, capped jars when a jar does not seal within 24 hours. The original lid must be removed and the food and/or liquid reheated as recommended by the recipe. The food and/or liquid must be packed into a clean hot jar and covered with a new clean lid with the screw band adjusted. The filled jar must then be reprocessed using the canning method and full length of processing time recommended by the recipe.

Rolling Boil
A rapid boil where bubbles continually break the surface of the liquid or food, causing it to spurt or foam. A rolling boil cannot be stirred down.

Salt (pickling or canning)
A fine-grained table salt without anti-caking agents or iodine additives that cause canning liquid to become cloudy and pickles to darken. Primarily used for pickling and canning, but may be used for cooking, baking, or serving.

Saucepan
An 8- to 10-quart heavy pot essential for cooking soft spreads. The pot must have a broad, flat bottom for good heat distribution and deep sides to prevent food from boiling over.

Sealing Compound
The red, shiny material found in the channel on the underside of the flat metal lid. The sealing compound is in contact with the rim of the jar in order to form a seal when the jar cools after processing.

Simmer
To cook food gently just below the boiling point (between 180° and 200°F). Bubbles will gently rise to the surface from the bottom of the saucepan, slightly disturbing the surface of the liquid or food.

Spice Bag
A small closeable bag, usually made of muslin or cheesecloth, used to hold whole herbs or whole spices during cooking, curing, or steeping. The bag allows herbs and spices to infuse flavor into a mixture. After the mixture is well-flavored, the spice bag is easily removed.

Spoilage
The evidence that microorganisms have not been completely destroyed in a food product. If microorganisms are present, the nutrients in the food product will allow them to grow and multiply. Spoilage occurs when food products have not been processed correctly. Signs of spoilage include broken seals, mold, gassiness, cloudiness, spurting liquid, seepage, yeast growth, fermentation, sliminess, and disagreeable odors. See page 188 for details on safely discarding spoiled foods, especially low-acid foods.

Sterilization
The process of killing all living microorganisms. For home canned foods, this is achieved by heating food in capped jars to a high enough temperature for a length of time sufficient to destroy the most heat-resistant microorganism known to be associated with the food.

Storage
A cool, dry, dark place where home canned foods can be kept until ready to be consumed. The ideal temperatures for storing home canned foods is 50° to 70°F.

Style of Pack
The form in which the food is prepared for canning, such as whole, slice, spear, chunk, piece, juice, sauce, or purée.

Syrup
A mixture of water (or juice) and sugar used to add liquid to canned or frozen foods.

Two-Piece Cap
A two-piece metal closure used to vacuum-seal home canning jars. The set consists of a threaded metal band and flat metal lid that has a flanged edge lined with sealing compound.

Vacuum Seal
The state of negative pressure within a jar of processed food. When a jar is closed at room temperature, the atmospheric pressure is the same inside the jar as it is outside the jar. When the jar is heated, the air and food inside expand, forcing air out and decreasing pressure inside. As the jar cools and the contents shrink, a partial vacuum forms. The sealing compound on the underside of the lid prevents the air from reentering the jar.

Venting
1. Forcing air to escape from a closed jar by applying heat.
2. Permitting air to escape from a pressure canner to create a steam environment (also called exhausting).

Yeasts
A group of microscopic fungi grown from spores that cause fermentation in foods. Yeasts are easily destroyed at a temperature of 212°F. Yeasts are inactive in foods that are frozen.

Index

Notes

_____

_____

_____

_____

_____

_____

_____

_____

_____

_____

_____